Feminist Perspectives on Family Care

FAMILY CAREGIVER APPLICATIONS SERIES

Series Editors

David E. Biegel, *Case Western Reserve University*
Richard Schulz, *University of Pittsburgh*

Advisory Board Members

Volumes in This Series:

1. **Family Caregiving in Chronic Illness: Alzheimer's Disease, Cancer, Heart Disease, Mental Illness, and Stroke**
   David E. Biegel, Esther Sales, and Richard Schulz

2. **Grandmothers as Caregivers: Raising Children of the Crack Cocaine Epidemic**
   Meredith Minkler and Kathleen M. Roe

3. **Balancing Work and Caregiving for Children, Adults, and Elders**
   Margaret B. Neal, Nancy J. Chapman, Berit Ingersoll-Dayton, and Arthur C. Emlen

4. **Family Caregiving Across the Lifespan**
   edited by Eva Kahana, David E. Biegel, and May L. Wykle

5. **Family Caregiving in an Aging Society: Policy Perspectives**
   edited by Rosalie A. Kane and Joan D. Penrod

6. **Feminist Perspectives on Family Care: Policies for Gender Justice**
   Nancy R. Hooyman and Judith Gonyea

Family Caregiver Applications Series
Volume 6

Feminist Perspectives on Family Care

Policies for Gender Justice

Nancy R. Hooyman
Judith Gonyea

Published in cooperation with the
Center for Practice Innovations,
Mandel School of Applied Social Sciences,
Case Western Reserve University

SAGE Publications
International Educational and Professional Publisher
Thousand Oaks   London   New Delhi

For information address:

SAGE Publications, Inc.
2455 Teller Road
Thousand Oaks, California 91320
E-mail: order@sagepub.com

SAGE Publications Ltd.
6 Bonhill Street
London EC2A 4PU
United Kingdom

SAGE Publications India Pvt. Ltd.
M-32 Market
Greater Kailash I
New Delhi 110 048 India

Printed in the United States of America

Library of Congress Cataloging-in-Publication Date

Hooyman, Nancy R.
   Feminist perspectives on family care: Policies for gender justice
/ Nancy R. Hooyman, Judith Gonyea.
      p.   cm.—(Family caregiver applications series; v. 6)
   "Published in cooperation with the Center for Practice
Innovations, Mandel School of Applied Social Sciences, Case Western
Reserve University."
   Includes bibliographical references and index.
   ISBN 0-8039-5142-6 (c: alk. paper).—ISBN 0-8039-5143-4 (p: alk. paper)
   1. Handicapped—Home care—United States.   2. Home care services—
Social aspects—United States.   3. Caregivers—Government policy—
United States.   4. Family policy—United States.   5. Sex role—
United States.   6. Feminist theory—United States.   I. Gonyea,
Judith.   II. Center for Practice Innovations.   III. Title.
IV. Series.
HV1553.H66   1995
362.1'0425—dc20   95-8958

This book is printed on acid-free paper.

95 96 97 98 99   10 9 8 7 6 5 4 3 2 1

Sage Production Editor: Diane S. Foster
Sage Typesetter: Andrea D. Swanson

Contents

To Naomi Ruth Gottlieb
1925-1995

Pioneer on Women's Issues and
Feminist Practice

Series Editors' Foreword

Caregiving has traditionally been defined as women's work, but should it be? And, what are the consequences of this value stance on social policy? These are the provocative questions posed by the authors of this volume.

It is well-established that most caregiving to family members with chronic illness, about 75%, is provided by women. Yet, equally important, the nature of care varies by gender. Women perform more direct, hands-on care, while men provide more care management. Not surprisingly, women are more likely than men to express feeling burdened by their care responsibilities.

In many cases, women are simultaneously providing care to more than one dependent family member. Women care for their children, for their husbands, for their parents, and even for their parents-in-law. Men typically take on the caregiving role only when there is no woman to relieve them of this responsibility. For doing this task, men often receive considerable praise for providing "extraordinary service," while women's caregiving work is rarely lauded because it is considered a normative role for them.

What are the implications for social policy of defining caregiving as a woman's role? Nancy Hooyman and Judith Gonyea offer a feminist critique of existing public policy in caregiving, arguing that current policies are unfair and oppressive to women and that substantial changes are needed to help eliminate gender-based inequities in this area. In the authors' view, caregiving is work and should be so recognized and rewarded through public policy.

Although there have been other feminist critiques of caregiving, this volume is unique in its comprehensiveness and scope. Caregiving is discussed from a broad perspective with a focus on analyses across three dependent adult populations—persons with developmental disabilities, mental illness, and the frail elderly. This broad perspective makes clear that caregiving is not restricted to any one chronological age, but rather occurs across the life span. The authors make a significant contribution with their rich discussion of the feminist perspective, and the importance of bringing this framework to the analysis of caregiving. They place caregiving in the context of broad societal changes—in family roles and lifestyles, in the economy and the workplace, and in health and long-term care. Also offered is an extensive review of the literature on the nature, extent, and consequences of caregiving.

The authors not only critique existing policies, but also present a number of thoughtful, provocative recommendations for comprehensive changes in both private and public domains, including health and long-term care policy, workplace supports, and in the provision of economic and social supports for caregivers.

The recommendations offered by Hooyman and Gonyea affect not only women but society as a whole. At a time of government retrenchment in human services, they are sure to engender considerable discussion and debate. The authors have done a great service by bringing this issue to the fore.

David E. Biegel
Richard Schulz

Acknowledgments

This book grew out of our personal and professional experiences as feminists who have worked in a variety of ways with women caring for persons with chronic disabilities. We have learned from their strengths as well as the burdens that they have faced. Their voices motivated us to seek to bring a feminist perspective to the public and corporate policies that intimately affect their lives and to propose alternative policies for gender justice.

We wish to extend our appreciation to:

David Biegel and Richard Schulz, Series Co-Editors, who encouraged us to articulate our feminist perspective on family care issues and patiently waited for the final version.

The Dean's office staff at the University of Washington, School of Social Work—Valerie Higgins, Christa Wells, E. Asantewa DeFreitas—for their ongoing support along with their tireless, behind-the-scenes assistance with production details. Special thanks to Valerie Higgins for her word processing skills, her humor, and her encouragement through the endless revisions; and to Fred Cox, our "retired" volunteer who shared his years of wisdom and experience as an author and assisted with tracking down the inevitable missing references.

To Naomi Gottlieb, colleague and friend, who was killed in a tram accident in Prague, The Czech Republic, May 1995. Naomi provided insightful feedback on the first draft; validated the importance of the work—even when we questioned whether we would ever finish it; and assited with the care of Gnanamani (Mani) Hooyman, who came from a crowded orphanage in India to join our busy family shortly before the book was due.

To Gary Gonyea, who shared in the many months of the book's creation, Judith's thanks and love for his good-humored encouragement and constant support. And to Gene, Kevin, Christopher, and Mani Hooyman, who patiently lived with Nancy's preoccupation and long absences during the final stages of completing the book.

To all those whose lives were touched by our hectic schedules in completing this book, our thanks.

Introduction

This book examines, from a feminist perspective, the phenomenon of family care for three populations of adult dependents with chronic disabilities across the life span: adults with mental retardation and other related developmental disabilities, adults with serious and persistent mental illness, and the frail elderly. For purposes of this book, our focus is on adults with chronic disabilities who have a limited capacity for self-care and thus may require long-term health and mental health care; personal care; economic support; and social, housing, and legal services. All three of these populations have been affected by the public policy changes of deinstitutionalization, shorter length of hospital stays necessitating home care for longer time periods, reductions in funding for social services, and greater civil rights through the enactment of the Americans With Disabilities Act. Of significance to this book, they are cared for primarily by unpaid and underpaid women (Kahana, Biegel, & Wykle, 1994).

With increasing life expectancy, the number of individuals with chronic disabilities is growing rapidly, intensifying the need for long-term care. In a 1993 poll by the American Association of Retired Persons (AARP), 43% of respondents experienced a need in their immediate family for long-term care, but only a minority were confident that they could handle the costs of such care (AARP, 1993). It is estimated that 11.3 million adults depend on others for some degree of care because of their chronic disabilities and that at least 10% of the U.S. population requires long-term care (Center for Vulnerable Populations, 1992; Ferber, O'Farrell, & Allen, 1991; Gimpel, 1991). Of household members with chronic disabilities in need of care, 12.4% are children and teenagers under 20 years of age, 31.7% are aged 20 to 49, 12.6% are ages 50 to 59, and 43.6% are aged 60 or older (Gimpel, 1991). Although the prevalence of disability increases with age and the elderly are the fastest growing segment of the population, there are slightly more people with disabilities aged 21 to 64 (5.8 million) than those who are over age 65 (5.5 million) (NASHP, 1992).[1]

1

The rapid growth of the proportion of the population with long-term disabilities is stretching the already constrained public resources to support their continuing survival and well-being. For example, dramatic gains in the average life expectancy of persons with developmental disabilities are resulting in a growing geriatric mentally impaired population, many of whom experience earlier onset of certain health-related problems such as respiratory disease, hearing loss, and dementia (Kelly & Kropf, 1995). Yet categorically based social and health care policies, as codified in the separate systems of aging and developmental disabilities, are neither structured nor prepared to address the quality of life of this proportion of the elderly population nor that of their aging caregivers. As a whole, long-term care in the United States is fragmented, inadequately financed, and biased toward skilled care needs and institutionalization, so that both personal and family funds must be used to finance nursing home, home health, and personal care (Estes, Swan, & Associates, 1993). The rapid increase in the number of individuals with chronic disabilities, particularly among those aged 60 years and over, raises fundamental policy and practice dilemmas regarding who should provide what types of long-term care assistance and at what costs.

These dilemmas relate not only to the needs of adults with disabilities but also to those of their caregivers. In most instances, family members are the primary carers, furnishing millions of hours of informal "unpaid" care and comprising the cornerstone of the provision of community-based long-term care (Estes et al., 1993). For example, it is estimated that 7.9% of adults (13 million people) have parents or spouses with disabilities and therefore are potential providers of long-term care (Stone & Kemper, 1989). And these figures do not recognize parents who, caring for adult children with mental illness or developmental disabilities, are experiencing their own age-related health and physical changes. Most estimates of national health care expenditures do not take account of the "costs" of informally provided care, especially the economic and psychological costs to family members. Yet without family care, the number of persons requiring publicly supported long-term care services, particularly institutional care, would increase dramatically. For example, it has been predicted that without family assistance, the number of elders in nursing homes would triple (Brody, 1985).

As examples of the extent of informal care, families provide 80% of the in-home care to elderly with chronic illness even when formal services are used selectively (Leutz, Capitman, MacAdam, & Abrahams, 1992; U.S. Senate Special Committee on Aging, 1992). Approximately 85% of individuals with developmental disabilities live with their families or on their own where they may still require some assistance of family members

(Center for Vulnerable Populations, 1992), and estimates of the percentage of individuals with severe and persistent mental illness who live with families range from 40% to 65% (March, 1992; Torrey, Wolfe, & Flynn, 1988). Increasingly, it is a normative expectation that at some point in a family's life cycle, it will face responsibility for the long-term care of members with chronic illness or disability (Zarit, Pearlin, & Schaie, 1993). When families do use formal services, it is usually as a supplement to or a brief respite from what they continue to provide. In fact, programs such as Medicare, Medicaid, and Supplemental Security Income, although presuming the cost-efficiency of family care, have sometimes created obstacles and disincentives to family care.

In most instances, *family caregivers* is a euphemism for *one* primary caregiver, typically female. Family members rarely share the work of caring. Even when work is shared, the networks of neighbors, friends, and extended kin tend to help only sporadically and irregularly (Dalley, 1988). Rather, a woman—mother, daughter, wife, granddaughter, grandmother—typically provides the majority of family care for adults with chronic disabilities (Finley, 1989; Older Women's League, 1989). Many women often care for more than one generation at a time, whether the "sandwiched generation" of an adult daughter caring for parents and children or a grandmother caring for her husband and grandchildren (Brody, 1985). From a feminist perspective, family provision of long-term care has less to do with families than with women in families. Although some men are "unsung heroes" as caregivers, they are less likely to be involved in direct hands-on care and more often provide indirect assistance with intermittent tasks, such as financial management or home repair. In fact, with the exception of the marital bond, men tend to assume primary responsibility for relatives with disabilities—and for household tasks—only when a female family member is unavailable (Hartmann, 1981). This pattern reflects the societal expectation and ideology that the home is women's domain and caring a natural female characteristic.

Throughout this book, caregiving work is defined as custodial or maintenance help or services, rendered for the well-being of individuals who cannot perform such activities themselves (Waerness, 1985). Yet caregiving work is more than meeting physical needs; the very use of the word "care" implies intimacy and connection (Graham, 1983). Caregiving typically involves "semicare," the emotional work of managing feelings and establishing and maintaining relationships, or what Bernard (1971) refers to as the "stroking" function, not just physical care (Hochschild, 1979; Lewis & Meredith, 1988). In examining the caregiving phenomenon, a useful distinction is between *caring for* and *caring about;* caring about involves affection and perhaps a sense of psychological responsibility, whereas caring for encompasses both the performance or supervision of concrete tasks and a sense of psychological responsibility. The fusion of caring about with caring for, between love and labor, often intensifies the stress experienced by family caregivers, particularly by women (Dalley, 1988; Lewis & Meredith, 1988).

The stress of caregiving is, in turn, affected by the changing demographic and societal context. As noted earlier, the number of adults requiring long-term care has increased in large part because of the success of medical technology. Both very young and very old individuals are now surviving conditions that 50 years ago would have been fatal. At the same time, the capability of traditional family caregivers to provide care is altered. Many factors have affected family structure and resources available for community care of relatives: geographic mobility; escalating divorce rates; greater public acceptance of single, cohabiting, and homosexual lifestyles; larger numbers of women in the paid labor force; and growth in unemployment, underemployment, contingent work, and poverty. The combined effects of these larger social and economic changes have placed pressures on contemporary families and make it less likely that they can provide long-term care. At the same time, public policy and normative attitudes advocating the cost-effectiveness of family care have increased. Yet, with the growth of single-parent families, who are often economically disadvantaged; blended or stepfamilies, who confront multiple loyalties; gay and lesbian families, who face legal and attitudinal barriers to services; and dual-income families, who feel constrained both by time and economic pressures, the expectation that families should provide the majority of care to relatives with disabilities is no longer realistic.

THEMES OF THIS BOOK

The past decade has witnessed an explosion in the research and literature on family care of dependents with chronic disabilities. Given this, why another book on family caregiving? What distinguishes this book from so many of the others?

The first distinctive theme is that our review and analysis of issues occur both *across disability groups and across the life span.* As noted earlier, this book draws on policy and practice dilemmas related to family carers of frail elders, adults with mental retardation and other related developmental disabilities, and adults with serious and persistent mental illness. Admittedly, these populations are not homogeneous in type and degree of dependency and thus in their need for care. Typically, physical disability requires physical care, often on a 24-hour basis, particularly related to problems of mobility; mental disability necessitates different forms of supportive assistance, such as employment training; and some chronic illnesses that usually affect the elderly, such as stroke, may require around-the-clock nursing care. These differences have significant consequences for the expectations that individuals hold for their lives and for the types of care that should be available. They also result in differences the caregiver experiences, especially in the kinds of stress and burden felt and in their interactions with isolated and fragmented service systems. For example, parents of adult children with developmental disabilities face the stress of "perpetual parenting," whereas those of adult children with chronic mental illness are "stigmatized parents" (Kelly & Kropf, 1995). Yet both groups of parents share concerns about the future care of their adult child when parents become incapacitated or die (Kaufman, Adams & Campbell, 1991).

Despite some differences among these three populations, there are common issues and needs in terms of quality of life; interactions with health and social service systems oriented toward acute, not long-term care; and how public policies—or lack of such—affect their lives and those of their families (Ansello & Eustis, 1992). For all three populations, their long-term disabilities, which are likely to persist indefinitely, result in continuous limitations in their ability to perform activities of daily living. Individuals may have multiple disabilities that cross traditional service system boundaries. For example, people with developmental disabilities also may have psychiatric conditions, including schizophrenia, personality disorders, and depression (Menolasciro & Potter, 1989). As individuals with developmental disabilities age, additional health care services are often needed, for both them and their caregivers (Kelly & Kropf, 1995). All these populations require a continuing system of services to address their multiple and complex needs, not only in terms of health and long-term care but also in terms of social supports, housing, and income, regardless of age and type of dependency. All three are vulnerable, at risk of decline and relocation, which means that their needs for care can shift dramatically over time. Finally, many are poor and depend on income-tested government assistance, thus lacking choice and flexibility in their care.

Similarly, those who provide for these three different populations confront shared issues, such as lack of flexibility and choice about whether and how to provide care and how to juggle both employment and caregiving. An advantage of this across-group perspective is the identification of common needs and issues in terms of long-term care and workplace policies, across both care receivers and caregivers; as such, it contrasts with our current categorical, fragmented, and sick-care-oriented service delivery systems in which the caregivers' needs are rarely considered.

This book emphasizes that family care of relatives with chronic disabilities is typically not a single, time-limited episode, but frequently spans the life course. For some family caregivers, particularly women, caring is a lifelong pattern. Providing support in old age to a husband with a disability often represents a continuation of caregiving from earlier phases in a woman's life, perhaps first as a mother, later as a middle-aged daughter for a chronically ill parent, and extending into demands in old age of caring for a partner with disabilities. Mothers of children with chronic mental illness or developmental disability face a special set of challenges. These women cannot anticipate that adulthood will bring their children complete independence and thus a cessation of their care responsibilities. Even when women are caring for children fortunate to be spared any disabilities, the stress from parental demands at earlier phases of their adulthood can affect how they later experience caregiving for dependent adult relatives in middle and old age. For many women, caregiving is experienced as a "career," continuous across their lives, regardless of the age of the relatives requiring assistance (Rossi, 1985). As caregiving needs and demands change over time, women's roles and responsibilities may shift; nevertheless, their employment and family choices, as well as their identities at all ages, tend to be shaped by their familial caregiving experiences (Hess & Ferree, 1987; Levy, 1988). Women's employment does not necessarily result in reduced assistance to dependent relatives but, rather, in "double duty" and less time for leisure (Brody, 1985, Estes et al., 1993).

The types of responsibilities and resultant burdens faced by family carers, regardless of the caregiver's age, are closely interconnected, highlighting the need for noncategorical long-term care policies that encompass the life span as well as cross-populations. The current preoccupation with intergenerational competition for scarce resources overlooks that women are the primary caregivers to both young and old and that women's interests bridge the needs of both groups across time.

Consistent with this across-population and across-life-span perspective, which seeks to identify commonalities, is the *feminist framework* or mode of analysis used throughout this book. We define long-term care of relatives with a disability as a central feminist issue, because such care depends on women's unpaid and often invisible labor. An underlying assumption of feminism is that women as caregivers have historically been oppressed within both the home and the labor market. Not only have women been relegated to the private sphere, but their lives within that sphere have been made invisible and their voices have been silenced

(Davis, 1994). Accordingly, women's place in the social structure is fundamentally different from men's because of women's daily experiences with oppression. A feminist analysis goes beyond simply recognizing the existence of such differences to asking what effect these have, and concludes with the absolute necessity of fundamental structural changes in social institutions, attitudes, and values to improve women's lives. Feminists argue that women's experiences as carers of adults with disabilities have often been invisible to or misrepresented by researchers, practitioners, and policymakers. The conceptualization of caregiving as unpaid domestic production has only recently appeared in the gerontological literature and is rarely mentioned in the research on developmental disabilities and chronic mental illness (Dwyer & Seccombe, 1991). Therefore, a feminist approach seeks to make visible and validate the importance of women's daily experiences as carers.

A feminist approach, aiming to eliminate false dichotomies or artificial polarities, recognizes that women's work both in and out of the home has been devalued. This is reflected in their low wages in the marketplace and the invisibility of their work at home. Women are expected to take on all family responsibilities without complaint, yet we know that long-term dependent care affects their physical and mental health and wreaks havoc on their economic welfare. Gender inequities are obvious when women are expected to be the caregivers and when little societal attention is paid to the effects—both psychological and financial—on women's lives.

Caring work cuts across the personal and political boundaries of family/employment and family/public policy. Recognition of the connectedness in women's lives as carers, of the interaction between the needs of the caregivers and the care receivers, and of interdependence and dependence across the life course, is fundamental to a feminist perspective. The life span perspective is central to feminist analysis because issues affecting younger women as mothers, especially their lower economic status, are played out across their lives in caring for adults with disabilities. A feminist analysis recognizes how caring for family across the life course has severe negative economic repercussions for them in old age, when many women lack choice in determining the conditions of their own aging. Feminists do not define the demographic and social changes, such as the growth of the proportion of the population with chronic disabilities or the large-scale entry of women into the paid labor market, as the "problems" occurring in community care. Nor is the stress experienced by many carers viewed as the primary problem of caregivers collectively. From a feminist analysis, inadequate and gender-biased policies (i.e., the socially constructed structural conditions) represent the problem in long-term care that must be addressed.

A feminist analysis also takes account of *variations* in family caregiving, not only by gender but also by race, ethnicity, socioeconomic class, and sexual orientation. There are multiple realities of the caring experience, shaped by the social constructs of class, race, ethnicity, and age cohort experiences. As noted by Hartsock (1990), the false "we" needs to be dissolved into its real variety, and "out of this concrete multiplicity build an account which can expose the falseness of the view from the top and can transform the margins as well as the center" (p. 171). By recognizing that not all women have the same experiences and view of reality, we acknowledge how inequities created by public policies differentially affect low-income women of color, for example. Although caring for adults with chronic disabilities is a growing issue in most other industrialized societies, the focus of this book is on caregiving cross-culturally within the United States rather than a comparative analysis with other countries. We attempt to address throughout the book how caring experiences vary with the sociocultural environment, socioeconomic class, and sexual orientation, although data about caregiving among these different groupings in the United States are, in some instances, relatively limited.

Central to this feminist analysis is the concept of *gender* and how it creates socially constructed structural, relational, and symbolic differentiations between men and women. Although this book examines the relative effects of gender on both male and female carers, including the amount and type of assistance given and the differential consequences of such gender-based responsibilities, the focus of our analysis is on the socially constructed definitions of women as natural caregivers and the negative economic consequences of the devaluation of women's work across the life course. Although women's experiences are documented more often than men's, a feminist perspective is "not for women only," but enhances our understanding of the interaction between men's and women's roles and responsibilities. Ultimately, feminism is concerned with (a) changing the roles of both men and women to insure choice regarding both caregiving and employment, and (b) altering social institutions, attitudes, and values so that caregiving is viewed as a societal, not an individual, responsibility. It is in this sense that gender justice is the focus of the feminist models of economic, social, and long-term care policies proposed in this book.

Familial, institutional, political, and societal norms, as codified in current long-term policies, tend to maintain and reinforce gender inequities in caregiving. Because of the role of policy in perpetuating gender inequities, the majority of this book focuses on *public long-term care policies* and *private workplace policies*. We first use a feminist framework to critique existing policies and then propose a social and collective model of care oriented toward gender justice. In fact, identifying gender inequities in caring is central to understanding both governmental and corporate policies related to families. A feminist model is oriented toward fundamental structural change that accords greater societal recognition to the work of caring and assures flexibility and choice for both those who require and those who provide it. By proposing policies to eliminate gender-based inequities in caregiving, it challenges a status quo that systematically disadvantages women within the home and in the paid labor force (Abel, 1991; Chavetz, 1988). Our feminist model is still incomplete and evolving, but it does provide the reader with criteria and principles to follow in thinking about and developing alternative strategies of care. To question existing arrangements is an essential first step in moving toward a social model of care built on gender justice.

ORGANIZATION OF THIS BOOK

Given the centrality of a feminist framework to our analysis, Chapter 1, "Why a Feminist Perspective?" begins by contrasting a feminist analysis with a more traditional psychological or "women's issues" explanation of care. The constructs that distinguish this framework from other progressive social welfare perspectives are then identified, including the social construction of gender, race, ethnicity, and class; patriarchy or domination of women within the family in capitalist societies; the ideologies of separate spheres and of familism; the interconnections between the public and private sectors, production and reproduction; and the empowerment of women through collective action that transcends traditional age and service delivery lines and takes account of the diversity of caregiving experiences by race, ethnicity, sexual orientation, and social class. Throughout, we acknowledge that other frameworks on long-term care, such as the political economy perspective (Estes, Girard, Zones & Swan, 1984; Estes et al., 1993; Hendricks & Leedham, 1992), may include some of the elements of a feminist framework, but typically they do not start from the assumption of women's oppression or have gender justice as their primary goal.

A feminist analysis of long-term care and workplace policies requires an understanding of the changing societal context for caregiving, specifically in terms of the increasing heterogeneity of the American family and the labor force. The nuclear family is no longer dominant, even though most public and corporate policies continue to assume so. As noted above, the family has dramatically altered in the past two decades while faced with increasing expectations, especially from the "New Right," to provide long-term care to relatives with disabilities. How family size, structure, roles, and responsibilities vary by race, ethnicity, socioeconomic class, and sexual orientation and interact with larger societal trends are examined in Chapter 2, "America's Changing Families." Despite profound economic, demographic, and social changes, the ideology of the nuclear family still influences public policies that assume that female relatives are available and willing to provide care.

Essential to our feminist analysis is the need to move *away* from policies centered on outdated notions of family, and *toward* policies that promote gender justice and community interdependency. At the same time that the family has altered dramatically, the nature and structure of work, the composition of the workforce, and the time demands of employment have also changed and are substantially different than even a decade ago. More women have entered the paid labor force, generally out of economic necessity, raising public concern about the diminishing ranks of traditional caregivers for relatives. From a feminist perspective, it is the socially constructed expectations of women to combine employment with care responsibilities that are problematic, not the entry of women into the workforce per se. Of particular significance to the issue of caregiving are the patterns of economic inequity and occupational segregation along race and gender lines, resulting in structurally based unemployment, underemployment, and poverty, which sharply constrain families' ability to care for members. Chapter 3, "The Changing American Economy and Workforce," examines the larger economic context; the shifts to both a global and service economy; growing workplace diversity, including a contingent workforce; modifications in the nature, structure, and time demands of work; and the gender-based occupational and economic inequities that underlie the feminization of poverty. Central to our feminist analysis is the recognition of the interaction between home and workplace lives, rather than viewing them as isolated spheres or artificial polarities.

As noted earlier, the success of medical technology in decreasing mortality rates at earlier phases of the life span and increasing life expectancy underlies the growing numbers of people with chronic disabilities. This growth has placed pressures on long-term care services, particularly community-based and home care resources, at the same time that public funding for such services has been constrained and deinstitutionalization of chronically dependent populations has been the norm. Of additional concern is the growing number of people moving into the community from hospitals or institutions, who lack health and long-term care insurance. Even among those who are insured, most policies do not cover the major long-term care need for chronic disabilities: home health care and social services. This gap most negatively affects women as family caregivers of relatives with chronic illness. The interaction between long-term care policies and the growing dependent populations resulting from improved medical technology and how these dynamics affect women as unpaid and underpaid providers of long-term care are the focus of Chapter 4, "Changing Health Care Needs and Long-Term Care Services."

Chapter 5, "The Social, Political, and Historical Context of Caregiving for Dependents," analyzes how cultural ideologies affect both the nature and extent of caring itself, as well as the types of incremental and residual policies formulated regarding caregivers. The development of long-term care policies in our society reflects an ongoing debate between those who argue for programs supportive of family caregivers and those who want to place even greater responsibilities on families as a means to reduce the rising costs associated with the care of dependents with chronic disabilities. These tensions are evidenced in the persistence of a "public burden" model of care, which emphasizes private responsibility; the existence of family responsibility laws and the ideology of familism; and the contemporary emphasis on deinstitutionalization and community care, particularly in terms of the cost-effectiveness of community-based service delivery models. These models rely on an implicit assumption of women's unpaid provision of care as the cornerstone of such support.

The cultural values underlying policies related to family caregiving, particularly principles of possessive individualism, private responsibility, and the historical ideologies of separate spheres and familism, mean that institutional or residential care is seen as the least desirable alternative for individuals who are viewed as simultaneously weak and deserving—in this instance, those with chronic disabilities (Dalley, 1988). How these values are played out structurally in terms of residual fragmented service systems of community care, the medicalization and privatization of services, and intergenerational competition for scarce resources are also explored in Chapter 5.

Within this social and political context, who needs family caregiving, who provides care across the life span, and how these patterns vary by gender, race, sexual orientation, and socioeconomic class, are reviewed in Chapter 6, "The Gendered Nature of Care." The interdependence between older women as care recipients and younger women as their unpaid and underpaid caregivers is a dynamic affecting the resources for care available to women across the life course. Chapter 6 explores how the differentiation between caring for and caring about affects gender-based variations in caregiving dynamics and stress across the life course. Caring for and caring about are presumed to be indissolubly linked as an integral part of women's nature, but this is not the case for men. When affective links get tied to servicing and maintenance functions, even menial tasks, such as washing the kitchen floor, are presumed to be invested with emotional significance (Dalley, 1988; Graham, 1983). Most community care policies tend to assert that caring for and caring about must be joined by placing primary emphasis on familial-based models of care. This linking underlies some of the stress experienced by caregivers, especially women.

The nature of care tasks, particularly their invisibility, unpredictability, and lack of rewards, also affects the consequences of caring, specifically the burden and stress of care, which are discussed in Chapter 7, "The Consequences of Caring." The intersections of class, race, and gender are analyzed in terms of increased vulnerability to both economic, physical, social, and emotional health costs, such as rates of poverty, depression, and physical illness among caregivers. Although the negative consequences of caregiving for women are carefully documented in Chapter 7, caring values per se are not under attack. Our commitment to gender equity is not incompatible with a willingness to nurture; the importance and necessity of caregiving work are taken as givens. For many women—and some men—family caregiving is their preferred life's work that they have deliberately chosen. For some families, there are benefits and opportunities that result from the carer role. It is the *ability to choose* caregiving and employment roles that is integral to a feminist model of care. Our critique is directed at the structurally based assumption that caregiving is women's unpaid and natural life work—an assumption that underlies many current care policies, particularly community-care initiatives—that blocks female caregivers' access to socially valued resources, thereby perpetuating their powerlessness across the life span. To question the nature of community care is to seek solutions that are equitable and acceptable for people who have chronic disabilities as well as for women as caregivers. As noted earlier, we aim to advance an agenda of gender justice that provides social and institutional supports for those men and women who do try to combine multiple roles within the home and labor market.

Chapters 8 through 10 in Part III, "A Feminist Critique of Current Policies and Programs," challenge the assumptions and goals of contemporary policies that emphasize community-based care and deinstitutionalization: family, long-term care, and workplace policies. Undergirding those policies are basic assumptions about the nature and structure of family life; the role of the family and the state; and the relative values of privacy, independence, and interdependence. The focus of this critique is on why these policies and the manner in which services are designed, implemented, and allocated often place unrealistic expectations on family caregivers of relatives with chronic disabilities and perpetuate gender-based inequities in care responsibilities and service use across the life span. The ideology of the traditional family, which is presumed to be unchanged, pervades current family policies—or what might more accurately be described as lack of a coherent and comprehensive family policy. U.S. health care and long-term care policies are strongly influenced by the medical model of care, which has promoted the negative aspects of institutionalized care of individuals with chronic disabilities. In critiquing these policies, recognition is given to the interaction between medical definitions of dependency, which have tended to produce institutional solutions, and social welfare definitions of dependency, which have created community or familial kinds of solutions. Consistent with our analyses throughout the book, our critique of policies examines how the intersections of gender, race, and class are created and perpetuated by existing policies that result in low-income women of color—both unpaid and underpaid—carrying the heaviest burden of care.

Chapters 11 through 14 in Part IV, "Toward a Feminist Agenda for Family Caregivers," conclude with a feminist model for family care, built on collective responsibility and an explicit goal of gender equality that takes into account the needs of both those who require care and their relatives. Central to this agenda is our vision of equity and justice. Policies to promote gender justice are proposed in the form of economic supports, social services and social supports, family-responsive workplace initiatives, and long-term care as part of national health care reform. Under such policies, caregiving is defined as legitimate work that is a normative part of the family life cycle and as a societal, not an individual, responsibility that protects rights and provides choices and opportunities for both women and men. Equity across the life span is promoted by efforts to balance the needs of carers and those who receive the care. In addition to setting forth a feminist or social model of care, these chapters identify barriers to more fundamental changes that lie in our societal priorities and our devaluing of care across both the public and private spheres.

Consistent with a feminist approach, in Chapter 15, "Feminist Strategies for Change: Toward a National Caregiver Coalition," we close with strategies for organizing caregivers to bring about structural change. Such feminist strategies recognize the interaction between the processes of personal and political change as well as the importance of intergenerational alliances across the life span that transcend traditional categorical, interest-group-based approaches to change. Models of broad-based coalition building among local organizations of caregivers are proposed as a way to make women's caring experiences public and visible.

We turn now to explain and identify the primary components of a feminist framework on caregiving of adults with chronic disabilities.

NOTE

1. Although the growing AIDS epidemic has increased the number of adults requiring long-term care, this book does not attempt to address their critical caregiving needs. Throughout this book, the term "long-term care" is used, rather than "community care," both to reinforce that the care often spans the life course and to avoid the false dichotomy of community-based and institutional care.

1

Why a Feminist Perspective?

In the 1960s and 1970s, feminists began to challenge deeply held societal beliefs of women's "natural" role as the carers for their family members' physical, social, and emotional needs. They argued that definitions of "mothering" and "fathering" were primarily socially constructed and not biologically determined. They contended that it was the gender stratification of home and market that led to women's disadvantaged status. However, beyond the mothering of young children, other types of family care in which women engage were largely ignored by these feminists. It was not until the mid-1980s that feminists began to extend their analysis of women's caring roles to include that given to adult members with chronic illnesses or disabilities and to define this as a women's issue as well. Yet the socially structured dependence on women's unpaid and underpaid labor to provide long-term care to adults and older persons with chronic disabilities clearly makes it a feminist issue.

Much of the existing literature and research in family care for adults with developmental disabilities, serious and persistent mental illness, or frail older adults employs either a *gender-neutral* approach or a *women's issues* approach. In a gender-neutral perspective, gender is neither brought into the analysis of caring nor seen as a relevant issue. Although implicitly understood that caring is about "women's work," gender-neutral terms such as "family" or "parent" are typically used rather than "wife" or "mother." A women's issues perspective often limits the analysis of caring to a single gender. These studies rely almost exclusively on female informants and thus only women's voices are heard. Men and their roles in the family are invisible, or presented through a female perspective. Typically, women are offered individual solutions or strategies to caregiving problems rather than the option of structural change through public policy solutions.

In this volume, it is our aim to bring a feminist perspective to viewing family care and to propose policy solutions to promote gender justice in community care responsibilities. A feminist perspective is not for women only, but instead seeks to understand the interaction between men's and women's roles, obligations, and rights. Central to our feminist analysis of family care is an exploration of how socially construed definitions of women as natural caregivers affect both women's and men's lives. Greater attention, however, is devoted to the negative psychological, social, health, and economic consequences of the devaluing of caring work, given the predominance of women as carers across the life span. This chapter thus begins with a brief definition of what we mean by a feminist perspective and identifies its central constructs.

WHAT DO WE MEAN BY FEMINISM?

A discussion of feminism starts from the assumption that the prevailing standpoint of social reality and knowledge about it has, by and large, been sexist (Krane, 1991). According to feminist theories, sexism refers to a picture of social reality shaped and influenced by a male perspective known as androcentricity—man as the norm (Eichler, 1987, 1988). Because we live in an androcentric social, political, and intellectual environment, women's concerns have often been absent or invisible, and their experiences—their reality and ways of making sense of the world—have been marginalized or misrepresented (Davis, 1994; Hawkesworth, 1989; Hooyman, 1994). What has been asserted as universal knowledge and truth are "meta-narratives," which falsely universalize white middle class males' lives as normative, and locate on the periphery the diverse experiences of women and people of color (Fraser & Nicholson, 1988; Mascia-Lee, Sharpe, & Cohen-Bellerino, 1989).

Feminists advocate a "deconstructive" strategy that questions the validity of "objective" or value-free knowledge and "universals" based on the white male experience. Deconstructionism leads to theories that are nonuniversalistic, explicit about values, and open to the multiplicity and diversity of experiences by gender, race, class, sexual orientation, and culture (Haraway, 1988). To reject a binary conceptualization of "man" and "woman," or "white man, including white woman," is to move to a conception of gender as one strand among others. This opens up the possibility of recognizing the diversity among men and women in specific historical, social, and cultural contexts (Fraser & Nicholson, 1988; Hurtado, 1989).

Rather than accept the worldview rooted in our culture based on the male experience, feminism aims to transform our ways of seeing and knowing in order to integrate male and female qualities, reason and emotion, thought and experience, and individuality and connectedness in women's and men's daily lives (Ackelsberg & Diamond, 1987). Feminist discourse provides a way of seeing and thinking about issues affecting women that is built on women's experiences, because women are the central figures, not the second sex, in a feminist framework (Brickman, 1984; Spender, 1985).

Feminism is not concerned only with women's issues. It is more than a list of problems relevant to women, and it is not inherently antimale (Collins, 1990); its goal of self-actualization and of eliminating oppression in any form cross-cuts concerns shared by women and men. Feminism originates in a belief in the worthiness of all individuals to have opportunities to develop to their fullest. Embracing both personal and social change, feminism aims to eliminate all hierarchies in which one category of human beings dominates or controls another, thereby releasing collective power for community-wide welfare (Morell, 1987). It provides both a mode of analysis and an action strategy for enacting social change that can and must contend with all the "isms" that threaten human well-being (Bricker-Jenkins, Hooyman, & Gottlieb, 1991). Feminist social work practice, for example, is designed to engage all persons in the process of personal and political transformation by changing institutionalized structures and beliefs that support inequity and by creating new structures that empower individuals (Bricker-Jenkins et al., 1991; Goldberg-Wood & Middleman, 1989). As transformational politics, feminism has the potential to change economic, social, and political structures (Van den Berghe & Cooper, 1986). Feminism means changing the whole system, not from the margins but from the center, with the participation of all women and men (Bernstein, 1994).

Within feminist theory, there is a range of political orientations: reformist, radical, and socialist (Bricker-Jenkins & Hooyman, 1986). Indeed, there is no one feminist perspective that encompasses the diversity of women's experiences. For purposes of this book, we draw on Hartsock's (1979) broad definition of feminism as a mode of analysis—a way of asking questions about existing structures and behaviors, and searching for answers by gleaning political insights from analyses of personal experiences. Feminism does not represent fixed political conclusions or a right or a wrong way. Rather, a theme in feminist theory is the recognition of the diversity of definitions, and one of its strengths has been a lack of orthodoxy or a fixed creed. Feminist ideas are constantly evolving and adapting to the varied experiences of women and are subject to continual self-scrutiny, challenge, and revision (Hartsock, 1979). The underlying bond among feminists is agreement that women's personal problems are affected by power inequities and injustices inherent in patriarchal structures, and that women's oppression and subordination must be eliminated.

Accordingly, feminism seeks to address issues of economic inequity and vulnerability to violence that in some way affect the lives of most women. It is this underlying assumption of women's oppression that differentiates a feminist approach from other progressive social welfare approaches, such as the political economy perspective that also advocates structural changes (Estes, Gerard, Zones, & Swan, 1984).

WHY CAREGIVING IS A CRITICAL FEMINIST ISSUE

Given this brief background on feminism, we turn now to discuss the need for a feminist perspective on care of adults and elders with long-term disabilities or chronic illness. Despite the large number of women providing unpaid and underpaid care, caregiving of adults with chronic disabilities was largely absent from the feminist agenda in the United States until recently. In 1963, Betty Friedan in *The Feminine Mystique* wrote of the "problem that has no name," because white middle class women's discontent did not fit into the categories of problems already named (by men). In the late 1960s and 1970s, consciousness-raising groups offered women a forum to express their discontent and to redefine it from personal to political (Hurtado, 1989). Societal emphasis was on youth, freedom, and self-expression. Young women's consciousness was being raised about their own personal situations—reproductive choice, marriage, child care, and entry into the paid-job market. When caregiving was discussed by activists within the women's movement, primarily as it related to motherhood, it was attacked for its oppression of women.

Because of the feminist movement's early focus on younger women, little attention was drawn to the caring functions of the family in relation to adults with chronic disabilities and the elderly (Dalley, 1988). This lack of attention may reflect the low status not only of the women who care for individuals with long-term disabilities, but also of those who receive the care—the frail elderly, individuals with chronic mental illness, and persons who are developmentally disabled. Although mothering may be viewed with ambivalence in our society, both romanticized and devalued, underpaid caregivers of the chronically disabled within institutions, and unpaid caregivers within the home, were for the most part not even visible to young feminists in the late 1960s and 1970s. Even more so than mothers, caregivers of adults were peripheral, and marginalized as the "other" (Freeman, 1990).

By focusing on issues primarily affecting women earlier in their life cycle, feminism in the 1960s and 1970s ignored the issue of family care across the life course and into old age. Early feminists did not articulate how aging, gender, race, and social class interact across the life span or how issues affecting younger women as mothers in the isolated nuclear family are also played out across the life span for adult dependents who need chronic care. Accordingly, feminist theory has not developed an adequate model of the female life cycle (Copper, 1986), and has overlooked how care for family members across the life course has severe negative economic consequences for women in old age. As has been the case with research in the social sciences generally, the first step in bringing a feminist analysis to the care of adult dependents was the recognition of its absence, and that the causes for this are structural, not individual.

This lack of attention to women's caregiving responsibilities across the life span began to shift in the 1980s. With the dramatic growth of the oldest-old requiring long-term care coupled with policy expectations that families provide such care, research focusing on family care of the elderly grew rapidly. As study after study consistently showed the predominance of women in the carer role, aging women's organizations, such as the Older Women's League and the National Forum for Mid-Life and Older Women, began framing elder care as a women's issue. (The National Organization for Women, however, has not defined caregiving of adult dependents as a priority issue.) The public policy of deinstitutionalization and the increasing emphasis on community-based and family-focused care for individuals with chronic mental illness and developmental disabilities fell heavily on women, particularly mothers who were often implicitly blamed for their children's mental illness or mental retardation (Wedenoja, 1991). As noted by Thurer (1983), as an extension of their culturally appointed nurturing role, mothers have unavoidably filled the vacuum left by the unmet promises of community care. Women were more frequently blamed if their caregiving "failed" than acknowledged if they were "successful."

To define family care as a women's issue was an important first step in raising the awareness of policy makers, service providers, and researchers about how caring affects women's daily lives. Definitions of caregiving as a women's issue, however, have tended to highlight the subjective stress and burden faced by caregivers and to focus on individuals rather than on the needs of women as a group. Accordingly, under a women's issues perspective, most suggestions for addressing stress have emphasized personal adaptation, education, counseling, and social support to enhance individuals' coping with adverse situations and incremental changes within service delivery models (Abel, 1991). Such interventions, directed toward women themselves rather than at systemic or structural factors, may inadvertently blame women caregivers for the burdens facing them (Gordon, 1992). Simply to acknowledge that the role creates individual stress and burden overlooks how gender-based care responsibilities have systematically disadvantaged women as a group across the life span.

This book moves beyond articulating family care as only a women's issue that requires personal remedies to defining it as a feminist issue necessitating basic structural changes. Using a feminist perspective fundamentally alters the way caregiving problems are approached and solutions are formulated. It includes demands for gender equality and community responsibility as well as the commitment to alter the process and manner in which public and private lives are organized and conducted. As noted by Abel (1991), the overriding issue is not how to relieve individual stress but how to organize society to achieve gender justice so that care for dependent populations across the life span is more equitable and humane for both those who give and those who receive care. To frame caregiving as a feminist issue is to make explicit the underlying social, economic, and ideological structures that devalue caring across populations and limit women's choices across the life span, both within the home and in the labor market, thereby systematically disadvantaging them economically. Bringing to bear a feminist perspective defines caregiving as a societal, not an individual, responsibility. A feminist vision of a society that assumes collective responsibility for all its members values the activity of caring and recognizes the worth of those cared for and those performing the caring (Dalley, 1988).

As feminist theorists have focused on women's work in the home and in the marketplace, there is also a growing recognition of the economic exploitation of women as paid carers in nursing homes and in community home care. From a policy perspective, feminists are now questioning how services for adults with disabilities can be offered in ways that do not rely primarily on women to do either the unpaid or underpaid work of caring. Questions about dependent care are especially salient for feminists who are often caught between the desire to challenge the exploitation of women's unpaid labor as carers and the desire to see that adults with impairments—many of whom are women, especially among the frail elderly—are cared for in nonpaternalistic ways (Dalley, 1988).

We turn now to examine the psychological explanations of care that have undergirded a women's issues approach and then to contrast this individualistic viewpoint with a feminist framework.

PSYCHOLOGICAL EXPLANATIONS OF CARE

Under a women's issues approach, most explanations of the prominence of women as family carers have been psychological (Walker, 1992).

From this perspective, women's caregiving is motivated by their emotional attachment to care receivers, by the fact that caring is central to their identity, and by their capacity for self-sacrifice and sense of altruism (Graham, 1983; Noddings, 1984). Early childhood socialization experiences and the mother's central role in personality formation are presumed to underlie gender differences in care.

Utilizing a psychoanalytic framework, Chodorow (1978) examines women's mothering as a central factor in the creation of gender differences. She argues that the sexual division of labor is rooted in women's mothering and results largely from unconscious psychodynamic processes that occur between mother and child in the earliest stages of development. Because women are themselves mothered by women, they grow up with the relational capacities and needs, and a psychological definition of self-in-relationship, which commits them to mothering. Men, because they are mothered by women, do not; men's emphasis on difference and individuation is partly a consequence of infantile experiences of difference and separation from their mothers. Women mother daughters who, when they become women, mother. In other words, the sexual division of labor passes from generation to generation through mothering in such a way that caregiving becomes identified with women. In addition, the affective links formed at birth are tied into the mechanical links of servicing and maintenance, first of children, but then later of nonchild dependents.

Gilligan (1982) extends Chodorow's argument, concluding that women have an ethic of care that reflects both their "sensitivity to others" and their "responsibility for caregiving." Each generation of women develops the capacity and need for close interpersonal connections and responsiveness to others' needs, whereas men generally form a *rights orientation*—the capability and need for separation and instrumentality (Lyons, 1983). Although men may be expected to take some responsibility for dependents, it is not assumed that they will provide the primary care themselves. They may arrange for the care to take place elsewhere, or pay for care to come into the home. For example, with regard to the elderly, sons are as likely to feel obligated to care for their parents as daughters are (Finley, 1989). However, the "good son" is one who typically provides for his parents or other relatives financially; the "good daughter" sacrifices herself (Dalley, 1988).

According to the psychological perspective, women's "nature" is characterized by "being" whereas men's is characterized by "doing" (Chodorow, 1978, p. 209). Caregiving work—performing expressive tasks within the home and attending to family member's socioemotional needs—is viewed as central to women's identity, whereas men tend to define themselves in other ways, most frequently as the economic provider for family members and mediator with the world outside the family (Dressel & Clark, 1990; Walker, 1992). The "caring about" nature of women justifies the "caring for" tasks that they perform, and are an expression of women's essentially passive nature. In turn, this assumption that caring is natural becomes a rationalization for women's choosing caring-for work in the public sphere—nursing, home health care, social work, teaching—resulting in women predominating as both unpaid and underpaid caregivers.

Women's stronger emotional ties with family members have also been advanced as a central motivation for their caregiving (Graham, 1983). The process of developing filial obligation is assumed to differ for women and men, with women's sense of filial responsibility containing an emotional component (Finley, Roberts, & Banahan, 1988). In general, men's lives are less involved with others' emotional needs (Wethington, McLeod, & Kessler, 1987). Men's concern for others may show itself in particular relationships, most frequently in horizontal ties to their spouse, but compared to women's concern with vertical ties to parents and children, does not extend as far into their social relationships (Troll, 1987). Men appear better able to distance themselves physically and emotionally from the care receiver, focusing primarily on economic responsibilities and concrete assistance. As a result, they typically experience caregiving as less stressful than women do (Gilligan, 1982).

Policy and practice interventions that have been developed within a women's issues perspective emphasize the individual carer and her internal barriers to more effective caregiving, such as lack of confidence, passivity, or inability to manage stress. In some instances using a psychological model, women's caring has been viewed as deficiency—a view that overlooks how caring is a product of structured power relations. For example, the psychological and behavioral characteristics of female caregivers should not be rejected per se, but instead defined as socially valuable qualities that men must develop as well. Person-centered interventions should not aim to change individuals by eliminating their concern for others, but rather free such concern from being placed at the service of their own subordination (Morell, 1987).

Psychological explanations can also be criticized for postulating a uniform feminine personality distinct from a masculine personality, thus oversimplifying empirical reality and underestimating differences and variations among women and among men as well as between them. Women are not uniformly nurturing and expressive, men are not a homogeneous group with uniformly underdeveloped emotional capacities who excel at instrumental tasks, and one gender is not "better" than the other or at least better suited for specific tasks (Gerson, 1985; Rossi, 1980). As noted by Ferree and Hess (1987), "the awareness of change and inconsistency within individuals as well as between them has rendered traditional theories of socialization inadequate" (p. 14). According to critics of socialization and personality models, women and men do not have inherently different capacities, needs, or desires. Instead, gender-based institutional norms and practices have historically denied women access to essential resources, including power, prestige, and property. As a result, they are offered different avenues for the expression or thwarting of their caring. In other words, male-female differences exist in caregiving within the home and in the paid workforce, not simply because men and women are treated differently as children, but because they also confront different gender-based socially structured opportunities as adults.

The differential distribution of women and men in the paid labor force, where women are less likely to be employed, is a consequence of these limited socially constructed choices, making it more likely that women will be the primary caregivers within a family. When employed, women generally earn less then men, and therefore, usually can leave the labor force to assume dependent care responsibilities at lower economic cost to their families (Spitze, 1988; Walker, 1992). They also continue to devote substantially more time to household and dependent care tasks, even when employed the same amount of time as their male counterparts (Spitze, 1988).

Another limitation of psychological explanations of caregiving is that the nuclear family is held as the ideal. Socialization theories tend to emphasize stable processes and fail to take account of larger societal changes, including economic and demographic conditions that affect the contemporary family. As an expression of dominant values, the nuclear family is presented to women as the norm to which all should aspire, even though this form, with the father as the sole wage earner and the mother a homemaker, no longer applies to 72% of family structures (Dalley, 1988). Such psychological explanations underlie the predominance of familism as an ideology that has influenced the development of long-term care problems, an ideology described more fully below.

In summary, from a psychological perspective, defining women caregivers as a special population with particular issues tends to focus on women's weakness and to isolate them, thereby representing little progression from the traditional sexist orientation toward women as "other" or the "second sex" (Freeman, 1990). By not taking account of underlying power dynamics and the need for structural changes, such individualistic approaches toward the problems faced by women ignore their life experiences with oppression. The women's issues approach does not fundamentally challenge the current power structure that overvalues men and masculine traits in the public sphere of the marketplace and that undervalues women and feminine traits within the private sphere of the home. Instead, personal issues of caregiving need to be viewed in a political and economic context so that solutions extend from the individual to the organizational and the institutional, as identified throughout this book in our recommendations for change.

A FEMINIST FRAMEWORK

In contrast to psychological explanations, feminists argue that women perform caring work not because it is natural but because of the dominant societal ideology of separate public and private spheres for men and women in our society, the low value placed on the work of women in the home, societal disregard of the economic costs of caring to women, and the lack of public support for governmental and corporate policies to meet the needs of dependent citizens. Feminists reject the traditional distinction between women's primary role in the family and men's in the workplace (Abel, 1986; Daniels, 1987). From a feminist perspective, such artificial distinctions have developed because our society extols the virtues of independence and individualism, seeks to distance itself from basic life events such as birth and dying, trivializes the domestic activities of women, and yet perceives paid or formal care as inferior to care provided by family members, i.e., women (Abel, 1991; Glazer, 1990).

We turn now to identify the central components of a feminist framework on family care, which underlies the analysis throughout this book. Our feminist analysis is empirical in its examination of women's caregiving experiences, but it is also ideological and normative by its critique of features of that experience that are oppressive and by its offering a new vision of gender justice and social models of care. In this view, caregiving is both a profound personal experience and an oppressive social institution that can interfere with women's sense of competence, economic independence and options, and equality in adulthood (Abel, 1986; Fisher & Tronto, 1990). The problems that women experience as carers are rooted in and influenced by societal expectations for women's behavior and in societal restrictions on their life possibilities. Feminism thus draws us away from what exists and challenges accepted ideas about gender, race, and class. A feminist perspective is central to achieving the vision of gender justice that attempts to address differences of race, class, and sexual orientation. As a worldview, feminism does not limit itself to only "women's issues," but has the potential to transform both men's and women's caring roles and relationships.

Constructs central to a feminist framework on caregiving across the life span and that are drawn on throughout our analysis are:

- Gender as socially constructed
- Patriarchy or domination of women within the family
- Interactions between production and reproduction with respect to gender within a capitalistic marketplace
- The ideology of separate spheres and of familism
- Interconnections between the public and private spheres, between employment and family, and between public policies and the personal experience of caregiving
- Women's shared consciousness from their caring experiences
- Variations in caregiving experiences by race, ethnicity, social class, and sexual orientation
- Women as collective agents of structural changes

Each of these constructs is discussed below and then drawn on in subsequent chapters in our analyses of the societal and political context; descriptions of the extent, nature, and consequences of caregiving; a critique of current public and corporate policies; and a proposed feminist agenda for gender justice and collective change.

THE SOCIAL CONSTRUCTION OF GENDER

Central to a feminist perspective on caregiving is the concept of the social construct of gender as a property of systems rather than individuals. In many studies of caring relationships, gender has been defined simply as an individual property or characteristic, either through the inclusion of sex as a variable in analysis or an expansion on the number of women in the sample. In other words, gender has been viewed as a biologically defined trait, with male and female taken as opposite ends of discrete and nonoverlapping categories reflecting immutable differences (Ferree & Hess, 1987).

With this gender difference approach of "adding" women onto studies, anomalies that appear in the analyses have sometimes been explained as sex differences, thereby reifying the immutable distinct nature of women and men. In such an approach, caregiving by women is implicitly defined as normative and men's performance is compared to it (Crawford & Maracek, 1989). This strategy of identifying gender differences can also serve to recreate an image of men as the dominant society and women as deviant from it (Andersen, 1983; Calasanti & Bailey, 1991; Walker, 1992). Gender is thus viewed as a fixed and natural property of individuals rather than a structural process based on power differentials that shape people's experiences, behavior, cognition, and social arrangements in both the public and private spheres (Calasanti & Bailey, 1991; Ferree & Hess, 1987; Walker, 1992). This view has served to reduce complex relations to fixed binary oppositions—male-female, good-bad, either-or. Many gerontological studies on caregiving that have included gender in their analyses have described rates and/or the extent of caregiving for wives versus husbands, and/or daughters versus sons, or gender differences in caregiving have been associated with demographic variables such as employment status (Walker, 1992). When the extent and type of caregiving by gender has been described under this approach, traditional theories and conclusions about women as carers have not been fundamentally challenged (Ferree & Hess, 1987).

A feminist approach begins with the perspective of gender as structural, relational, and symbolic differentiation between women and men. As a product of interpersonal interaction, gender is created and recreated in men and women's relationships to one another (Hendricks, 1990). Differences between men and women are defined in social structural, rather than individual, terms: "gender is a property of the social structures within which women and men forge identities and through which they realize their life chances" (Hess, 1990, p. 12); accordingly, structures of gender subordination systematically affect interactions and shape definitions of reality (Glenn, 1987). When the social constuct of gender is made explicit, our attention is directed away from the individual and toward the structures and processes that shape experience and meaning, give people a location in the social world, and define and allocate economic and social rewards. Rather than the individual being seen as the basic unit with social organization added on, individuality itself is a social product (Ferree & Hess, 1987). With the focus of analysis on structural factors, we recognize that it is the gaps in social welfare and long-term care policies that compel many women to provide unremunerated services for their families, not that they are naturally more nurturing. Because of the limited availability of in-home services for long-term care, women have tended to lack choices about whether and when to provide care, to control the intrusions of caring into their lives, or to delegate responsibilities that have become overwhelming. Such deficiencies in the long-term care system have the most profound negative effect on low-income women and women of color (Abel, 1991).

In a feminist analysis of such inequities, gender is not a rigid analytic category imposed on human experience reflecting immutable differences, but a fluid one whose meaning emerges in specific social contexts as it is created and recreated through human actions (Gerson & Peiss, 1985). In other words, gender is that construct recognized as masculine or feminine by a social world. Further, these definitions have historically reinforced power relations of men over women because masculinity is traditionally associated with traits of authority and mastery, whereas femininity is connected with passivity and subordination (Gould & Kern-Daniels, 1977). Gender relations, like class and race relations, are ones of power, a "hierarchical structure of opportunity and oppression as well as an affective structure of identity and cohesion" (Ferree, 1990, p. 870). As noted by Spitze (1988), "It is difficult to speak of power in the context of an individual household without taking into account the societal context of women's lower status" (p. 698). Thus, individual problems experienced by women as carers have structural, historical, and cultural bases, not only psychological ones.

PATRIARCHY OR DOMINATION
OF WOMEN WITHIN THE FAMILY

The concept of patriarchy as a system of social structures and practices in which men dominate women is central to a feminist analysis of gender relations in family care (Baines, Evans, & Neysmith, 1991; Walby, 1989). The nuclear family is often regarded as the fundamental unit of patriarchy, and it is also the central locus for the caring work that women do (Curtis, 1986). Thus, the family is both the locus of personal attachments and the primary arena of economic and power relationships (Baines et al., 1991). Patriarchal relations in families create inequities that interact with specific economic systems to produce a dominance of men in both the economic and domestic workplace. Particularly important to an understanding of patriarchy is the view of women's role in reproduction (giving birth and rearing the next generation and nurturing those already in the workforce), which has resulted in the development of a "woman's sphere" (Curtis, 1986). Restriction of women to a private sphere denies them societal power by definition, and even reduces their power within the family. Men not only possess societal power, but by bringing economic resources produced outside the family into it, they also acquire internal power by controlling these resources. As an antipatriarchal ideology, feminism challenges these assumptions about power and privilege in the social world and argues for the elimination of women's oppression and subordination (Sands & Nuciro, 1992; Tice, 1990).

INTERACTIONS BETWEEN PRODUCTION AND
REPRODUCTION WITH RESPECT TO GENDER
WITHIN A CAPITALISTIC MARKETPLACE

Understanding the structural roots of caring as a woman's role requires that attention be given to the interrelationship of patriarchy and capitalism.

From a feminist perspective, gender relations operate in relatively autonomous yet interrelated spheres of social life. Accordingly, a feminist framework examines the interplay of the social relations of production and reproduction with respect to gender, asking who controls women's labor and who benefits from it (Calasanti & Bailey, 1991). Gender itself embodies a power relationship in both public (marketplace) and private (domestic) spheres (Coleman, 1988).

As noted by Gailey (1987), the origins of gender inequality can be located in the history of other forms of stratification, primarily the emergence of the organized capitalist state. The development of modern industrial society and the ideological foundation of individualism on which capitalism is based have shaped contemporary expectations regarding women's caring. Capitalism heralded the emergence of a new role for women as reproducers. Unlike preindustrial societies in which men, women, and children all contributed to the family economy, capitalism created a sharp division between the public world of men centered in the waged labor market and the locus of women's domestic labor within the private domain of the household, producing the artificial duality of public versus private or political versus personal (Abramovitz, 1988; Acker, 1989; Baines et al., 1991; Dalley, 1988;). The primary change in the mode of production, which is the defining characteristic of capitalism, thus caused the fragmentation and separation of production, reproduction, and consumption by removing production from the domestic domain. The market economy's emphasis on the "productive" value of men's work helped to obscure the significance and visibility of women's work within the home (Baines et al., 1991). This gendered division of labor serves to undervalue women's participation in the labor market and plays a major role in determining who performs household labor.

In contrast to precapitalist periods, domestic labor under industrialization became responsible for the social and biological reproduction of a form of manpower that was to become engaged in wage labor. As noted by Dalley (1988), the tasks traditionally allocated to women are central to survival, in the most basic terms. The function of bearing children—biological reproduction—and the emotional bonds associated with it become indissolubly linked with the tasks of servicing, maintaining, and succoring the domestic group (social reproduction) within which childbearing takes place. Social reproduction is the continuation of those who are alive whereas biological reproduction insures the succession of generations. Although this reproductive role was and is crucial, it was rendered invisible by the way it was socially constructed and relegated to the private sphere under capitalism (Dalley, 1988).

Recognizing the necessity of the functions of both biological and social reproduction, feminists do not reject them per se. What they object to are the ways that these functions have historically been relegated to the private domestic sphere, with women confined along with them, and how they are replicated in the public world, where women's jobs have traditionally served men's jobs as secretaries, aides, nurses, and support staff. Even though more women in the past two decades have moved into higher-level positions comparable to their male counterparts, they still predominate among administrative support and services. In sum, women, especially low-income women and women of color, generally absorb the cost of caring—they provide free labor in the home and cheap labor power in the public sphere, leaving society as a whole unaware of the true costs of care, such as lost salary and retirement benefits, lost potential for financial equity in interpersonal relationships, or lost taxes to federal or local government (Dalley, 1988; Glazer, 1990).

Patriarchy and capitalism can thus be conceived as analytically separate but interrelated realms of social oppression. Under capitalism, patriarchy expanded from the private sphere of the home into the public arena of the marketplace, with men dominating and exploiting women in both realms (Acker, 1989; Hartmann, 1981). Capitalism continually presents the possibility of women's independence through the ability to move into the labor market, although it must be done according to the demands of capital. At the same time, it engenders conditions and responses that have tended to constitute a fully dependent form of family unit—the dependence of middle and working class women on individual men's salary or wage. It is the social organization of women's labor in the home and outside it, and the relations between the two, which have been at the base of women's inequality in terms of salary and occupational status (Smith, 1987). Fundamental to this relationship between home and employment under capitalism are the ideologies of separate spheres and of familism.

THE IDEOLOGIES OF
SEPARATE SPHERES AND OF FAMILISM

Capitalism during the Industrial Revolution also spawned the ideology of separate spheres, which has major consequences for the way in which care of dependents with chronic disabilities is viewed in our society. This ideology, referred to as the "cult of true womanhood," the "domestic code," and the "romantic solution," accepted profit as the sole operating principle of the marketplace and exonerated the public sphere from obligations of community responsibility. Caregiver values were removed from the mainstream of public life and sequestered in the home as an antidote to the public sphere rather than as a central force in shaping it.

The family or the female world represented nurturing—enduring and contingent relations governed by feelings of morality, love, or duty ethos—whereas market relations, the cash-nexus ethos of the male world, were characterized as impersonal, competitive, contractual, and temporary (Voydanoff, 1988). Although the ideology of separate spheres elevated caring to new importance as a function of family life (the family has a moral duty to care), caregiving remained a private activity to be performed in isolation, behind closed doors. Nonmonetized and nontechnological, caregiving became devalued in a society that increasingly defined work in terms of measurable output and wages rather than nurturing and maintenance (Bernard, 1983).

This dualism continues to operate in the current ideologies reflected in the "family ethic," or ideology of familism, which functions as a principle against which all social organizational forms are measured and judged at both the domestic and public level, especially in terms of public policy and social care. Familism, which delegates to women the principal responsibility of caring for family members, combines with the "work ethic," which values activities performed in the "productive" market, to contribute to the invisibility of women's work in the home (Abramovitz, 1988; Dalley, 1988). Women's place in the private arena and men's dominance in both the private and public spheres are affirmed as natural. Accordingly, nonfamilial forms, such as residential or institutional care for dependents of any age, are viewed as deviant. Even when society does assume responsibility for providing care, it promotes a familial model as the ideal. Collective responsibility residing in the state becomes merely a backup to private provision, playing a residual role in supporting private effort rather than taking a lead (Dalley, 1988).

The ideology of familism is rooted in the principle of possessive individualism (Dalley, 1988), with its emphasis on self-determination, privacy, and freedom from intrusion. Contemporary social service, workplace, and long-term care policies are based on this individualized approach, valuing self-reliance, independence, and minimal state provision with families assuming most of the burden. Privacy and independence are regarded as goals to be prized and achieved, and are assumed to best be secured by remaining in one's own home.

In summary, failure to recognize the interconnections between the public and private spheres has meant that *work* has traditionally been defined as "paid labor," based on men's experiences (Acker, 1988). Women's life work—the work of caregiving—is regarded as nonwork. The invisible work that contributes to and creates family is thus largely ignored, unexamined, and undervalued (DeVault, 1993; Voydanoff, 1988). Women are expected to perform unpaid work that underpins the economy, yet is considered peripheral to the economy as defined by the cash-nexus criteria of the male world. But caregiving work is not intrinsically of low worth. Many would argue that it is the most important work that women and men can do. The low status of women and the low value attached to their work generally, the caring role in particular, mutually reinforce each other because they have been divested of power—a power that has been invested in men and that has attached to the roles men perform (Abel & Nelson, 1990; Dalley, 1988).

INTERCONNECTIONS BETWEEN THE PUBLIC (EMPLOYMENT) AND PRIVATE (FAMILY) SPHERES

A feminist perspective on caregiving moves beyond the dualities or polarities of home and the marketplace, recognizing the interconnections between employment and the family, the public and private spheres. Women's work in the home is essential in shaping women's employment, the family's class position, the development of the economy, and the moral order (Gerstel & Gross, 1987). Women's caring responsibilities for dependents are inextricably connected to their disadvantaged position in the labor market. In the marketplace, occupational segregation provides men access to the best paid jobs at the expense of women. When women do achieve access to public spheres, they are often shunted into women's occupations—social work, teaching, nursing, home health care, and secretarial work. In the public sphere, women continue to experience ideological pressures to be social reproducers and social servicers. In fact, men's careers are structured on the premise that women will provide the servicing functions that allow men to pursue their career interests single-mindedly. If women refuse to assume subordinate roles and seek to achieve success in the male world or on male terms, they have been viewed as deviant and atypical (Dalley, 1988).

Even when jobs in the workplace are evaluated as comparable in terms of skill and responsibility, occupations in which females dominate command only about 70% of the wages earned in the male occupations (U.S. Bureau of Labor Statistics, 1991). Women's concentration in low-wage occupations is the most important factor in explaining male-female differences in income. Women's time spent out of the labor market on household chores explains about 12% of the earnings gap between men and women (Evans, 1991; Kalleberg & Rosenfeld, 1990; Shelton & Firestone, 1989). Given these salary disparities across time, it is not surprising that woman-headed families currently represent 53.1% of all poor families and account for most of the increase in the poverty rate generally (Sands & Nuciro, 1992).

Changes within society at large, specifically the movement of more women into the marketplace, do not necessarily presage changes in the household. The growing participation of women in the labor force as well as the government policies that aim to increase opportunities for women in the public sphere may result in greater equality in the domestic division of labor over time, but this connection is not a necessary one (Hardesty & Bokemeier, 1989). Even when women have paid employment, they continue to do more labor than men within the household, resulting in men's privileges and women's longer total work week and shorter leisure time (Hartmann, 1981; Rexroat & Shehan, 1987; Shelton, 1990; Spitze, 1988, 1986; Thorne, 1982). In other words, as women have entered the paid labor force or public sphere, their domestic responsibilities have not diminished proportionately, but instead have resulted in a normalization of double duty or the "double day of work"—both home and employment. Because men have not moved into the domestic arena to the same degree, the domestic division of labor has not been substantially altered. This arrangement continues to benefit men, because those with greater resources in the labor market will do less domestic labor in order to devote more of their efforts to obtaining greater marketplace rewards (Kalleberg & Rosenfeld, 1990).

Women's oppression within the home and in the marketplace act to reinforce each other: women's disadvantaged position in paid work puts them in the more vulnerable position in making marriage arrangements, and their gender inequality in the household disadvantages them in paid work, especially in terms of income earned. Family obligations that keep women out of the paid labor force for periods of time, and the restricted opportunities and incomes available to them when they do enter the marketplace, work in tandem to promote women's economic dependence across the life span and particularly in old age (Acker, 1988; Coverman, 1983). To some extent, this becomes a tautology; women do more domestic work because they earn less than men in the labor market, but one reason they earn less is that they have—and are perceived by their employers as having—greater family responsibilities (Kalleberg & Rosenfeld, 1990).

A woman depending on a man for survival is more than a residual effect of other processes. It is a continuing experience, reproduced on a daily basis in the higher poverty rates for women of all ages, especially among female heads of households and older women (Baines et al., 1991). As noted by Graham (1983), "poverty and caring are, for many women, two sides of the same coin. Caring is what they do; poverty describes the economic circumstances in which they do it." A feminist framework defines poverty as the result of the intersecting processes of the ethic of familism and capitalism that assign men to work in the public world and women to work in the private domain of the household. Therefore, any analysis of women and poverty must be based on an understanding of the interrelationship between the labor women do in the home and in the paid marketplace. Efforts to improve women's economic position must include more than incremental workplace changes, although family-responsive workplace policies can be an important first step.

INTERCONNECTIONS BETWEEN THE PERSONAL AND THE POLITICAL

Consistent with the feminist premise that the public and private spheres are interconnected, political and economic forces in the public arena affect the most intimate family relationships within the home. What happens within the home is not exempt from the political forces that affect the rest of society. Throughout the history of the feminist movement, women—primarily white women—have gained political consciousness about gender oppression by examining their personal lives and their everyday interactions with men. The notion that the "personal is political" identifies and rejects the public versus private dichotomy by which women are excluded from public participation (Hurtado, 1989). The ideology of separate spheres, or the "romantic solution," created the duality of the loving home and the impersonal public domain. Yet, personal relationships within the home are not invariably governed by warmth, concern, and affection. Relationships of domination and subordination prevail, as shown most vividly by the incidence of interpersonal violence within families across the life span, including abuse of adults who are chronically disabled and frail. Feminists have tended to emphasize the underside of the family, calling attention to the oppression, conflict, abuse, and violence hidden behind a portrait of love and nurturing (Thorne, 1982). They suggest that rather than being an aberrant form of family life, this is perhaps an inevitable consequence of the patriarchal structure itself (Dalley, 1988). Accordingly, as is reflected in instances of caregiver neglect or abuse, caregiving can reflect fear and obligation as well as concern and affection (Abel, 1986).

Although caring involves an intensely personal relationship between individuals, it cannot be examined apart from the public policies surrounding it. The personal is political: women's experiences as carers are shaped by their interactions with the public social service, health, mental health, and long-term care systems and policies. Our public welfare and long-term care systems are sustained and legitimized by the ideology of familism—by the assumption that the nuclear family is the proper locus of care for relatives and by the family ethic that women will deliver a broad array of unpaid services in the home (Abel, 1991; Abramovitz, 1988; Baines et al., 1991; Dalley, 1988). It is also presumed that the nuclear family is unchanging. As a result, many current community care policies appear to be based on principles to which feminists are opposed— the primacy of the conventional family and the home-bound status of women within it, resulting in minimal or little choice for many women (Dalley, 1988).

Because women provide numerous care services free or at low cost, these needs for care do not compete for scarce available resources and do not become a political demand on the system (Balbo, 1982). Instead, because it is assumed that a person's needs for care can and should be met individually within the family, services designed to replace or supplement familial care, such as adult day care, have been found to be minimal, to be distributed according to the availability of female kin, and to build on and reinforce family-based care (Baines et al., 1991). It is not surprising that a comprehensive public policy to support family carers does not exist in our society. The role of the state is itself subject to feminist debate between those who see government intervention as buffering the impact of capitalism and patriarchy and those who are more skeptical about the efficacy of public policy (Ferree & Hess, 1987).

Within a feminist framework, the goal is to break down the dichotomies of public versus private and impersonal workplace versus loving home, and to challenge the gendered division of labor in all its forms. Such a framework must also resolve the implicit contradiction between feminist demands for independence and equality for women, and for sharing and interdependence across the life span inherent in a social care model.

SHARED CONSCIOUSNESS AND DIVERSITY
OF WOMEN'S CAREGIVING EXPERIENCES

Rather than focus only on who performs which concrete tasks of caregiving, a feminist view attempts to understand women's common experiences of providing unpaid and underpaid care services, and the meaning that caring has for them. To emphasize primarily the stress of caring and the mental and physical health status of the caregiver is to impose a narrow medical model on women's experiences, ignoring the larger social and economic forces in the marketplace and home that have subordinated women as a class (Estes & Binney, 1989; Riessman, 1989). Likewise, this medical perspective defines caregiving as an individual rather than a societal responsibility (Abel, 1991). Using a feminist model, women have begun to claim their power, to speak in their own voice, and to use their shared identities to act politically. One way in which women have spoken collectively about their common experiences is through the process of consciousness-raising. The concluding chapters of this book build on such collective experiences to propose a feminist agenda for fundamental changes in societal priorities oriented toward gender justice and reflected in new long-term care and workplace policies and programs.

The inclusive nature of feminism sees the universality of women's experiences with oppression as well as the diversity within the unity. With a feminist lens, diversity of all kinds is valued as a source of strength (Hooyman, 1994). In listening to women's experiences, feminists attempt to attend to the range of voices, for there is not "a" woman's standpoint on caregiving, but multiple realities shaped by class, race, ethnicity, sexual orientation, and age cohort experiences (Collins, 1990). The early stages of the contemporary women's movement minimized such differences by focusing on the economic mobility of relatively privileged white women who were restricted on the basis of gender, but not race or class. Any current feminist discussion of gendered relations and family care must take account of the different perspectives of women of color. These variables are rooted in the fact that the domestic and labor market experiences of women of color are different from those of white women because of racist structures that further economically disadvantage women of color. As an example of such difference, poor, immigrant, and minority women are more likely to have been employed across the life span out of economic necessity, and thus do not inhabit the same separate sphere of the home occupied by white native-born middle-class women (Gerstel & Gross, 1987). Nor, as noted by Buechler (1990), was movement into the workplace necessarily seen as liberating for minority and working-class women, whose experiences often suggested that paid labor created a double burden. As another example, for many families of color, the nuclear family model does not fit their experience, even though it may be held up as a norm to which they should aspire. But the nuclear family model may not have its basis or roots in their consciousness or social forms. In fact, the nuclear family may symbolize the oppression of many families of color, held up as an unrealistic ideal to which all families should aspire (Dalley, 1988). As Dalley (1988) notes, a task for many women of color, which differs from that of white women, is to resist this imposition and to question those ideologies of daily living that derive from the structure and culture of their own milieu in the context of their own groups.

For women of color, the family—often of extended or fictive kin—may be both a source of gratification and a site of resistance and solidarity against racism, not a locus of oppression (Glenn, 1987). Also, the public versus private distinction has a different meaning for women of color than for Caucasian women because of the frequency of government intervention in their lives. For example, some welfare programs have discouraged family life, and sterilization projects have restricted reproductive rights. It has been argued that there is no such thing as a private sphere for people of color, except that which they manage to create and protect in an otherwise hostile environment. For women of color, their political consciousness "stems from an awareness that the public is personally political" (Hurtado, 1989, p. 849). From a feminist perspective that attends to diversity, the aim of structural changes is not to reduce inequalities based only on gender across the life span, but also those deriving from class, race, and sexual orientation.

WOMEN AS COLLECTIVE
AGENTS OF STRUCTURAL CHANGE

Giving voice to collective concerns is a first step toward changing gender inequities in care responsibilities. For individual experiences of stress to be transformed into publicly expressed claims for change, it is necessary that people talk about and share their difficulties and develop a sense of collective consciousness and identity (Baines et al., 1991). As long as women continue to accept caregiving as their individual responsibility and see the existing gender inequities in caring as "natural," their privately experienced strains are not moved into the public realm and given public voice and visibility. As long as caring remains isolated and viewed as a private responsibility, most women will continue to bear the burden in silence and not see the political aspects of their situation. Women with sufficient financial means often resort to the individual solution of hiring caregivers from a pool of marginal workers. Seeking to reduce their immediate stress, they may establish exploitative relationships with underpaid caregivers, many of whom are recent immigrants and women of color.

A feminist perspective is oriented toward structural change that will challenge a status quo that systematically disadvantages women and will accord greater recognition to the work of caregiving (Abel, 1991; Chafetz, 1988). However, the view of women as agents of change rather than passive victims of circumstances points to how women both interpret and respond to structures of opportunity and constraints and also to the limited alternatives for action facing women who wish to resist oppression (Ferree & Hess, 1987). Strategies for organizing for structural change must recognize the interaction between personal and political change as well as the importance of intergenerational approaches across the life span that transcend categorical approaches. Women's political involvement has long been contingent on their experiences as members of primary groups—families, friendship networks, and neighborhoods (Ferree & Hess, 1987). Such experiences are central to their mobilizing as political actors around gender-based caregiving issues, not just being objects of public policy.

Within this context of the constructs central to a feminist approach to care, we turn now to examine the larger demographic, familial, and economic changes in our society that partially shape gender-based differences in caregiving.

PART I

The Changing Societal Context for Caregiving

The 1980s and 1990s have been characterized by rapid change in family structures, economic and workplace conditions, and health care. It is within this context that researchers, practitioners, and policy makers first began to recognize the issues concerning caregivers of the chronically disabled, particularly the frail elderly. Because of such dramatic changes in three primary structures—the family, the workplace, and the health care system—families are experiencing growing and often unrealistic pressures to provide in-home care for dependent relatives.

This section reviews the major changes in these three arenas. We begin by documenting the decline in the nuclear family, along with the increasing diversity of family structures—including dual-income, single-parent, step-parent, ethnic minority, and gay and lesbian families. The growing heterogeneity of family structures is due largely to three trends: increasing life expectancy; changing marriage, divorce, and remarriage patterns; and declining fertility rates. Concurrently, the economic well-being of the American family as a whole has deteriorated. Despite these changes, the nuclear family continues to be the societal ideal, an ideal that intensifies the expectations upon women to provide care to chronically disabled adults, even though they may be employed, caring for younger dependents, or both.

Changes in the economy and the workplace have also increased pressures upon family members. In the past two decades, the U.S. has shifted from a national economy to a global one and from a production economy to a service one. These macrolevel changes have profoundly affected the nature of the workplace along with the economic well-being of the majority of families. The feminization of the workforce has also occurred, with growing numbers of women, including those with young children, entering the labor market, often out of economic necessity. When women have moved into the workforce, they have encountered persistent gender-based inequities, specifically occupational segregation. With women still concentrated in lower-paying, lower-status service jobs, they have less access to promotional opportunities and benefits. The dramatic expansion of the contingent workforce—part-time and contractual work—also directly impacts women, who are more likely than men to engage in part-time and hourly contract work. At all ages, women are more likely to be poor than their male counterparts. These inequities often reflect lifelong patterns affecting not only women's current economic well-being but also their economic status in old age, when they are less likely to have adequate Social Security or private pensions than are older men.

Whereas the workplace has changed dramatically with the increasing numbers of women employees, there have not been concomitant changes in workplace policies and procedures that adequately take account of family roles. Historically, work and family have been viewed as separate spheres, so that employers have rarely been concerned with how their employees' work lives are affected by their family roles. Women who have entered the workforce have typically been expected to manage their family responsibilities on their own, with little support for their dependent care tasks. Because men rarely assume as many domestic or dependent care responsibilities as women, women typically carry the double duty of employment and caregiving, often sacrificing their leisure and their physical and emotional health. The burden of multiple roles is intensified when caring for chronically disabled relatives for whom there is little anticipation of increasing independence and improved well-being.

These changes in the family and the economy interact with the dramatically changing health care arena. With escalating health and long-term care costs and increasing numbers of families who lack adequate health and long-term care insurance, many families are unable to afford adequate care for their disabled relatives and face financial burdens from providing care. Part I concludes by describing the health and long-term care arena with an overview of the three populations requiring long-term care, which are the focus of this book: the frail elderly, the developmentally disabled, and the chronically mentally ill. Their needs for care have intensified due to a number of factors, including (a) the success of high-tech medical interventions that have sustained their lives, and (b) deinstitutionalization, a process that has moved many chronically disabled out of institutions into the community without providing adequate community-based supports to reduce the stresses faced by family caregivers.

As we examine the health and long-term care arena, a major theme is the lack of fit between the needs and the preference of the chronically disabled for community-based care and the institutional bias of service systems, given the primary methods of government funding—Medicaid, Medicare, Social Services Block Grant, Older Americans Act, and private long-term care insurance. The limitations of the current long-term care system and the isolated funding streams have resulted in a nonsystem of fragmented services, characterized by: care oriented to acute medical needs rather than chronic, long-term care; insufficient community-based services to support both the chronically disabled and their family members; cutbacks in federal funding and the shifting of responsibility to the state level; privatization of services; and increasing expectations on the informal sector of family and friends to shoulder the burden of care. Overall, Part I lays the foundation for our later review of how the rapid changes in the family, the economy, and the health care arena have not been met by adequate governmental or corporate policy to address the needs of chronically disabled adults or their caregivers.

2

America's Changing Families

During the past four decades, American families have experienced tremendous changes that affect their ability to provide care to members with serious mental illnesses, developmental disabilities, and frailties associated with aging. The "traditional" nuclear family, with the man in the workplace and the woman at home providing care, is in decline. Dual-income, single-parent, and stepfamilies represent significant portions of contemporary American families. Although American families are experiencing a "quiet revolution," which is transforming many family roles, the role of carer has not shifted away from women (toward either men or institutions). Although the majority of women are now in the workforce, the burden of caregiving remains predominantly on the shoulders of women.

In this chapter we explore the increasing diversity of the composition and structure of American families—across racial groups and by sexual orientation—throughout the past four decades. The increasing diversity reflects three trends: increased life expectancy; changing marriage, divorce, and remarriage patterns; and declining fertility rates. We also examine the decline in the economic well-being of American families, a trend that particularly affects women and that has profound implications for caregiving. Finally, we discuss why the traditional family, despite its declining prevalence, remains the cultural ideal and continues to influence long-term care policies for individuals with chronic disabilities. We then argue for the adoption of a broader definition of family as a basis for the development of public and corporate policies and programs.

INCREASING DIVERSITY OF
FAMILY STRUCTURE AND COMPOSITION

The "typical family," comprising two adults in a lifelong marriage with the father working and the mother remaining at home raising the children, is a vanishing phenomenon. Married couples with children under 18 declined from 40% of U.S. households in 1970 to 26% in 1991 (U.S. Bureau of the Census, 1992ba). Even this statistic overestimates the number of "traditional families" in that it encompasses households in which married couples bring children from previous marriages. High divorce and remarriage rates in recent years have resulted in about 20% of the children in two-parent households actually living with one natural and one stepparent. The percentage of U.S. two-parent households comprising a breadwinner father and a homemaker mother has also fallen, from 43% in 1976 to 28% in 1987 (U.S. Bureau of the Census, 1989). Thus, today the "cultural ideal of the family" as a sole wage-earner father, a full-time homemaker mother, and at least one child living at home in fact represents only approximately one out of every ten U.S. households. Yet, as we will elaborate in Chapter 5 in our discussion of the ideology of familism, the cultural ideal continues to affect the development of social policy.

America's growing racial and cultural diversity also shapes the extent and nature of caring that families can provide. Cultural norms about the nature of familial bonds and responsibilities, as well as available resources, influence the different caring roles families assume. In 1950, almost 90% of the total U.S. population was Caucasian; by 1991, it had become 75% non-Hispanic Caucasian; 12% African American; 9% Hispanic (all races); 3% Asian or Pacific Islander; and 1% American Indian or Eskimo (U.S. Bureau of the Census, 1993b). Projections suggest that the nation will continue to become racially more diverse. During the 10-year period of 1981 to 1991, the average annual population growth rate by racial group was: 0.4% for non-Hispanic whites; 1.4% for African Americans; 4.1% for Hispanics (all races); 6.4% for Asian and Pacific Islanders; and 3.6% for American Indians and Eskimos (U.S. Bureau of the Census, 1993b). Both the Hispanic and Asian American populations' greater growth rates are the result of a higher fertility rate and a sustained flow of international migration.

Indeed, the America of 2050 will be a very different place. It is estimated that by 2050, the non-Hispanic Caucasian population will decline to 53% of the total U.S. population, the African American population will increase to 16%, the Asian population will grow to 11%, and the Hispanic population will reach 21% of the total population (U.S. Bureau of the Census, 1992e). In developing caregiving policies, it becomes crucial to understand how the family experience is shaped by the intersection of race, class, and gender. A number of African American feminists argue that rather than family being a source of oppression (as presented in the feminist literature), African American women have relied on the family as a support system to challenge the racist social structure. Hispanic feminists also note that the dominant culture bias to define "family" as the "nuclear family" neglects the importance of Hispanic extended family relationships such as the *comadre* (godmother). Shaping effective social policies and programs for families thus depends on a valuing of diversity.

The number of homosexual families in the United States is also increasing, with growing public acceptance of homosexuality over the past 25 years since the Stonewall Rebellion by gays and lesbians in New York City. Accurate national statistics on the number of homosexual individuals or households, however, are difficult to obtain. It was only in 1990 that the U.S. Census Bureau revised its survey questionnaire to allow couples of the same or opposite sex residing in the same household to distinguish whether or not they were involved in an intimate relationship. It is currently estimated that 5.2 million heterosexual persons and 3.2 million homosexual persons are cohabiting or living in domestic partnerships (Issacson, 1989). Historically, the most frequently cited statistic, based on Kinsey's 1948 study of human sexuality, is that approximately 10% of the population is homosexual (Kinsey, Pomeroy, & Martin, 1948). This figure is being challenged by recent European and Canadian studies, as well as the U.S. Battelle study, which report only 1% to 4% of the population to be homosexual (Painton, 1993). Critics of these recent studies, however, cite methodological factors that contribute to lower estimates. Most social scientists argue that there are simply no good figures on either homosexual or heterosexual activity. The population or sample queried, the type of interview or survey techniques, and the tendency of some persons to deny or exaggerate their sexual behaviors call into question the validity of most findings (Schneider, 1993).

Estimates of the number of lesbians in the U.S. who are mothers range from Hoeffer's (1979) figure of 200,000 (3% of the 6.6 million female-headed households) to Martin and Lyon's (1972) statistic of 3 million (30% of an estimated 10 million lesbians). Most studies have found that approximately 33% of lesbians have been heterosexually married, and almost all had their children during these marriages—although an increasing number of lesbians are seeking parenthood through insemination or adoption processes (Kirkpatrick, 1987). Similarly, it is estimated that 25% to 50%, or 1.1 to 2.3 million, of gay men are biological fathers (Bell & Weinberg, 1978; Miller, 1979). Again, this figure may underestimate the number of gay fathers because it does not include men who adopted children, have stepchildren, or had children outside of marriage. Studies show that approximately 20%, or 4.6 million, gay men have been previously married (Bozett, 1989).

What is the impact on caregiving for gay and lesbian families? Because such families are not legally recognized, they have fewer rights and less protection than traditional families. Both government and employer-provided benefits are generally restricted to family members related by blood, marriage, or adoption. Thus, many gay or lesbian partners lack access to health insurance, pensions, and Social Security benefits. Homo-sexual families may also encounter homophobia and discrimination from professional health and social service agencies. Parents may not recognize or may repudiate their son's or daughter's partner and offer no support when care is needed. On the other hand, the felt responsibility for caring in the lesbian and gay communities often extends beyond blood relations. Gender roles in homosexual communities are less rigid than elsewhere and it is less rare for a carer to be a man.

DEMOGRAPHIC SHIFTS

Life Expectancy

People are living longer than ever before. At the turn of the century, average life expectancy in the United States—the average length of time one could expect to live if one were born that year—was 47 years; in 1950 it was 68 years. By 1990, Americans' average life expectancy had reached 78.8 years for women and 71.9 years for men. Individuals can now expect to reach age 65, at which point there is a better than 50% chance of living past 80 (Kingson, Hirshorn & Cornman, 1986). Projections suggest that average life expectancy will increase to 78 years by 2005 and to 81 years in 2080 (U.S. Bureau of the Census, 1992f). Increase in life expectancy has occurred among persons with developmental disabilities as well, which has extended the years of caregiving responsibility among aging parents, particularly mothers who are the primary caregivers. It also means that many adults with developmental disabilities will outlive their parents.

A gender and racial gap exists in life expectancy. Life expectancy at birth in 1990 was 79 years for Caucasian females, 74 years for African American females, 73 years for Caucasian males, and 65 years for African American males. This gender difference has contributed to a large sex ratio imbalance in old age. For persons aged 65 to 74, there are 83 males for every 100 females; among the very old—those 85 years and older—there are only 43 males for every 100 females (U.S. Bureau of the Census, 1992f). Although there are fewer older men, they are much more likely to be married than their female counterparts and, if disabled, are often cared for by their wives. In contrast, the growing number of older women living alone puts many of them in a precarious situation vis-á-vis caregiving. Primarily because they live alone, older women are at a greater risk for institutionalization. Approximately 75% of nursing home residents are women (Dolinsky & Rosenwaike, 1988).

Increased life expectancy accompanied by lower fertility rates has contributed to the rise in the median age of the U.S. population from 28 in 1970 to 33 in 1990. The 1990 census counted 31 million elderly (aged 65 or older), representing 12.5% of the total U.S. population. One age cohort, the "baby boomer" generation (persons born between 1952 and 1964,) will dominate the U.S. age distribution well into the next century. Between 2010 and 2030, we will experience a "senior boom" as these baby boomers enter the ranks of the elderly. It is anticipated that one out of every five Americans will be 65 or older by 2030 (U.S. Bureau of the Census, 1992f).

Finally, it must be underscored that the fastest growing segment of the U.S. population is the very old or oldest-old (Longino, 1988). In 1990, of the 31.2 million persons aged 65 and over in the United States, 32% were aged 75 to 84, and another 10% were aged 85 and older (U.S. Bureau of the Census, 1992f). Those over age 85 have increased by 300% from 1960 to 1990, with their numbers expected to reach 4.6 million in the year 2000 and 8 million in the year 2030 (U. S. Bureau of the Census, 1992c). This tremendous growth in the oldest-old will take place before the influx of baby boomers reaching old age, because this group will not begin to turn age 85 until after 2030. By the year 2050, when the survivors of the baby boom generation born between 1946 and 1965 are aged 85 and older, they are expected to number 15 million or 5% of the population, with more Americans aged 85 and over than children under the age of 5 (Taeuber & Allen, 1993). This represents a 500% increase within 60 years, resulting in a dramatic impact on the demand for both formal and informal long-term care services. The exponential growth of the population of elderly, especially the oldest-old, will profoundly increase the caregiving responsibilities of their offspring, particularly if the gender roles of their daughters remain rigid.

Marriage, Divorce, and Remarriage

Increased educational and labor force opportunities for women, greater birth control availability, and public acceptance of single and cohabitation lifestyles have contributed to women and men across racial groups marrying later. In 1950, the median age at first marriage was 20 for women and 23 for men; by 1990, the median age reached 24 years for women and 27 years for men (U.S. Bureau of the Census, 1992c). Again, gender and racial differences exist in the proportion of persons who have never married. For example, among adults aged 25 to 29, Caucasian and Hispanic males have a larger proportion of never married persons (46%) than their female counterparts (29%), whereas African American men (65%) and women (60%) are more similar (U.S. Bureau of the Census, 1992c).

Divorce patterns in the United States have also changed dramatically. In 1950, slightly less than 33% of marriages ended in divorce. In contrast, at least 50% of all persons marrying today will divorce (Furstenberg, 1990). Approximately 4% (4.3 million) of all adults who had ever been married were divorced in 1970; this rate increased almost threefold to 11% or 16.3 million adults by 1992 (U.S. Bureau of the Census, 1992c). The median duration of first marriage before divorce is about 6.3 years for women aged 20 to 54 years (U.S. Bureau of the Census, 1992d). Marital disruption, however, "is not randomly distributed" (Furstenberg, 1990, p.382); couples who married in their teens or early twenties, couples in which one or both partners dropped out of high school, and previously married couples are more prone to divorce. Primarily because of socioeconomic status, the rate of marital disruption is about 50% greater among African Americans as compared to whites (Sweet & Bumpass, 1987).

Yet for many individuals, divorce is a transitional state. Remarriage in the United States has become fairly common. Slightly more than 40% of all current marriages are second or third marriages (U.S. Bureau of the Census, 1992c). Nearly 75% of men and 60% of women eventually remarry. Although it is typical for men to remarry more quickly than women, the length of the interval between marriages has increased for both sexes during the past decade (Spanier & Furstenberg, 1987). The implications for caregiving demands from remarriage and the concomitant creation of blended or reconstituted families are profound. These individuals, typically the women, often face the dilemma of how to fairly distribute time and divide loyalties and responsibilities among family members, including relatives from former marriages who remain emotionally close. Loyalties may be particularly "put to the test" when extraordinary demands occur as a result of chronic illness or disability.

Fertility Rates

Families today are smaller than they have been at any time in history primarily because families have fewer children. In addition to delayed entry into first marriage, medical advances have offered women greater control over their bodies in achieving, preventing, and terminating pregnancies. Birth control options have widened for women. Medical technologies allowing sperm and egg donation, in vitro fertilization, and surrogate parenting offer heterosexual and homosexual couples and single individuals of a wide range of ages greater options regarding parenthood.

U.S. Census Bureau data charting the average number of children borne by American women (referred to as the total fertility rate) reveal striking shifts over time. The total fertility rate declined from a high of an average of 3.6 children during the "Baby Boom Period" (1952-1964) to a record low of an average of 1.8 children from 1975 to 1988. Since 1988, there has been a rise in total fertility levels to 2.1 births per woman (U. S. Bureau of the Census, 1992e). Historical data suggest that although trends across racial groups vary in the same manner over time, convergence will not occur in the future. Projections of total fertility rates for 1995 are: 1.9 births to Caucasian women; 2.3 births to Asian American women; 2.5 births to African American women; and 2.7 births to Hispanic women (U.S. Bureau of the Census, 1992e).

Later age at first marriage coupled with earlier sexual intercourse has contributed to the rise in single women bearing children. In 1940, approximately 12% of all births occurred outside of marriage; by 1989, this figure reached 29% of all births (U.S. Bureau of the Census, 1992b). There are significant differences by race. In 1940, 6% of Caucasian babies were borne by single women compared with 38% of African American babies, and by 1985, 15% of Caucasian babies and 60% of African American babies were born to single mothers. Spain (1988) argues that "this set of statistics is more politically charged than any other, and has the greatest relevance of planning for the 21st century" (p. 6). Single mothers represent the vast majority of single-parent households; we will consider the implications for caregiving in the following discussion about single-parent households.

Over the past decade, the percentage of women who are childless has also increased. Among women aged 30 to 34 in 1985, 26% were childless as compared to 16% 10 years earlier. Approximately 50% of these women report they expect to have children, but demographers predict the actual percentage will be much lower (U.S. Bureau of the Census, 1992b). The declining fertility rate, including the increase in childless marriages, has fueled public and policy makers' concerns about the caregiving capability of families in the future. Childless women do not, of course, have care responsibilities for young children, but they also lack traditional family resources (i.e., daughters,) to draw on for assistance in their old age.

FAMILY DIVERSITY

These demographic shifts have contributed to the growing diversity in family structure and composition. Across all racial groups and sexual orientation, changes in life expectancy, marriage and divorce, and fertility have increased the prevalence of such family forms as: the verticalized family, the age-gapped family, the age-condensed family, the truncated family, the single-parent family, and the blended or reconstituted family. A brief discussion follows on these different family types, their potential effects on generational and intergenerational relationships, and the ability of family members to provide care to relatives with chronic disabilities.

The Verticalized Family

Increased life expectancy and declining fertility have resulted in a general trend of the verticalization of American families—a pattern of an increasing number of living generations in a family accompanied by a decreasing number of family members within a single generation (Hagestad, 1988). This phenomenon is often referred to as the "beanpole family structure" (Bengtson, Rosenthal, & Burton, 1990). It is not uncommon for many young people today to have four living grandparents and even several great-grandparents. One direct consequence of the verticalized or beanpole family is that current and future cohorts of adult children face having a greater number of aging frail parents and grandparents to care for at the same time that they have fewer siblings to call on for assistance. In other words, kin networks are increasingly top heavy.

Because women have a longer average life expectancy than men and because women are traditionally the caregivers within families, the verticalization of the family has a greater impact on women. Watkins, Menken & Bongaarts (1987), using U.S. Census data, illustrate how declining fertility rates and increasing life expectancy has changed the nature of women's caring roles. In 1800, women spent 56% of their adult lives raising children under 18 years of age; in 1980, this figure declined to 43%. Conversely, in 1800, a woman spent only 15% of her adult years with parents over 65 years of age, on average; by 1960, this percentage almost doubled, to 29% of a woman's adulthood.

> In 1800, 1900, and 1960, the middle generation spent more years with children under 18 than with parents over 65. By 1980, the seesaw tipped in the other direction: years with parents over 65 exceeded years with children under 18. (Watkins et al., 1987, p. 352)

Thus, although women are spending a smaller percentage of their married years raising children, the "freedom" they have gained is, in many cases, replaced with parent or grandparent care.

The Age-Gapped Family

The media have popularized the notion that the current cohort of adult daughters are the "sandwich" generation. They characterize the typical middle-aged woman as caught between the duties of child care and elder care (Brody, 1990). Yet the 1984 National Long-Term Care Survey found that only about 7% of all women in the U.S. were potentially faced with simultaneously caring for children under 15 years of age and elder parents (Cantor, 1991). Such women caught in the middle are often from age-gapped families in which there has been a pattern of multiple generations delaying childbearing until their 30s or 40s. This is more typical of white families than families of color. Women who were born to mothers in their 30s and who delayed childbirth until their own 30s or 40s now find themselves in the position of caring for young children at the same time that they are increasingly being called on to help their aging parents or parents-in-law. A "sandwiched" adult daughter may be frantically searching for child care for a preschool-aged child at the same time she is seeking home health care for her frail, widowed mother—both services that may be difficult to find and expensive to procure.

One consequence of the age-gapped family structure is a larger than average age difference between each generation. This generational age difference of 30 or 40 years may contribute to difficulties in building affective bonds across multiple generations, due to different values or life orientations (George & Gold, 1991). For example, grandparents who came of age during the Great Depression may experience value conflicts with grandchildren who entered their adolescence during the 1980s "decade of excess." Such value differences and weakened affective bonds may reduce the sense of responsibility for caring in the younger generation or may introduce such responsibilities at an age—the late 20s or early 30s—when the lifestyle changes required for caregiving seem inappropriate.

Age-Condensed Family

The age-condensed family reflects a pattern of multiple generation childbearing in the teen or early 20s years. In contrast to the age-gapped family, the smaller age difference of only 13 to 20 years between generations may lead to less value conflict and thus to stronger affective bonds across generations (George & Gold, 1991). Census data suggest that due to earlier childbearing among African American women as compared to Caucasian women, the age-condensed family structure is more prevalent in the African American community. Because in many of these cases the mothers are single, unmarried adolescents, the workload and responsibility for these children often fall on the older women in the family. Burton and Bengtson's (1985) study of adolescent childbearing in multigenerational African American families revealed that early transitions to grandmotherhood were not welcomed by the majority of women. Rather, "the burden of care was often pushed up the generational ladder to the great-grandmother" (Burton & Dilworth-Anderson, 1991, p.316; Minkler & Roe, 1993). At the same time, the great grandmother may be experiencing age-related changes that reduce her ability to provide care for younger generations and may leave her own need for care unmet. This suggests that the age-condensed family structure may result in the blurring of generational roles and relationships and create highly stressful caregiving situations.

The Truncated Family

Census data suggest that as the Baby Boomers age, there will be an unprecedented number of individuals who have remained childless through-out their lives (U. S. Bureau of the Census, 1991). The question is, Who will these childless elders turn to for assistance with care in the future? Spouses and children (particularly wives and daughters) are the two most frequent providers of support for the elderly. But never-married older men and women who remain childless, as well as childless married older women who outlive their husbands, do not have these informal resources. For these individuals, their siblings, nieces, and nephews may provide some assistance. Yet, with the verticalization of the family, elders will have fewer siblings to turn to for help, and these siblings may already be assisting frail parents and parents-in-law. Extended kin may also place greater limits on both the intensity and duration of such assistance than immediate family members do (George & Gold, 1991; Johnson & Catalano, 1981).

Divorced noncustodial fathers who did not remarry and who retreated from their parental responsibilities may also experience a truncated fam-ily in old age. Furstenberg and Cherlin argue that "many men view marriage and child care as an inseparable role-set. Accordingly, men often sever ties with their children in the course of establishing distance from their former wives" (Furstenberg, 1990, p.388). There is little research on the aging parent-adult child relationships of these absent fathers and their children, and it is unknown whether these fathers will call on their children or whether these children will step forward to provide assistance in later life.

The Single-Parent Family

The rising numbers of single women bearing children and rising di-vorce rates have caused the single-parent family group to become more prevalent. In 1970, only 10% of households with children under 18 were maintained by one parent; by 1990, about 30% of households were so headed. This trend exists across all racial groups. However, the magnitude varies. In 1990, single-parent families accounted for 23% of all Caucasian families, 33% of all Hispanic families, and 61% of all African American families (U.S. Bureau of the Census, 1992d). Thus, although the one-parent family is common for all children, for African American children it is now the most common family structure. The great majority of single-parent households are headed by single mothers; women represent 88% of all single-parent households. However, the percentage of single-father households is increasing—from 9% in 1970 to 12% in 1992 (U.S. Bureau of the Census, 1992c).

The political rhetoric surrounding single parents ignores the reality that they are a heterogeneous group. Although a minority, 21%, of female-headed households have yearly incomes of $35,000 or greater (U. S. Bureau of the Census, 1992g). The rhetoric also overlooks the fact that some single mothers have extensive family networks to turn to for support. For a number of African American single mothers, the availability of a relatively young grandmother or great-grandmother to help nurture the child of a young daughter helps to alleviate some of the stresses of single parenthood. (Although it may burden the grandmother or mother who is dealing with her own age-related changes.) Moreover, a women carrying the role of sole breadwinner and sole parent has a full load that hardly permits caregiving to her parents' generation or to a sibling with a developmental disability or serious mental illness. This may leave aging parents or vulnerable siblings with fewer caregiving resources.

The Blended or Reconstituted Family

High divorce and remarriage rates have resulted in many children living in families with one natural and one stepparent. In 1990, 5.3 million married-couple households had at least one stepchild under 18, which represented almost 21% of all two-parent households (U.S. Bureau of the Census, 1992d). These families often create a complex series of relationships involving step, half, and full siblings as well as stepgrandparent and grandchild relationships. The literature on stepparenting suggests that stepmothers face greater difficulty in integrating themselves into the blended family than do stepfathers because of the cultural perception that the bonds between mothers and children are more deeply embedded by nature. Stepfathers seem to more easily assume the "father" role (Johnson, Klee, & Schmidt, 1988). Less well-explored is how these different step-bonds affect the nature of generational and intergenerational support when an adult family member is confronted with a chronic disabling disease.

ECONOMIC SHIFTS

Until the mid-1970s, the vast majority of American families experienced tangible gains in their income with each successive year. Shifts in the nation's economy during the past 15 years, however, have led to a declining standard of living for many families. As Abramovitz (1991) suggests, for many, the American dream has become deferred as "the middle class has lost its economic footing and the ranks of the poor have soared" (p.484). Taking inflation into account, a worker who earned $187 a week in 1970 made just $173 in 1980 and only $167 in 1989 (Schmidt, 1990). In most families, the income of a second earner has become essential to maintain an adequate standard of living.

In 1989, after decades of constantly rising, the median household income began to drop. Over the past 2 years (1990-1991), real median household income declined 5.1%—from $31,203 to $30,126. This change in real median household income differed across racial and ethnic groups. For Caucasian households, the decline was 3%, to $31,569; for Asian households, the decline was 9%, to $36,449. Although African Americans' and Hispanics' median household incomes did not decline significantly, their household incomes are much less, at $18,807 and $22,691 respectively (U.S. Bureau of the Census, 1993a). The Center on Budget and Policy Priorities Report (1989) confirmed what many Americans had been feeling for quite some time—that the income gap between rich and poor families grew wider in 1988 than in any year since the Census Bureau began gathering these data in 1947. Currently, more families are falling out of, rather than rising into, the middle class. In 1970, 43% of American families earned between $15,000 to $35,000, but by 1988 only 35% of families reported incomes in this range.

As economic pressures have increased, the situation has become even more dismal for lower-income families. Although the U.S. poverty rate declined between 1960 and 1970, it has increased steadily since that decade to 13.5%, or 33.6 million persons, in 1990. Analysis by race reveals that the 1990 poverty rate for Caucasians was 10.7%; for Hispanics, 28.1%; and for African Americans, 31.9% (U.S. Bureau of the Census, 1992b). Two-parent families, regardless of race, have much lower poverty rates than do one-parent families. The incidence of poverty is greatest for female-headed households, especially African Americans and Hispanics, who have a poverty rate of about 60% (U.S. Bureau of the Census, 1989). Of course, poverty, whatever the cause, has negative implications for caregiving.

One group—America's aging population—has experienced economic gains throughout the past 30 years. In 1959, approximately 35% of elders were below the poverty line as compared to about 20% of the general population; by 1990, 12.2% of elders were poor in contrast to 13.5% of the general population (U.S. Bureau of the Census, 1991). Many of the economic gains experienced by the older population are the result of government income-maintenance programs, primarily Medicare and the cost-of-living increase automated to Social Security. Yet Census data reveal these economic gains were not evenly distributed throughout the older population. Prior to the 1960s, men and women faced an almost equal one-out-of-three (33%) chance of living in poverty; by 1990, older men had a 7.6% poverty risk as compared to older women, who had a 15.4% poverty risk (Gonyea, 1994). This differential improvement in the economic status of older men and women is, in part, a result of gender bias in our nation's public policies. For example, Social Security rewards persons who remain in couple relationships throughout their lives. Women who violate the norm of being married, whether through divorce or widowhood, ultimately pay a much greater price than men, given that Social Security is based on marriage as an economic partnership in which the husband is the breadwinner (Gonyea, 1994). Analysis by race reveals that older African Americans are three times as likely (33.3%) and older Hispanics are twice as likely (22.5%) than older Caucasians (10.1%) to live in poverty. The interactive effects of gender, race, and age on the risk of poverty are illustrated by the fact that the poorest group of elders are African American women over 75 (43.9%) followed by Hispanic women 75 years of age and older (30.1%) (U.S. Government Accounting Office, 1992a).

It is important to underscore how economic factors influence families as we move forward with our discussion of their ability to care for members with disabilities. For many families, the lack of an adequate income often leads to poor or substandard housing, poor nutrition and diet, and minimal or no health care. Many of the stresses contemporary families face derive, directly or indirectly, from pressures created by the lack of economic resources. Typically, structural inequities, not personal inadequacy, limit families' ability to provide care. As we will elaborate, these structural inequities especially affect women, due to the gender-segregated nature of the American work economy.

THE FAMILY IDEAL

Social and economic trends, as well as structural changes in the family, are transforming the family life experience for women and men across all racial groups. Feminists argue that the continued use of the monolithic term of "the family," as opposed to "families," implies that there is one legitimate form of family life. This ideal family form is nuclear, hetero-sexual, and based on a prescribed gender-based division of labor, in which women's roles are defined as being within the private sphere of home and men's roles are seen as within the public sphere of work. Further, this ideal family is reified to be seen as natural or biologically determined, not culturally or structurally created.

Yet, as we have seen, a growing number of contemporary families find their own life experiences depart radically from this ideal family form. Historians argue that this ideal form also distorts family experiences of the past. Families have never been as uniform, stable, or harmonious as the cultural ideal would lead us to believe. Desertion, illegitimacy, and remarriage were common events throughout America's colonial and pre-industrial-industrial periods (Baca Zinn & Eitzen, 1987). Feminists argue that when contemporary families are measured against the norm of the mythical ideal family, those who differ are labeled deviant or even pathologi-cal, even though they may possess numerous strengths (Anderson, 1991).

We pose two fundamental questions within our feminist framework. First, why does society continue to uphold this view of the family ideal in the face of the tremendous changes in family structures? And second, what are the costs of maintaining this ideology of the family? Gittins (1986, p. 70) argues that we as a society have strong "beliefs about sexuality, reproduction, parenting relations, and power relationships be-tween age groups and between the sexes. The sum total of these beliefs makes up a strong symbol system which is labeled the family." Thus, rethinking or redefining the family threatens many of society's most fundamental beliefs and values that, in turn, underlie the individualistic, residual approach to U.S. public policy. As discussed in Chapter 1, Thorne (1982) suggests that the ideology of the family reinforces women's proper role in the home, and thus promotes the economic exploitation of women. She argues that "beliefs that most people live in a nuclear family, that adult women usually have husbands to support them, and that motherhood is women's central vocation are used to legitimate the subordination of women in the economy" (Thorne, 1982, p. 4). Anderson (1991) contends that the "conservative climate in which we live actively supports the traditional family ideal. . . . Ideology about the family has been actively promoted through conservative movements and through state-based attempts to formulate policies that encourage traditional arrangements" (p. 244). In fact, the New Right's emphasis on women remaining within—or for em-ployed women, returning to—the home reflects this underlying ideal.

The cost of maintaining the ideology of familism is experienced by women and men who seek to construct meaningful lives but feel conflicted by the discrepancies they perceive between their own families and what has been held up as the ideal. These persons may view themselves and their families as devalued by society. Moreover, because policies have historically been built on the assumption of the traditional family and have sought to enhance it, families who deviate from this artificial norm may be penalized either in terms of eligibility for, or level of, entitlements. Because this universal ideal no longer holds for most American families, both governmental and corporate policies must be developed or modified to take account of how gender, race, and class shape the family experience.

What is a family? is not an easy question to answer. Historically, only family relationships based on blood ties, marriage, or adoption were legally recognized. "Courts and legislatures established policies that were designed to promote so-called traditional families. Any alternative form was viewed as a threat to not only the family but also to the state" (Wisensale & Heckart, 1993, p.199). As a result, traditional families generally experience more rights than nontraditional families in areas such as health insurance, worker compensation, bereavement leaves, and neighborhood zoning. The growing numbers of new forms of relationships such as gay and lesbian partners, heterosexual and homosexual cohabitation, and surrogate parenting, however, have increasingly blurred this narrow legal definition of family (Scanzoni & Marsiglio, 1991). Throughout the next decade, the courts will undoubtedly continue to struggle over the legal definition of family. These future legal decisions regarding the questions of what is a family and who is responsible for meeting families' needs, especially those of dependent and vulnerable members, are of critical importance because they may ultimately determine the condition of the family at the beginning of the 21st century (Wisensale & Heckart, 1993).

3

The Changing American
Economy and Workforce

In the past several decades, profound changes in the American workplace have accompanied modifications in the structure and composition of American families. The shifting composition of the U.S. workforce—a growing number of women, single-parent, and dual-earner households—has led to a reassessment of how dependent care responsibilities, traditionally the onus of the family alone, can be carried out, particularly given the entry of carers into the workplace.

> For most families today, it is no longer possible to assume that employees have someone at home to care for those who are dependent (i.e., children, elders, chronically ill) and to insure that these problems do not intrude into the workplace. (Googins, Gonyea, & Pitt-Catsouphes, 1990, p.1)

Many policy makers, especially those of the New Right, have sought to define women's employment as a problem because of the loss of potential caregivers. Our feminist analysis, however, stresses the larger structural factors in the economy that underlie both the economic necessity of employment for many women and the gender-based division between employment and family, the public and private roles that have been historically perpetuated by the ideology of separate spheres.

Feminists have sought to redefine women's struggle to maintain a balance between their home and work lives as a public concern. Arguing for a fundamental shift in our deeply rooted cultural beliefs in the traditional boundaries between work and family, Kanter (1977) conceptualizes the two worlds as highly interactive domains. Most employees do not simply abandon their family concerns at the company doorstep, nor do they leave behind job demands at the office, plant, or shop. Stresses and successes can spill over into both one's home and one's work life (Gonyea, 1991).

During the past five decades, the United States has experienced dramatic changes in the organization of its economy that have altered the nature of the workplace and the work experience for countless Americans. These changes impact workers'—especially employed women's—private lives at home. In this chapter we identify three trends in the U.S. economy that have profoundly affected American workers and their families. These trends are: (a) the shift from a national economy to a global economy, (b) the change from a production economy to a service economy, and (c) the feminization of the labor force. In addition, we explore structural factors that underlie persistent gender inequities, including occupational segregation and the dramatic expansion of the contingent (part-time and contractual) workforce. We then begin to examine the difficulties and challenges that the current organization of the American workplace creates for today's employed caregivers.

GLOBALIZATION OF THE U.S. ECONOMY

Technological advances in the second half of this century, such as jet airplanes, satellites, and fiber-optics communication, have rendered meaningless large geographic distances and different time zones between countries, and have led to the creation of a world economy (Johnston & Packer, 1987). Many nations—including the United States—are experiencing massive growth in the number of global corporations, foreign investments in real estate and businesses, and labor contracts that are going across borders or overseas. As economist Milton Friedman asserts, the world has been shaken by a technological revolution "making it possible to produce a product anywhere, using resources from anywhere, by a company located anywhere, and to be sold anywhere" (Magnet, 1993, p. 54).

As global trade has grown in importance, the U.S. economy has become tied to the world economy. Over the past 25 years, as the global economy grew or shrank, the United States has experienced economic booms and recessions; yet, although it has mirrored the world's economy, the U.S. economy has often lagged behind. For American government officials, corporations, and workers, these changes have required coming to terms with the erosion of the United States' economic preeminence and the "loss of our economic sovereignty" (Johnston & Packer, 1987, p. 3). In the 1960s, American companies virtually dominated international trade, and the U.S. dollar was the international standard of exchange; by the 1980s, the United States' economic status had clearly declined. America's share of world exports has dropped considerably. Our national economy is now just as affected by world events—the OPEC oil prices, the German discount rate, the strength of the U.S. dollar relative to the Japanese yen—as it is by events in the our own country—the federal interest rate, savings and loans banking failures, labor contracts. Globalization has had positive effects on the American work economy. It has contributed to the creation or expansion of markets for U.S. products. Yet, for American workers, globalization has also been associated with corporations' movement, or threat of movement, of jobs outside the United States in a deliberate attempt to depress wages.

POSTINDUSTRIALIZATION OF THE U.S. ECONOMY

The Bureau of Labor Statistics' data reveal strikingly different growth trends for the three major sectors of the U.S. economy—agriculture, goods, and services—between the 1950s to the 1980s (Urquhart, 1984). Not surprisingly, both the number of persons and the percentage of the U.S. population employed in the agricultural sector has steadily declined from 11.3% of employed persons in 1952 to only 3.6% in 1982. In contrast, until the 1980-1982 recessionary period, when approximately 3 million jobs were lost, the goods sector created approximately 30 million new jobs between 1952 and 1979. In spite of the actual job gains in the goods sector, its share of total employment declined from 35.5% in 1952 to 27.2% in 1982, primarily as a result of the service sector's considerably faster growth. In 1952, the service sector represented slightly more than half (63.3%) of the employed population; by 1982, the service sector's relative share was more than two thirds (69.2%) (Urquhart, 1984).

These trends have continued throughout the past decade. The agriculture sector has slipped to less than 3% of employed persons (U.S. Bureau of Labor Statistics, 1991). The manufacturing sector has slashed millions of jobs due to plant closings, relocation, and layoffs. The Fortune 500 industrial companies, which generally pay the best wages and offer the best benefits, have downsized and eliminated approximately one out of every four jobs. Fewer than one fifth (18%) of American jobs are now found in the manufacturing sector (U.S. Bureau of Labor Statistics, 1991). About 80% of the all-new jobs created between 1982 and 1992 were in services and retail sectors, and most of these jobs paid only one half of the average manufacturing wage. Currently, 78% of employed Americans work in the service sector. It is projected that by the year 2000, the service sector will account for 92% of all jobs (Schuping, 1992). Although the greatest expansion of jobs will continue to be in services, it is not anticipated that this heterogeneous sector—encompassing such diverse fields as transportation, information technology, retail services, and banking and financial services—will experience equal growth rates across all segments. The Labor Department predicts that some of the fields that will experience the greatest growth between 1988 and 2000 include retail services, janitors and house cleaners, waiters, receptionists, hospital orderlies, and clerks (O'Reilly, 1992). These jobs typically offer low wages, few insurance or retirement benefits, and little opportunity for promotion. In many cases, the growth of lower-wage service sectors depends on the availability of women to work (Spakes, 1992).

The dilemma is no longer simply an issue of too few jobs, but one of too few good jobs. Although the United States added 13.6 million jobs between 1979 and 1989, almost half were low-wage jobs. A Fortune analysis of Labor Department wage data reveals that nearly 5 million of these jobs paid less than $250 a week, or $13,000 a year, after adjusting for inflation, which is below the official poverty level for a family of four. More than 1.6 million of these jobs are in restaurants, stockrooms, and retail sales, where the chances for promotion are low (O'Reilly, 1992). U.S. Census data reveal that in 1979 less than 20% of workers had low-wage jobs; this figure grew to 25.7% of the workforce by 1990. According to Labor Secretary Robert Reich, the generation of new jobs is not the challenge that confronts us; rather, "our bigger long-term problem is creating good jobs" (Swoboda, 1993a). This failure of the U.S. economy to generate a substantial number of new high-wage jobs has contributed to families falling out of the middle class. Dislocated workers have slid into lower-wage jobs that yield smaller family incomes (Shapiro & Greenstein, 1991).

FEMINIZATION OF THE U.S. WORKFORCE

The fundamental demographic shifts occurring in our society—increased racial diversity and the aging of the population—are mirrored in the workplace, yet perhaps the most significant change in the American workplace has been the increased participation of women in the labor force. At the turn of the 20th century, the labor force participation rate for men was 84% and 18% for women, of which only 5% were married women. Significantly different labor patterns, however, existed for women of color and immigrant women: Approximately 25% of African American women—single and married—were employed, and 33% of married immigrant women took boarders or lodgers into their homes (Matthaei, 1982). In 1900, 39% of all working women performed domestic work. Of these, 33% were African American, 33% were foreign-born white, and

16% were Asian (Blau & Ferber, 1986). Another 25% of working women worked in the textile, millinery, or tobacco industries. Slightly less than 20%, almost all of which were African American, worked in the farms and fields primarily of the rural South. About 8% were teachers or nurses, two professions that were open to women at that time (Blau & Ferber, 1986).

Between 1890 and 1940, women's rate of labor force participation experienced only modest gains, from 18% (over three quarters single women) to 28% (over two thirds single women). The country's mobilization for World War II, and the need to fill civilian jobs left vacant as men joined the armed forces, led to the large-scale entry of women into the paid workforce. By 1945, more than one third (35.8%) of American women were earning wages, and, despite some initial decline in the immediate postwar period, women's labor force participation has continued to increase steadily (Blau & Ferber, 1986). Approximately 34% of women were working in 1950, 38% in 1960, 43% in 1970, and 52% in 1980 (Chadwick & Heaton, 1992). Currently, labor force participation rates of women vary little by race or ethnic origin: In 1990, 57.8% of African American women, 57.5% of white women, and 53% of Hispanic women were in the labor force (Ries & Stone, 1992). Projections suggest that by the year 2000, more than 60% of women will be in the labor market.

Women are now in the workforce in unprecedented numbers, and equally important, their patterns of participation in the paid labor market over the life cycle have changed radically. Prior to the 1940s, most women workers were young and single. Women generally left the workforce permanently on marrying and having children. However, between 1950 and 1990, the labor force participation rate of women in their 30s and 40s soared, whereas the rate among women aged 20 to 24 remained almost constant. Middle-aged women have entered and reentered the workforce in increasing numbers. Today, married women (57%) are almost as likely as single women to be employed (68%) (U.S. Bureau of the Census, 1992a). In the past two decades, one of the most notable trends has been the increased labor force participation of women with children under the age of six. In 1975, slightly more than one third (36.7%) of married women with children under six were working; by 1990, this figure had jumped to more than half (58.9%) of married women. The 1990 rate of employment for single women with children under six was slightly less than one third (29%). In 1980, fewer than 25% of married women with toddlers (children under 3 years) were full-time workers; in 1990, the figure exceeded 33% (U.S. Bureau of the Census, 1992a). In 1994, the percentage of women in the workforce between ages 20 and 44 is dropping for the first time in more than 25 years. Whether or not this shift is temporary, it has been partially explained by the high cost of day care, corporate downsizing, and the increased demand for temporary workers (Joyner, 1994). From a feminist perspective, this shift illustrates how women's lives are profoundly affected by larger societal changes, especially those in the economy.

GENDER DIFFERENCES IN OCCUPATIONS

Although the proportion of women in the labor force has increased steadily, declines in occupational or job segregation by gender have occurred at a much slower pace. Approximately 20 million women joined the U.S. workforce between 1975 and 1990. Most of these women entered traditionally female occupations. The U.S. Bureau of Labor Statistics (1991) data reveal that despite some inroads into traditionally male occupations, more than 66% of all employed women are still found in just two sectors—services (45%) and wholesale and retail trade (22%). These data are made even more striking by breaking the service sector into two components: administrative support and services. Three quarters of the women employed in administrative support are either clerical workers (45%) or secretaries, stenographers or typists (31%); and women in the services field are primarily found in either food services (34%), cleaning or household services (23%), personal services (21%), and health services (20%).

Men, in contrast, are more evenly distributed across occupations. The ratio of men to women is at least two to one in the fields of manufacturing; transportation and public utilities; and finances, insurance, and real estate (U.S. Bureau of Labor Statistics, 1991). Even today, some occupations remain almost exclusively male or female. Women still represent just 2% of workers in construction or fire fighting, whereas only 1% of secretaries and 5% of registered nurses are men (U.S. Bureau of Labor Statistics, 1991). As Blau and Ferber (1986) stress, "data on the major occupational categories do not reveal the full extent of occupational segregation by gender" (p. 159). For example, 22% of employed women and 21% of employed men are found in sales, but women are more likely to be involved in retail sales, whereas men are more often manufacturing sales representatives. Similarly, a 1984 study of California firms found that approximately 50% were completely gender-segregated by job category— that is, not a single woman or man shared the same job title (Baron & Bielby, 1984). Analysis by race suggests that women of color as compared to white women are overrepresented in the lower-paying service jobs and underrepresented in professional positions (U.S. Bureau of Labor Statistics, 1991).

GENDER DIFFERENCES IN WAGES AND BENEFITS

In 1963, after an 18-year battle in Congress, President Kennedy signed into law the Equal Pay Act, making it illegal for women employed in the same jobs as men to receive lower wages. Since that date, the gap between female and male earnings has narrowed somewhat. In 1963, women typically earned 59 cents for every dollar men earned; by 1990, women were earning 72 cents for every dollar of men's wages (U.S. Bureau of Labor Statistics, 1991). Although, at first glance, this shrinking of the female-male earnings gap seems to be encouraging, Susan Bianchi-Sands, Executive Director of the National Committee on Pay Equity, argues that "being 30% behind after 30 years is not great. At this rate, it will take us another 90 years to have equal pay" (Mollison, 1993).

One important reason that the gap has not narrowed further is that the Equity Pay Act did not affect hiring, promotions, or wages for people in unequal jobs or different occupations. The recent reduction in the female-male earnings ratio is as much a function of declining male salaries as it is a result of rising wages for women. Ries and Stone's (1992) analysis of 1983 and 1990 Labor Department statistics revealed that men's average wages increased substantially for only one of the eight major occupational categories—managerial and professional employees.

Differences in the size of the female-male pay gap vary across racial, age, and occupational groups. For example, in 1991, African American women earned 62 cents and Hispanic women 54 cents for every dollar earned by Caucasian men. For persons aged 16 to 24, women earned 90% of men's wages; however, for individuals between 25 and 54, women earned just 73% of men's wages, and for those 55 and older, the earning gap widened to 65% (U.S. Bureau of Labor Statistics, 1991). Also, the female/male earnings ratio is larger in certain fields, such as production inspectors and examiners (63%) and financial managers (67%), as compared to other professions such as police and detectives (94%) and engineers (90%).

Identifying the exact proportion of the earnings gap that is due to discrimination against women in the labor market is difficult. "Nonetheless, the findings of most studies provide strong evidence of pay differences between men and women that are not accounted for by sex differences in qualifications, even when the list is extensive" (Blau & Ferber, 1986, p. 234). Even after taking into account gender differences in such factors as formal education, years of training completed on the job, labor force attachment, and other employment history, over 50% of the variation in men's and women's wages remains unexplained (Blau & Ferber, 1986). Thirty years after the Pay Equity Act, even in the female-dominated professions (i.e., nurse, waitress/waiter, elementary-school teacher, secretary), women on average earn less then men (Saltzman, 1991).

In addition to wages or salaries, fringe benefits such as health insurance and pension coverage are critical to ensuring a family's well-being, yet the proportion of all American workers—male and female—who have health insurance or pension plans provided through their job has actually declined in recent years. Moreover, women of all races are less likely to have this coverage than their male counterparts. In 1987, 48% of Caucasian women, 51% of African American women, and 41% of Hispanic women had employer- or union-sponsored health insurance. In contrast, 65% of Caucasian men, 54% of African American men, and 47% of Hispanic men received this benefit (Ries & Stone, 1992). These days, even workers who have employer- or union-sponsored health insurance are paying for a greater share of their health care costs out of their own pockets. Companies are requiring their employees to absorb the rising health care costs either by having workers pay a greater share of the plan fees or by restricting what medical procedures are covered by the plan. This decision has a profound impact on families with members with a chronic illness or disability who often have substantial medical expenses. Nearly 60% of companies require employees to pay an average of $107 a month for family coverage, as opposed to $69 in 1989 (Samuelson, 1993).

Private pensions represent an important source of income in later life. Persons who do not accrue pension benefits face a much greater risk of poverty in old age, yet the number of American workers covered by employer- or union-sponsored pension plans is also declining and, once again, women workers are more disadvantaged. In 1987, 46% of white men, 40% of African American men, and 29% of Hispanic men in the workforce had pension coverage in contrast to only 36% of white women, 39% of African American women, and 28% of Hispanic women. Pensions are part of the compensation package, and thus employees with higher-wage jobs are more likely to have coverage. Women's lower pension coverage is a result of their concentration in lower-wage jobs. More than 67% of women earn less than $20,000 a year. These workers had the lowest pension coverage rates in the workforce (Korczyk, 1993). Among the current cohort of older adults, men are twice as likely as women to receive a private pension. Of the approximately 13 million retirees receiving private pension benefits, 66% are men (Hess, 1990). Women's lack of pension income has contributed in part to gender differences in economic well-being in later life. In 1988, the median income for older men was $12,471 as compared to only $7,103 for older women (Moon, 1990).

Membership in unions or labor organizations correlates with both increased wages and fringe benefits. Union membership for men and women has declined in recent years, however. In the 1950s, more than a quarter (27%) of U.S. workers were union members, but in 1990, slightly less than 17% of U.S. workers were unionized (Bureau of National Affairs, 1990). Women have always been underrepresented in labor organizations. One primary reason for the lower numbers of women in unions is that historically, unionization has been highest in the blue-collar manufacturing jobs where fewer women are employed. However, the lack of women leadership in the labor organizations, as well as union policies or strategies for emphasizing issues of concern to male workers at the bargaining table to the neglect of female workers' concerns, have also contributed to women's underrepresentation (Blau & Ferber, 1986). "It is tough to be a union leader because so much union work takes place at night or after work hours," said union president Lenore Miller, who started out as a clerical worker 35 years ago at the Retail, Wholesale and Department Store Union's central offices. "You're doing a double job, and we are the caregivers. We are the wives and mothers, too," she said (Franklin, 1993, p. C1).

THE GROWTH OF THE CONTINGENT WORKFORCE

A recent shift within the American labor force has been the rapid expansion of the contingent workforce. During the 1980s, American companies, seeking to maintain or increase profitability, attempted to gain greater control over their labor costs by quickly adjusting the size of their workforce in response to shifting market conditions. To do this, companies began to rely more heavily on part-time and temporary workers as well as contracting out for services previously performed in-house. These various flexible work arrangements are increasingly referred to as contingent work.

A two-tiered workforce has always existed in the United States. The first-tier is comprised of a core of salaried employees who have a high degree of job security, health and pension benefits, and opportunities for training and advancement. The second-tier, historically described as peripheral workers, secondary workers, or reserve workers, and more recently as contingent workers, represents employees who have only weak ties to a particular company, few or no employee benefits, and few opportunities for career development. What is new is the dramatic expansion of the contingent workforce, the growing practice of companies laying off their own employees and hiring them back (at lower wages and without benefits) as independent contractors, and the spread of contingent workers into white-collar positions. "Examples abound in the publishing, television, insurance, and advertising industries of employees laid off from the core tier and hired back as independent contractors, euphemistically referred to as freelancers, or supplanted by temporary workers" (Christensen, 1990, p. 1428).

Within the United States (and in other developed countries), in the 1980s, part-time and temporary employment grew at a much faster pace than did full-time permanent employment, and this trend is expected to continue throughout the next decade. Today, contingent workers represent more than 25% of the U.S. workforce, or one out of every four Americans. Indeed, Manpower, Incorporated, a temporary-employment firm with 560,000 workers, has replaced the General Motors Corporation as the largest employer in the United States (Rosenblatt, 1993). There are now an estimated 35 million contingent workers with lower-paid women and people of color disproportionately filling their ranks (Bryant Quinn, 1991). Howe's (1986) analysis of the temporary-help industry revealed that women make up 65% of these workers, as compared with 35% for men; almost 20% of temporary-help workers are African American, which is double the representation of African Americans in all other industries. Women's strong presence in the contingent workforce makes it a feminist issue.

Some of the growth of contingent work results from individuals voluntarily seeking part-time or project work, but most contingent workers would prefer to be in the first tier of the labor force. The primary impetus for the expansion of contingent work is corporate America's desire to cut company costs through the elimination of employee benefits and through reduced payroll tax obligations. When companies outsource their own employees— i.e., firing them and hiring them back as independent contractors or part-timers—they are freed from "having to provide any benefits or worry about other workplace laws or regulations" (True, 1993, p. 7). A recent study by the International Labor Organization revealed that these part-time workers are, on average, paid lower wages than full-time workers, especially if the part-time employee is a woman, and that these workers are typically excluded from benefits such as sick pay, overtime, health insurance, pension plans, and unemployment insurance (Swoboda, 1993b). *Newsweek* columnist Jane Bryant Quinn (1991) emphasizes the following:

> All employment today is colored by this new "contingent" workforce. . . .
> They're the human equivalent of the inventory control system known as "just in time." Widgets, for example, now enter factories moments before they'll be

> called for on the assembly line. Similarly, almost any type of worker—from data processor to auditor to sales executive—can be signed up as needed, then shown to the door when business slows. (p. 41)

Nor is the growth of the contingent workforce limited to the private sector; both federal and state governments are increasingly eliminating jobs through the use of temporary employees or the contracting out for services. True (1993) cites a recent embarrassing case for the federal government, in which an 8-year employee of the National Park Service suffered a fatal heart attack while caretaking the Lincoln Memorial. Because the employee was a "temporary" employee (i.e., he signed a new contract yearly,) despite his length of service and death on the job, the surviving family was not legally entitled to federal employee benefits.

The growth in the number of contingent workers in both the private and public sectors has led to many individuals finding themselves living from one job to the next. Although there are advantages to companies (and to some individuals) in having greater flexibility in work arrangements, for numerous Americans, contingent work has resulted in greater job insecurity, lower wages, fewer benefits, and greater burdens. As Bryant Quinn (1991, p. 41) suggests, there are social costs to the contingent workforce growth: According to Quinn, nearly 5 million people are working part-time because they cannot find full-time jobs. They have no affordable source of medical and disability benefits, and will reach the end of their working lives with no company pensions and minimal Social Security checks. A "disposable" workforce appeals to employers, but it builds in long-term social costs. For many American families—especially female-headed households—employment within the contingent labor market has led to an erosion in their standard of living and resulted in a greater sense of "living life on the edge." Job insecurity in the 1980s and 1990s has basically led to economically insecure families.

THE AMERICAN WORK EXPERIENCE

Juliet Schor's 1991 book, *The Overworked American,* provided statistical evidence of a historical trend in the decline of leisure in American lives; it spoke to the hearts of many Americans who perceived themselves as caught in a rat race and experiencing a decline in the quality of their lives. They were working longer and harder, earning less, and spending less time with family and friends.

According to Schor's estimates, "the average employed person is now on the job an additional 163 hours, or the equivalent of an extra month a year" as compared to the worker in 1969 (Schor, 1991, p. 29). One of Schor's most interesting findings is that this trend of increasing work hours is a distinctly American response to global economic stagnation. West European and Scandinavian countries have also experienced economic downturns; however, workers' hours in these countries have continued to decline and their wages have increased. In contrast, American businesses have disproportionately passed on their fiscal problems to their employees. During the 1980s and 1990s, U.S. businesses are increasingly downsizing and striving to become "lean and mean." The remaining core workers are often asked to work overtime or forgo vacations to meet company deadlines. Fearful of being the next to be laid off, workers feel they have to constantly demonstrate their organizational commitment by arriving early, working late, through lunch or illnesses, and/or postponing or canceling vacation plans. A 1992 survey of a large high-technology company found that 20% of the workforce had not taken a single vacation day in the previous year (Googins & Litchfield, 1992).

People are also working longer because they are being paid less, especially in the contingent workforce.

> Workers paid by the hour—a majority of U.S. employees—saw their average wages peak in 1973. Since then, it (the average wage) has declined substantially and now stands at its mid-1960s level; just to reach their 1973 standard of living, they must work 245 more hours, or 6-plus extra weeks, a year. (Schor, 1991, pp. 80-81)

For many families, a second income has become absolutely necessary to maintain their standard of living. Approximately 63% of married couples are dual-earner families—that is, both the husband and wife are in the labor force (Chadwick & Heaton, 1992). Moreover, in almost 20% of dual-earner households, the husbands and wives work different shifts. For some of these families, the choice of working different shifts is a child care solution, especially in light of the costs of day care, which frequently absorb the majority of the mother's salary (Joyner, 1994). It allows parents the opportunity to care for their children in their homes rather than having to purchase child care services.

For other families, especially single-parent households, additional income is generated by one person holding multiple jobs. In fact, the number of persons working several jobs has increased 400% between 1970 and 1989 (Ries & Stone, 1992). Approximately 40% of women and 32% of men holding multiple jobs indicated that they were doing so in order to meet regular household expenses (U.S. Bureau of Labor Statistics, 1991). Because one of the primary reasons persons hold multiple jobs is inadequate wages, it should not be surprising that a greater proportion of women are working more than one job. In 1989, women were almost twice as likely to work for minimum wages than men. Approximately 7% of women and 3.5% of men earned less than $7,000 a year (Ries & Stone, 1992). Some persons seek out several jobs because they are unable to secure a single full-time, permanent position.

CORPORATE AMERICA'S
RESPONSE TO EMPLOYED CAREGIVERS

Despite almost daily features in the media concerning women's entry into the workforce, employment-family conflicts, and the aging of the U.S. population, less than 1% of the 17 million U.S. companies have instituted family-responsive benefits. Even fewer companies are working to change the American management culture that grew out of the white male workforce of the 1950s (Gonyea & Googins, 1992). After two decades of highly publicized, innovative corporate programs, there is still not a widespread adoption of work-family benefits in corporate America (Galinsky, Friedman, & Hernandez, 1991). We will elaborate the reasons for the persistence of this pattern in Chapter 10.

Why has corporate America been reluctant to respond to the concerns of employed caregivers? Corporate managers may not even recognize work-family conflicts as an issue to be addressed. Consistent with our feminist analysis outlined in Chapter 1, this lack of awareness results from the dichotomy between work and family life created by the ideologies of separate spheres and of familism. It is presumed that family or personal concerns are isolated from and do not influence what occurs in the workplace. Another reason for the lack of awareness is that top-level management's demographic characteristics and family structures do not resemble those of the average worker. Senior management remains a white male preserve. Managers are unlikely to confront some of the work-family dilemmas experienced by their employees. It is true that women have made significant gains rising into middle management; still, only 3% of top executive jobs are held by women. A "glass ceiling" of subtle gender discrimination has effectively kept women out of the executive suites.

> Even companies that win awards for enlightened work and family policies have made little progress in bringing women into the upper ranks. In *Working Mother* magazine's most recent list of the top 75 companies, fewer than 10% of officers or vice presidents in 48 of the firms were female. (Saltzman, 1991, p. 44)

Women are also underrepresented on corporate boards: A 1989 survey of Fortune 500 companies revealed that less than one out of every eight board members is a woman (Ries & Stone, 1992).

Most corporate leaders are not convinced that assisting employed caregivers will benefit the company. Top management generally views work-family responsiveness as a marginal component of strategic human-service management (Lobel, 1992). Corporate America will remain reluctant to act unless they perceive that their failure to become more "family-friendly" will cost companies in terms of their ability to recruit and retain a highly qualified workforce or to raise productivity levels. There are four key policy issues for companies: (a) How many workers have caregiving responsibilities, and do these demands affect work absenteeism, tardiness, job performance, and productivity? (b) Are there certain types of caregiving or perhaps critical points in a family's life cycle that result in greater work-family stress? (c) What resources are needed by employed caregivers, and do these benefits make a difference in terms of workplace and family life consequences? and (d) What are the respective roles and responsibilities of the family, the workplace, and the community in meeting these needs? (Neal, Chapman, Ingersoll-Dayton, & Emlen, 1993). Until these policy questions are addressed, we anticipate that U.S. businesses will, at best, respond to employed caregivers' concerns in a piecemeal manner (e.g., on-site child care, information and referral services, support groups) rather than take on the larger challenge of how to reinvent the workplace to change the existing workplace culture, which grew out of the 1950s, and to allow for the greater integration of home and workplace, private and public.

AMERICAN HOUSEHOLDS' RESPONSE TO WORKING WOMEN

Corporate America's general lack of response to the needs of employed caregivers means that the responsibility for balancing work and family still rests squarely on the shoulders of individual employees. The next logical question to ask is whether, with women's entry into the labor force, American families have reorganized the performance of household and caregiving tasks. Are men and women sharing more equally in these domestic roles within the private sphere? In short, no. Women still disproportionately shoulder the responsibilities for home and family. Research reveals that like reports of Mark Twain's death, "the commonly held belief that men's roles at home and work have changed dramatically in recent years is greatly exaggerated" (PR Newswire, 1991). Although a

1990 Roper Organization poll found that 69% of women and 64% of men felt the single easiest solution to the time crunch in two-income families was increased housework for men, rhetoric still does not match or equal performance (Clark, 1992).

Data collected from 60,000 employees at 15 major corporations by Work/Family Directions Inc. between 1986 and 1991 found that employed wives spend nearly twice the number of hours per week on child care and household tasks compared to employed husbands. The average employed mother spends 44 hours at work and 31 hours on family responsibilities each week as opposed to the average employed father's 47 hours on the job and 15 hours of family responsibilities (Rodgers, 1992). Based on her in-depth study of 50 San Francisco Bay Area families over a 7-year time period, Hochschild (1989) concluded that the majority of women work one shift at the office or factory and a "second shift" at home, which leads to a "leisure gap" between the sexes. On average, mothers, as compared to fathers, worked an extra 13 hours each week, which ultimately added up to an extra month of 24-hour days each year. Hochschild argues that the second shift or leisure gap is the result of a stalled revolution in gender relations. The revolution in the role of women by entering the workplace has occurred without a revolution in the role of men within the home and without a revolution in the institutions that define the workplace or family. Accordingly, public and corporate policies have failed to support women and men in trying to alter stereotypical sex roles.

Time diaries kept by households (one of the most accurate data sources) reveal that although men have been increasing their share of household duties, the division of responsibilities is still not equal. In the 20 years between 1965 and 1985, men's share of the household or child care tasks rose from 20% to 33% (Pleck, 1985). When housework is shared, women continue to have responsibility for the tasks that must be done daily or at someone else's convenience (e.g., cooking, cleaning, bathing) whereas men tend to do tasks that can be carried out at their own convenience (e.g., yard work, bill paying). A 1990 Roper Organization Poll revealed that "the more unpleasant the task, the less likely men do it . . . toilet scrubbing, floor washing, laundry, and oven cleaning are things men would rather save for females" (Levine, 1990, p. E1).

The negative effects of the stalled revolution of gender relations are felt by all family members (Hochschild, 1989). Tensions between the sexes have increased.

Ongoing polls by the Roper Organization indicate that women's anger at men has risen steadily over the last 20 years. Instead of mellowing, relationships between the sexes get grittier as more women work outside the home—and find they still have to work inside the home as well. Husbands and lovers talk a good game about sharing chores, the studies show, but their actions don't match their words. (Levine, 1990, p. E1)

Such tensions are likely to be even greater when women must provide care for dependent relatives with chronic disabilities.

Obviously, the costs of this stalled or incomplete revolution are greatest for women and occur across the life span. Because our society, according to the ideology of familism, has continued to define the second shift for women as normal family life, women's fatigue, role overload, anger, and resentment are all viewed as personal problems as opposed to political or public concerns. Rather than reorganize the workplace or family life on a societal or macro level, women are told to seek individual solutions to these problems. For many, work-family conflict is seen as an issue relevant only to affluent baby-boomer women trying to "have it all." But *Wall Street Journal* columnist Sue Shellenbarger stresses the following:

Work-family conflict reaches far beyond this stereotype about the two-career couple. More than five million American households with children under 18 are headed by working single parents. . . . Thus, regardless of gender or political persuasion, more and more workers are caregivers, and more and more caregivers must work. (Shellenbarger, 1992, p. 158)

The Women's Bureau of the U.S. Labor Department's (1994) survey of 250,000 working women recruited through businesses, unions, magazines, and community groups, and their parallel scientific study of 1,200 working women, underscore the magnitude of the problem. America's employed women remain overworked and underpaid. Asked to cite the biggest problems at the work site, both surveys revealed that: 59% of the women identified too much stress, 49% cited not getting paid what the job is worth, and 44% noted the need for better benefits. The Women's Bureau concluded that America's working women are exhausted (Naylor, 1994). Commenting on the survey, Secretary of Labor Robert Reich said that "women are giving 110% to their work and 110% to their families and they feel as if most of what they do goes unnoticed" (Lewis, 1994, p. 69).

The long-term costs of society's reduction of work-family conflict to "a woman's problem" contributes greatly to women's increased risk of poverty in later life. The problems and choices women face in the public economic sphere and the private domestic arena throughout their lives— the tensions between breadwinning and caregiving—shape their economic status in old age. Across the life span, women are disadvantaged by their predominance in the secondary sector of the labor market—a sector composed of jobs that offer low wages, little job security, and few fringe benefits. As Perkins (1993, p. 5) notes, "women's workplace poverty is recycled into poverty during retirement." Women are also disadvantaged by the fact that they receive no economic credit under Social Security for the years they delayed entry into or left the workforce to care for children, spouse, aging parents, or other relatives with chronic disabilities (Gonyea, 1994; Minkler & Estes, 1991). As we will elaborate in Chapter 11, both Social Security and private pensions are based on an outdated male-model of family and work that systematically penalizes middle-aged and older women. It is the way in which underlying societal values interact with structural factors in the workplace and in the home that oppress women in terms of their health and economic status and is at the heart of the feminist critique throughout this book.

4

Changing Health Care Needs
and Long-Term Care Services

We turn now to examining the changing health and long-term care needs of three populations with disabilities that are the focus of this book: the frail elderly, adults with mental retardation and other related developmental disabilities, and adults with serious and persistent mental illness. We also describe the long-term care system for dependents with chronic disabilities, the major methods of financing, and how these structural and regulatory factors have affected families. Changes in the family, the economy, and the health and long-term care needs of individuals with disabilities all interact to create increasing burdens on family caregivers.

Many individuals in these three groups have survived as a result of the success of medical technology. Pursuit of the "perfect" technology, oriented toward cure, has created the paradox that although these populations are now living longer, they face serious, often debilitating or life-threatening disabilities that create the need for care. This need is often intensified by the interaction of race, gender, and poverty along with changes in the economy and the family described in Chapters 2 and 3. Although disability per se does not create dependency, growing numbers of these persons have multiple disorders and are dependent on the assistance of others as well as medical and nonmedical services. This constellation of assistance and social services required to perform activities of daily living—bathing, dressing, using the toilet, cleaning, shopping—combined with skilled care for medically related problems constitute what is defined as long-term care. The extent of the need for assistance from others is not static, but varies over time. People requiring long-term care frequently move in and out of acute-care settings, using about twice as much acute care as do their same-aged peers (National Committee to Preserve Social Security & Medicare, 1993).

Despite these fluctuating needs for support, growing numbers of persons and their families in our focus populations lack the health and long-term insurance essential to quality care. Even when they have access to federal reimbursement for care, such as Medicare or Medicaid, their complex needs for custodial and maintenance services are often inadequately met through existing service delivery and financing systems. Most prefer to remain in a homelike setting rather than in an institution. In fact, Fischer and Eustis (1994) suggest that being cared for in one's own home is a universal value. There are few resources, however, for paid home care. All three populations have been affected by the process of deinstitutionalization and the ideology of community care—the movement of individuals from large institutions to the community, without adequate development of a "safety" net of community- and home-based support services.

To fill these gaps, family members, not formal services, are the primary providers of care, yet as shown in Chapters 2 and 3, many families are less able to provide care because of economic changes. The growth in the number and seriousness of the needs of these dependent persons is placing tremendous demands on both the formal and the informal long-term care systems at the same time that public funding has declined and expectations of private responsibility have grown. With policy makers increasingly concerned about how to deal cost-effectively with the disabled's multifaceted needs, family members, typically women, face growing expectations to carry the burden of custodial care even though more women are employed (Aday, 1993: Estes, Swan, & Associates 1993).

In this chapter we describe the three focus populations and their growth as a result of "high-tech" medical interventions. We review the institutional bias of service systems, particularly their emphasis on acute care, and the gaps in systems that result in their failure to meet the needs for long-term care. Our review of the primary funding mechanisms highlights how separate funding streams result in (a) the lack of a comprehensive and coordinated system of community-based home care services, (b) service fragmentation and gaps intensified by recent cutbacks in public funding for long-term care services, and (c) the devolution of funding responsibilities at the local level. At the same time, medicalization and privatization of services and informalization of care for the dependent individuals and their families have intensified structural gender and racial inequities in care. We do not attempt to provide equal coverage of each of these populations and the relevant policies and programs, given the comprehensive and complex nature of such a task. Instead, we include selected examples from the fields of aging, developmental disabilities-mental retardation, and mental health to highlight general trends and issues.

THE GROWTH AND NEEDS OF
ADULT POPULATIONS WITH CHRONIC DISABILITIES

The Frail Elderly

As we noted in Chapter 2, the major demographic change of the 20th century has been the increase of the population age 65 and over from approximately 4% of the population in 1900 to nearly 13% in 1990 (U.S. Bureau of the Census, 1991b). This growth reflects the increase in life expectancy, most of which has occurred because of advances in medicine, specifically the eradication in this century of many diseases, such as influenza and pneumonia, that caused high infant and childhood mortality. Chronic disease being the dominant pattern of illness today, death from acute disease is rare. Maternal, infant, and early-childhood death rates have also declined considerably, resulting in a growing number of people who survive to old age, often facing chronic disabilities requiring long-term care and eventually resulting in death (Hollingsworth & Hollingsworth, 1994; Verbrugge, 1989). Death rates due to hypertension and heart disease have started to decline, which may result in significant increases in survival beyond age 65, when heart disease and cancer become more chronic and less fatal.

Mortality decreases accompanied by a significant increase in disability have resulted in a growing need for medical interventions during the increased years of life expectancy that are spent in disability. Estes et al. (1993) refer to this as the paradox of the demographic imperative: The medical care that has contributed to expanded longevity is the same care that threatens to eliminate the provision of community-based care and long-term care support services. At the same time, escalating health and long-term care costs are indicators that the United States can no longer afford to provide everything that medicine has to offer. The medicalization of service systems, which is incongruent with older adults' need for custodial services, is further compounded by insurance schemes that pay for failing kidneys, lungs, and heart, but not for personal care or home-maker services essential to supporting disabled elders and their families in the community.

As we have indicated in Chapter 2, even more significant than the general increase in life expectancy is that the population aged 85 and older, the "oldest-old," has grown more rapidly than any other age group. What poses challenges for long-term care is not just the growth in numbers, but the fact that the oldest-old are likely to have multiple health problems that result in physical and mental frailty and consequent dependency on long-term care services and family members for assistance.

Individuals aged 85 and older are 4 to 5 times more likely to be disabled and to require assistance with personal care activities than those aged 65 to 74. Of persons over age 65, about 46% are disabled; of these, about 13% are aged 65 to 74 and 25% are aged 75 to 84 (McBride, 1989).

Needs for long-term care vary by gender, race, and income. The least healthy and most disabled elderly tend to be older, poorer, single, minority, and female. Elderly persons of color experience greater degrees of functional and chronic impairment than whites but utilize fewer long-term care services (Abel, 1987; Leutz, Capitman, MacAdam, & Abrahams, 1992). This suggests that they rely more heavily on informal care providers. People aged 85 and over are most often women living alone on inadequate incomes, a consequence of the fact that more men than women die earlier from major chronic illness such as heart disease, stroke, and cancer. Among those living with such disabilities, women face more difficulties in carrying out their normal daily routines. Accordingly, these oldest-old women are frequently dependent on both unpaid and underpaid younger women for their care. For example, older women have been found to have higher utilization rates for home health aides and other paraprofessional home care providers (Leutz et al., 1992). Overall, the disabled occur disproportionately among the poor, with 60% of the elderly who require long-term care having incomes in the poverty or low-income range (Leutz et al., 1992).

Long-term care policies over the past two decades have significantly increased the institutionalization of the elderly and have developed caretaking institutions into private, profit-making enterprises (Estes et al., 1993). Of the 5.5 million elderly with disabilities in 1990, about 1.5 million lived in nursing or residential care homes, with women comprising 75% of nursing home residents. Although only about 5% of adults aged 65 and over live in nursing homes, this rate increases to 25% among those over age 85, where they form more than 50% of the population of nursing homes (Bould, Sanborn, & Reif, 1989; Leutz et al., 1992). It has been estimated that for every disabled elder residing in a nursing home, two or more equally impaired elders live in the community (Brody, 1985).

Of the 4 million noninstitutionalized elderly, approximately 20% have at least one limitation in their ability to perform daily personal care (e.g., bathing, dressing, walking, toileting) or home management activities (e.g., handling money, shopping, meal preparation), resulting in a mild degree of disability in their activities of daily living. Approximately 4% are severely disabled, unable to carry on major activities without the assistance of family members or professionals. Consistent with the increase in chronic disabilities with age, the prevalence of limitations in daily activities increases to 56.8% among the oldest-old compared to

9.9% among the young-old—those aged 65 to 69. These rates of limitations are also higher among women and African Americans than among men and Caucasians (Aday, 1993). The number of persons 65 years or older who need assistance in order to remain in the community is expected to increase from 5.2 million to 7.2 million by the year 2000, 10.1 million by 2020, and 14.4 million by 2050, with approximately 66% of this group having severe limitations in their ability to perform activities of daily living (McBride, 1989; U. S. Senate Special Committee on Aging, 1990).

Family caregivers provide the primary source of assistance to the disabled elderly living in the community. As an indication of the limited public funding for community-based services, only about 36% of government long-term care expenditures for the elderly in 1993 were for home care, primarily through Medicare home health benefits, which are generally for post-acute rather than long-term care (Wiener, Illston, & Hanley, 1994). As a result, only about 25% of older people with disabilities receive paid home care services, either alone or in combination with care from family members; of these, only 5% are cared for solely by paid helpers (Leutz et al., 1992). Another 15% to 20% receive other types of paid community-based services, such as adult day care, home-delivered meals, transportation assistance, or telephone checkups (Center for Vulnerable Populations, 1993). Of those who use paid helpers, out-of-pocket spending finances more than 50% of the care (Leutz et al., 1992). Those who pay out-of-pocket for assistance tend to be the most medically and functionally vulnerable, isolated, and medically confused. At any given time, 7 out of 8 disabled elders in the community are relying on informal care and whatever formal care they can find and pay for themselves (Leutz et al., 1992).

Although use of services correlates with level of disability, even at very high levels of disability, most older persons primarily receive informal care from relatives rather than formal assistance. A 1990 survey found that among severely disabled elderly who had difficulty performing three or more activities of daily living, including about 125,000 persons who lived alone, more than half did not receive any formal paid services and depended solely on unpaid helpers (Leutz et al., 1992; National Medical Expenditure Survey, 1990). And when relatives, primarily female, attempt to fill this gap through their unpaid care, the elders' needs for assistance with activities of daily living may not be adequately met (Leutz, et al., 1992).

Some exceptions to this pattern of informal care have been identified. Kemper (1992) found that disabled persons with spouses or adult children receive more home care than those living alone. Also, family caregivers tend to be selective and modest in their requests for paid services. The use of formal services is not necessarily associated with less stress, because families still face the pressure of locating and coordinating outside help (Orodenker, 1990). Although disability rates are much higher for the elderly, at least 25% of the adults with disabilities who have trouble performing activities of daily living but who still live in the community are under age 65 (Wiener, Illston, & Hanley, 1994). We turn now to the two largest groups of individuals with disabilities under age 65: adults with developmental disabilities and those with chronic mental illness.

Adults With Developmental Disabilities

Persons with developmental disabilities have a severe, chronic physical or mental impairment that is (a) first manifested in childhood (prior to age 22), (b) is likely to continue indefinitely, (c) results in substantial functional limitations in three or more areas of major life activity, and (d) reflects a need for care, treatment, or services of extended duration (Public Law 91-517, Developmental Disabilities Services and Facilities Construction Amendments of 1970, 84 Stat. 1316, 1970). Individuals with mental retardation comprise the largest group of persons with developmental disabilities. Other conditions that cause developmental disabilities include impairments to the bones and muscles, chronic illness of the internal body systems, and central nervous system disorders such as cerebral palsy, autism, epilepsy, and spina bifida. These conditions tend to be overlapping. Of individuals with mental retardation in residential care, about 30% have epilepsy, 12% have cerebral palsy, 4% have autism, .5% have spina bifida, and about 7% are deaf and/or blind (Center for Vulnerable Populations, 1993).

Approximately 1% of the U.S. population is mentally retarded, with about 1,260,000 persons with mental retardation living in the community and 330,000 living in supervised residential settings in 1992 (NASHP, 1992). Not all persons with mental retardation have substantial functional limitations; only about 20% need assistance in performing basic life activities such as dressing and bathing. Similarly, many persons with epilepsy are not limited in major activities (Center for Vulnerable Populations, 1993).

A major effect of medical advances in the treatment of diseases of infancy, childhood, and young adulthood is that persons with developmental disabilities are living longer, thereby suffering the double jeopardy of aging and developmental disability, this creates the nonnormative experience of the oldest-old caring for the old-old (Neal, Chapman, Ingersoll-Dayton, & Emlen, 1993) and the phenomenon of continuous or perpetual parenting by older parents who cannot look forward to the increasing independence of their adult children (Kelly & Kropf, 1995).

The dramatic increase in numbers of older adults in general has been paralleled by the increase of older adults with mild to moderate developmental disabilities (from approximately 350,000 in 1970 to 1,577,340 in 1989) (U.S. Bureau of the Census, 1991a), despite the fact that the average life expectancy of people with mental retardation remains less than that of the general population (Eyman, Grossman, Tarjan, & Miller, 1987). Although there is not agreement about the minimum age at which people with developmental disabilities are considered old, age 55 is frequently identified as the threshold for entry into "old age" for these individuals (Martinson & Stone, 1993).

Life expectancy has improved even among those more severely retarded: for persons with Down's syndrome, it has increased dramatically—from 9 years in 1929 to 18.3 years in 1963 to 55 years today (Adlin, 1993). This increase is due primarily to improvements in health care and decreased rates of institutionalization. Deaths among people with Down's syndrome were previously attributed to respiratory and other types of infectious disease, malignancy, and congenital heart disease. The improved availability of antibiotics reduced deaths due to infection; the increased use of residential services rather than institutions reduced exposure to potentially lethal infections, leading to the prevention of morbidity and later mortality. Today, the primary causes of death in persons with Down's syndrome are stroke, dementia, and infection; approximately 40% of persons with Down's syndrome develop the dementia symptoms associated with Alzheimer's disease, with the average age of onset between 53 and 55 years of age (Adlin, 1993). Alzheimer's disease appears to progress more rapidly among individuals with Down's syndrome, and the incidence of seizures increases dramatically compared to the general population, placing additional pressures on family caregivers who may be ill prepared to handle the presenting behaviors.

Approximately 12% of individuals with developmental disabilities are aged 65 and over, with the population of developmentally disabled people aged 55 and over projected to double by 2030 (Spencer, 1989). Prior to the Omnibus Budget Reconciliation Act of 1987 (OBRA, Public Law 100-203), the nursing home was the primary placement for adults with developmental disabilities over 65 years of age. OBRA, however, mandated the diversion of people with developmental disabilities out of nursing homes. This mandate, combined with the demographic trend of increasing life expectancy in the developmentally disabled and their movement out of state institutions generally, has placed pressures on families who provide the majority of care.

An underlying barrier to the use of services by the developmentally disabled elderly and their families is that most agencies have no special provisions for older people with developmental disabilities, and services between the Aging network and the Developmental Disabilities network remain uncoordinated. This barrier persists despite the fact that the 1987 Developmental Disabilities Act Amendments established the welfare of older adults with developmental disabilities as a new priority and the Older Americans Act Amendments of 1987 recognized new definitions of disability, thereby increasing the opportunity for older adults with developmental disabilities to use the services offered by the generic aging network.

In the future, older adults with developmental disabilities will place additional demands on already overburdened, fragmented, and costly service systems as parents and sibling caregivers die or become too infirm to provide care. For example, 3,300 adults with developmental disabilities aged 30 and over who are living with aging parents in the state of Illinois are projected to require another residential arrangement over the next 15 years (Heller & Factor, 1988). Community care options—adult homes, group homes, and foster families—are a particularly pressing need (Martinson & Stone, 1993).

The major types of services needed by people with developmental disabilities are residential, employment, and social support (e.g., financial, mental health, transportation, recreation), not medical care. Yet almost 50% of persons with developmental disabilities never enter a formal program through the states' developmental disabilities service delivery system. The majority depend on families for assistance (Lakin, Hayden, & Abery, 1993; Morton, 1988): Only about 15% of individuals with developmental disabilities live in supervised residential settings, whereas 85% live at home with relatives or on their own (Center for Vulnerable Populations, 1993). Most adults with developmental disabilities have been cared for by their families in the community, typically for many years across the life span, rather than by professional care providers in formal settings. It has been estimated that 70% to 80% of the continuing care received by developmentally disabled adults is provided by family members, often unassisted and unrecognized by the formal care network (Krauss, 1986; Martinson & Stone, 1993). Increasingly, these family caregivers are elderly who have seen services shift from an institutional system to a community-based paradigm, but have not necessarily benefited from this shift (Rowitz, 1987). Services, when available, have tended to be oriented toward the developmentally disabled person, not toward supporting the family system of informal care.

Persons With Severe and Persistent Mental Illness

The chronically mentally ill—approximately 2.5 million individuals aged 18 and over—account for about 6% of the mentally ill living in the community (Lefley, 1987; Marsh, 1992). Chronic mental illness, as distinguished from shorter-term conditions, is a severe or persistent mental or emotional disorder that seriously impairs functional ability with regard to self-care in aspects of daily living, such as personal relations, living arrangements, and employment, for an extended period of time. Individuals with chronic mental illness require prolonged mental health care—typically 24-hour residential treatment and social support (Goldman & Manderscheid, 1987). Their disorders include some form or combination of schizophrenia, psychosis, major affective disorder, depression, anxiety, or phobia (Center for Vulnerable Populations, 1993). Prolonged functional disability caused or aggravated by severe mental disorder, not former hospitalization, is the chief distinguishing characteristic of chronic mental illness from more short-term conditions (NIMH Steering Committee on the Chronically Mentally Ill, 1980).

It has been estimated that the lifetime prevalence rate—the number of individuals who experience a mental health problem at some time in their lives—is 32.2%, with 1% of the total population estimated to suffer from severe mental illness (Aday, 1993; Hollingsworth, 1994). The baby boom phenomenon has meant an increase in percentage in the age group vulnerable to the onset of serious mental illness (persons 18 to 35 years) (Hollingsworth, 1994). Gender, race, socioeconomic status, and age increase the risk of mental illness among women, persons of color, and low-income individuals, with a disproportionately high number of chronically mentally ill persons relative to nondisabled persons being older, female, African American, and not married (Ashbaugh, 1983). Social or environmental stressors associated with greater risk of chronic mental illness include limited educational and employment opportunities, which typically result in poverty and family disruptions. Individuals with persistent and severe mental illness also manifest higher rates of mental retardation and substance abuse than the general population. Such persons with "dual diagnosis" are particularly likely to "fall through the cracks" of service systems (Center for Vulnerable Populations, 1993).

There is a complex interaction between poverty and disability. Although persons in poor families report higher rates of disability among all age groups, the differences become larger as age increases, indicating that people also become poor as a result of being disabled (Center for Vulnerable Populations, 1993). Given this interaction among mental disability and socioeconomic status, mental health care is only one type of service required by the chronically mentally ill. Housing, social and rehabilitation services, medical care, and basic minimum maintenance needs also have to be met (Dickey & Goldman, 1986). One of the most pressing needs is for community-based housing (Aday, 1993). As noted by Hollingsworth and Hollingsworth (1994), it is probably not very useful to provide psychotherapy to someone with serious mental illness if the person lacks a home (p. 8).

Many people with persistent and severe mental illness do not receive formal services. It has been estimated that 30% of individuals with a diagnosable mental disorder go untreated, whereas 56% to 59% receive care in the general medical care sector, and only 8% to 12% in the specialty mental health sector (Aday, 1993). The majority of individuals with major chronic disorders, who may also be dangerous and dependent, have never been hospitalized (Hollingsworth, 1994). Rates of untreated disorders are higher for the elderly, children, African Americans, and Hispanics. According to Hollingsworth (1994), of those with the highest level of need, only a minority are served by the mental health service system.

Many adults who are chronically mentally ill live a marginal existence in urban settings, and they increasingly form the homeless population. Their marginality is often a result of deinstitutionalization, a process that has moved adults with mental illness out of institutions into community settings without providing adequate community-based support services. As noted by Lewis, Shadlish, and Lurigio (1989, p. 174), deinstitution-alization created "policies of inclusion"—forcibly including back into society patients who were formerly excluded by institutional placement. The Community Mental Health Center Act of 1963 signaled the official opening of the era of community care of the mentally ill.

A number of factors underlie the large-scale deinstitutionalization or discharge of adults with mental illness from public and private hospitals. One is the ideology that community care is desirable, combined with the belief that it is less expensive, and another is the wider availability of psychotropic drugs to control or modify behavior on an outpatient basis. Two additional factors are (a) federal programs—Medicare, Medicaid, and Supplemental Security Income—that allow states to shift costs to the federal government by moving patients from state institutions, and (b) the civil liberties movement on behalf of the rights of the mentally ill and court decisions guaranteeing institutionalized patients rights to treatment that many states determined to be too expensive to continue to assure (Aday, 1993; Hatfield, 1978; 1987). As a result, in the two decades between 1955 and 1978, the state hospital census was reduced by two thirds, and when patients were hospitalized, the length of stay declined. Patients who formerly might have been hospitalized for extended periods of time are now returned home in several weeks or months (Goldman, 1982; Hatfield, 1987a). Many have been placed in nursing homes, some-times inappropriately so.

As with other populations with chronic disabilities, the lives of the chronically mentally ill and their families have been profoundly affected by technological advances, specifically the discovery in the 1950s of effective psychopharmacological agents for treating psychosis. Medications made it possible for many patients to live free of restraints and locked doors, to move about freely. Paralleling the development of the new drugs, new psychosocial technologies were generated with the intent of fostering more open therapeutic communities. However, medications are not a "cure," and federal reimbursement programs are generally inadequate to support community psychosocial rehabilitation services. As a result, many formerly institutionalized patients discharged to their families or single-occupancy residences were ill-prepared for living successfully in the community. Their difficulties and the stress on their families have been intensified by the lack of adequate community-based services, fragmented and uncoordinated services, community resistance to their presence, and the doctrine of "least restrictive environment" whereby families cannot hospitalize a relative involuntarily (Hatfield, 1987a).

The Community Support Program (CSP) was initiated by the National Institute of Mental Health in 1977 to foster support services for the chronically mentally ill for whom long-term skilled or semiskilled nursing care is inappropriate. It focused on direct care and rehabilitation through a system of services among existing community agencies rather than the construction of new types of facilities. The community support movement also fostered the development of the National Plan for the Chronically Mentally Ill and the passage of the Mental Health Systems Act of 1981.

Since the 1987 Omnibus Budget Reconciliation Act's repeal of the majority of provisions of the Mental Health Systems Act, however, all federal funds for mental health programs were consolidated into a block grant, funded at a level below previous appropriations. Subsequently, Medicaid funds were capped, limiting the availability of federal funds for mental health services for the poor. In fact, government funding for the chronically mentally ill has been decreasing since the early 1980s (Hollingsworth, 1994). The elimination of categoric support for community mental health centers resulted in a number of centers closing or greatly reducing the scope of services provided, with less than one third of funds controlled by state mental health programs being spent on community programs (Hollingsworth, 1994). The shortage of community-based service has been intensified by the lack of case management and coordination across service systems. Despite the overall decline in mental health funding, almost every state has developed some type of community support program, although still falling short of the extent of need.

The deinstitutionalization of mentally ill individuals without sufficient development of alternative community-based systems of care led early on to a revolving-door pattern of readmissions as discharged patients relapsed, and patients who had never been institutionalized repeatedly relapsed (Kane, 1994). A Massachusetts study found that between 50% and 75% of admissions to the state's mental health hospitals could be avoided if adequate community services were available. Such high admission rates are costly, because initial admission days cost 150% of the usual per diem (NIMH Steering Committee on the Chronically Mentally Ill, 1980).

More recently, concerns have been raised about the "reinstitutionalization" or "transinstitutionalization" of the severely mentally ill to an array of institutions, such as board-and-care homes, nursing homes, adult homes, residential treatment centers, or jails and correctional facilities (Aday, 1993; Morrissey & Goldman, 1984). These predominantly private, profit-making facilities, reimbursed through federal programs—SSI and SSDI payments and Medicaid—serve custodial and treatment functions once performed almost exclusively by state mental hospitals, but may, in some instances, be less appropriate settings than were the state hospitals (Marsh, 1992). One indicator of this reinstitutionalization process is that whereas the number of state and county mental hospitals has declined since 1950, the number of private psychiatric hospitals, nonfederal general hospitals with psychiatric services, and residential treatment centers has grown substantially. In addition, because of the availability of Medicaid reimbursement for nursing home care but not for care in state hospitals, nursing homes are now the main institutional providers of long-term care for adults with chronic mental illness (Binney & Swan, 1991). As noted earlier, the transinstitutionalization process has also occurred with respect to people with developmental disabilities, with their transfer to somewhat smaller public institutions such as nursing homes or large intermediate-care facilities. According to Lewis et al. (1989), the policies of inclusion, created by deinstitutionalization, meant that decisions about the mentally ill affected new areas—nursing home care, Medicaid, housing, and the "household economies of families that must now find a way to support and care for a family member who can no longer be excluded by institutional placements" (p. 174).

Families have been left as the primary community-based providers of care, faced with creating solutions to new problems on their own (Amado, Lakin, & Menke, 1990; Anthony & Blanch, 1989; Francell, Conn, & Gray, 1988; Hatfield, 1987a). In the initial period of deinstitutionalization, approximately 65% of all patients—and 25% of those who were severely ill—who were discharged from mental hospitals returned to their families

(Geiser, Hoche, & King, 1988; Goldman, 1982; Marsh, 1992). Although estimates vary widely, it appears that nearly 33% return home to live, with 50% to 90% residing in a variety of community settings, and remaining in contact with their families (Anthony & Blanch, 1989; Grellar & Grusky, 1989; Marsh, 1992; Torrey, Wolfe, & Flynn, 1988). This means that each year, approximately 1 million discharged patients, 25% of whom are defined as chronically mentally ill, return to the care of family members. As Thurer (1983) notes, because women provide the majority of care, deinstitutionalization of the mentally ill is primarily a women's issue. Many of these caregivers are older adults, a pattern that will increase as society in general ages (Kelly & Kropf, 1995). The concomitant changes of growing older, such as declining health or widowhood, make older parents especially vulnerable to stresses of caring for an adult with chronic mental illness (Belcher, 1988).

Family support programs have often aimed to help families become more effective caregivers so that their relative does not relapse and return to the hospital; this goal of cost-effectiveness and prevention of institutionalization, however, overlooks the stress faced by many families in their caring roles (Hatfield, 1987a). Innovative community-based programs that maintain patients out of the hospital and indeed improve patient outcomes have nevertheless produced about the same amount of family burden as standard hospital treatment plus aftercare. Nor does longer hospitalization of their chronically mentally ill relative appear to significantly reduce family burden (Marsh, 1992).

Families have identified their needs as follows: an adequate system of community-based care for their relative, information about mental illness and available resources, suggestions about how to cope with problem behaviors, opportunities to relate to other families with similar problems, family respite, a place other than home in which the patient can live, and financial relief and therapy for themselves (Marsh, 1992). Traditionally, there has been a poor fit between family caregiver needs and the mental health system, and families often experience isolation and alienation from services (Kelly & Kropf, 1995; Marsh, 1992). As Lefley (1987) observed, caregiving for one group at the expense of another can scarcely be considered a desirable mental health objective.

Limitations of the Long-Term Care System

As noted earlier, our three focus populations all require long-term health or mental health services. Although their particular needs differ, all are affected by structural limitations in the provision of services. The language of fiscal crisis frequently appears in discussions about long-term care costs and future directions. Families are viewed as a way to save money in public budgets. The escalating costs are real. In 1991, federal and state governments spent $90 billion to help provide long-term assistance to adults with chronic disabilities (NASHP, 1992). Most of this support—over 80%—went to institutional care, even though public institutions serve a small and decreasing number of frail elders and persons with developmental disabilities or chronic mental illness (NASHP, 1992). Despite the escalating expenditures associated with long-term care, federal and state funds are not meeting the greatest needs of the chronically disabled to enable them to remain in the community and to reduce the burdens on family caregivers. In fact, the current "nonsystem" of care is extremely expensive in both fiscal and human terms, with families financing out-of-pocket about 55% of long-term care (Hendricks & Hatch, 1993).

The most basic problems of our current financing system for long-term care services for adults with chronic disabilities are the large out-of-pocket payments for nursing-home care, often in the proprietary sector, and the lack of either publicly or privately funded support for home care. The system begins with the assumption that the individual is financially responsible for long-term costs until his or her assets and income have been virtually exhausted, at which point welfare in the form of Medicaid takes over. However, Medicaid pays primarily for institutional care. Whereas Medicaid and private payments together finance about 96% of long-term care, Medicare and private insurance together pay less than 4% (Chan, 1992). Benefits from government programs cover about 66% of the care costs of older persons and only 25% of persons under age 65 (AARP, 1993a).

These structural limits reflect the system's institutional and medical bias, which results in inadequate community-based supports for performance of activities of daily living; the lack of coordination and consequent fragmentation of services; and the shifting of services to the state and local level. This has resulted in a wide variability of services by geographic location and increased competition for scarce resources. Instead of a national service delivery system or policy to address the needs of dependent populations with chronic disabilities, each population has discrete services available to it, and each service, funded by different federal and state programs, has different eligibility requirements and limited available resources. As Leutz et al. (1992) maintain, there exists less a system to finance long-term care than simply several ways to pay for it.

To understand the limitations of the current long-term care system, it is necessary to briefly review these major sources of funding for services for populations with chronic disabilities: Medicare, Medicaid, the Older Americans Act and Social Services Block Grants, and private insurance.

FUNDING MECHANISMS

Medicare

As a social insurance system, Medicare is intended to provide financial protection against the costs of hospital, nursing home, and physician care for people aged 65 and over. Although Medicare is a major payer for hospital and physician services, its focus on acute care limits its role in financing long-term care for those with chronic disabilities; in fact, 65% of Medicare dollars cover hospital care, typically for catastrophic illness (Kane & Kane, 1990), and 30% of Medicare expenditures cover costs of eligible recipients in the last year of life (Binstock, 1990). Medicare covers virtually none of the outpatient custodial or personal assistance (nonmedical) services provided to people with chronic disabilities by nonphysicians, such as visiting nurses, home health service providers, and home health aids. It provides only skilled nursing for acute care needs of homebound elderly, for a limited time. Individuals who have long-term, irreversible loss in physical and social functioning are unlikely to meet Medicare's restrictive eligibility criteria of "medically necessary" and potential for rehabilitation. Consistent with this medical focus, the physician is the gatekeeper who authorizes "medically necessary" services under Medicare. As a result, home care services comprise only 3% of Medicare benefit payments. The elderly and their families pay directly for almost 75% of all noninstitutional care (e.g., home health care, homemaker services, and adult day care) (Kane & Kane, 1990).

Despite this small percentage of home-care benefits, Medicare home health expenditures have grown dramatically since 1989, in part because of the prospective payment systems or Diagnostic Related Groupings (DRGs) enacted under Medicare in 1983. DRGs have meant that hospitals are reimbursed by the diagnostic category in which each patient is placed, not by fee-for-services, because their fixed rates are based on expected length of stay for such conditions.

DRGs have resulted in many elderly and disabled individuals being discharged early into the community without adequate posthospitalization care; this has created 21 million more days of care annually that must be provided in the home or community, largely by unpaid female caregivers (Binney, Estes, & Ingman, 1990). DRGs have thus placed increased pressures on nursing homes, families, and home health agencies to provide care (Mantron, Vertress, & Wrigley, 1990). At the same time that hospital discharges to home health care have risen 37% since the passage of DRGs, the rate of growth in community-based home health services to the Medicare enrollees has slowed, largely as a result of inadequate

Medicare reimbursement policies (Estes, Wood, & Lee, 1988). More stringent cost-sharing provisions associated with Medicare through coinsurance, deductibles, and the Part B premium have also increased the financial burden on many chronically disabled beneficiaries and their families, including those in need of psychiatric services (Dickey & Goldman, 1986).

Much of the funding for the treatment and rehabilitation of the mentally ill is embedded in medical insurance and federal programs conceptualized and organized in terms of illness and disabilities of a nonpsychiatric kind. As a result, Medicare coverage for mental health services is limited. What exists is primarily for inpatient care (88% of expenditures) versus outpatient facilities (12% of expenditures), suggesting that "care in the community for mental disorders is far from reality" (Sherman, 1992). Part A of Medicare imposes a lifetime limit of 190 days of care in freestanding psychiatric hospitals and 90 days in a general hospital within a benefit period. For outpatient services, Medicare covers only 50% of approved charges for treatment of mental disorders, compared to 80% of charges for physical disorders. In addition, Medicare charges a higher coinsurance rate on outpatient mental health care than on other types of services. Mental health services excluded under Medicare are custodial care for Alzheimer's patients and others not requiring skilled nursing care, and outpatient prescription drugs, including psychotropic drugs. Furthermore, for persons who are chronically mentally ill, negotiating the paperwork of Medicare can itself limit access to services. Not surprisingly, less than 3% of the Medicare budget is spent on mental health services, whereas payments for mental health services represent 20% to 50% of total health expenditures made by private insurers (Sherman, 1992).

Medicaid

In contrast to Medicare, Medicaid is not a health insurance program for the elderly, but rather a federal and state means-tested welfare program of medical assistance for the categorically needy, regardless of age (e.g., to recipients of Aid to Families with Dependent Children and Supplemental Security Income). Every state must provide Medicaid to recipients of Supplemental Security Income (SSI), a federal-state program of public assistance to the elderly and disabled. Often viewed as a "safety-net" program and administered through state welfare departments, Medicaid eligibility criteria and benefits, based on financial need, vary widely among states. With reductions in the federal funds allocated to states since the passage of the Omnibus Budget Reconciliation Act in 1981, states have cut back Medicaid benefits, eligibility, and utilization, and have increased copayments (Harrington, Estes, Lee, & Newcomer, 1986). Consequently, Medicaid, similar to Medicare, provides only 80% to 85% of daily health care charges (Marsh, 1992).

Medicaid is the primary public source for funding nursing-home care, with over 40% of nursing home revenues coming from Medicaid (Leutz et al., 1992). Medicaid's eligibility policies and benefit structure have created financial incentives to use nursing homes rather than community services, because home care benefits are limited and the income eligibility is higher for nursing home residents than for those categorically needy who are living in the community. Nursing home costs account for about 45% of total Medicaid expenditures and 68% of Medicaid funds spent on older people, despite the fact that only 13% of Medicaid recipients are aged 65 and over (Waldo, Sonnefeld, McKusick, & Arnett, 1989; Wolfe, 1993). Nursing home expenditures are increasing at an average annual rate of 10% and form the fastest growing category of Medicaid expenses. At the same time, only about 2% of Medicaid expenditures go to community-based home health services. Given the relatively small proportion of dependent persons with chronic disabilities who are in nursing homes, expenditures are thus concentrated on very few individuals. Less than 35% of older Medicaid recipients account for over 80% of the total Medicaid expenditures for nursing homes (Hendricks & Hatch, 1993; Pepper Commission, 1990).

Medicaid also creates certain inequities in terms of access to services: about 25% of physicians refuse to treat Medicaid patients, and most will accept them as no more than 20% of their load. Because the number of Medicaid beds in nursing homes is limited, Medicaid patients must often wait longer for placement than private-pay patients, and the proprietary homes available to them are frequently of lower quality. Individuals must "spend-down" their assets in order to be eligible for Medicaid; elderly who have been private-pay patients in a nursing home may find that the facility will no longer accept them after they have spent-down. Some 40% of the elderly whose incomes fall below the poverty line set by state policies on eligibility do not qualify for Medicaid, yet they typically lack the resources to pay out-of-pocket for long-term care (Wiener, Illston, & Hanley, 1994b).

A pervasive inequity is the wide variability among states vis-à-vis access to "optional" benefits such as physical therapy and personal care—benefits that may not be optional if a disabled person is to remain in the community. Because Medicaid expenditures are outrunning the capacity of many states to pay them, most states have revised eligibility requirements and reduced the scope of services. Accordingly, a majority of states have adopted some form of prospective reimbursement for nursing care, thereby setting a limit on the amount of care.

From the perspective of families and their disabled relatives, a positive development in 1981 was the passage of Section 2176 of the Omnibus Budget Reconciliation Act that permits the waiver of Medicaid statutory requirements so that states can provide community-based alternatives to institutionalization to the elderly and persons with developmental disabilities. The waiver program specifies seven core services that may be included in the states' community-based service plan: case management, homemaker services, home health aide services, personal care, adult day health services, rehabilitation services, and respite care (Kemper, Applebaum, & Harrigan, 1987a,b).

The primary criterion is that states must demonstrate that the costs of home and community-based services do not exceed the cost to Medicaid for care in institutions, and also that they serve to divert from nursing home placement those who are at risk of institutionalization. Because the Medicaid waiver program assumes that home care is less expensive than placement in a nursing home or intermediate care facility, the target for benefits must meet the "but for" criterion; that is, the person would be in a Medicaid-financed institution but for the services provided by the community-care program. Because a person without family to provide care will receive a higher benefit under the waiver program than an equally disabled person who is receiving family assistance, this "but for" approach discounts the unpaid care of families from the benefits to be paid and creates structural inequities for family caregivers. It also overlooks that home care may be the best option even for those who are not at risk of institutionalization and that those who can benefit from home care differ from those residing in nursing homes. For example, in a study of 16 demonstration sites, services were being provided to those who would not otherwise be institutionalized (i.e., not at risk of institutionalization) and did not reduce the amount of care provided by family and friends (Kemper et al., 1987a).

Although 42 states have covered an array of health and social services under Section 2176, its cost containment goals mean that waivers have been granted sparingly. The availability of community alternatives to institutional care has been expanded only marginally, although noninstitutional care does appear to improve clients' quality of life (Kemper et al., 1987a; Kemper et al., 1987b). The waivers are optional, with the result that they are denied to many eligible individuals. The Home and Community-Based Care Program, under the Omnibus Budget Reconciliation Act of 1990, provides a loophole to the 2176 waiver by incorporating community-based services as optional for individuals with severe physical or cognitive impairments who are eligible for Medicaid and who would otherwise require more costly institutional care (Lipson & Laudicina,

1991). Both programs are constrained by their limited government funding relative to the extent of need (Leutz et al., 1992).

For adults with developmental disabilities, Medicaid is the single largest federal program that funds community-based housing options, primarily through Intermediate Care Facilities for People with Mental Retardation and Related Conditions (ICR/MR) program. Eighty-eight percent of the institutional "placements" in the current developmental disabilities residential services system are financed by the ICR/MR program. In contrast, only 25% of the community-based living arrangements are supported by Medicaid, including both the ICR/MR and Home and Community-Based Care Services Waiver. Of the $5.6 million ICF/MR expenditures in 1987, 75% went for care in large state institutions, even though residents in these facilities account for less than 5% of all persons with mental retardation-developmental disabilities (Martinson & Stone, 1993; NASHP, 1992).

Adults between the ages of 18 and 65 who have severe and persistent mental illness are ineligible for Medicaid-financed care in mental hospitals, although Medicaid will cover limited nursing home care. Accordingly, they also are ineligible for most services available to the elderly under the Medicaid Home and Community-based Care Waiver Program for the chronically mentally ill. Only minimal support for community-based social services is available through Medicaid, and home care services are rare, with a very limited amount covered by Medicare. Given these funding limitations, it is not surprising that of the three populations, the programs, resources, and access to services are least well-developed for the chronically mentally ill (Hollingsworth & Hollingsworth, 1994).

Social Services Block Grants and The Older Americans Act

In addition to the limited allocations of Medicare and Medicaid, Title XX Amendments to the Social Security Act (Social Services Block Grants) and Title III of the Older Americans Act are the primary sources for funding nonmedical, custodial services for older persons with disabilities.

Title XX was established in 1974 to provide social services to all age groups; entitlements are means-tested, with most services to older persons going to those who receive Supplemental Security Income. Title XX services are viewed as basic life-sustaining, self-care services to compensate for loss in health and the capacity for self-maintenance. These include homemaker and chore services, home-delivered meals, adult protective services, adult day care, foster care, and institutional or residential care. Under the federal Omnibus Budget Reconciliation Act of 1981, Title XX was converted to the Social Services Block Grant program at the same time that federal funds to the states were reduced on the average by 20%. This has resulted in increased competition for decreasing funds at the local level.

Title III of the Older Americans Act (OAA) is the sole federal social service statute designed specifically for older people. Entitlements to services are universal, with the only eligibility criterion that one be over age 60, although states are required to target assistance to persons with "greatest social or economic need." This has the advantage that OAA services may be provided without the restrictions of Medicare and without the means test of Medicaid. In-home services are designated by the OAA as a priority service for states to provide. Long-term care services funded at the local level by OAA funds include information and referral, case management, transportation, homemaker, day care, nutrition education and congregate meals, respite care, and senior centers. These services under OAA overlap the goals and provisions of the Social Services Block Grants.

Both programs are limited in their effect by the relatively small allocation of federal resources (Leutz et al., 1992), with $1.2 billion appropriated to OAA in 1992 as compared to $15 billion for Medicaid (AARP, 1992b). Moreover, the Omnibus Budget Reconciliation Act, which intensified the tilt toward medical services, reduced federal funds and removed state matching funds and state reporting requirements for these programs (Bergthold, 1987). In 1992, states spent an average of 21% of their block grant money on long-term care for older people (AARP, 1992). Community agencies that relied heavily on Title XX funds tried to recover their losses by restructuring their programs toward the medical services reimbursed under Medicare. The programs most likely to be eliminated or reduced were homemaker, chore, and personal care services—the very programs that could minimize demands on family caregivers. These changes in the Social Services Block Grant and the Older Americans Act, along with those in Medicare and Medicaid, have sharply reduced the elderly's access to long-term care; this is particularly the case for low-income elderly, thereby increasing gender and racial inequities in terms of access and availability of services. The general approach under these two programs has been to give a few services to as many people as possible, which does not necessarily reach the most vulnerable elderly.

Private Insurance

Whereas our long-term care system is based on the assumption that individuals are first responsible for paying for their care, 37 million persons, or approximately 15%, of the total civilian noninstitutionalized population lack health and long-term care insurance. Many of the uninsured are employed, with 25% of adults workers under age 65 and their families lacking work-related coverage through employers or labor unions; in fact, the number of two-worker families without insurance has risen in the past decade to 52%. Most of these workers are employed by small businesses or are owners of small sole-proprietorships (National Medical Expenditures Survey, 1990; Short, Monheit, & Beauregard, 1989; Wiener et al., 1994b). Among persons aged 55 to 64, 13% (2.7 million) are uninsured and comprise a large segment of the medically "high risk" uninsured (Jensen, 1994). For those workers with insurance, firms have raised employee premiums and copayments, creating underinsurance as a pervasive problem.

For elderly who can afford more extensive coverage than is provided by Medicare under Social Security, private "medigap" insurance is available. Over 70% of the older population have purchased some type of private supplemental insurance; of these, about 33% have employment-related coverage. Retirees over age 75, as well as women and minorities, are less likely to have access to such insurance (National Medical Expenditure Survey, 1990). Of the poor or near-poor elderly, who suffer from more chronic illness and disability than do their higher-income peers, only 47% have private insurance, compared with 87% of the high-income elderly. Also, less than 18% of elders of color have private medigap coverage compared to 48% of poor elderly whites. And women are less likely to have had access to group health insurance through employment than their male counterparts. Only 20% of all retirees who lack private coverage are able to obtain Medicaid or other public health insurance, such as Veterans' Assistance (National Medical Expenditure Survey, 1990).

Even those who carry supplemental coverage can suffer burdensome medical expenses if they are seriously ill, because Medicare does not cover the full costs of care. This burden was acknowledged by the 1988 passage of the Medicare Catastrophic Coverage Act, which was subsequently repealed. Few medigap policies pick up physician charges in excess of Medicare's allowable fees, nor do they ordinarily cover prescriptions, dental care, or nursing home care—all services essential to the long-term maintenance in the community of elderly with chronic disabilities. As a result, supplementary private insurance plans, on the average, cover only about 7% of the elderly's health care bills (Davis & Rowland, 1991).

Out-of-pocket health care costs for the elderly, adjusted for inflation, consume a higher percentage of the elderly's income (18.1%) than prior to the passage of Medicare in 1961 (11%). Those with lower incomes expend an even greater proportion on health care expenses than the elderly in general. Out-of-pocket health care costs for the elderly in 1988 were estimated to average $2,934 per person. Among the elderly who incurred $3,000 or more in out-of-pocket expenses, 82.5% was due to uncovered outlays for nursing home expenses, thus reflecting significant gaps in the long-term care system (Rice, 1989).

With over 130 firms selling one or more long-term care options, an increasing number of private long-term care insurance schemes are available. Most policies cover nursing home care (at a range of $40 to $120 a day), with home health and adult day care services usually reimbursed at 50% to 80% of the selected nursing home benefit. Less than 1% of the disabled elderly are covered by private insurance; the high premiums and copayments mean that most policies are out of the financial reach of up to 20% of Americans age 55 to 79. Indeed, high quality policies cost as much as $2,500 at age 67 (Wiener & Illston, 1994a). Not surprisingly, women are less likely than men to be able to afford private insurance and they spend a higher percentage of their income when they do, reflecting both gaps in coverage and their lower median income (Allen, 1993). Those individuals most likely to purchase and benefit from long-term care insurance are those with assets and a spouse to protect. Although insurance is likely to be more affordable in the future, by the year 2018, only an estimated 20% of the elderly will be able to purchase private long-term care insurance. Even if private policies were to become more affordable, questions have been raised about their quality (Wiener & Illston, 1994a).

With regard to insurance available to individuals with chronic mental illness, private psychiatric hospitals and general hospital psychiatric units are mainly supported through private insurance and patient fees (Taube, 1990). The extent of coverage and rates of reimbursement for providers under private systems are less for mental health than for general medical services, with relatively few employment-related insurance systems covering psychiatric inpatient care in full, and even fewer covering outpatient psychiatric care. Data from the National Center for Health Statistics and National Institute of Mental Health indicate that a larger proportion of psychiatric patients than of medical-surgical patients are uninsured. Even when coverage is available through medium and large firms in the private sector, it is subject to severe limitations on the numbers of visits or dollars covered, or to high coinsurance rates. Another services barrier is that people are less likely to purchase mental health care out-of-pocket than medical care generally. The more people have to pay out-of-pocket, the less likely it is that individuals who need mental health care services will obtain them (Frank & McGuire, 1986). Problems created by the lack or inadequacy of coverage are greatest for adults who are chronically mentally ill and require both inpatient and outpatient mental health as well as related social services and who are likely to be referred to already overburdened public systems and shuttled between the public mental health system and corrections (Aday, 1993; Dickey & Goldman, 1986). Capitated systems of financing, based on payments per enrollee (such as Health Maintenance Organizations and Social-Health Maintenance Organizations), are increasingly being used as a mode of financing mental health services for groups of employees or program participants. However, the nonmedical support services most needed by individuals who are chronically disabled are unlikely to be offered through such systems because of the costs entailed (Dickey & Goldman, 1986). Similarly, the habilitation services and therapy essential to the community support of adults with developmental disabilities are not covered by most private insurance plans.

FRAGMENTATION OF SERVICES

Because chronic disabilities are long-term and usually involve gradual changes in functional ability, the long-term care system should ideally offer a continuum of care, from institutional care to community-care services that could support both the dependent person and their family caregivers. Instead, in part because of isolated funding streams, the community care system is a patchwork (Leutz et al., 1992); services are uncoordinated, resulting in gaps that create a "no-program land" or "no-care zone" of fragmented population-specific services (Estes et al., 1993; Wallace, 1990). As noted by Leutz et al. (1992), having services available does not make a system of care, when systems of financing and coverage to ensure equitable access are missing.

Underlying such gaps is the lack of a coherent federal strategy and management system to administer programs. Fragmentation exists within and among federal departments. Definitions of responsibilities are unclear among the federal, state, and local levels of government. Categoric funding streams and related financial incentives have tended to encourage the formation of competitive agencies or programs operating in discrete noncollaborative sectors rather than an integrated system of care for individuals in need of services from a variety of agencies, institutions, and funding streams (Ada, 1993).

Case managers are increasingly being utilized to create and coordinate systems of care for dependent individuals. For example, Public Law 99-660 mandated that state mental health authorities provide case management services to every person identified with serious and persistent mental illness, which has resulted in a wide range of case management models to serve adults who are mentally ill. According to the Case Management Society of America, which has developed standards for practice, the case manager performs the roles of assessor, facilitator, planner, and advocate. However, some case management services have been devices for insurers to contain costs rather than for clients to gain expanded access to services (Birenbaum, Guyot, & Cohen, 1990; Capitman, 1988). Moreover, some families have felt that they were being managed by professionals rather than collaborating with them (Bradley, Knoll, & Agosta, 1992). In Chapter 13, we discuss case management as a mode for brokering, coordinating, and monitoring existing services.

COST-SHIFTING AMONG LEVELS OF GOVERNMENT

Paralleling such fragmentation, states have the lead role in formulating long-term care policy, although federal funding sources of Medicaid, Medicare, and SSI are often the driving forces behind state decisions regarding who gets what service. Instead of a national long-term care policy, we have 50 state systems of care with wide variation within and among them. Critics of the current system maintain that eligibility for long-term care is determined not so much by physical or financial need, but by geographic location. (Hollingsworth, 1994; Quadagno, Meyer, & Turner, 1991). States differ in criteria for eligibility, benefit design and coverage, and financing options that increase the potential for preventing action or policy change, and for lack of coordination between financing and program administration (Marmor & Gill, 1989). For example, with regard to home and community-based services for dependent populations, large differences exist across and within states in access, quality, and coordination of services, resulting in large inequities (Pendleton, Capitman, Leutz, & Omata, 1990).

In the 1980s, under the "new federalism" and cutbacks in federal funding of the Republican administrations, even more responsibility for dependent populations was shifted to the state level or away from government entirely. Redirection of federal outlays for a range of health and social service programs into block grants at the state and local levels was designed both to reduce federal spending and to place programs closer to the people. Cutbacks in federal funds have forced state and local governments to restrict services and to increase the burden borne by the recipients and their families (Estes et al., 1993). Block grants at the state and local level, deregulation, and restricted federal funding encouraged states to seek competitive bids from for-profit health care enterprises for provision of services under contractual arrangement, thus furthering market competition in the health care sector.

THE INSTITUTIONAL BIAS OF CARE

As noted earlier, the patchwork of services is increasingly characterized by an institutional orientation. The institutional bias of current systems of public and private financing is reflected in the extent to which nursing homes provide care to persons across the three vulnerable populations focused on in this book. Approximately 40,000 persons with mental retardation are in nursing homes, many of them inappropriately placed due to lack of other community alternatives. At least 50% of older residents in nursing homes suffer from mental disorders of some type; about 150,000 nursing home residents under age 65 and about 180,000 persons over age 65 have mental disorders other than dementia. Placement of adults with mental illness in nursing homes is related to the availability of Medicaid reimbursement for nursing home care, but not for care in state hospitals (Amado et al., 1990).

Addressing the fact that many mentally ill and developmentally disabled individuals are inappropriately institutionalized, the Omnibus Budget Reconciliation Act of 1987 required preplacement screening as well as an annual review of nursing home residents for mental illness and mental retardation. New applicants or residents who had been in the home fewer than 30 months who were not deemed to need active mental treatment would not be covered by Medicaid and would be considered for placement in other "less restrictive settings." It has been estimated that 37,890 to 65,600 nursing home residents could be displaced as a result of this process, many of whom do not have adequate provisions for their housing or personal care needs in the community (Freiman, Arons, Goldman, & Burns, 1990).

Across all three dependent populations, an ideology of community care has supported deinstitutionalization, moving individuals out of institutions to the community, but without public dollars following them. More than 80% of long-term care dollars are spent on nursing home care for the elderly, even though less than 20% of elders with disabilities use nursing homes (Hallfors, 1992). For low-income people, the government subsidizes only 25% of noninstitutional care. Even among older persons with severe disabilities, only 50% use nursing home services (Leutz et al., 1992). As the number of elderly in nursing homes has been decreasing, the total dollars for institutional care for the elderly has continued to increase, with Medicaid spending growing from approximately $7 billion in 1980 to over $18 billion in 1991 for institutional care for the elderly (Center for Vulnerable Populations, 1993).

As noted earlier, a primary reason for the disproportionate funding of institutional care has been the availability of Medicaid funding for medically oriented treatment programs in nursing home settings. In contrast, public funding for community-based and in-home care is limited. For the frail elderly, most formal home care is publicly financed under the highly restrictive Medicare home health care benefit, Medicaid, the OAA Programs, the Social Services Block Grant, and state general revenue programs. Home health care has typically accounted for less than 2% of Medicare and Medicaid reimbursements (Estes et al., 1993).

Similarly, over 50% of all public spending for mental retardation and developmental disabilities services is allocated for institutional care in Medicaid-funded Intermediate Care Facilities, despite the fact that residents in these facilities account for less than 5% of all persons with mental retardation-developmental disabilities. As another indicator of the institutional bias of the current long-term care delivery systems, the federal government finances almost 50% of all institutional care (typically nursing home facilities with more than 15 beds), but only 25% of all community-based services for persons with mental retardation-developmental disabilities. In fact, operating public facilities for the developmentally disabled is the fastest growing component of Medicaid, even though about 8,000 fewer developmentally disabled persons resided in large institutional settings in 1991 than in 1977 (NASHP, 1992). Accordingly, residential gaps persist for those with severe disabilities and those who live at home while awaiting services (Lakin, Hayden, & Avery, 1994).

The pattern for services to adults who are chronically mentally ill is comparable. Although 75% of adults with chronic mental illness live in community-based settings and the absolute numbers in institutions continue to decline, 70% of the dollars available to State Mental Health Authorities through Mental Health Block Grants fund public institutionalization of this population (Center for Vulnerable Populations, 1993; Marsh, 1992; NASHP, 1992). Only about 5% of state funds support community residential programs such as halfway houses, and about 19% of state mental health agency budgets are used to finance ambulatory services such as community mental health centers, outpatient clinics, and day treatment (Bachman & Drainoni, 1992).

TRENDS INCREASING THE
BURDENS ON FAMILY CAREGIVERS

Along with the cutbacks in federal funding, increased shifting of responsibilities to the state and local levels, and a persistent institutional bias, three other interconnected trends are increasing the burdens on families who provide care to dependent populations: privatization of services, medicalization or high-tech care, and informalization of care (Estes et al., 1993). Whereas these trends have been most extensively documented in terms of Medicare-reimbursed acute care services to the elderly, they have also affected the long-term care services available to adults with developmental disabilities-mental retardation and to those with chronic mental illness. We briefly discuss these trends to lay the foundation for a more detailed discussion in our feminist critiques (Chapters 8 to 10) of current public and corporate policies.

PRIVATIZATION

The trend toward privatization is most pronounced among home health care agencies, nursing homes, board-and-care homes, and hospitals. For nearly all sectors of health and community-based care, Reagan's policies during the 1980s brought a decline in the role of the public provider and an infusion of for-profit providers into the service delivery system (Estes et al., 1993). Public providers have been the major source of less profitable, nonreimbursable social and custodial services that are essential to the long-term maintenance of dependent populations in the community, particularly for low-income populations. As states, regions or counties turned programs over to private agencies, new quasi-public organizations emerged (e.g., voluntary sector agencies providing care paid with government dollars) (Hollingsworth, 1994). The decline in public sector provision of services has reduced access to low- and moderate-income elderly; the availability of a full spectrum of services beyond high-tech, postacute services reimbursed under Medicare has been reduced as well.

The trend toward providing health care services in the home has accelerated in the past decade. From 1986 to 1992, home care grew 20% in the United States, compared to a 2% increase in nursing home care and a declining use of hospital beds nationwide (Haracznak, 1991). In 1990, home health care grew faster than all other industries in the United States, in terms of number of agencies and volume of visits and services—even faster than the health care field in general (Halamandaris, 1991).

Home care has shifted from the domain of public and private nonprofit organizations to proprietary firms, often chains oriented toward meeting acute care needs (Leutz et al., 1992). These firms have been responding both to the increased demand for home care created by discharges through DRGs and by the 1980 Omnibus Budget Reconciliation Act that allowed for-profit agencies to qualify for Medicare reimbursement and at the same time restricted eligibility criteria. Accordingly, for-profit agencies are able to negotiate lower rates of reimbursement because they can spread overhead costs over more services. It is the high-tech medical services—skilled nursing, physical therapy, and speech therapy—that are most likely to be reimbursed, not the "low medical" services of home health aides or medical social work that are integral to comprehensive long-term care. Because of the rapid growth of Medicare-funded home health costs subsequent to DRGs, in 1985 the Health Care Financing Administration (HCFA) restricted Medicare funding for home health benefits by reducing the ceilings on allowable costs per visit as well as the number of visits by home health aides, thereby more strictly defining "medical necessity." By tightening Medicare home health eligibility, the number of beneficiaries receiving home care has declined, and the services funded are increasingly high-tech medical ones oriented toward the short-term care of persons with acute illness rather than toward a continuum of care for chronically ill persons. Accordingly, home health agencies competed more intensely for clients eligible for Medicare reimbursement or who could pay privately, and there has also been an increase in competition among independent providers of personal care services.

Privatization in services to adults with mental illness has meant the growth of the private mental health care system, including specialty mental health outpatient clinics operating on a profit-making basis, private psychiatrists and psychologists, private for-profit psychiatric hospitals, and modest numbers of other for-profit facilities. Yet the private system is far from the lives of most persons with chronic mental illness (Hollingsworth, 1994). The main private health system providers serving adults with chronic mental illness are hospitals. Because Medicaid will pay for psychiatric care in community hospitals, many patients are directed to such hospitals. A secondary provider has been nursing homes, although as a result of the 1987 Omnibus Budget Reconciliation Act, fewer adults with serious mental illness are in privately owned nursing homes. Adults with persistent mental illness are unlikely to be clients of private mental health outpatient clinics, particularly because Medicaid's low reimbursement rates make them financially unattractive. As with services to older people, those adults with mental illness who are low-income and have the most severe disabilities are most likely to be negatively affected by the current privatization of services. Paralleling the trends toward privatization and community-based care is the decrease in constant dollars spent on funding for the chronically mentally ill (Hollingsworth, 1994).

THE MEDICALIZATION OF CARE

According to Estes et al., (1993), the medicalization of care, which refers to the corresponding biomedicalization of aging—the propensity of the health care industry to maximize high technology as a means to extend life regardless of the costs—is a product of an expanding home health industry based on profit and specialization. As we have described, individuals who previously would not have survived beyond childhood are now living longer, but without the nonmedical services essential to the quality of those additional years. Costly medical procedures to prolong life have spurred debates about the rationing of health care. Low-technology nonmedical needs have been minimized, resulting in Medicare funding for acute care needs and inappropriate application of expensive medical care when social and psychological supportive services would be preferable (Binney et al., 1990). Thus, aging and other dependencies across the life course are defined as medical problems—individual problems requiring individual solutions—not as structural problems requiring societal changes.

INFORMALIZATION OF CARE

Given the emphasis on high-tech care for acute needs, families have assumed increasing responsibility for nonacute care, thus creating informalization, where care is transferred from the formal delivery system of hospitals and agencies to the informal arenas of home and community (Estes et al., 1993). This trend is consistent with the ideology of community care and of familism, which has assumed that family care is more cost-effective and more attuned to the needs of the care receiver. The medicalization of care combined with the prospective payment system under Medicare for the elderly has resulted in increased expectations on families to perform high-tech tasks previously done by professionals in institutional settings. So, a theme throughout this book is that a well-documented result of informalization is the transfer of a large portion of the provision of long-term care to women—unpaid relatives, neighbors, volunteers, and underpaid aides, nurses, and social workers.

In conclusion, meeting the needs of growing populations with chronic disabilities requires new solutions that affect the social structure and functioning of society. Given the magnitude of both the need and the potential changes, it is not surprising that no other part of the health care system generates as much passionate dissatisfaction as does long-term care (Wiener & Illston, 1994a). The trends toward privatization and informalization of care via family members raise critical questions about the proper balance between public- and private-sector initiatives and whether public funds should be allocated to institutional or noninstitutional services. Differences over the emphasis to be placed on each sector reflect underlying and conflicting values of individualism, familism, and societal good. In the next chapter, we turn to an examination of how such values have resulted in a residual and incremental approach toward long-term care based on an outdated model of the nuclear family.

PART II

The Context, Extent, and Nature of Caregiving for Dependents

To understand the nature, meaning, and consequences of care within our society, it is first necessary to examine the social, political, and cultural context that has shaped expectations and policies related to long-term care responsibilities. The development of public and corporate policies in our society reflects an ongoing debate between those who argue for programs supportive of family caregivers and those who want to place even greater demands on families as a means to reduce the rising costs associated with the long-term care of dependents. These tensions are evidenced in a "public burden" model of societal welfare, which emphasizes private (family) responsibility along with the contemporary ideology of community care, with its focus on cost-effectiveness. Chapter 5 documents how this model has resulted in fragmented and incremental residual services that have not adequately addressed the needs of family caregivers and often served to pit different age groups against one another in intergenerational competition for scarce public resources. Integral to this context are historical and current values and assumptions about the role of the family and, in particular, of women. We examine how these values, particularly the ideologies of separate spheres and of familism, are played out structurally, resulting in differential expectations about men's and women's roles and unequal economic opportunities.

Chapter 6 documents the resultant gender-based nature of care, with women predominating as both unpaid and underpaid caregivers. Men and women differ in the frequency with which they perform caring roles, and also in the ways that gender influences both the objective (or behavioral) and subjective (or cognitive and emotional) dimensions of care. Cultural ideologies and assumptions about women's roles are translated into women's and men's sense of obligation to family members, with many women and men accepting the gender-based division of roles as natural and not subject to question. Women are more likely than men to feel both psychologically and physically responsible for the care of their chronically disabled relatives, which affects the nature and extent of stress experienced in the role.

Chapter 7 describes researchers' efforts to define *caregiver burden,* particularly the differentiation between *objective* and *subjective burden.* Objective burden focuses on behavioral phenomena associated with performing the caring role and most frequently includes the problematic behavior of the care receivers and the disruption of family relations and daily patterns, including health problems and financial stress. Subjective burden refers to how family members feel about fulfilling their care responsibilities. Caregivers differ, particularly between men and women, in what they experience as stressful or difficult in care. Throughout the analysis of the caregiver burden literature, we draw attention to how structural factors influence the nature and consequences of care. Because of the gender-based nature of care, caregiving tasks remain largely invisible and unrewarded by public or corporate policies, resulting in women's differential opportunities as unpaid carers in the home and underpaid carers who service others in the marketplace.

5

The Social, Political,
and Historical Context of
Caregiving for Dependents

This chapter explores the values of individualism, independence, and familism that underlie the residual approach to public policy in the United States—values that are currently played out in the trends toward privatization and informalization of care. Closely related to these values is the historical development of the ideologies of separate spheres and of familism (the family ethic) that have perpetuated the expectation that women's major role is to provide uncompensated care to dependent relatives. The societal value of individualism, played out in debates about family and governmental responsibility in a period of fiscal restraint, is also reflected in the current public preoccupation with issues of generational equity and intergenerational competition for scarce resources.

Ideology—the relatively coherent set of beliefs and values about human nature and social life generated by a society for itself—can profoundly influence individual thoughts and behavior, institutional practices, and societal organization (Abramovitz, 1988). By appealing to economic necessities, ideologies are integral to sustaining dominant views about the role of social welfare and public interventions and thus can contribute to structural inequities by gender, race, and class (Estes, 1991). We contend that the ideologies of familism and of separate spheres have profoundly influenced the lives of family caregivers. They have articulated women's expected work and family behavior, and defined women's (unequal) place in the public and private spheres. The economic dependence of women on men and the continued economic vulnerability of many older women are outgrowths of these ideologies that have been supported and enforced by public long-term care policies and regulations as well as by corporate unresponsiveness to personal or familial concerns.

In this chapter we analyze the societal, historical, and political context for public and corporate policies to provide a framework for understanding the devalued nature of caregiving in our culture and the resultant inadequate policy responses and burdens and costs of caring. These values contrast sharply with the collective approach to social justice formulated in our feminist models of economic and social supports, workplace policies, and long-term care, discussed in Chapters 11-14.

THE VALUES OF INDIVIDUALISM, PRIVATE RESPONSIBILITY, AND THE "PUBLIC BURDEN" MODEL OF WELFARE

Public policies in the United States have historically been organized on the premise of private responsibility; families have the primary and natural responsibility for the care of dependents with chronic disabilities. This assumption of private responsibility is consistent with the larger cultural values of individualism, self-determination, independence, privacy, and freedom from intrusion—values that are legacies from our 19th-century past and are still widely embraced. American culture is based on the core values of self-reliance, economic initiative, and productivity; this has created a profound fear of dependency among many Americans. A major component of the ethic of self-reliance is the obligation of citizens to avoid being a burden to others; citizens are expected to support themselves, or if they are dependent, they should depend only on someone who has voluntarily assumed the obligation of support (Winston & Bane, 1993). In the context of long-term care, an individualistic orientation emphasizes the duties and responsibilities of individuals to provide care for others. People who fail to provide for their own health and long-term care or that of family members are viewed as failures (Gill & Ingman, 1994).

The preeminence of the individual in the United States is ingrained in our national identity and championed in the notion of individual rights. Clark (1993) notes that individualism is the American quality that, more than any other characteristic, defines who we are and how we organize our relationships and lives. Individualism is frequently drawn on as the moral basis for distrust of government assistance and underlies the current popularity of interventions such as self-help, social support, and voluntary associations. This configuration of values runs counter to the idea of an individual relying on publicly funded social and health services at different phases of the life cycle. In fact, the cultural value of independence is antithetical to issues concerning infirmity, death, and dying that are inevitably raised by chronic disability and illness.

When public policies are developed within this individualistic value system, assistance, when absolutely necessary, is often packaged in such a way as to reaffirm the ethic of self-reliance, as in "workfare" as a basis for welfare reform (Winston & Bane, 1993). The individual serves as both the unit of need and service and as the core organizing principle. Problems are defined in individual, not social, political, or economic, terms; the individual is seen as primarily responsible for meeting his or her own needs. Assistance to a needy individual should be temporary and oriented toward achieving or recovering his or her independence. When the individual cannot attain independence, family members are the next level of responsibility. The family is thus defined as part of the problem, either as the cause (as incapable caregivers), as barriers to successful treatment, or as responsible for the solution. The family is rarely defined as the client system in need of resources (Moroney, 1980).

At the extreme, families are held responsible both for providing care, and also as the cause of their dependent relatives' problems. This has occurred in definitions of familial etiology of mental illness (Lefley, 1986; Wedenoja, 1991). Chronic disability is not seen as individual misfortune, but is attributed either to the dependent persons themselves or to those who reared them, especially their mothers (Kane & Kane, 1994). Family responsibility laws for the elderly are another example. These require adult children to contribute to nursing home costs and remain on the books in 34 states, although rarely enforced. The Supplemental Security Income Program (SSI) penalizes family members for sharing living expenses with SSI recipients, thereby inadvertently supporting institutionalization over community-based living situations. Such focus on family responsibility serves to divert attention from the problems of an inadequate care system. By overlooking the structural causes of problems, these individualistic definitions of cause and responsibility reduce the likelihood that far-reaching reform toward universal policies for the collective provision of social care will occur.

Our cultural values on individualism and personal responsibility also underlie the widely held belief that institutional or residential care is the least desirable care alternative for individuals and groups who are viewed as weak and deserving (Dalley, 1988). When privacy and independence are regarded as goals to be prized and achieved, they are best secured by remaining in one's own home, even at the expense of other family members' well-being. Our societal value of independence is evident in many of our approaches to care. Institutional, day treatment, rehabilitative, and aftercare services for the chronically mentally ill stress high expectations for success, with the aim of returning the person to "independent functioning" in the community. As noted by Lefley (1986), the very language used—"transitional," "halfway," and "step level"—conveys our fear of dependency. We contend that policies based on individualistic values of self-care and self-help, personal initiative, and independence run counter to the norms of reciprocity, exchange, and interdependence that should underlie the provision of comprehensive care to the chronically disabled across the life span. As noted by Zaretsky (1982), mutuality and interdependence "are an inevitable part of the structure of any society, even one . . . ostensibly organized around individualism and independence" (p.193). From a feminist critique, the fact that helplessness and dependency are part of life for all persons tends to be hidden by many policy initiatives and by the fact that these needs have often been relegated to an invisible and marginalized women's culture. As a result, it is women who bear the costs of individualism (Pascall, 1988).

Inherent in this residual approach to social welfare is the presumption that family life is and should be a private matter, an area not to be encroached upon by the state (Moroney, 1980). By viewing the family's private domain as natural and normal, government creates the impression that nonintervention is justified and acceptable; governmental assistance is not regarded as a right, but as an exception and privilege (Walker, 1985, 1991). Accordingly, government has generally intervened and provided publicly funded services only after family resources have been exhausted, or the family has proven itself incapable of meeting certain standards of care, as in instances of abuse or neglect—after the individual has tried to provide care and failed (Kane & Kane, 1994). When it is assumed that a person's need for care can and should be met within the family, then formal services designed to replace or supplement familial care are limited, and those that exist tend to build on and reinforce family-based care (Baines, Evans, & Neysmith, 1991). Minimal services are justified on the basis of preserving the family's freedom to make their own decisions about care; yet, as Osterbusch, Keigher, Miller, and Linsk (1987) portray, the privacy of such decisions is illusory because the capacity of female caregivers to choose freely whether to provide care is severely limited by the paucity of other care alternatives. From a feminist critique, it is in the government's interest to secure as much of women's free labor as possible because it relieves the public costs of providing adequate long- term care (Arendell & Estes, 1991).

This overall policy approach has been characterized as a *public burden model* of welfare, where expenditures for public services are defined as a drain on the economy (Titmuss, 1968; Walker, 1990). The economic objectives of profit maximization, growth, and cost-effectiveness are defined as legitimate, whereas achievement of the social objectives of good health and community care are believed to rest ultimately on sound economic policy (Titmuss, 1968). Because of the growing preoccupation with ways to reduce public expenditures, the equity concerns of social welfare policy become subordinate to the efficiency criteria that dominate economic policy. Priority is placed on finding the least expensive and most efficient way to provide care. This reasoning provides a justification for strengthening the family's capacity to do even more work than they are already performing (Walker, 1985). Collective responsibility as it resides in the state becomes merely a backup to private provision; government performs a residual role, supporting private effort, rather than taking a lead in promoting social welfare (Dalley, 1988). Debates about family responsibility and caregiving stress can serve to deflect attention from broader structural problems and from social, economic, and political inequities by race, gender, age, and class (Estes, Swan, & Associates, 1993; Minkler & Estes, 1991).

THE IDEOLOGY OF FAMILISM

Closely related to these values, the ideology of familism—or the family ethic—is also rooted in the principle of individualism, with its emphasis on self-determination, privacy, and freedom from intrusion (Abramovitz, 1988; Dalley, 1988). The ideology of familism operates as a principle of social organization at both the domestic and public levels, especially in the arena of social care, by affirming women's place in the domestic sphere as natural and appropriate and family care as superior. The current media and partisan preoccupation with "family values" is the ideology of familism dressed in new clothes, with "the onus of responsibility for caring cloaked in the ideological sanctity of family values" (McDaniel, 1993, p. 139). The New Right's neoconservative appeal to authority, allegiance, tradition, and the free market attempts to meld the interests of capitalism and patriarchy and to justify government intervention only for purposes of national defense and law enforcement (Arendell & Estes, 1991). This neoconservativism is reflected in recent criticisms of feminism for its inadequate attention to the issues affecting families and children. Appeals for traditional family values hide efforts to restore and regulate patriarchal modes of family life, particularly to control women's lives in order to ensure a continuing supply of women's free labor, which is viewed as essential to the reproduction and maintenance of the paid workforce (Abramovitz, 1988). The often-expressed fear of family disintegration is, to some extent, a manifestation of the fear that women are abandoning their historically prescribed caregiving roles and that men are losing their dominance as heads of households (Binney & Estes, 1988).

The ideology of familism is based on an outmoded, unrealistic (and actually never-existent) model of the middle-class nuclear family as a private place where all caring occurs, which assumes the total availability of the family's free domestic labor and time (Clark, 1993). Such a model presumes demographic trends and economic realities of earlier decades. Specifically, it assumes that women are at home with free time, willing and available to provide care to dependent relatives and simply waiting to be called on—assumptions that, as we have seen, are false. As noted by Estes et al. (1993), the magnitude of the sacrifices entailed by women's caregiving is unrecognized because family labor tends to be viewed as free labor, if it is recognized as labor at all. As we will elaborate, familism, with its prescriptive assumptions about the "natural" and "right" position of women, constrains women's actions and results in economic gender-based inequities across the life span.

If a "good" family is one that is autonomous and takes care of its own, then government interference is presumed to weaken the fiber of the family. Under the ideology of familism, the state's primary responsibility toward the family is to assure freedom from state intrusion (Linsk, Simon-Rasionowitz, & England, 1992). Upholding "family values" and family-based models of care means preserving a separation between the public and private spheres of responsibility. By maintaining the illusion of the family as a private domain, presenting the traditional family as responsible for dependents and a gender-based division of labor as normal and natural, the state supports and sustains the inequities of these relationships without appearing intrusive. Like the English Poor Laws, familism assumes that intergenerational dependence is essential for the maintenance of family ties. At the extreme, formalization of caregiving functions are viewed as a source of disintegration of the modern family, which needs to be preserved—if not strengthened—for the survival of society (Estes et al., 1993). If formal services must be provided, then temporary community care is preferred; nonfamilial forms of care, such as residential or institutional care, are viewed as deviant, undesirable, and to be avoided as much as possible. As noted in the preceding discussion about the effect of individualism on public policy, the target of these benefits is the dependent individual whose autonomy is to be fostered, not the caregiver or support system's well-being. Accordingly, those without available family are more likely to qualify for government assistance than those with informal supports (Linsk et al., 1992).

This ideology of familism underlies some policymakers' misconception that family care of the chronically disabled is underused and simply needs to be activated (Briggs & Oliver, 1985). Familism reinforces the belief that families must "spend-down" their resources before publicly funded, needs-based programs such as Medicaid will step in to offer assistance. Policy makers may use the ideology of familism to cloak their goals of cost containment, claiming that provision of services would threaten familial ties and the traditional role of families. When services are provided, the rationale is to prolong the family's caring capabilities through replicating the family form of care as closely as possible, not necessarily to enhance caregivers' well-being (Dalley, 1988; Lewis & Meredith, 1988). As an example, the state's objective in providing home-care services is to avoid or delay institutionalization and thus curtail costs to government (Linsk et al., 1992). The deinstitutionalization movement—which has affected all three focus populations—has affirmed the family model of care as the appropriate policy goal.

Critics of the familial ideology have noted the following limitations (Abel, 1987; Dalley, 1988; Estes et al., 1993; Qureshi & Walker, 1989). Although the public burden model of welfare has taken the harmony and security of family life for granted, care within the family is not necessarily loving nor in the best interests of the disabled persons; instead, as poignantly illustrated by cases of abuse and neglect, dependent individuals can experience emotionally destructive or physically damaging relationships within the privacy of the home. As noted by Abel (1987), caregiving of adult dependents can fracture family ties, resulting in conflicts, anger, and bitterness. Instances of interpersonal violence indicate that for many women, home is not a place of safety but, rather, a center of intense human emotions where males assert power over them. Because of their lack of resources outside the family, many women have no alternative but to live with the daily experience of violence.

Another limitation is that policy makers' tendency to set up artificial polarities between the emotional relations of the informal sector and the instrumental ones of the formal sector overlook the fact that personal benefits can be associated with formal service delivery. For example, an older person may experience the receipt of formal services as an expression of caring by relatives, not as an abdication of care (Qureshi & Walker, 1989). Similarly, formal service providers, such as home health nurses or nurse's aides, frequently become personally attached to those to whom they provide care; they may express their caring by working longer hours, cooking favorite meals, or giving physical affection. As we see, the formal sector is not "uncaring," nor is the informal sector always "loving."

A fundamental limitation of the ideology of familism is that it derives from a middle-class model of the family, based on individualism, self-improvement, and amassing wealth and private property. As such, it does not fit with the experiences and consciousness of low-income persons and women of color, nor with gay and lesbian families. When familism is presented as a standard and an ideal to which to aspire, it negatively affects those for whom it has little meaning in their daily lives (Dalley, 1988). As noted by Hendricks and Rosenthal (1993b), people who do not fit this middle-class ideal, such as single-parent families, are frequently defined as deviant and blamed for social problems. Under this ideology, it is believed that policies should not support "alternative" family forms. In contrast, a feminist perspective grapples with how policies can best meet the emerging needs presented by the diversity of family forms created by poverty, race, single-parent families, and the growing number of homosexual families.

THE IDEOLOGY OF SEPARATE SPHERES

Inextricably interconnected with the cultural value of individualism and the ethic of familism is the ideology of separate spheres or the "cult of domesticity" (Cott, 1977). As noted in Chapter 1, this ideology has had major consequences for the way in which care of chronically disabled relatives is viewed in our society and, accordingly, for the economic and health conditions of women across the life span.

The expectation that women are primarily responsible for work in the home and men for that in the marketplace is a relatively recent phenomenon. The care responsibilities traditionally assumed by women did not become social norms until around 1820, after the Industrial Revolution, when the moralistic ideology of separate spheres as a "romantic solution" to the negative consequences of industrialization and flourishing capitalism was spawned (Erhrenreich, 1983). Women's caregiving became invisible when industrialization made paid labor outside the home the only way to produce something of value. Whereas men controlled the technology, women were to preserve the values of love and nurturing within the home. Under capitalism, production was moved out of the home, and gender-based separate spheres—the family and the work ethic—were created. Economically dependent on men, women as domestic laborers became responsible for both the biological and the social reproduction of labor power (Abramovitz, 1988; Dalley, 1988). Children were to be raised and workers "serviced" through women's unpaid labor. Not only were women to reproduce and service those engaged in productive labor in the public arena, but also those not able to be productive—the chronically disabled. Central to capitalism was a dichotomy between the public and private spheres, a polarity that has been largely taken for granted and continues to influence the formulation of public and corporate policies today.

Under this ideology, nurturance and maintenance were romanticized and honored for meeting fundamental needs for affection within the family, needs that presumably could not be met by paid care providers within the public arena. Catherine Beecher and other mid-19th century feminists argued for women's moral superiority, based on their highly developed capacity for self-sacrifice (Hayden, 1981). For many women, then, gaining a sphere of influence under industrialization and capitalism was perceived as progress, because prior to the 19th century, men retained dominance both in the home and in the marketplace (Ryan, 1987). Although the ideology of separate spheres, or the cult of domesticity, did provide opportunities for women to exercise more power at home, it limited their options for participation in life outside the home. As a largely middle-class ideal with its emphasis on self-sacrifice as a virtue, the ideology of separate spheres, by defining labor force participation as deviant for married women, has had profound negative consequences for economic opportunities for women of all classes (Cott, 1977; Degler, 1980; Hooyman & Ryan, 1987).

From the Industrial Revolution through the 1960s, efforts to expand women's roles into the public sphere repeatedly met with opposition based on fears that gender equity in the workplace would destroy the family. Women gained access to education, suffrage, and paid employment only by arguing that an expansion of women's spheres would enhance rather than undermine their caregiving and would extend their moral influence into public life (Degler, 1980; Hooyman & Ryan, 1987). The perception that married women's participation in the paid labor force was deviant began to shift only in the 1960s, when government officials became concerned that the economy was not growing fast enough. Nevertheless, women's caregiving roles were still to be primary, as illustrated by the recommendation of the first President's Commission on the Status of Women for "women to continue with roles as wives and mothers while working and making a maximum contribution to the world around them" (President's Commission on the Status of Women, 1963, p. 1).

Under the separate spheres ideology, caregiving became defined as women's mission to save civilization from moral ruin in the new industrial age. In order to preserve morality and decency, women had to be sheltered from the corrupting forces of the outside world, and the value placed on the privacy, self-sufficiency, and autonomy of the family reinforced the isolation of women and resulted in the lack of recognition and financial remuneration for caring work (Arendell & Estes, 1991; Ryan, 1987). Caregiving values of love, nurturing, and self-sacrifice were sequestered in the home as an antidote to the public sphere of the marketplace. The home was to be a haven, a repository of warm, caring human relationships based on affection, and thus a private protection against the harsh realities of a cold, hostile outside world (Cott, 1977; Dalley, 1988). In fact, 19th-century advice books to women exhorted them to temper the effects of the public work place with their virtue, love, and selflessness (Cott, 1977; Degler, 1980; Ryan, 1987; Strasser, 1982).

With workers' affiliative and affective needs to be met within the family, the public sphere was exonerated from any obligations of social or care responsibilities, and profit became defined as the sole operating principle of the marketplace. Because all that women earned belonged to their husbands, the only means for extending their influence with the men who controlled their lives was to assert the moral superiority of self-sacrifice (Cott, 1977). The virtues of compassion, support, and affection enshrined in the home could compensate for but not shape the public sphere (Cott, 1977; Erhrenreich & English, 1979; Ryan, 1987). Caregiving was thus viewed as a private activity to be performed in isolation within the home, away from public scrutiny. Home life became an antidote to marketplace competition rather than a central force in shaping society.

Although presumably elevating the importance of caregiving to the sanctity of family life and providing women with moral leverage with men (Hooyman & Ryan, 1987), this separation of caregiving from the public arena actually served to devalue it. Caregiving is often viewed with contempt, in part because it does not resemble the time-regulated tasks of the industrial marketplace (Cott, 1977). Nonmonetized and nontechnological caregiving became devalued in a society that defines work primarily in terms of measurable output and wages, and that values independence and productivity, not long-term maintenance of dependent individuals. In the most basic sense, the ideology of separate spheres took two conflicting philosophies—the pre-Industrial Revolution value of community, reciprocal rights and responsibilities, and duty; and the newer one of individualism, progress, and competition—and resolved the conflict along the lines of gender: Women would nurture as the carers in the home, men would achieve as the breadwinners in the public arena. The domestic sphere of women became culturally linked to expressiveness, nurturing, and emotion, whereas the public sphere of men became characterized as instrumental, competitive, and rational (Chodorow, 1978).

From our feminist perspective on caregiving of dependents with chronic disabilities, the long-term consequence of this ideology is that women have been expected to perform the unpaid work in the home that underpins the economy; yet their work is viewed as peripheral to the marketplace norms of competition and financial gain as defined by men. Their life's work has been regarded as nonwork, unrecognized and undervalued. Even when women have moved into the marketplace, assuming the roles of underpaid caregivers—teachers, nurses, social workers, nurse's aides, home care workers—it is still presumed that women should give generously rather than be adequately compensated for their work. This is reflected by the wage inequities still experienced by the majority of employed women. The need to restructure the basic division of labor between the private and public spheres on the one hand, and women and men on the other, cuts deep into the political agenda and is at the core of our feminist critique of public and corporate policies related to the chronically disabled (Hernes, 1984).

GENERATIONAL EQUITY AND INTERGENERATIONAL CONFLICT

With policy making increasingly framed in the language of economics and driven by concern for cost containment, the issue of informal caregiving has been conceptualized in terms of generational equity and intergenerational conflict, especially with regard to older people with chronic disabilities (Estes et al., 1993). The growing perceived public policy polarization between the young and the old, "kids versus canes," reflects different interpretations about the relationship between the family and the state as well as the societal value of individualism (Binney & Estes, 1988). Underlying this debate is a zero-sum notion that services are finite and limited, so that one generation inevitably benefits at the expense of another. Consistent with the ideology of familism, this debate is also propagated by those who claim a crisis of the family, relying on an outmoded model of the nuclear family extolled by the popular media and by the New Right. Inaccurate perception of generational inequity, especially with regard to health care costs, has also been fueled by the media (Cohen, 1994).

As noted earlier, the values of individualism and private responsibility, the definition of problems in individual terms rather than social ones, and the ideology of familism have resulted in incremental, residual policies that are particularized and compartmentalized along lines of individual or group-based need. In the past two decades since the Reagan era, these trends have been compounded by the erosion of basic entitlements and the targeting of increasingly limited benefits (Binney & Estes, 1988). The core values of individual rights and family responsibility, along with the bifurcation of formal and informal care in a period of fiscal austerity, are being played out presently in intergenerational competition over what are defined to be limited residual resources. The intergenerational debate is connected with debates about health care financing and rationing. The elderly are frequently implicitly blamed for escalating health care costs, even though old age and expensive high-tech care do not necessarily go together (Cohen, 1994).

Such a victim-blaming approach has a number of fundamental limitations. By blaming the elderly for the poverty among women and children, it overlooks the real causes of increasing poverty among younger age groups. The large increase in poverty among children is a result of the growth in female-headed households, and the inability of women heads of households to support their families adequately. Women's low earning power is, in turn, a consequence of a gender-segregated labor force in which women are concentrated among the lower-paying service jobs—which, as we have seen, is a product of the ideologies of familism and separate spheres (Quadagno, 1989). Those who predict that younger age groups will never enjoy a standard of living comparable to their parents' overlook that it is stagnation of production and low investment in the United States that underlie this gloomy prognosis, not the elderly per se (Minkler, 1991; Walker, 1990). Both young and old have been negatively affected by reductions in public social spending under the cover of deficit reduction (Binney & Estes, 1988). Within age groups, there is considerable heterogeneity regarding economic status, as for example, with the high poverty rates among older minority women. This perspective also overlooks inequities within age groups by class, race, and gender, and deflects attention from the basic issue, which is that the main cause of poverty is income inequity, not intergenerational inequity (Kingson, 1988; Minkler, 1991).

The intergenerational inequity debates overlook the interdependence and shared interests of different generations, different classes, and different racial groups with regard to publicly funded programs such as Social Security, Medicare, and Medicaid. For example, public funding for home care can benefit all age groups who face chronic disabilities. Under the perspective of finite resources, common interests have been disaggregated, false dichotomies established, and within-group differences obscured. This has prevented the building of coalitions and broad-based grassroots support systems and has permitted the state to abdicate social responsibility for human needs (Binney & Estes, 1988). As noted by Kingson (1988), such interest-based, pluralist politics do not lead to social or economic justice. Our society's fragmented, group-based "nonsystem" stands in sharp contrast to more comprehensive policies of other Western industrialized societies, especially the Scandinavian countries, that meet the changing needs of families over the life course. From a feminist perspective, a primary goal is to reduce such fragmentation and build coalitions across different population groupings as discussed more fully in Part IV.

In conclusion, given the fundamental value differences reflected in current debates about public policies and caregivers of dependents with chronic disabilities, it is clear that ending the social and economic inequities experienced by family caregivers will require deep structural and political changes, challenging the very nature of our social institutions of the government, the workplace, and the family. For example, funding more home care services, as put forth by President Clinton in his health care proposal, confronts traditional assumptions about the distribution of public and private rights and responsibilities (Minkler & Estes, 1991; Neysmith, 1991; Ungerson, 1987). The nature of the contemporary debates about health care and long-term care reflect increasing recognition that care of dependents is not just a private obligation, although as a society, we have not yet reallocated such care to the arena of public responsibility, in part because of our societal ambivalence about the nature of and responsibility for care. Whatever the outcome of the debate, those most affected will be women as underpaid workers, unpaid caregivers, and beneficiaries of public programs, given the gendered nature of care. We turn now to a more detailed analysis of the gender-based division of care responsibilities.

6

The Gendered Nature of Care

One of the most consistent findings in family research is that, across the family life cycle, the vast majority of carers for relatives with chronic disabilities are women. Although both masculine and feminine roles within American families have changed in the past few decades, women are still the primary nurturers, kin keepers, and carers of family members. Moreover, it is women in the middle generation who are most centrally involved in maintaining family contact and cohesion across generations (Gonyea, 1995). Gender—more than kin ties—determines who assumes the caring role. Although some men are "unsung heroes" as caregivers, they tend to shoulder this role only when a female family member is unavailable. Of all family caregivers to the elderly, for example, 23% are wives, 29% are daughters and daughters-in-law, and 20% are more distant female relatives (Older Women's League, 1989; Stone, Cafferata, & Sangl, 1987). Thus, feminists assert that social scientists' continued treatment of the family as the smallest unit of analysis has "served to hide from view the complex and gendered nature of caring" (Traustadottir, 1991, p. 212). Social scientists' use of gender-neutral terms such as *parent, spouse, sibling,* and *family-caregiver* has obscured differences in men's and women's roles and has led to "gender insensitivity" in policies and programs (p. 212).

A gender-blind approach renders opaque our value system, which, according to Abel and Nelson (1990, p. 4), "enshrines the virtue of independence, defines instrumental work as superior to emotional work, seeks to distance itself from basic life events and devalues the activities of women." Such values have also led policymakers to ignore the experience of caregivers. Within the public policy arena, caregivers—mostly women—have historically been invisible, a situation that both reflects and reinforces their powerlessness. This circumstance is, however, beginning to change. As British researchers Twigg and Atkin (1994, p. 1) note, "carers are no longer the Cinderellas of social policy. One of the striking developments of the last decade has been the increasing reference to carers in public policy documents." Although they go on to temper this statement by noting that "despite this greater visibility of carers in the policy debate, policy itself has not engaged in any sustained way with their incorporation, remaining undeveloped and seldom going beyond bland statements of the importance of supporting carers." Politicians may offer platitudes to carers, but little strategic thinking exists regarding their roles and needs.

In this chapter, we explore how men and women differ, not only in their enactment of the caregiving role, but also in the ways gender influences the meaning of caring, the social context of providing care, and the consequences of performing the carer role. We argue that although caring for a family member is a profoundly personal experience, it is shaped by a broader social and political framework. We explore how the prevailing cultural ideology that women are "natural caregivers" alters both women's and men's lives. Consistent with our feminist approach, we emphasize that in order to understand the caregiver role, it is necessary to take account of structural factors and the ways public policies affect both the nature and consequences of family caregiving.

According to Dressel and Clark (1990), when social scientists have discussed family care, they have historically drawn a distinction between families' routine daily life and stressful events and life crises. As a result of this dichotomy, Dressel and Clark point out that separate bodies of literature, each with their own language or terminology, have emerged within the family field. Studies concerned with everyday family life focus on the division of household labor, child care, and kin keeping; research on stressful family events (e.g., assistance to members with physical, psychological, or cognitive disabilities) examines the nature of caregiving and the role of social supports or social networks. Even in the caregiving literature, little cross-fertilization has occurred across the fields of mental health, developmental disabilities, and gerontology. In fact, the developmental disability and mental illness literature rarely uses the specific term "caregiver," and refers primarily to "families."

Although there may be distinctions between routine and nonroutine family experiences (and thus a value to this dichotomy), Dressel and Clark (1990) and Abel (1991) suggest there are also a number of commonalities across these experiences. These include the concept of choice or options available to women, the connection between women's caregiving roles and their disadvantaged positions in the labor market, and the societal devaluation of caring (Abel 1991). Indeed, it is the structural assumptions that women's primary orientation is toward the family and the extension of women's "natural" role of mother that prescribe their role as primary caregiver for disabled members.

Some feminists argue that gender has been reified in discussions of family care—that is, the social construction of gender predetermines who will assume the caregiving role. Women are viewed or assumed to be the natural carers because women are expressive, whereas men are instrumental—women do emotional labor, whereas men do goal-oriented labor—and according to the ideology of separate spheres, women's domain is the home and hearth, whereas men's is the external world of paid work and community (Abel, 1991). A theme throughout this book is that this cultural ideology of the gendered nature of caring profoundly shapes both women's and men's lives. As Hochschild (1975) emphasizes, feelings are not random experiences; they are highly structured and tied to normative frameworks. American culture's gender-based dichotomy of caring influences how both men and women who care for family members with disabilities experience this role and the meaning they attribute to it.

The gendered nature of family labor has not been explored equally across the different bodies of the family caregiving literature. Abel (1991) criticizes feminists for their "lavished attention on motherhood" but their slighting of other forms of caregiving. Although the division of routine family work—household chores and child care—between husbands and wives (spurred on by women's increasing entry into the paid labor market) has emerged as an important topic within the family field, the gendered nature of family caregiving, with the exception of elder care, has been neglected in the disabilities field. Traustadottir (1988, p. 8) maintains that, "Women's informal caring work has rarely been the center of focus within the disability field. . . . The sexual division of caring for people with disabilities is largely an unstudied topic." The neglect of gender as an important variable in the field of mental illness is echoed by Cook (1988, p. 44), who states, "Until this time, empirical studies concerning the influence of gender on familial reactions to mental illness had been limited to scattered findings." As noted in Chapter 4, "although gender was not viewed as a major feature in understanding familial reactions to mental illness, it was a central underpinning of theories of causation of psychiatric disturbance with mothers typically blamed for their children's mental illness" (Cook, 1988, p. 44). Feminists assert that it is precisely this cultural expectation of caregiving being a woman's responsibility that has resulted in the lack of study of the sexual division of family labor in long-term illness management as well as the lack of policy supports for caregivers.

GENDER ROLE EXPECTATIONS AND CAREGIVING

Within the family caregiving literature, family division-of-labor models are often advanced to explain existing gender differences in caregiving: the time-available hypothesis, the gender-role socialization or ideology hypothesis, the external-resources hypothesis, and the task-specialization hypothesis (see Finley, 1989, for a detailed discussion of the four explanatory models). The time-available hypothesis posits that competing roles and time demands restrict the amount of time an individual has available for family labor. The external-resources hypothesis predicts that assets obtained externally, such as education, occupation, and income, determine the power dynamics within the family. In contrast, the ideology hypothesis suggests that gender role attitudes learned in the socialization process, rather than resources, influence the division of labor. Finally, the specialization of tasks hypothesis asserts that men and women perform different but complementary tasks in order to maximize the well-being of the family.

Findings for these four hypotheses are inconsistent. Regarding the time-available hypothesis, a number of studies have found that employed caregivers provide as many hours of care as those who are not employed outside the home (Brody, Johnson, Fulcomer, & Lang, 1983; Cantor, 1983; Soldo & Myllyluoma, 1983), but other studies suggest that employed caregivers provide less assistance (Giele, Mutschler, & Orodenker, 1987; Matthews, Wekner, & Delaney, 1989). Interestingly, Stoller (1983) found that both employment and number of children reduced men's assistance to aging parents, but did not alter women's care to parents.

In research on 1,760 adult children (men and women) with older parents or parents-in-law, Finley (1989) explored whether any of the four family division-of-labor hypotheses were adequate in explaining why females were more likely to be involved in caregiving than males. Finley's study is important because she was seeking to understand, after controlling differences between the sexes in available time, gender role ideology, external resources, or task specialization, whether there was still a significant difference in the level of men's and women's caregiving involvement.

The results of Finley's (1989) research are profound. Her data reveal that "neither the time available, attitudes of obligation nor external resources seem to account for gender differences in caregiving. The direct relationship between gender and caregiving remains significant after these variables are controlled" (Finley 1989, p. 84). Women experience more role conflict than men, and although men and women share a similar sense of filial obligation, men are less likely to act on it to the extent that women do. In terms of task-specialization, Finley concludes that men are not specializing in certain types of tasks. Her data suggest that in every task category, females are more likely than males to provide help. "The gender difference is statistically significant in only two categories, activities of daily living and cognitive assistance; however, there is no category in which males are significantly more likely to be caregivers" (Finley 1989, p. 84).

Finley's (1989) study underscores that gender differences in caring have become institutionalized in American society. Our culture's assumptions or expectations of the gendered nature of care influence the experiences of both men and women who perform the caregiver role. A feminist analysis of caregiving thus requires that gender be at the center of our inquiry, that the carers' behaviors not be separated from their understanding of their actions (Cook, 1988; Gilligan, 1982), and that we examine how social institutions built on gender role differentiation impact the caring experience.

THE PERSONAL AND SOCIAL MEANINGS OF CAREGIVING

Each of us is a member of a family, and at some point in our lives has either given or received care from another member. For this reason it is often assumed that the meaning of family care is self-evident, that everyone knows what care is and what it means. It is surprisingly difficult, however, to define the phenomenon of family caregiving, which reflects the complex nature of caring. Family caregiving transcends traditional boundaries between private and public domains, between work and leisure, and between productive and reproductive relationships (Graham, 1983). It is also important to keep in mind the distinction between caring about someone and caring for them. Caring about involves primarily a psychological connection—the expression of affection and love—whereas caring for involves carrying out tasks such as personal assistance, paying bills, and transportation. Because these two aspects of caregiving are fused and the affective side is romanticized, the carer's experience remains invisible. Wives, mothers, and daughters are expected to be self-sacrificing and nurturing, and the tasks involved in caregiving are assumed to require minimal effort or time (Hooyman & Ryan, 1987). Caregiving tasks such as cleaning, transportation, and doing laundry are not respected as real work because, as Cott (1977) notes, they do not resemble the time-regulated, task-structured work of industrial production.

Guberman, Maheu and Maille (1992) argue that it is the confusion of these two concepts, caring about and caring for, that results in policies that place undue pressure on families to assume the "daily hands-on physical and psychological care for dependent members on the pretext that families should 'care.' . . . Because it is considered 'natural' for families to care about, it seems 'natural' that they assume the tasks linked to caring for" (Guberman et al., 1992, p. 607). The personal meaning of family care not only reflects one's own unique family culture, but also incorporates the values of the broader culture's social, political, and economic spheres. As noted in Chapter 5, our societal values underlie the expectation that family care is a private responsibility to be carried out, as much as possible, on one's own.

OBJECTIVE DIMENSIONS OF CAREGIVING

There are both objective and subjective dimensions of caregiving. Much of the relevant research has focused on the objective or behavioral aspects of caring—the type, frequency, and duration of caregiving activities. The impetus for social scientists' focus on the objective dimensions of caring has been the need or desire to dispel two prevailing social myths. The first cultural myth is that families have, or wish to, abandon their members who are frail or have disabilities. The second is that the introduction of public programs leads families to neglect their caring responsibilities. Despite more than three decades of research consistently documenting that persons with developmental disabilities or chronic mental illness and frail elderly individuals receive the vast majority of their care from families, the myth of family abandonment remains.

Across all three vulnerable populations, the intensity and duration of family care are typically dictated by the nature and degree of the disability. Differences do exist among the three groups, however, in terms of the time of onset of the disability and hence, for many, the onset of the caring role. For parents of children with developmental disabilities, their caregiving responsibilities begin at birth and often become a lifelong pattern. Most of these individuals would describe their role in terms of parenting rather than caregiving. The overwhelming majority of the developmental disabilities literature focuses on young families. It was not until the mid-1980s that concerns of older caregivers—typically, parents of developmentally disabled adults—began to appear in the literature (Janicki & Wisniewski, 1985; Seltzer & Krauss, 1987). In contrast, many of the most severe and disabling mental disorders, such as schizophrenia, are characterized by onset in late adolescence or early adulthood. Ironically, just when they may have begun to anticipate or experience greater freedom, parents of children with severe mental disorders often find their caring role increasing. For these families, the launching of the children into the adult world may never be completed. The consequences of caring for someone with a mental health problem clearly depend on the type of illness. Schizophrenia and other psychotic conditions are typically thought of as mind disorders involving impairment of cognitive functioning, particularly in relation to perception, thinking, and insight. Neurotic conditions are characterized by feelings of depression, anxiety, or phobic, obsessive, or compulsive behaviors. Finally, for older spouses, the role of caregiver often occurs very late in life after many years of sharing healthy and independent lives.

Research has consistently documented that a hierarchical or sequential model of social support exists based on both kinship ties and gender. In times of need, people generally turn first to their most intimate relationships—the bonds between spouses and between parents and children. If these most intimate relations are not available, assistance is then sought from more distant relations. Thus, among the frail elderly, spouses provide the most care for the married; adult children (daughters and daughters-in-law before sons and sons-in-law) for the widowed; and siblings (sisters before brothers) for the unmarried and childless (Cicirelli, 1985; Coward & Dwyer, 1990; Johnson, 1983; Johnson & Catalano, 1981; Matthews, 1987). The crucial role of gender in the hierarchy of obligation to elderly family members is reflected in the fact that after spouses and daughters, it is daughters-in-law and not sons who are the next lines of resort (Qureshi & Walker, 1989).

Unlike most adults, persons with severe mental illness or mental retardation generally lack a spouse or a child to whom they can turn for support (Horwitz, 1993; Seltzer & Krauss, 1987). It is estimated that only 10% of the individuals with serious mental illnesses are married (Grusky, Tierney, Manderscheid, & Grusky, 1985). Parents, especially mothers, are the primary source of support for adults with mental disabilities. As we have noted, it is increasingly common for these parents themselves to be among the ranks of the elderly. In a British study, Grant (1986) found that among 100 adults with mental disabilities living at home, 90% of the family members with primary responsibility were parents, of which 40% were aged 65 or older, and nearly 60% of those carers had suffered the loss of a spouse. Regardless of age, 9 out of 10 carers were women.

Although parents, especially mothers, are an important source of support for these individuals, most adults with a developmental disability or mental illness will outlive their parents. Thus, in middle age, as a result of either their parents' declining health or death, siblings become the primary source of support for most of these individuals. Horwitz (1993, p. 631) suggests that because adults with a mental health problem typically outlive their parents and because their friendships are often frail and unstable, "in the long-term, siblings may be the only possible source of informal support for the seriously mentally ill." Despite the importance of siblings, researchers have only recently begun to explore adult siblings as sources of support for persons with chronic disabilities.

Whether caring for a person with a physical, mental, or cognitive disability, the clinical literature emphasizes that the nature of the relationship, or kinship tie, between the caregiver and recipient influences patterns of assistance. The literature also suggests that spouses, offspring, siblings, and other relatives experience the caregiver role quite differently. For instance, children who were raised by a parent suffering from a mental illness bring a different family history to caring for this person in their later years than does an aging parent of an adult child with a mental illness. Moreover, siblings often enter into the caregiving role with a very different set of expectations than do parents of an adult child with a developmental disability (Seltzer, Begun, Seltzer, & Krauss, 1991) or a seriously mentally ill adult child (Horwitz, 1993).

The types of tasks performed by families with members who are developmentally disabled, mentally ill, or physically frail are often similar. The caregiving literature often notes four types or categories of assistance: activities of daily living, instrumental tasks, cognitive assistance, and expressive tasks (Brody & Schoonover, 1986). Activities of daily living focus on the personal care needs of the disabled or frail individual, such as dressing, bathing, toileting, walking, eating, and bed or chair transfer. Instrumental assistance encompasses housekeeping chores (i.e., cooking, cleaning, and laundry), maintenance of the home or yard, transportation, and financial assistance. Cognitive assistance refers to linkage or brokerage services such as appointment scheduling, checking medication schedules, financial management, and monitoring personal health and home safety. The expressive tasks focus on emotional support such as personal contact, telephone check-in, offering comfort, and insuring that the care recipient feels loved, connected, and valued by the family.

Even without the presence of a member with a disabling condition, the gender-based division of family labor is well documented. When couples share household and child care responsibilities, women typically perform the tasks that are unrelenting, repetitive, and routine, whereas men choose the tasks that are infrequent, irregular, and nonroutine (Berk, 1985). This gender-based division is intensified when the family includes a member with a disability (Cook, 1988). Research reveals that the amount of family labor performed by mothers of children with disabilities is both qualitatively and quantitatively different from that performed by fathers (Baldwin & Glendinning, 1983). In interviews with 50 two-parent families, Mardiros (1985) found that although all the mothers had been active in the workforce prior to the birth of a child with disabilities and 75% had originally planned to return to work, only 8% ultimately returned to their jobs after the child's birth.

As the mother assumed more traditional responsibilities related to homemaking and child care, husbands were found to become more "traditional" and more removed from the family. . . . Mothers who had seen themselves as being self-reliant now felt dependent on their husbands for social and intellectual stimulation. Mothers also reported an obvious division of labor regarding household tasks and the ways in which interpersonal and personal needs were met within the marriage. The rules and expectations were now altered. (Mardiros, 1985, p. 25)

A study comparing 49 married mothers and 50 single mothers of children with developmental disabilities suggests little difference in the amount of instrumental support these two groups of women receive. Married women were given no greater amount of support either with daily household chores or baby-sitting for the child with the disability than their single counterparts (Marcenko & Meyers, 1991). Marcenko and Meyers (1991, p. 189) conclude, "In terms of day-to-day responsibility for the care of the child with handicaps, that job seems to fall to mothers, regardless of marital status."

Although both of these studies focus on families with minor children, it is reasonable to hypothesize that this gender-based division of family care extends across the family life cycle, given what we know about elderly mothers caring for adult children with developmental disabilities. Whether or not they are employed outside the home, women generally provide more "high-intensity" care than do men (Foster & Brizius, 1993). Miller and Cafasso's (1992) meta-analysis of seven gerontological caregiving studies reveals that women are much more likely than men to provide the personal hygiene care of bathing, dressing, and toileting as well as the daily tasks of cooking and cleaning. A gender division of family labor appears to be particularly true of adult daughters and sons caring for aging parents (Kaye & Applegate, 1990). Studies consistently reveal that adult daughters or daughters-in-law as compared to sons or sons-in-law are three times more likely to provide personal care assistance (Coward & Dwyer, 1990; Finley, 1989; Stoller, 1983).

Caregiving covers a wide spectrum of services that depend on the degree of disability as well as the family's resources. The 1982 National Long-Term Care Survey revealed that almost 11% of caregivers left the paid workforce specifically to provide care to older family members with disabilities (Stone et al., 1987). Because women earn less than men as a rule, it is not surprising that if one spouse must give up employment in order to care for a family member with a disability or chronic illness, it is usually the wife who does so, not the husband. It is also important to underscore that for women, working outside the home does not necessarily translate into receiving more family support. In their study of families with children with developmental disabilities, Marcenko and Meyers

(1991) found that although employed mothers received greater assistance with baby-sitting than did mothers who were not working outside the home, enabling them to pursue paid employment, employed mothers did not report receiving more help with daily household chores.

More recently, research has focused on how living arrangements affect patterns of care. Through a comparison of 445 spouses, offspring, and other relatives caring for frail elders, Tennstedt, Crawford, and McKinlay (1993a) examined whether coresidence status rather than kinship was a more important predictor of assistance. Based on their data, the researchers conclude that it is, in fact, coresidence that provides the basis for similarity among informal caregivers in relation to provision of instrumental (housekeeping) assistance. "Spousal caregivers are distinct only from other caregivers who do not live with the care recipient in what they do and the impact of that care" (Tennstedt et al., 1993a, p. S82). The authors caution, however, that although coresidence emerged over caregiver relationship as the more important determinant of the pattern of care, "caregiver relationship might operate indirectly on patterns of instrumental care through its influence on the decision to share a household" (Tennstedt et al., 1993a, p. S82).

The results of the study by Tennstedt et al. (1993a) have special significance in relation to families of color, given that multigenerational households are more prevalent among African American, Latino, and Asian American families as compared to Caucasian families. Beck and Beck (1989) found that almost 50% of African American women lived in a three-generation household at some point between 1969 and 1984. Hispanic families have been found to have more households of extended families than either African American or Anglo families (Mindel, 1980). Burr and Mutchler's (1993) analysis of the living arrangements of unmarried females aged 55 and older, based on 1980 U.S. Census data, revealed that whereas only 33% of whites coresided or lived in complex households with other kin and nonkin, 55% of Japanese, 69% of Chinese, 84% of Koreans, and 89% of Filipinos coresided.

Economic resources, level of acculturation, health status, and the availability of kin all influence living arrangement choice (Burr & Mutchler, 1993; Lockery, 1991). Considerable diversity exists within each racial group. The greater prevalence of the pattern of coresidence or complex families in communities of color may, in part, explain the higher levels of assistance to frail elders reported by Latino, African American, or Asian American families as compared to Caucasian families. For example, Greene and Monahan (1984) found that when families were questioned about the twelve types of instrumental support, although Hispanic care recipients were actually less functionally impaired than their Caucasian counterparts, Hispanic elders obtained help in an average of six service areas as opposed to 3.5 service areas for the Anglo group. Clearly, more research is needed to determine how the structural phenomenon of a shared household affects both the intensity and patterns of care. Whereas some social scientists have emphasized the role of the extended family among African Americans, Hispanics, and Asian Americans, others have argued that the role of the extended family is overexaggerated or disintegrating in populations of color (Purdy & Arguello, 1992).

SUBJECTIVE DIMENSIONS OF CAREGIVING

Although the vast majority of research has focused on the objective or behavioral aspects of caring, several qualitative researchers have begun to explore the subjective, cognitive, and emotional dimensions of caregiving in greater depth. These studies underscore how cultural ideologies and assumptions about women's association with family caring are translated into both genders' sense of obligation to family members. As Aronson (1992, p. 12) suggests, "Prevailing ideologies provide images, vocabularies, and symbols that powerfully shape our thinking about ourselves and our social worlds, defining our conceptions of what is right or desirable and what is possible and thinkable."

Aronson's (1992) interviews with 28 adult daughters of aging mothers reveal that these women had internalized the cultural message that women are the "natural" caregivers; they simply accepted as natural the limited roles of the men in their families and of the government regarding supportive services. Although all of these women had husbands or brothers, they thought it so obvious that daughters would naturally step in to assist their mothers as to be unremarkable—"I've never thought of it before" (Aronson, 1992, p. 17). The women offered two explanations for their lack of expectations for support from their husbands and brothers. First, that men's primary attachment is to the work world; and second, that men do not provide the same quality of care as women do. In terms of public services, "subjects spoke at length about their awareness of the current pattern of care in which families are encouraged to look after their members' welfare with minimal public supports. Normative expectations about family obligations were so assumed as to be practically unnoticed." Aronson (p. 25) argues that the recurring theme of "Who else is going to do it?" reflects the lack of choice and constraints women face as providers of care.

Traustadottir (1991) collected data over a 2-year period through both participant observation and in-depth interviews with 14 families of children with disabilities. Like Aronson, she discovered the gendered nature of family care. Whereas the mother's principal role was to be the doer or provider of care, the primary role of father was to be a supporter. Families defined father's support by three types of activities: to provide financial support, to recognize and appreciate the mother's caring work, and to be willing to discuss options and help make decisions around care issues. Mothers either provide the care themselves, search out community services, or both. If a father performs these three roles, "the mother sees him as being very supportive and involved" (Traustadottir, 1991, p. 221).

In contrast to Traustadottir, Mardiros's (1985) ethnographic interviews with 50 parents of children with disabilities reveal that most women found they could not turn to their husbands to discuss their concerns arising from child care demands.

> Typically, the mother felt that she could not burden the father with many of the problems she experienced, that his work was more valued than hers, and that she was to meet his emotional needs, especially where the child was concerned, whereas she must find other ways to have her needs met. (Mardiros, 1985, p. 25)

These women identified other mothers of children with disabilities as their most significant social support rather than their husbands.

Traustadottir's (1991) interviews with the mothers reveal three different meanings of *caring*. The first two meanings, *caring for* and *caring about,* were discussed earlier in this chapter. *Caring for* refers to the work of caring, whereas *caring about* refers to relationships and emotions. Like Guberman et al. (1992), Traustadottir found that the intertwining or confusion of these two meanings provides the justification for others to pressure mothers into doing caring work or leads to feelings of guilt within the mother. The third meaning of care Traustadottir noted in these women's lives was that of the extended care role. In this capacity, mothers extended their caring beyond their own child to the broader community or society, often in the role of advocate. "They start caring about what happens to people with disabilities in general and the way that society as a whole treats them" (Traustadottir, 1991, p. 217). This is significant in that it demonstrates these women clearly understand the interrelationship of the private and public realms in shaping both their children's and their own lives.

Guberman et al. (1992, p. 607) argue that, although social scientists recognize the importance of gender as a predictor of caregiving, "there is no real questioning of the 'naturalness' of family caregiving, nor of the fact that it is primarily women who assume this task." Through open-ended thematic interviews with 40 nonspousal (primarily adult children and parent) female caregivers for a relative with a mental illness or a frail elder, Guberman et al. (1992) explored the "motives" of these women to take on the caregiver role. The researchers specifically chose to use the term "motives" as the concept that best reflects the fact that actions can be derived both from within the individual (i.e., the internalizing of the dominant culture's norms) and from the social context (i.e., the individual's own set of circumstances).

Consistent with a feminist approach, their analysis revealed that 3 of the 6 primary factors that appear to be determinants of a woman's decision to provide care represent external or structural constraints: the inadequacy of institutional and community resources, the imposition of the decision by the dependent person, and women's economic dependency. Guberman and her colleagues conclude that the lack of community resources, the use of pressure tactics by professionals on families to provide the care, and the refusal of the dependent person to use community resources suggest that the formal and informal sectors continue to mutually reinforce the cultural assumption that women are the "natural" carers.

Women's lack of financial autonomy also influences their decision to provide care. Several female respondents expressed that they felt compelled because of their economic dependency—either on a husband or the state—to provide care. These women included a homemaker wife who felt she had no choice but to abide by her husband's wishes that she care for his frail mother, and a divorced woman who took her mother into her home in order to have access to her mother's old-age pension. Their interviews reveal that "these women were resigned to their caregiving role but would not have chosen it had they been financially independent" (Guberman et al., 1992, p. 612). Consistent with other researchers's findings, the remaining three primary factors identified as motivating women to adopt the caregiver role were derived from within: feelings of love and family ties, a need to help others, and a sense of obligation and duty. These factors represent women's internalization of the dominant culture's ideology of women as the expressive kin-keepers and those who perform the emotional labor.

Feminists emphasize that this ideology creates a dichotomy between feminine love and masculine self-development, which results in different ways of caring for men and women (Cancian, 1987). Thompson (1993) argues that

> the image of feminine love gives women responsibility for love and defines love as self-sacrifice, emotional warmth, expressiveness, vulnerability, and sensitivity. . . . The image of masculine autonomy does not allow men to admit

their need for care, and the image of feminine love does not offer men gender-appropriate ways to display care. (p. 559)

Just as women's role as caregivers for adults is an extension of the culturally defined role of motherhood, so is men's role as carer (and their much lower participation in caregiving) an extension of the culturally defined role of fatherhood. Historically, the dominant image of father has been as a distant breadwinner. LaRossa (1988, p. 451) poses the question of whether fatherhood has changed in the wake of the social and economic changes that have taken place in America since the turn of the century. Interestingly, the answer he forms to this question is both yes and no. Although a new image of father as nurturer has emerged, a review of the research reveals that how fathers behave with their children in terms of engagement, accessibility, and responsibility has not changed significantly. He concludes that "the culture of fatherhood has changed more rapidly than the conduct" (LaRossa, 1988, p. 451).

One of the few studies specifically focused on men as caregivers is by Kaye and Applegate (1990). Although Kay and Applegate did not explore what factors motivate these individuals to assume the carer role for an elderly relative, their research provides valuable insights into how men both perform and experience caregiving. Not surprisingly, the vast majority of men in their study were caring for a spouse. Only with the spousal relationship does the nature of the bond supersede gender in seeking aid. A married person will almost always turn to his or her spouse first for assistance, regardless of whether the partner is a man or a women. Beyond the spousal bond, however, gender becomes critical. As we have noted, the hierarchy of support passes from spouse to daughters, sisters, and nieces (if they are available) before sons, brothers, and nephews become involved.

Although we do not know if these particular men who stepped forward to assume the carer role are unique or different from men who do not, Kaye and Applegate's findings do underscore that the men who are primary caregivers do provide a broad spectrum of services "from hand holding to home repair" (Kaye & Applegate, 1990, p. 83). Further, more than 50% of the men reported providing more than 60 hours of care each week. Even though they were primary caregivers, these men had nevertheless internalized the dominant culture's ideology of women as the "natural" caregivers:

Asked about differences in the ways men and women give care, for example, one man caring for his wife declared that "women are more sensitive and knowledgeable [about caregiving]. They relate better. . . . Men are more brutal

[and] try to put things out of their minds." Another believed that male caregivers are "more efficient and less tender." Another thought that "women in general have a more loving approach. Men are more matter-of-fact.". . . Repeatedly, terms like tender, patient, intuitive, and compassionate appeared as men talked about female caregivers, whereas they characterized men as efficient, tough-minded, or even insensitive. (Kane & Applegate, 1990, p. 115)

Although the men's attitudes toward the appropriate gender allocation of different caregiving tasks reflects considerable androgyny, most thought women should assist with personal care tasks whereas men should help with home repairs, transportation, and other instrumental aspects of daily living. This gender-based distinction of roles is important. Men ranked the care recipient's mental and emotional health as the primary barrier to the amount of care they provided, but "the caregivers' responses suggested that gender-related factors ranked next in importance as caregiving barriers. Their own and others' opinions of what appropriate male behavior should be appeared to be related to the amount of care they provided" (Kaye & Applegate, 1990, p. 84). This theme of men's adoption of the belief that women possess "natural" caregiving skills is also echoed in Grant's (1990) British study of family carers for adults with mental disabilities. Grant cites the example of the Evans, a couple in their seventies caring for their daughter, in which Mr. Evan reaffirms both women's natural superiority to men in caregiving and the inappropriateness of men in performing personal care assistance.

Of course, I hope nothing happens to my wife, but the mother can do things a father can't. For instance, a father wouldn't like to bathe her would he? She's a young woman, you know what I mean. She's 41 years of age. (Grant, 1990, p. 364)

The research suggests that men and women ascribe different personal meanings to the caregiving role. Because both genders appear to accept the adage that "housework is women's work," women often feel that any assistance with these chores is unnecessary or inappropriate, whereas men who perform these tasks feel entitled to help with them (Twigg & Atkin, 1994). The difficulties experienced in providing personal care reflect both the intimate nature of the tasks and cultural taboos about touching and nakedness. Relationship and gender clearly influence the meaning of personal care. Different norms apply to different relationships. For example, what a parent can do for a child is different from what a child can do for a parent.

Cross-gender tending of an intimate character threatens conventional expectations concerning what a man should see and touch in relation to a woman and vice versa. These cross-gender rules have an asymmetrical character to them. What men may do for women in relation to bodily contact is more highly constrained than women for men. (Twigg & Atkin, 1994, p. 32)

These inhibitions apply to spouse carers as well. Parker (1993) cautions that it should not be assumed that marital intimacy extends to other forms of physical intimacy. Based on their study of 90 British family carers for adults with learning disabilities, mental health problems, or frailties associated with aging, Twigg and Atkin (1994, p. 32) conclude that "men either found it more difficult to undertake cross-gender tending than women, or felt more justified in refusing to do it. Male carers were more likely to define specific boundaries around what they would or would not do."

In summary, not only do women and men differ in terms of objective dimensions of caregiving—the type and intensity of caring activities in which they engage—but also in the meanings they give to their caring roles. These gender-based differences in caregiving experiences can lead to substantially different costs and consequences for women and men who adopt the caregiver role, as explored next in Chapter 7.

7

The Consequences of Caring

In this chapter, we explore the emotional, physical, social, and financial costs of assuming the caregiving role as well as the rewards and gratifications. During caregiving years, a considerable variation exists in the types of assistance provided. Consistent with our life course approach, Montgomery and Hatch (1986) suggest that the concept of a caregiving career best captures this notion that the caregiving role is "never established or immutable" but rather it shifts as changes occur in either the carer's or recipient's needs and resources (Montgomery & Datwyler, 1990, p. 36). The social, emotional, physical, and financial consequences of performing the caring role may also change over the course of the illness or disability, the caregiver's or recipient's life span, or the family life course.

LIMITATIONS OF THE LITERATURE

Before discussing the findings regarding the consequences of caring, we need to point to four limitations of existing family caregiving literature that greatly affect the nature of the information we present in this chapter. First, as we have noted, social scientists have often hidden the gendered nature of caregiving behind gender-neutral terms such as *family, caregiver, parent, spouse, or child*. This is especially true within the developmental disabilities and mental health fields where it has been implicitly assumed that the caregiver is a woman, and few researchers have included gender as a relevant variable in understanding the caring experience. Although gerontologists have increasingly incorporated gender into their analyses, their research is also limited. They tend to conceptualize gender as only a property of individuals rather than a principle of social organization or structure. Interpretations of male-female differences in the caregiving experience are based on sex-role socialization theory versus a gender-dominance model. Turner (1994, p. 7), however, argues that "gender relations, like race and class relations, are power relations." Feminists generally identify three stages to psychological and sociological research on gender. The initial emphasis was on sex differences, followed by a focus on sex roles and sex as a social category, and most recently there has been a shift to a gender-dominance model (Ferree & Hess, 1987; Turner, 1994).

> The concept of "sex role" became an omnibus term for female-male differences in behaviors, such as role enactments, as well as differences in internal dispositions, such as personality, values, attitudes, and other characteristics. . . . The transition during the 1980s from a sex role perspective to a gender perspective is a transition from a "difference" to a "dominance" model. (Turner, 1994, pp. 5-6)

Second, our understanding of family caring is primarily derived from information gathered from one member of the family, typically a woman. The designation of caregiving as a "woman's role" has resulted in the fact that respondents to research surveys and interviews have been overwhelmingly women. This gender imbalance in respondents cuts across the fields of aging, developmental disabilities, and mental health. In their study of caring for frail or disabled elders, Miller, McFall, and Montgomery (1991) note that 79% of their adult children respondents and 68% of their spouse respondents were women. Similarly, in Finley's (1989) study of elder caregiving, 77% of adult children respondents were women, whereas Barusch and Spaid (1989) and Pruchno and Resch (1989) found that 70% and 68% respectively of spouse respondents were wives. Within the developmental disabilities field, the respondents are also more likely to be women. In reviewing the literature on family carers of adults with developmental disabilities, Roberto (1993a) identified 14 major empirical works published between 1986 and 1992. Of these, 10 studies had samples that were either exclusively or "mostly" female. Scheyett (1990) drew a similar conclusion regarding the mental health literature and family care.

> Responses to research surveys sent to families with such relatives are answered predominantly by women; Franks (1987) found that 73.3% of her respondents were women, Hatfield (1978) noted that "mostly" women responded to her survey and McElroy (1987) found that 71% of her respondents were mothers. (Scheyett, 1990, p. 35)

In fact, Greenberg, Greenley, McKee, Brown, and Griffin-Francell (1993, p. 206), in their study of families with an adult child with schizophrenia, acknowledge that although previous research has revealed significant gender differences, "too few fathers were respondents ($n = 16$) to investigate or control for gender differences." The limited participation of men in most research studies means that not only is it difficult to disentangle the gendered nature of care, but also that our understanding of the family roles and dynamics of caregiving is constructed almost exclusively from women's voices or perspectives. Although acknowledging gender differences, researchers have often relied on women to explain their husbands', brothers', and sons' experiences in the family management of a chronic illness or disability.

Third, although supporting a family member can be a rich and rewarding experience, the majority of the professional literature focuses on the negative effects of assuming the caring role. Although recognizing that this emphasis represents an attempt by professionals "to argue that families cannot absorb additional obligations and that the government must devote adequate resources to support them," Abel (1991, p. 8) criticizes the current caregiving research agenda "which has focused almost exclusively on the issue of stress." She argues that "this preoccupation with stress has denied us a full understanding of the experience of caregiving" (Abel, 1991, p. 8). A more complex view of caring is needed, one that recognizes that taking on the caregiving role has both positive and negative implications for an individual's life. As Walker (1992) notes,

> Feminists have yet to develop a completely satisfactory perspective on caregiving. . . . [It] can contribute to a person's sense of connection, yet it can also interfere with the activities that contribute to a sense of competence in adulthood and economic independence. Caregiving can reflect concern and affection, but it can also reflect fear and obligation. (pp. 44-45)

Our own discussion of the benefits or rewards of caring is hindered by this limited exploration of caregiving gratifications and rewards.

Fourth, despite general acceptance of the notion of a caregiving career, longitudinal studies in the field remain relatively sparse. With few exceptions (i.e., Haley & Pardo, 1989; Montgomery & Kosloski, 1994a; Morycz & Biegel, 1993; Schulz, Williamson, Tennstedt, Crawford, & McKinley, 1994b; Townsend, Noelker, Deimling, & Bass, 1989; Zarit, Todd, & Zarit, 1986;), most of the conclusions regarding the long-term effects of providing care are based on cross-sectional data and must be viewed as tentative. Two alternative and contradictory hypotheses have been offered to explain the effects of long-term caregiving. One is an adaptational model positing that, over time, caregivers develop effective coping strategies that ultimately lead to stability or improvement in their mental health (Townsend, Noelker, Deimling, & Bass, 1989). A second hypothesis is a "wear and tear" model that suggests that prolonged exposure to stress results in a decline or depletion of psychological resources (Johnson & Catalano, 1983; Pearlin, Lieberman, Menaghan, & Mullan, 1981). In this chapter we present evidence supporting both hypotheses.

THE CONCEPT OF CAREGIVER BURDEN

It is often assumed that the meaning of family care is self-evident (i.e., everyone "knows" what care is) and that the burdens of caring are fairly obvious. Yet defining just what constitutes caregiving burden has proven to be challenging. It is difficult to offer a concise definition because it is a multidimensional concept that encompasses a wide range of stressors, including "the physical, psychological or emotional, social, and financial problems" that may be experienced by family members caring for a relative with a disability or impairment (George & Gwyther, 1986, p. 253).

Focusing on the effects of mental illness on the family, British researchers Grad and Sainsbury (1963) were the first investigators to conceptualize and measure family "burden." In her review of the caregiver literature, Braithwaite (1992, p. 4) notes "two [subsequent] major theoretical efforts to define the burden concept more precisely are widely acknowledged." The first major theoretical effort was the distinction drawn between objective and subjective burden. This differentiation was first noted by Hoenig and Hamilton (1966) in their study of the effect of an adult with schizophrenia on the household and was subsequently adopted by other investigators in the mental health field (Platt, 1985; Thompson & Doll, 1982) as well as researchers in the gerontology and developmental disabilities fields (Marsh, 1992b; Montgomery, Gonyea, & Hooyman, 1985).

Objective burden refers to the reality demands that confront the family member who takes on the carer role. Bulger, Wandersman, and Goldman (1993, p. 256) suggest that "objective burden most commonly consists of two elements; worrisome patient behavior, such as hostility, reclusiveness, and overdependency; and disruption of family life in areas such as leisure activities, domestic routine, and opportunity to socialize." Marsh (1992a,b) notes that dimensions of objective burden can include the symptomatic behaviors of the relative; disruptions in family relations; problems with the social, health, and legal systems; and alterations in family identity and roles.

Whereas objective burden focuses on behavioral phenomena associated with performing the caring role, subjective burden refers to feelings aroused in family members as they fulfill their caregiving functions (Braithwaite, 1992). Bulger et al. (1993, p. 255) conceptualize subjective burden as "emotional reactions to caregiving such as worry, tension, sadness, resentment and difficulty sleeping." Marsh (1992a,b) cites subjective burden as encompassing a wide range of emotions such as anger, guilt, loneliness, depression, withdrawal, and empathic suffering.

The second major theoretical effort noted by Braithwaite (1992, p. 5) was "Poulshock and Deimling's (1984) work [that] recognized burden as a subjective phenomenon. What was difficult for one caregiver need not be difficult for another: Burden lay in the experiences of the caregivers." This distinction was important because it helped explain the confusion regarding why carers did not experience the same phenomenon as "burdensome." For example, when two adult daughters are providing similar levels of assistance to a frail elder, such as bathing and dressing, one might report feeling "very burdened" while the other might cite experiencing "little stress."

THE EXPERIENCE OF CAREGIVER BURDEN

Much of the caregiving literature has attempted to understand the nature, prevalence, and predictors of carer burden. A number of studies have consistently documented that a significant proportion of families experience burden or distress as a result of their performance of the caregiving role. The findings regarding the predictors of caregiver burden, however, are inconsistent and contradictory. These contradictions may partly reflect the fact that, across studies, different definitions and, thus, different measures of burden are used. They may also reflect variations in the populations studied, such as type of impairment, and the caregiver's gender and relationship to the recipient, whether the bond is as a wife, husband, daughter, son, sister, or brother.

Discussions of the predictors and nature of objective burden generally include the care recipient's symptomatic behaviors and the caregiver's physical health, economic pressures, employment restrictions, and constrictions of leisure and social relationships.

Symptomatic Behaviors of the Illness or Disability

Whether one is caring for an adult or elderly relative with a serious mental illness, a developmental or cognitive disability, or a chronic physical illness, the care receiver's disruptive behaviors and impaired social functioning appear to be some of the most difficult behaviors for caregivers to accept. Indeed, one of the greatest fears expressed by families with members with a serious mental illness is that the individual will harm him- or herself or others. Families of the mentally ill report having to cope with symptomatic behaviors such as hostility, mood swings, self-destructive behaviors, physical abuse, and property destruction (Hatfield & Lefley, 1987; Marsh, 1992a). Greenberg et al. (1993, p. 206) suggest that "these fears may have powerful effects on the family member's health by creating a condition of chronic anxiety in which the parent feels compelled to constantly monitor the mentally ill child's environment to protect the patient and others."

Physical violence or fear of physical violence is a particular source of stress for women who are often physically smaller and weaker than the family member for whom they care (Cook, 1988; Scheyett, 1990). Cook (1988) argues that women's greater fears are justified in that

> [They] are on the "front lines" of caregiving. . . . Mothers are likely to be in direct contact with the child during periods of decompensation . . . and mothers more often assume responsibility for administering medication, so that problems surrounding compliance often turn into a struggle between mother and child. (p. 46)

In fact, Cook's (1988) interviews with mothers and fathers of a child with a psychiatric disability revealed that when the child directed violence toward only one parent, it was typically toward the mother rather than the father.

Because women are on the front lines as caregivers, it should not be surprising that mothers of adult children with developmental disabilities rank their child's associated disabilities as more severe than do their fathers (Brubaker, Engelhardt, Brubaker, & Lutzer, 1989). Seltzer and Krauss's (1989) study of 462 older mothers caring for an adult with mental retardation revealed that having an adult child in poor physical health was associated with both poor physical and emotional well-being for the mother. It is also important to underscore that mental disorders and psychological problems are 3 to 4 times as prevalent among the mentally retarded population than they are among the general population (Marsh, 1992b; Matson & Frame, 1986). Such behavioral symptoms and disorders include: low frustration tolerance, aggressiveness, poor impulse control, hyperactivity, self-injurious behaviors, and psychotic and personality disorders. Marsh's (1992b) research suggests that families of children with mental retardation coping with such problems experience much higher levels of stress; it is likely that such stress continues across the life span for carers of adults with mental retardation.

Families caring for relatives with Alzheimer's disease report having to contend with socially embarrassing acts, sudden mood changes, wandering behavior, incontinence, and reversal in sleeping patterns. George and Gwyther (1986) found that carers of older adults with memory impairments exhibited 3 times as many stress symptoms as age-matched noncaregiver peers. In Skaff and Pearlin's study of spouses and adult children caring for a relative with Alzheimer's disease, one of the strongest predictors of caregiver role engulfment or "loss of self" was problem behaviors: "Those who must mobilize their attentions and energies around the surveillance and control of potentially dangerous or troublesome behavior were more likely to experience a loss of self" (Skaff & Pearlin, 1992, p. 660).

Physical Health and Caregiving

There is growing evidence that family members, especially the women who have taken on the role of caregiver, experience increased personal health problems, including physical exhaustion and deterioration of their own health status (Biegel, Sales, & Schulz, 1991; Fengler & Goodrich, 1979, Grad & Sainsbury, 1968; Haley, Levine, Brown, Berry, & Hughes, 1987). Early investigators into the effects of chronic mental illness on the family system noted that over 33% of the family carers studied reported their own physical health as negatively affected (Brown, Bone, Dalison, & Wing, 1966; Grad & Sainsbury, 1968). Their symptoms typically included headaches, stomachaches, insomnia, and weight losses or gains. In their study of 203 families coping with a serious mental illness, a significant number of the health problems individuals cited were stress-related health conditions such as insomnia, hypertension, heart attacks, ulcers, exhaustion, and alcoholism (Holden & Lewine, 1982).

Comparisons of self-reported health between caregivers (mostly women) for the frail elderly and age-matched noncaregiving peers reveal that the former group reports poorer physical health (Biegel et al., 1991). A study of caregivers for relatives with Alzheimer's disease and matched noncaregivers found that the individuals involved in care generally had poorer immune responses (Kiecolt-Glaser, Glaser, Shuttleworth, Dyer, Ogrocki, & Speicher, 1987). Similarly, caregivers of the elderly, when compared to matched noncaregivers, reported more chronic illness, poorer overall health, and greater use of prescription drugs (Haley et al., 1987). Although not conclusive, the literature suggests that wives caring for disabled husbands are more likely than others to suffer adverse health effects (U.S. House of Representatives, 1988). Moreover, poorer physical health or lower physical stamina has been found to be associated with depression (Schulz, Tompkins, & Rau, 1988) and less patience and less ability to cope with caregiving demands (Cohler, Pickett, & Cook, 1991).

Schulz (1990, p. 43) cautions that although "taken together, all of the research on the physical health effects of caregiving are suggestive," they should not be regarded as conclusive due to the number of methodological limitations in the research. Determination of causality is difficult because (a) health status may be an important selection factor in who assumes the caring role, (b) the existing data are primarily cross-sectional (as opposed to longitudinal) in nature, and (c) the studies are typically based on purposive (versus random) samples. However, Snyder and Keefe (1985) note that more than 66% of interviewed family members caring for a frail or disabled elderly relative attribute the decline in their own physical health specifically to their caring activities. Silliman (1984) also found that 75% of 89 family caregivers of elderly stroke patients worried about the consequences of the caregiving on their own health. Engelhardt, Brubaker, and Lutzer (1988) reported that healthier caregivers of adults with developmental disabilities felt better able to provide care their relatives needed. Caregiver's health can be perceived as either a resource or a demand. "Good health can help caregivers cope with their responsibilities, but poor health among caregivers can be associated with increased stress" (Neal, Chapman, Ingersoll-Dayton, & Emlen, 1993).

The Financial Burden of Caregiving

The unpaid care that women provide to their dependent relatives is of substantial economic value. In the mid-1980's, the typical family caregiver for an older relative with a cognitive impairment was a women providing 6 hours and 28 minutes of assistance with the activities of daily living each day (Hu, Huang, & Cartwright, 1986). Using $29.15, the daily median wage of a nurse's aide, along with $3.00 per day in agency administrative costs, Hu et al. (1986) conservatively estimated the costs of women's caregiving labor at, on average, $11,735 a year.

In addition to women providing this care "free," families also incur financial burden through the direct costs of medical care, adaptive equipment, hired help, or a combination of all three. For example, mental retardation is associated with an increased risk of a wide range of medical problems. Epidemiological studies suggest that epilepsy, cerebral palsy, or both may be present in 30% of cases of retardation (McLaren & Bryson, 1987). There is also a greater risk for sensory disorders such as blindness, hearing loss, and motor dysfunctions. Many of these families face major medical problems that have the potential to deplete their financial resources completely. In their survey of 388 caregivers of adults with mental retardation, Brubaker and Brubaker (1993) found that 48% of families viewed the financial costs of caring as the greatest concern. Caregivers identified financial concerns in the areas of medical care, transportation, out-of-home respite care, in-home care, and equipment needs (Brubaker & Brubaker, 1993).

The financial burdens of providing care are consistently cited by families caring for an adult with a developmental disability and by a significant proportion of families caring for an adult or an elder with a chronic physical, psychological, or cognitive disability. Few studies have explored gender differences in the experience of financial burden as a result of caregiving, although a major argument of this book is the long-term negative economic consequences for women, especially in old age. Barusch and Spaid's (1989) study of 92 elderly wives and 39 elderly husbands caring for a spouse with a chronic illness or disability found that, when questioned about financial concerns, wives indicated that they worried more about currently not having enough money (38%) than did husbands (25%), and worried more about future finances (69%) than did husbands (56%). More than 3 times as many women (38%) as compared to men (14%) reported currently experiencing a loss of income. Whereas no older men in their study admitted that they were "not sure how to manage," 10% of older women expressed this concern (Barusch & Spaid, 1989, p. 672).

Employment Restrictions

Another aspect of the economic burden of caregiving is the indirect cost of lost income families experience as a result of either temporary or permanent withdrawal from, or restricted engagement in, the workforce. Among heterosexual couples, the woman usually leaves or reduces her number of hours in the paid labor market in order to assume the carer role. Data from the National Long-Term Care Survey (NLTCS) indicate that about 9% of persons—primarily wives and daughters—left the labor force to care for an elderly relative with a disability (Stone, Cafferata, & Sangl, 1987).

In this chapter, we explicitly separate employment restrictions from financial burdens. Our rationale is that limited employment opportunity not only restricts women economically, but also restricts them emotionally and socially. As Scheyett (1990) argues, when caregiving responsibilities do not allow a woman to seek paid employment or remove her from it, she loses income and forfeits the opportunity to find meaning, stimulation, and companionship outside the home. For many women forced to leave the workplace to care for relatives with disabilities, the loss of contact with fellow workers and friends results in loneliness and comes with social as well as economic costs (Sommers & Shields, 1987).

The research concerning how individuals experience or balance the dual roles of paid worker and family caregiver is inconclusive and contradictory. Tennstedt and Gonyea (1994) suggest that much of the employment and family research is plagued with methodological limitations (i.e., low response rates, lack of caregiver comparison groups, retrospective self-report measures) that restrict the ability to generate accurate estimates of the prevalence and consequences of these dual roles. It is generally assumed that the competing demands of caregiving and employment are burdensome to individuals. Scharlach and Boyd (1989) found that caregiving employees indicate greater job-family conflicts than noncaregiving employees. Stone et al. (1987) report a greater likelihood of stress and emotional burden from the dual demands of caring and work. For employed caregivers, there simply may not be enough hours in the day to complete all the tasks associated with both paid work and caregiving. Other researchers have argued that employment may buffer the negative effects of caring by offering the caregiver a respite from its continuous demands, providing social opportunities, or enhancing feelings of self-esteem (Baruch & Barnett, 1986; Enright & Friss, 1987; Giele, Mutschler, & Orodenker, 1987). As Spaniol (1987) notes, meaningful outside employment may help caregivers achieve a better balance in their lives.

The vast majority of caregivers remain in the paid labor force—either by necessity or choice—but they make a number of workplace accommodations in order to meet dual demands. They restrict their work schedules, reduce the number of hours they work, and often miss opportunities for career development or job promotion. In exploring the intersection of paid work and elder care, both Scharlach and Boyd (1989) and Anastas, Gibeau, and Larson (1990) found that approximately 2% to 11% of employees reported that they had missed opportunities for job training, new work assignments, job relocation, and career promotions and that they had taken leave without pay because of their caring roles. Similarly, the NLTCS data revealed that 29% of employed caregivers rearranged their work schedules and 21% reduced their number of work hours to balance the dual demands of work and caring (Stone et al., 1987).

The Financial Effects of Restricted Employment

All of these work accommodations have negative implications for women's immediate and long-term economic well-being. A British study of married mothers caring for young adults with severe disabilities found the employment patterns of these women to be "strikingly different" from those of married women in the general population (Hirst, 1985, p. 297). Mothers caring for a disabled young adult were twice as likely to lack paid employment than married women in general (between 30% to 50% for the former as compared to 60% to 75% for the latter). Moreover, when these women did seek outside work, less than 30% engaged in full-time employment. Consequently, these married women with young adult children with serious disabilities earned on average £12.70 a week less than married women in the general population. Hirst (1985) concluded that

> Caring for young disabled adults appears to limit women's employment capacity in two crucial ways: by making it less likely that they would seek paid employment and, where they did, by making it less likely that they would seek full-time work. Restriction to part-time work affected earning because of fewer hours worked and possibly lower hourly rates of pay. (p. 299)

Mutschler's (1994) study of how employees' occupational status influences their balancing paid employment and elder-care responsibilities also illustrates the tensions women face between breadwinning and caregiving. Her data reveal that all workers constrained by elder-care responsibilities had fewer hours of paid employment than did their unconstrained counterparts, and that this difference was greatest among service or sales workers—a sector in which 80% of all women work. Service or sales workers worked only 26 hours per week as compared to the overall (across occupations) average of 31 hours. Using a conservative estimate of 5 dollars per hour, Mutschler (1994) estimates these five lost hours per week cost an average of $1,300 each year.

These tensions between breadwinning and caregiving have long-term effects on women's economic status. The average woman now spends nearly 33% of her life fulfilling the caregiving role, leaving the paid labor force for approximately 11 years as compared to only 1 year for her male counterpart (Older Women's League, 1990). Because of these interruptions, older women are less likely to have an employment history that provides adequate Social Security benefits or a private pension. A retired woman's average Social Security benefit is only about 75% of a man's (AARP, 1988b). Analyzing data from the Social Security Administration's 1982 New Beneficiary Survey, Kingston and O'Grady-LeShane (1993) found that early- and late-life caregiving reduced the Social Security benefits of women workers. Each child raised was associated with a loss of $8 to $16 in the 1983 Social Security Primary Insurance Amounts

(PIAs). The 1983 PIAs of women leaving their last jobs to care for others were $127 lower than the PIAs of women who left because of the availability of Social Security benefits, to receive a pension, or because they wanted to retire. Moreover, leaving paid work to provide care was more costly for low- and moderate-wage-earning women than for women with high earnings.

Similar gender differences exist with regard to private pension benefits. More than 40% of older men are covered by private pensions as compared to less than 20% of women who have been employed. And those women with pensions receive approximately 50% of the benefit income of men (Older Women's League, 1990). Discontinuities in employment carry severe economic costs for women across the life span. Ultimately, caregiving places women in greater jeopardy for poverty in their later years. Understanding these economic costs of care is central to our feminist analysis as well as to our proposals for economic supports for family caregivers (see Chapter 11).

Social Relations, Leisure Activities, and Caregiving

Caring for a relative who has a cognitive, psychological, or physical impairment can disrupt family life and strain family relations. It is increasingly recognized that one family member's disability reshapes each family member's life (Featherstone, 1980). Marsh (1992a, p. 121) reports that among mothers caring for a child with mental retardation, "some mothers reported adverse effects on their relationship with that child (21%), with their other children (8%), among their other children (14%), [and] with their spouse (27%)." Thompson and Doll (1982) found that almost 30% of carers perceive that their assistance to their child with a mental illness resulted in neglect of their responsibilities to other family members.

According to Strawbridge and Wallhagen (1991), family conflict is an often overlooked aspect in caring for frail elders. Their data reveal that 40% of the 100 adult respondents caring for a frail parent or in-law experienced a relatively serious conflict with another family member, usually a sibling who was unwilling to provide the amount of assistance the caregiver expected. A greater proportion of female caregivers experienced conflict than did their male counterparts. This gender difference may reflect the fact that fewer male caregivers had a living sibling available, but it may also reflect differences in gender-based expectations regarding the appropriate roles of men and women in the care of family members. Thus, for instance, a married working daughter with children may resent the fact that her brother with fewer responsibilities (simply as a function of gender) is not asked to do more, or volunteers so little.

Gender differences have also been found in marital satisfaction among parents of children with a severe mental illness (Cook, Hoffschmidt, Cohler, & Pickett, 1992). The researchers found that even after other significant variables were controlled, such as degree of mutual comfort, family size, income, and severity of illness, mothers still report lower levels of marital satisfaction than do fathers. They attribute this difference to this fact:

> Severe mental illness is a "family matter" in contemporary American society, [therefore] the gender division of labor in the family assumes critical importance in molding mothers' and fathers' experiences. Mothers are burdened by caregiving demands at all points in the family life cycle, and this burden appears to be related to their lower satisfaction with marriage. (Cook et al., 1992, p. 560)

Changes in social relationships extend beyond the household or the family. Individuals who have taken on the caregiving role often report restrictions in social and leisure activities, such as opportunities to visit or relax with friends, take vacations, engage in hobbies, attend church or community activities, and participate in volunteer work or community service. The loss of such opportunities leads to a greater sense of isolation and loneliness among caregivers. Indeed, social contacts have been shown to have an important mediating influence on the relationship between stress and well-being (Antonucci, 1985).

Noting that social or personal limitations is one of the most frequently cited consequences of caring for an elder (ranging from 33% to 75% of caregivers across empirical studies), Miller and Montgomery (1990) attempted to examine what factors were associated with perceived social limitations, using the NLTC data set. Their findings underscore once more the importance of exploring the gendered nature of the caring experience. Their data reveal that "subjective assessment of time and task demands was a more important influence than objective caregiving activities" and that "daughters and wives were more likely to report such limitations than sons and husbands" (Miller & Montgomery, 1990, p. 72). Two potential interpretations of this gender difference might be that (a) women's internalization of their appropriate role as nurturer results in their placing a higher priority on the caring role (relative to their personal needs) than do men, or (b) women have less money and fewer social resources than do men; it is this relative lack of resources that results in women's perception of greater constraints imposed by caregiving.

Constriction of social and leisure opportunities occurs because the caregivers feel a loss of personal time or the inability to leave their relatives with disabilities, and also because of feelings of stigma. Families with relatives with a serious mental illness or developmental disability may be reluctant to invite friends and neighbors to their home, or may curtail their involvement in community activities, because they fear the unpredictability of their relative's behaviors or the cruelty and insensitivity of others to their loved one (Link & Cullen, 1990). Thompson and Doll (1982) found that 20% of families caring for a relative with a mental illness report strained relationships with their neighbors. Baxter (1989) notes that despite changing societal attitudes toward mental retardation, for families with a relative with a mental deficiency, the presence of stigma remains one of the most difficult of experienced burdens. Because stigma is often associated with feelings of self-blame, and mothers in American society are held more accountable for the raising of their children than fathers, women more often than men express feelings of guilt, self-blame, and shame (see Cook, 1988, for a discussion of "mother blaming").

THE INTERRELATIONSHIP OF
OBJECTIVE AND SUBJECTIVE BURDEN

As we have discussed, objective burden refers to the more tangible or behavioral aspects of care, such as loss of income or social restrictions, whereas subjective burden refers to the distress or strain experienced by the family in response to their relative's physical, cognitive, or psychological disability. It is difficult, however, to completely separate out these two types of burden. In our earlier discussion of the objective phenomena that caregivers confront, such as symptomatic behaviors and disruptions of family life, we could not avoid touching on many of the emotional reactions that caregivers experience, such as worry, anger, guilt, loneliness, and depression. Researchers attempting to explore the relationship between objective and subjective burden have, however, discovered the correlation between the two burdens to be fairly small (Hoenig & Hamilton, 1966; Montgomery, Gonyea, & Hooyman, 1985; Thompson & Doll, 1982). For instance, Thompson and Doll (1982) found that 50% of families with relatives with a mental illness who were both symptomatic and disruptive of family life (high objective burden) did not perceive their relative as causing great distress or strain (low subjective burden). However, 66% of asymptomatic mentally ill relatives (low objective burden) were perceived by their families as causing great distress and strain (high subjective burden).

THE STATE OF BURDEN RESEARCH

The literature regarding the predictors or determinants of caregiver burden is inconsistent and contradictory. Again, one explanation for differing outcomes stems from methodological bias. Lack of comparability across studies in terms of definitions of caregiver and measures of burden, recruitment processes of subjects, and research designs or strategies may explain the contradictory evidence regarding the phenomenon of burden or distress. Inconsistent findings may also represent some true or real differences. Variations in caregiving outcomes may exist, for example, by type of impairment. Two key differences that we have already highlighted are (a) the social stigma of mental illness or cognitive disabilities in contrast to social acceptance of frailty associated with aging, and (b) the fear of violence or concern for their own physical safety experienced by some families with a relative with a serious mental illness—a feeling not shared by most families caring for physically frail elders.

Families experience very different kinds of grief or loss depending on the type of disability. Parents of a mentally retarded child may grieve for the child who will never be; parents of an adolescent or young adult with schizophrenia may grieve for the adult who will never be; and an adult child caring for a frail parent may grieve for the loss of the mother or father one could always lean on. Hatfield and Lefley (1987) suggest that the cyclical nature of mental illness—periods when the individual is functioning well followed by periods when the individual is symptomatic—makes the grieving process more difficult because families' hopes are constantly being raised and dashed. Others have suggested that families of individuals with a cognitive disability such as Alzheimer's disease face a special hardship (Poulshock & Noelker, 1982). Many of these families report that the gradual and irreversible loss of a relationship with their loved one who has dementia is more difficult to accept than the loss experienced through death.

Montgomery and Kosloski (1994b) put forth this caution even though a great deal has been learned about the effects of caregiving:

> As researchers, we may be too fond of measuring sociodemographic variables such as the caregivers' relationship to the elder, marital status, gender, urban/rural residence, ethnicity and so on. . . . The drawback is that these variables are almost certainly not the causes of caregiving outcomes. More likely, sociodemographic variables merely vary with the underlying causes. In other words, being a member of a particular ethnic group is unlikely to cause an individual to provide care longer; in contrast perceiving certain normative demands and holding particular personal expectations may. (p. 130)

Similarly, Lee (1992) argues that although female dominance in caregiving is well-established empirically, it is poorly understood theoretically. We may understand least the subjective experience of caring—the meaning of caregiving felt by the caregiver (Parks & Pilisuk, 1991). Sociodemographic variables such as gender, race, and social class are only proxies for understanding the meanings individuals endow to their caring roles. Moreover, the treatment of these variables by most researchers as individual properties rather than social constructs fails to acknowledge that caregivers' motives, sense of personal obligation and responsibilities, feelings of affection for the care recipient, and perceptions of the costs of not caring are all shaped by societal expectations and norms regarding appropriate roles.

Zarit (1994, p. 11) suggests that most caregiving research "has been guided, either implicitly or explicitly, by theoretical models about how stressors affect well-being and how the effects of stress may be modified or mediated." A growing number of studies have utilized the stress process model (Pearlin, Mullan, Semple, & Skaff, 1990) as a framework for understanding how different levels of stressors as well as individual and environmental resources influence individuals' adaptation to the caregiving role. Two distinctions made by Pearlin et al. (1990) have special relevance to understanding the gendered nature of the caregiving experience. The first distinction, which is congruent with our feminist analysis, is the recognition that attributes such as gender, race, and class present different structural opportunities and barriers to caregivers. Reflecting the cultural ideology that caregiving is rightfully the province of women, health and social service professionals often place greater pressure on daughters than sons to assume, or continue, caring for frail parents. The second distinction is the differentiation between objective and subjective measures of stressors: stress research suggests that the meaning or value that a person attributes to a stressor is a stronger predictor of its effect than objective measures (Zarit 1994; Pearlin & Schooler, 1979). Thus, the stress process model offers a framework for analyzing the effects of the different roles, resources, and values that men and women may bring to the caregiving experience.

GENDER DIFFERENCES IN
CAREGIVER BURDEN AND COPING

A leader in bringing a feminist perspective to the study of family care for persons with severe and persistent mental illness, Cook (1988, p. 43) argues that the literature is "scanty, much of it characterized by scapegoating of families, particularly mothers, and failure to investigate the father's parenting behaviors and effects." In her study of 50 families with a child who has a chronic mental illness, she focused on nine emotional reactions: stress, anxiety, resentment, grief, depression, fear, emotional drain, hopelessness, and anger (Cook, 1988). Her data reveal that a majority of parents—both fathers and mothers—experienced all nine negative emotions. However, mothers report significantly higher levels of anxiety, depression, fear, and emotional drain than fathers, even after controlling for the effects of parent education, age, ethnicity, and offspring's gender and illness length. Two factors may partially explain these gender differences. First, in American society, women are on the front lines in providing care; as a result, mothers may have more realistic assessments of their child's functioning and are more likely to be the recipients of their child's antisocial, abusive, and violent behaviors than are fathers. Second, because mothers are held more accountable for their children's behaviors, they may feel more responsible for the behavior than do fathers.

Within gerontology, Miller and Cafasso's (1992) meta-analysis of the results of 14 descriptive studies of gender differences in caregiving undertaken between 1980 and 1990 is especially important in determining both the size and significance of gender differences in caregiving stressors and burden. Female and male carers did not differ either in their elder's severity of functional impairment or in the level of total care involvement, but a significant gender difference was found in terms of type of task involvement and level of caregiver burden. Although the size of the gender effect was small, female carers were more likely to perform personal care and household tasks and were more likely to report greater burden than male carers. Based on their data, the researchers suggest that "what is needed may be less documentation of specific gender differences in isolated components of caregiving and more attention to the role that gender-role expectations play in assigning meaning to the caregiving experience" (Miller & Cafasso, 1992, p. 506).

Social scientists have recently begun to move beyond bivariate analyses of gender differences in stressors and burdens to engage in a more in-depth analysis of the gendered nature of care. Because the quality of the relationship between caregiver and care recipient is an important predictor of stress for the caregiver, it is necessary to be aware of the forces that impede those relationships. The demands placed on women's caring, and the lack of support and recognition it receives, seriously strain the relationship between those caring and those in need of care. The devaluation of caring, coupled with its invisibility, can place those who are cared for, whether by family members or human services organizations, in a position of extreme dependency on others. Thus, it is not caring per se that becomes the problem, but the burden of caring experienced both by women who care and by those who are cared for (Baines, Evans, & Neysmith, 1991). Parks and Pilisuk (1991) examined gender differences in the psychological costs of providing care to a parent with Alzheimer's disease in relation to the caregiver's coping style, social supports, and sense of control. The researchers discovered that (a) women had a higher self-report of stress than did men, although the two groups did not differ significantly in terms of depression or anxiety; and (b) women predominantly used fantasy to cope, whereas withdrawal was the more common technique for men. Perhaps more interesting is the differential effectiveness of these coping strategies for men and women in adapting to the carer role. Significant predictors of anxiety among the women were an external sense of control and the use of fantasy as a coping style. The women's use of internalization as a coping style predicted feelings of resentment, but internalization was not a significant predictor among the men. For men, anxiety was predicted by lack of social support coupled with the use of either fantasy or withdrawal as a dominant coping style (Parks & Pilisuk, 1991, p. 507).

Research, such as Parks and Pilisuk's, suggests that men and women approach the caregiving role from different perspectives and that it takes on very different meanings for the two groups. These studies underscore the fact that gender does make an important contribution to understanding how differences in the caring role are experienced. We need research that moves beyond treating gender as an individual property to an exploration of the social construction of the gendered nature of caregiving.

THE BENEFITS OF CARING

As we have noted, Abel (1991) has been critical of the dominance of the burden and stress research in the caregiving literature, which has resulted in the overshadowing of other aspects of caregiving. Caregiving research has consistently documented variability among families with respect to the effect of a physical, cognitive, or psychological disability. Marsh (1992b) found that a significant proportion of mothers reported that mental retardation had a positive effect on their relationship with their child (39%), with their spouse (28%), and with their other children (25%). Some of these mothers also reported that the retardation had a positive effect on their mental health (23%), on their physical health (12%), and on their social life (7%). Marsh (1992b, p. 139) comments that "it is noteworthy that the mothers who completed the survey reported comparable levels of positive and negative consequences."

In interviews with 50 wives caring for husbands with dementia, Montenko (1989) found that continuity in the closeness of the marital relationship was associated with perceived gratification from caregiving. Two groups of wives—those who were close to their husbands before the illness and remained close and those who were not close to their husbands before the illness and continued not to be close—derived gratification from caring. However, wives who were close prior to the onset of the illness but were not close after reported little caregiving gratification. Montenko (1989, p. 171) interprets these data as showing that "perception of continuity in marital closeness lends meaning to caregiving roles." No association was found between sociodemographic variables (i.e., income, socioeconomic status, age) and wives' caregiving gratification.

Bulger et al. (1993) assessed 60 parents' appraisals of the burdens and gratifications of caring for an adult child with schizophrenia. Their interviews revealed that parents experienced gratification and intimacy much more frequently than they felt burden or conflict. Burden was highly correlated with conflict and intimacy with gratification. Moreover, the quality of the relationship (as measured by intimacy and conflict) was more highly associated with burden and gratification than was the severity of schizophrenic symptoms or the level of caregiving involvement.

Sociodemographic variables, especially socioeconomic status and race, also correlated with burden and gratification. Caregivers with higher incomes and more education reported greater burden and less gratification. White caregivers reported greater burden, whereas African American caregivers indicated greater gratification. As a group, Caucasian caregivers had substantially more education and income than did African American caregivers. Bulger et al. (1993) offer two explanations for the fact that more economically disadvantaged individuals report greater happiness with the caregiving situation. First, for poorer families, the approximately $400 monthly Social Security payment the patient received was probably a main source of income for the family. Second, families with more income and education have more options available to them and may have been more willing to acknowledge their dissatisfactions.

The literature increasingly suggests that families of relatives with a cognitive, physical, or psychological impairment can simultaneously experience both burden and satisfaction from their caregiving roles. Similarly, feelings of conflict and intimacy can coexist for the caregiver. There is growing evidence that the satisfaction or gratification experienced may be linked to the subjective meanings attributed to the caregiving role. Skaff and Pearlin (1992), in their study of role engulfment or loss of self in caregiving, report that one of their more intriguing findings is the lack of relationship between loss of self and self-gain:

The independence of these two indicators of the impact of caregiving on the individual suggests that loss and gain are not opposite points on the same continuum. . . . Some caregivers may feel that they have grown as a result of their experiences, but whatever personal enrichment they might experience doesn't protect them from suffering a loss of identity. (Skaff & Pearlin, 1992, p. 659)

THE LONG-TERM EXPERIENCE OF CAREGIVING

Although social scientists refer to "caregiving as a process" and to the "caregiving career," the field is plagued by a limited number of longitudinal studies. As we have stated, two contradictory hypotheses are often posed to explain the long-term consequences of the caregiving role: The *wear and tear hypothesis* suggests that the repetitive nature of caregiving will take its toll and deplete an individual's physical and emotional resources. The *adaptational hypothesis* suggests that, with experience, caregiving may get easier or become more bearable. At this time, due to reliance on primarily retrospective self-reports by caregivers or on cross-sectional samples, the issue of how time affects the relationship between caregiving and outcomes, such as caregiver distress or burden, remains unresolved.

In the developmental disabilities literature, both retrospective self-report and cross-sectional comparison methodologies have been used to explore changes over time in caregiver perceptions. Roberto (1993b) asked 48 older adults caring for aging family members within their homes to rate changes in 14 aspects of their caregiving role over the past 10 years. The data revealed a general pattern of stability in caregiving situations over time. The most frequently cited changes were in terms of physical burden (40% increase), emotional burden (41% increase), social activities (26% decline), and financial burden (21% decline). The strongest predictors of changes in the caregiving situation were declines in either the caregiver's health or the care recipient's level of impairment. Although acknowledging the limitations of a small volunteer sample and of retrospective information, Roberto (1996, p. 48) concludes that "the picture that emerged from this study . . . is one of stability in many facets of the caregiving situation. It seems that this group of caregivers has accepted their role and has learned to cope with the responsibilities placed on them."

In contrast, Heller (1993) explored the life span perspective through a cross-sectional study of families grouped into five age phases based on the age of the person with mental retardation—preschooler, young child, adolescent, young adult, and older adult. Her data reveal that perceived burden was lowest for caregivers of the youngest (under 6 years of age) and oldest (30 years and older) members with mental retardation, and adolescence was perceived as the most difficult. Noting that although one cannot control for cohort effects in a cross-sectional design, Heller (1993) makes this suggestion:

> As the child becomes an adult and the parent ages, families experience less burden. Perhaps at this stage there is greater acceptance of the family member and greater reciprocity in caregiving as the child with mental retardation is often a strong support for the parent. (p. 29)

The research agenda within gerontology has been strongly influenced by policy makers' persistent fears that the provision of public or formal services will lead to families' abandoning their elder-care responsibilities. Much of the previous longitudinal research on caregiving has focused on identifying predictors of nursing home placement or institutionalization risk. Despite policy makers' fears, research indicates a great deal of stability in family care over time. Zarit, Todd and Zarit's (1986) 2-year follow-up study of husbands and wives who were caregivers for a spouse with senile dementia suggested the following:

> Caregivers' ability to tolerate problem behaviors actually increases, even as the disease progresses...many of those providing home care in this sample genuinely seemed to have established a daily routine that while not without its stressors, also was not excessively demanding or burdensome. (p. 265)

Haley and Pardo (1989, p. 389) argue that both the wear and tear and the adaptation hypotheses assume that "with the progression of dementia, behavioral problems and caregiving stressors develop in a linear, mounting fashion." Their 29-month longitudinal study of caregivers suggests that it is critical to account for the changing nature of caregiving stressors:

> For example, longitudinal decreases in caregiver depression may represent successful adaptation, but may also be related to decreases in such patient problems as wandering or dangerous behaviors. Caregivers in poor health may be especially vulnerable during later phases of dementia that require direct ADL care, such as help with transfer. (Haley & Pardo, p. 392)

The importance of studying the caregiving trajectory is underscored by Schulz et al.'s (1993) longitudinal study of depression in caring for relatives with Alzheimer's disease. Their data revealed the following:

The capacity of some caregivers to cope with the demands of caregiving is gradually eroded over time. . . . Gender and concern about financial resources are important early in the caregiving process but less so later on. Problem behaviors and social support are important determinants of caregiver well-being throughout the caregiving process. (p. 138)

Jette, Tennstedt, and Branch (1992) found that when one family member is no longer able to provide care, another person, usually from the same or the next generation, steps forward and assumes the role. There is, however, some evidence that high stress levels or subjective burden are associated with an increased risk for institutionalization (Colerick & George, 1986; McFall & Miller, 1992; Zarit, Todd, & Zarit, 1986). Montgomery and Kosloski's (1994b) longitudinal analysis of over 500 informal caregivers offers new insights into the nursing home placement process and underscores the importance of the subjective meaning of caregiving. Their data suggest that the contextual differences spouses and adult children bring to the adoption of the caregiving role and their perceptions of this role result in significantly different predictors of placement for elders cared for by these two groups. Finally, one recent longitudinal study (Tennstedt, Crawford, & McKinlay, 1993b) has moved beyond the focus on institutionalization risk to explore family care and the use of community-based formal services (i.e., home health aide or nurse, homemaker, home delivered or congregate meals, transportation, financial management, and case management). The availability of formal services did not result in families permanently relinquishing their roles.

Typically the change or loss was due to death or illness (an involuntary situation) of the caregiver rather than to competing demands or interpersonal conflict. . . . The data also indicate that substitution of care was temporary rather than permanent, and that informal care was again in place by the time of the next contact. This suggests that, in these cases, service substitution was beneficial in that it met the elder's needs for care during a transition in informal care, thereby possibly avoiding nursing-home admission. (Tennstedt, Crawford, & McKinlay, 1993b, p. 620)

In conclusion, the caregiving literature underscores the persistence of families in caring for their relatives who have either physical, cognitive, or psychological impairments. Yet performance of the caregiving role often entails substantial costs, especially for women. These costs may be physical (i.e., the deterioration of one's health, stress-related health disorders, increased reliance on psychotropic drugs), social (i.e., increased isolation, the loss of friends, recreation, and leisure activities), financial (i.e., additional medical costs, lost income), and emotional (i.e., fear, anxiety, depression, anger, loss of self, resentment).

As a result of researchers' failure to include gender as a relevant variable or researchers' use of predominantly female respondents, it is difficult to fully disentangle or understand the gendered nature of the caregiving experience. However, we do know that women are especially at risk of being the primary caregiver. This is consistent with the ideologies of separate spheres of familism because in American culture, caregiving remains the province of women. Braithwaite (1992, p. 23) argues that "women are particularly at risk, not only because they are more likely to be caregivers, but because they are being denied the opportunity to be something other than a caregiver." Society's definition of care of the dependent members as a family issue rather than a community-care policy issue, coupled with society's acceptance of the gendered division of family labor, ensures that responsibility for care will continue to fall squarely on the shoulders of women in their roles as wife, mother, daughter, and sister. Until caring for dependent members of society is defined as a public policy issue and there is a broadening of the base of societal responsibility, women, in their role as caregivers, will be required to sacrifice their own needs and development.

PART III

A Feminist Critique of Current Policies and Programs

This section draws upon a feminist framework to critique three types of policies that daily affect the experience of families caring for dependents with chronic disabilities: family policies, long-term care policies, and workplace policies. Constructs integral to a feminist framework on caregiving underlie this critique. To briefly review, these are as follows:

- The social construction of gender that has created historical differentiations of power between men and women.
- The interactions between production and reproduction with respect to gender within a Western capitalistic marketplace, which have isolated and oppressed women within the private sphere and resulted in the devaluing of their unpaid caregiving work in the home and underpaid work in the labor market.
- The interconnections of the ideologies of familism and separate spheres within a capitalistic, individualistic system that have created the breadwinner-dependent model of the family. Public policy has traditionally supported this model, which is at the heart of the way women experience oppression.
- The interconnections between the private and public, the personal and political, the informal and the formal, and thus the interplay between women's subordination in the family and in paid work.
- Women's shared consciousness from their caregiving experiences, and also the variations in their realities by race, ethnicity, social class, and sexual orientation.
- The necessity to empower women as collective agents of structural changes in order to move toward a feminist model of social care.

The recognition that women are oppressed by their caring roles is at the heart of our feminist critique; as noted by Pascall (1988), women are dependent because they care for dependents. As emphasized throughout, women predominate as unpaid carers within the home and underpaid carers in the secondary market or service sector. Caregiving is a critical feminist issue because gender-based inequities in care responsibilities have limited women's economic independence and personal rights, resulting in women's lower economic status and higher rates of poverty across the life span and particularly in old age. A feminist analysis focuses on the structural—not the individual—causes of women's oppression in the home and workplace. Structural factors underlie both how caregiving work is organized in our society and how policies perpetuate the power differentials and inequities in who performs and who is rewarded for such work.

The way in which caregiving tasks are allocated and performed is not "natural" or "immutable"; it is socially constructed. The norms that define women's role as carer within the family and that underly their poverty result from processes that are mutually interacting and that reinforce: (a) our underlying cultural values on individualism, productivity, and independence, which have resulted in a public burden or residual model of welfare; (b) the interaction of the ideologies of familism and separate spheres within a capitalist economic system, which then affects how reproduction and production are organized in our society, with men assigned to work in the public sphere and women in the private and invisible domain of the household; and (c) the manner in which problems are individually defined, incremental policies are constructed, and public programs are funded and regulated (Abramovitz, 1988; Allen & Pifer, 1993). The inequitable allocation of care responsibilities is also a result of dichotomous conceptualizations of the formal versus the informal and the public versus the private as antithetical spheres, a bipolarization that has pitted the needs of the caregiver and the person who requires care against each other.

A feminist perspective begins by examining (a) values and assumptions underlying family, long-term care, and workplace policies; (b) how problems within each of these domains are defined, oftentimes in individualistic, victim-blaming terms; and (c) how solutions are socially constructed and inadequately funded. We do not take policies at face value, but rather critique them in terms of their objectives and their effect upon family caregivers, whether intentional in their consequences or not; such a critique can lead to a rethinking of the nature and goals of public and corporate policy. For example, our review of family policy illustrates that some recent family- and community-based policy initiatives, which appear to "support the supporters," are motivated more by a desire to save costs and to enhance the family's efficiency and productivity within the home or the workplace than to enhance the caregivers' well-being through tangible support (Brody, 1985). Support for the family is frequently interpreted to mean support for a rigidly demarcated breadwinner-dependent model of the family. Such policies do not sustain families per se, but only particular kinds of families, to the exclusion of others—especially low-income families, families of color, and homosexual families. Policies that do not take account of a variety of family structures and needs tend to further class, racial, and gender inequities.

A holistic perspective regarding the interconnections between different spheres is fundamental to feminism. A feminist framework recognizes that public and corporate policy and the intensely personal experience of caregiving are inextricably connected. As noted by Abel (1990), all activities, including those that we think of as political, involve caring; conversely, all caring activities, however intimate and personal, entail the political dimensions of power and conflict, and raise practical and real questions about justice and equality. Private life is not private from social, long-term care, and corporate policy; personal life, in turn, affects public policy (Ungerson, 1987). The division between private and public spheres is neither unchanging nor unchangeable (Pascall, 1988). A feminist analysis recognizes the interaction between the personal and the political, between the private sphere of the home and the public sphere of the marketplace, between the informal and formal sectors of care, and attempts to break down the artificial dichotomy between them by integrating these domains.

The ways in which policy fundamentally affects personal life are evidenced in our critique of how current long-term care, family, and workplace policies serve to limit women's choices in the home and in the marketplace. Chapters 8 to 10 focus on how inequities in dependent care responsibilities interact with and are perpetuated by inadequate long-term care, workplace, and family policies. The outcome of this interaction furthers societal dependence on the unpaid labor of female family members to provide care across the life span. Public life reflects the division of labor in the home. To the extent this occurs, current policies serve to control women (Abramovitz, 1988).

A feminist approach also means understanding public and corporate policy as part of wider social, political, historical, and economic processes (Pascall, 1988). The interactions between the larger economic and social context and family caregiving are recognized. When economic and social policies result in unemployment and economic insecurity, this works against the creation of caring relationships, both within families stressed by too few economic resources and in the larger society where groups compete for limited resources.

From a feminist perspective, growing public concern about caregiving is not just a problem for individual families to solve as a private trouble, but a public issue demanding a collective response and a social model of care. A feminist critique of policy leads to a profound rethinking of how policy is formed and a recognition that there are no simple solutions or straightforward answers to shifting women's economic dependence without changing dependent relationships in the private sphere (Pascall, 1988). An overall goal of social policies should be the development and support of gender, race, and class equity regarding the performance of caregiving responsibilities.

Following our critique of the underlying values and assumptions of policies that impact dependent care, Part IV presents a feminist agenda for a social model of care that promotes equity across the life span by finding a balance between the needs of carers and those who receive the care; such an approach is consistent with the feminist goal of new visions of society in which caring is a central value and institutions truly facilitate care (Abel, 1987). Whereas this agenda provides overall direction, it is nevertheless incomplete and evolving, and may raise questions more than provide answers. Such an evolving analysis is consistent with feminism. The authors do not claim to provide all the answers, but offer "another set of truths" and a way of viewing the world that is fundamentally different from prevailing worldviews rooted in our culture (Hartsock, 1979).

8

A Feminist Critique
of America's Family Policy

Many Western European and Scandinavian countries have a "long and self-conscious history" of family policy, but the concept of a national family policy has never achieved widespread acceptance in the United States (Aldous, 1980 p. x). The absence of an explicit and coherent federal family policy, however, does not mean that the United States lacks family policy. Policies for taxes, education, health, housing, social services, and so forth, all affect the lives of families and, accordingly, of women. As Hendricks and Rosenthal (1993a, p. 1) note, "from prenatal health care to old age pensions, domestic policies structure the financial, physical and social well-being of families." The lack of an explicit family agenda also does not signify that the United States has failed to recognize the family as the primary institution of society. Indeed, domestic policies are predicated on the notion of "families first" to meet the needs of citizens. Formal alternative surrogates are perceived as necessary only when families are unavailable or unable to perform their responsibilities (Hendricks & Rosenthal, 1993a).

We begin this chapter by exploring two questions: (a) What is family policy? and (b) Why does the United States, unlike many industrialized countries, lack an explicit family policy? Policy is generally viewed as "a statement of values to be employed in guiding action toward desired ends" (Moore, 1971, p. 41). Central to our discussion, therefore, is an examination of how values and ideology enter into any discussion of family or family policy. The lack of an explicit family agenda reflects the absence of a shared national vision of the American family and a lack of consensus about what is in the best interest of the family. Conservatives and members of the New Right emphasize the return to the traditional nuclear family and a reduction of the role of government in family life. In contrast, liberals and feminists stress the plurality of family forms and the need for the development of cohesive family policy and programs (Granger, 1990).

We argue that the "war over the family" is not simply about the family. Rather, it is a debate about the respective roles of state and family as well as a conflict about gender roles—particularly the roles of women. Women's policy is central to family policy. By contrasting the perspectives of the New Right with those of feminists regarding the family, gender roles, and public policy, we show that a key element of the debate over family is women's autonomy and their choices within and outside the family. Current family policy has been defined as if it was gender-neutral, thereby serving to make women invisible.

Within the United States, family policy is defined as being concerned with families and children. Because this definition excludes the care of adult and elderly dependents, we do not focus on specific public programs. Rather, we address how prevailing ideologies influence the role of government in supporting families (usually the female members) caring for members with disabilities across the life span.

DEFINING FAMILY POLICY

Defining *family policy* is a difficult task. No country represents family policy by a single policy; instead, a collection of policies is directed at the family (Kamerman & Kahn, 1989). Moreover, unlike many public policy areas such as education or health care, family policies lack clear boundaries. The family is the central institution in people's lives; thus, in the broadest sense, anything the government does that affects families can potentially be construed as family policy. For example, transportation and environmental policies, such as where communities build roads or locate waste sites or how government subsidizes public transportation services, directly affect the quality of families' lives. In this chapter, however, our focus will be restricted to government actions specifically designed to affect families' lives. In defining family policy, we draw heavily on the work of two leading pioneers in this arena, Sheila Kamerman and Alfred Kahn (1978), who distinguish between *explicit* and *implicit* family policy and offer three alternative definitions.

Countries that develop explicit family policies view the family as the key unit of analysis. Countries that develop implicit family policies institute policies and programs affecting families, but the individual members of the family are the typical unit of analysis (i.e., children, the aged, the physically disabled, the juvenile delinquent). Kamerman and Kahn (1978) note the following:

> The explicit-implicit dimension clearly is interesting, reflecting as it does whether a society has enough internal homogeneity to announce objectives for

this most intimate of institutions, enough power to do something about such objects, and a value system which supports such actions. (p. 477)

Countries such as the United States and the United Kingdom, in which rhetoric about the traditional family (two parents, one breadwinner) predominates, are more likely to reject a national family policy, as compared to countries such as France, Sweden, or Norway that support the concept of family diversity.

Kamerman and Kahn (1978, 1989) also distinguish among three dimensions of family policy. Family policy as a field, they argue, focuses on defining certain objectives regarding the family, such as achieving healthier children, less financial burden attached to raising children, or greater equality for women. Based on the specified objectives, the parameters of family policy may include such domains as income-transfer programs, tax policy, health, housing, personal social services, and education. Family policy as a social instrument encompasses population policies, labor market policies, and social control policies (Kamerman & Kahn, 1978). Recent government interest in developing policies to support families in providing care to relatives with disabilities represents an example of family policy as an instrument of social control (Kamerman & Kahn, 1989). Despite women's changing social roles, Kamerman and Kahn (1978, p. 7) suggest that the "assumption here is that family care is cheaper and may be more humane." Thus, government should actively encourage family caregiving (usually meaning women's caring) to prevent the transfer of responsibility to the state. Finally, family policy as a perspective assumes that debate on all public policies should include an exploration of their potential consequences or effects on families' well-being. This type of investigation, similar to the environmental field, is often referred to as "family impact analysis" (Kamerman & Kahn, 1989).

For our discussion, it is also important to emphasize that, across countries, family policy is largely defined as benefits directed toward families and children. Although Wilensky (1985, p. 56) views family policy as "a wide umbrella of providing shelter across the life span," most policy makers, family advocates, and social scientists exclude adult and elderly dependents from family policy discussions. Analysts often justify this perspective by arguing that the family's economic situation is most likely to be strained when children are young (Kamerman & Kahn, 1989). They tend to ignore the extent and cost of caring for dependent adults, particularly the cost to women. Moreover, this socially constructed dichotomy may add fuel to the current conflict presumed to exist between generations (Binney & Estes, 1988; Quadagno, 1989; Wisensale, 1988). The focus on the nuclear family obscures the widespread phenomenon of intergenerational support—support flowing in both directions across generations. It also ignores commonalities in the caring experience across the life span, promotes special-interest mentality (i.e., "kids versus canes"), and discourages the adoption of "a principle of life course entitlement" to basic human needs (Binney & Estes, 1988).

UNDERSTANDING AMERICA'S
LACK OF AN EXPLICIT FAMILY POLICY

Cultural ideologies and values provide the context both for how countries define problems and how they seek solutions. As Clark (1993, p. 33) underscores, "Ethical principles guide our development and implementation of policies and programs. . . . The moral dimension of public policy . . . influences our perception of acts, our loyalties, and our assumptions about human nature." Public policy is inevitably tied to empirical data; it is our interpretation of these data that is key. Empirical data become the instrument to advance a particular social agenda based on an ideological understanding of the nature of family and state.

In attempting to understand the United States' lack of an explicit, coherent, and comprehensive family policy, analysts have often used a cross-national perspective. As Meyers, Ramirez, Walker, Langton, and O'Connor (1988, p. 139) note, "modern societies differ in their construction of the public, and in particular the way in which the state becomes linked to private life." They distinguish between three forms of modernization: organic corporatism, communal corporatism, and liberal individualism (for a detailed discussion of this typology of modernization, see Meyers et al., 1988). Many Latin American countries are models of organic corporatist societies, in which the traditions of natural law and the church dominate, and individualism is deemphasized. The family is viewed as a natural entity worthy of public protection. The state does not penetrate the internal side of family life and therefore intrafamilial conflicts are invisible to public organizations. "The internal arrangements of family life are determined by what is conceived to be natural or religious. . . . The conflicts between women and children as putative individuals are handled in more traditional ways . . . and do not much enter the public agenda" (Meyers et al., 1988, p. 144). The state concerns itself mainly with women and children who are not in families.

Northern European communities offer examples of communal corporatism. Within these societies, "modernization is built on a perception of the state as a national community, rather than a nation of free individuals" (Meyers et al., 1988, p. 144). Instead of being hidden within the family, individuals are viewed as having rights and responsibilities in the public sphere based on one's own personal status as women, men, children, the aged, homosexuals, etc. Public organizations recognize the natural characteristic of conflicts between groups (based on differing capacities and needs) and expect that they "may be called upon to clarify or redefine mutual rights and obligations" (Meyers et al., 1988, p. 145).

The United States represents the liberal individualistic society. The state, the economy, culture, and religion all emphasize the concept of individual choice and freedom. Ironically, this society overlooks women as individuals by presuming that women will assume traditional roles and caregiving burdens, thereby limiting their choices. Meyers and his associates argue that "liberal society is built on the myth of the individual who is free to choose and act—free beyond age, gender and family relations" (Meyers et al., 1988, p. 146). They contend that familial conflicts are redefined as public issues when persons assert their individual rights against situations that constrain them, such as marriage, fatherhood, motherhood, and filial obligation.

In his comparison of the United States' and Canada's domestic policies toward older families, Clark (1993) notes that both countries possess an ideology of familism, that is, an assumption of the primacy of families in meeting the care needs of their members. Canada's emphasis on collectiveness or a sense of community, however, tempers familism; whereas America's stress on individualism heightens familism (and reduces options for women as individuals). Clark stresses that this preeminence of the individual is ingrained in our national identity. America's founding document, the Declaration of Independence, emphasizes "life, liberty and the pursuit of happiness." In contrast, Canada's founding legislation, the British North American Act, stresses the importance of "peace, order and government." He argues the following:

> [The United States] particularizes and compartmentalizes social policies along lines of individual or static group-based need, rather than seeing public programs as responding to changing life course needs across the entire society . . . [Thus] the United States has spawned the generational equity debate. (Clark, 1993, p. 34)

Canada's emphasis on a sense of community responsibility—a concern for the welfare of others versus a concern directed mainly toward self—makes the development of more universal policies such as a national health care system much more possible.

As we have previously noted, it is these values of individualism and familism that form the basis for the residual approach to public policy in the United States. Residualism—meaning the state becomes involved only after the family has assumed as much responsibility as possible—especially serves the current federal government's goal of cost containment. Faced with an increasing federal deficit and growing interest in cost effectiveness, "familism offers a convenient justification to cloak the real reasons for withholding support" (Clark, 1993, p. 27). As feminists stress, those most affected by such withholding of government support are women. It is women who, in the great majority of cases, are the caregivers; therefore, legislation strengthening family obligation restricts women's lives.

History, social and cultural traditions, and economic and demographic circumstances shape each country's approach to family policy. The interest of Western European countries in family policy came about in part due to the heavy loss of life during World War I. Governments created policies and programs that made having children less of a financial burden to families. Following World War II, more financial aid for families was seen as "part of a push for social equity by socialist and church-related parties represented in post-war governments" (Aldous, 1980, p. x.). Thus, in Europe the concept of family policy has an extensive history of being employed as both income redistribution policy and population policy—a means to promote higher fertility rates and larger families. Resurgence of interest in family policy in Europe reflects the recent "demographic panic" about declining birth rates in many European nations (Kamerman & Kahn, 1989). Current European fertility rates are significantly lower than the United States' 2.1 births for each woman. Only one European country, Ireland, has a similar fertility. Spain and Italy (1.2 births) presently have the lowest fertility rate of the European Union (Le Monde de l'education, 1994). Thus, European family policy is viewed as offering families incentives for childbearing and child rearing.

This pronatalistic value underlies most countries' family policies that feminists have argued are restrictive of women's choices. Most European family policies were instituted to promote reproduction. "They do not give people choices of whether or not to have children. They seek to provide supports for the family roles of women as mothers and men as fathers" (Spakes, 1989a, p. 612). Of European nations, only France includes a couple without children in its definition of family. All other countries with an explicit family policy have in their definition of family the presence of at least one parent and at least one child (Kamerman & Kahn, 1989).

Although the United States has not experienced concern with fertility decline or population size as has Europe, the pronatalistic value has been incorporated into many of our social policies. "AFDC (Aid to Families with Dependent Children) provides an example. . . . The program is clearly pro-natalistic. No forms of financial support are available for low-income women without children" (Spakes, 1989a, p. 616). In the United States, interest in family policy emerged primarily during the mid-1970s in response to growing public concern about the disturbing number of children living in poverty.

THE EVOLUTION OF THE
FAMILY POLICY DEBATE IN THE UNITED STATES

The concept of a national family policy was not broadly promoted in the United States until the Carter-Mondale administration (1976 to 1980). Drawing on the experiences of European and Nordic nations, the Carter administration suggested that the federal government should assume a more proactive role through the development of comprehensive policies and programs to support all families in performing their functions. Increasing public concern about the state of the American family focused primarily on three issues (Bane & Jargowsky, 1988):

- The large number of children who live in poverty. The poverty rate for children is greater than any other age group in this country. More than 20% of all children, and nearly 25% of children under 6 years of age, live in poverty in the United States. In fact, children are worse off than they were two decades ago when America undertook its "war on poverty."

- Children living in single-parent families are at greatest risk for poverty, and the percentage of children who spend at least part of their lives in single-parent families continues to increase.

- Rising divorce rates and greater acceptance of heterosexual and homosexual cohabitation are leading many adults to fail either to form, or to stay in, "families" in the traditional definition. This situation may reflect the declining importance of the institution of family in our society.

Bane and Jargowsky (1988) note that there is general agreement on the first point, that poverty among children is a problem, but less agreement on the second two points: whether single-parenthood is a problem or whether the family is in decline. Feminists argue that the single-parent family structure per se is not the problem. Instead, the association of poverty with single-parent families reflects the following: (a) only with both parents working are families able to enjoy the same standard of living as single-earner families a generation ago; (b) the inability of the majority of women to earn an adequate family wage due to gender-based occupational segregation and pay inequity; and (c) in many cases, fathers' failure to assume economic responsibility for their children. Feminists also emphasize that the plurality of family forms does not mean that essential family functions are less important than they were a generation ago. Critical functions of the family remain: economic security; nurturance, affiliation, and emotional support; socialization and education; and procreation.

These ideological disputes dominated the 1980 White House Conference on Families. Convened by President Carter to address the growing problems of children and families in America, the Conference is best remembered for the polemics between conservatives and liberals on the definition of the family, the passage of the Equal Rights Amendment, and the issue of abortion and reproductive choice for women. Whitehead (1993, p. 48) notes that "no president since has tried to hold a national family conference." During the 1980s, as the Reagan administration entered the White House and the Republican party took control of the U.S. Senate, the notion of a national family policy disappeared from debate. The Right carried the dual messages of being "profamily" and "antigovernment" (Langley, 1991). Under Reagan, the emphasis was on eliminating government programs viewed as "undercutting the family" (Seaberg, 1990). For instance, Reagan appointed administrators to the Department of Health and Human Services who were antiabortion and opposed to recognition of adolescent sexuality. As a result of these appointments, new federal regulations were introduced under Title X requiring federally funded family planning agencies to notify both parents or legal guardians within ten days of giving birth control technology to any minor.

The Reagan administration also instituted major cutbacks in the levels of benefits and the coverage of income maintenance programs. Especially hard hit were the means-tested programs for those in poverty, such as AFDC, food stamps, and Medicaid. During Reagan's first term, the total reduction in income maintenance programs was $57 billion, representing 33% of all federal cuts, in programs that accounted for only 10% of the federal budget (Abbott & Wallace, 1992). The changes in AFDC that resulted from the Omnibus Budget Reconciliation Act (OBRA) of 1981 made life worse for most women and children on welfare. Particularly devastating were the diminution of the work-incentive provisions and the imposition of limits of $75 per month for work expenses and $160 per month for child care. As noted by Miller (1990, p. 36-37), "restricting [AFDC] eligibility to the third trimester of pregnancy is a punitive measure directed toward single mothers, and is ironic in view of the Reagan administration's position that a fetus is a person from the moment of conception."

A similar philosophy continued with the Bush administration. Although seeking a "kinder, gentler" society, Bush's message of "a thousand points of light" emphasized the role of family, church, charitable organizations, volunteers, and business—as opposed to government's responsibility—for the well-being of citizens. For example, although the Family Support Act of 1988 mandated (a) the establishment of procedures to assure that center-based child care met health and safety standards and (b) the development of guidelines for family day care, the Bush administration's Department of Health and Human Services' regulations emphasized, instead, the use of free informal sources of care (Miller, 1990).

The current Clinton administration stands apart from the previous two administrations in suggesting that the federal government should play a greater role in safeguarding and promoting the well-being of American families. There is symbolic importance in the fact that the first Act signed into law by President Clinton was the Family Medical and Leave Act (FMLA), which offered job protection to workers requiring short-term leaves from their jobs to care for ill or disabled family members. Moreover, the number one priority of the Clinton administration has been health care reform, an issue of great concern to many American families. It is important to note, however, that Clinton has chosen not to structure his reforms, whether in health, housing, welfare, or education, around a family policy framework. This decision may reflect a desire to avoid some of the intense debate that surrounds the changing American family and the role of government in family life.

> Family policy in liberal circles is understood to mean economic assistance and social services that will put a floor under family income and lead the way to self-sufficiency. . . . For [conservatives], family policy appears to involve the use of national resources to legitimize behavior not concomitant with behavior typical of the American family. Right-minded national policy should reinforce traditional American patterns, but not abide deviations that smack of irresponsibility. (Steiner, 1981, p. 17)

Such "deviations that smack of irresponsibility" presumably include nontraditional forms of families as well as any choices women make away from traditional caring roles.

THE NEW RIGHT'S PERSPECTIVE
OF FAMILY AND SOCIAL POLICY

The 1980s represented a decade in which the appropriate role of government was being reevaluated, not just in the United States, but globally (Hula, 1991). Eastern Europe and the Soviet Union experienced the collapse of socialist and communist governments, and in United Kingdom and the United States, dominant themes were government retrenchment and privatization. Hula (1991) suggests the following:

> Given the importance of family in the framing of social welfare policy, it is hardly surprising that current political debate often focuses on the effects of social policy on the family. . . . It is apparent that family is a symbol of fundamental importance in American politics and it is equally clear it offers no guide to action. (p. 3)

Both those who argue for less federal intrusion into families' lives and those who advocate for increased public spending to strengthen the family view themselves as "profamily." Central to the debate about social policy is whether the traditional nuclear family should serve as the guiding symbol.

The New Right idealizes the traditional patriarchal nuclear family, a family composed of a male breadwinner, an economically dependent female homemaker, and socially and economically dependent children. The appeal of the New Right is one of nostalgia for a time when marriage was for a lifetime, children obeyed their parents, crime was low, and families felt safe in their neighborhoods. Feminists argue that what is ignored by the New Right is that for many families, especially working-class families, immigrant families, and families of color, this image was never a reality. Throughout U.S. history, working-class women and children were frequently in the labor force, often employed long hours in unsafe or unhealthy environments. Working-class women and women of color have seldom had the luxury of opting out of paid employment. These families have often lived in substandard housing, in neighborhoods lacking adequate sanitation, or in high-crime areas.

Gender roles, defined by the ideology of separate spheres, are central to the Right's view of the family:

> A man's responsibility to his family is best met by his success in the market, his ability as a wage earner to support his wife and children; a woman's worth is measured by her dedication to her role as wife and mother. (Cohen & Katzenstein, 1988, p. 26)

Neoconservatives Brigitte and Peter Berger (1983), as well as New Right author George Gilder (1981), emphasize the importance of the bourgeois or traditional heterosexual nuclear family to both capitalism and democratic order. Gilder argues that married men contribute more to society by virtue of their stable work patterns than do bachelors, who dissipate their energies in nonproductive sexual and economic concerns. The Bergers suggest that the bourgeois family's promotion of individualism of male members is conducive to entrepreneurial capitalism and democracy. Although they maintain that women will need to decide on their own priorities, the Bergers express a strong wish that women come to recognize that "life is more than a career and that this 'more' is above all to be found in the family." They warn women that "they should not expect public policy to underwrite and subsidize their life plan" (Berger & Berger, 1983, p. 205).

Understanding the New Right's views on gender relations and the family is crucial to understanding their argument that reducing the role of the state is the way to solve economic and social problems.

> The family is seen as the linchpin of New Right economic and social policies because, within this discourse, men are seen as the "individuals" of economic liberal thought whereas women are seen as outside the market place, a part of the dependent family, not citizens in their own right. (Abbott & Wallace, 1992)

The Right sees the family as the cornerstone of society, crucial to maintaining stability. It views the diversification of family forms as the moral and economic decline of the family and, in turn, defines this as leading to the moral and economic decline of society. Similarly, the Right sees legislation allowing abortion, instituting easier divorce procedures, permitting sex education in the schools, and mandating equal opportunity in the labor market, along with welfare programs that offer benefits to never-married or divorced single parents, as sabotaging the traditional nuclear family and validating alternative family forms and lifestyles. The New Right views the breakdown of family life in its idealized form as the cause of the high rates of criminal activity, substance abuse, school drop-outs, and unemployment.

Whitehead (1993) begins her *Atlantic Monthly* article, "Dan Quayle Was Right" with this statement:

> The social-science evidence is in: though it may benefit the adults involved, the dissolution of intact two-parent families is harmful to large numbers of children. . . . Family diversity in the form of increasing numbers of single-parent and stepparent families does not strengthen the social fabric but, rather, dramatically weakens and undermines society. (p. 47)

For evidence, she cites poverty statistics such as that children in single-parent families are 6 times more likely to be poor and they are also likely to stay poor longer. The empirical data are correct, but Whitehead and other conservatives err in their interpretation. They falsely assume that correlation equals causality (Cowin, 1993). It is beyond dispute that single-parent families are at greater risk for poverty, but the Right chose to "blame the victim" and ignore the synergy of social forces that place these families at risk. The Right fails to consider alternative causal hypotheses for the economic and social stresses experienced by these families, such as the worldwide economic upheaval, the decline in real wages for American workers, gender inequality in the labor market, and social policies that penalize nontraditional families. They do not see the connection between women's traditional caring roles and the poverty of women and children.

Within New Right thinking, Abbott and Wallace (1992) identify two conflicting ideologies: *economic liberalism* and *traditional authoritarian conservatism.* (For an in-depth feminist analysis of the New Right, see Abbott & Wallace, 1992.) Economic liberalism argues a laissez-faire position, in which government should not intervene in the economy nor in individuals' lives unless they endanger the rights of others. In contrast, traditional authoritarian conservatism emphasizes the need for government to reinforce traditional patterns of authority (i.e., institutions of family and church) in order to protect a strong central state. They note that these contrasting ideologies do not conflict in practice. For example, the economic liberal objectives of reducing public spending for welfare implies traditional roles for women and the family (Abbott & Wallace, 1992).

Much of the writing of New Right intellectuals, George Gilder, Charles Murray, Martin Anderson, and Lawrence Mead, has criticized income maintenance programs, particularly AFDC. Common to most of their writings is the view that the welfare programs of the Great Society "undermine the moral responsibility of individuals by removing their incentives to work and support themselves and by discouraging marriage" (Abbott & Wallace, 1992, p. 97). They reject the liberal view that poverty is derived from structural disadvantage and argue instead that it arises from individuals' own behaviors. In establishing a behavioral basis for poverty, Murray and Mead distinguish between the deserving or respectable poor and the undeserving or underclass of poor. They view the underclass as complacent about illegitimacy, inadequate parents, and lacking a strong work ethic (Mead, 1986; Murray, 1984, 1988). Moreover, they assert that government programs have fostered dependency in the underclass. Mead (1986, p. 38) suggests that "especially since the late 1960's on, millions of female-headed families and other low-income groups signed up for AFDC, food stamps, and other programs rather than continue to struggle to support themselves without assistance." Interestingly, Abbott and Wallace (1992) note that Murray and Mead view the problem similarly but they would seek different solutions. Murray sees the solution as getting, or keeping, women married and supported by a male wage-earner. Mead proposes welfare mothers enter the workforce, although he advocates that they should furnish their own child care arrangements rather than rely on government to do so. Abbott and Wallace (1992, p. 96) conclude that "neither position is particularly helpful to women, especially poor women."

The New Right's attitude toward care of America's elderly is also based on a mythical past in which families supposedly lived in multigenerational households (Ford, 1991). Gerontologists have consistently found, however, that within the United States, multigenerational households have never been the standard. In the past, fewer persons survived to old age, and those who did most often lived in a two-person household with their spouse. It is the normative preference of older persons, even in widowhood, to maintain a household independent from their children (Daniels, 1982; Treas, 1975; Troll, Miller, & Atchley, 1979). Members of the New Right argue that both the responsibilities and costs of long-term care should be shifted back to the family rather than incurred by the state. "Family responsibility, therefore, has become the central underpinning of current long-term care policy implementation and formulation. . . . The ideological constructs of the New Right exert tremendous influence on current policy development" (Ford, 1991, p. 100). "Family," as used here, is essentially a euphemism for women, who carry most of the burdens and costs of caregiving.

Filial responsibility—the concept that the state is not responsible until children (in practice, female children) have made the maximum effort— dominates the New Right's philosophy regarding long-term care. Evidence suggests, however, that family responsibility laws regarding elder care are neither beneficial nor cost-effective. Forty states currently have, but do not enforce, laws requiring financial support of elderly parents (Hagestad, 1987). In general, these family responsibilities have not produced substantial revenues for the states, have been found to be time-consuming and difficult to administer, and have entailed substantial administrative and judicial costs (Bulcroft, Leynseele, & Borgotta, 1989; Schorr, 1980). Gilliland (1986, p. 33) posits that, "the impact of filial responsibilities will be greatest on adult children who, although not denying their filial responsibility, must impoverish themselves and their children to make a financial contribution to their parents' care." She also notes that elder abuse is more common among families who are forced into elder care, and suggests that, on a societal level, mandated filial responsibility will only heighten intergenerational tensions and conflicts (Gilliland, 1986).

FEMINISTS' PERSPECTIVES
OF FAMILY AND FAMILY POLICY

Feminists argue that the traditional nuclear family should not be the guiding metaphor for American social policy. For more and more families, the traditional nuclear family is simply no longer a reality. Focusing only on family structure (and not family roles), a 1994 U.S. Census Bureau Report confirms that only 50% of American children now live in the traditional nuclear family and that there is considerable variation by race and ethnicity. As we have seen, approximately 56% of Caucasian children live in a traditional nuclear family, but only 38% of Hispanic children (who can be of any race), and 26% of Black children do so (*Boston Globe*, 1994).

Despite demographic and social changes such as the diversity of family structures and women's entry into the labor force, policy makers have been reluctant to modify existing policies or to create new ones because such proposals are often perceived as being "antifamily."

> While there is no doubt that the traditional family has become less common, it continues to have enormous normative power. That is, such families are seen as being the ideal, the model to which reasonable citizens strive. Such an argument underlies the demands that social policy continue its traditional posture toward families even as its central model becomes a statistical rarity. (Hula, 1991, p. 3)

It is questionable whether public policy can be used to strengthen the traditional nuclear family. Bane and Jargowsky (1988) contend that although family support and welfare policies may substantially affect quality of life, the evidence suggests such policies will not bring about much change in family structure. Their analysis of European countries' pronatalistic policies and fertility rates reveals that even substantial policies had minimal effect. They suggest that "both conservatives and liberals should find this analysis, if they believe it, troubling," but also insist that "this conclusion does not imply that policies for families are of no importance or should not be pursued. . . . Improving the well-being of families and the general environment to support families also is important" (Bane & Jargowsky, 1988, p. 245).

Feminists maintain that if policies are to truly support women, they cannot be based on the system of patriarchy that currently underlies our social welfare programs—patriarchy being a system of sexual hierarchical relations maintained by law, culture, and societal norms in which masculine dominance is upheld (Miller, 1990). Although first-wave feminists of the 19th century fought for women's emancipation, women's rights to choose marriage or a career, and to vote, they did not challenge women's place in the family. Second-wave feminists of the 1960s and 1970s, however, focused on sexual politics in both the public and private spheres. Rapp (1978) makes this assertion:

> One of the more valuable contributions of feminist theory has been its effort to "deconstruct" the family as a natural unit, and to reconstruct it as a social unit, as ideology, as an institutional nexus of social relationships and cultural meanings. (p. 280)

Women's roles in the family and the consequences of a male-dominated power structure for women are central to these discussions. Simone de Beauvoir (1968) conceptualized woman as "Other" to describe women's second-class status in a patriarchal society in which man is "Subject" or "Absolute." She noted that within the economic sphere, women's lower standing resulted in men holding the better jobs, getting higher wages, and having greater opportunity for success than their female competitors.

Miller (1990, p. 23) uses the concept of *patriarchal necessity*—"the need among the collectivity of men to separate the sexes and devalue and control women"—as the driving force of the social welfare system's treatment of women. The Social Security Act of 1935, the foundation of our national social welfare system, is predicated on a notion of family in which a breadwinner father and a homemaker mother are committed to each other in a lifelong marriage. Thus, women who find themselves living outside of marriage—whether from personal choice, divorce, or widowhood—are often penalized for these circumstances. Women who are not under the protection or control of men through marriage are generally viewed as falling under the protection or control of the state.

AFDC (originally entitled Aid to Dependent Children), for instance, was enacted as part of the Social Security Act to be a small, temporary program for widows with young children. For the first 20 years, the majority of recipients were widows; however, by the 1960s the vast majority of recipients were divorced or never-married women with children (Segal, 1989). The shift in the AFDC population led to a change in public opinion. Rather than being seen as the "deserving poor," AFDC mothers were blamed for their own condition and stigmatized as amoral, lazy, and unsuitable parents. AFDC is now regarded as, at best, a subsistence program that keeps women and children in poverty.

Social Security's Old Age and Survivor Insurance Program (OASI, but commonly referred to as Social Security) also may penalize older women who are alone. Because women usually earn lower wages and have more interrupted work histories (due to caregiving) than men, the majority of older women choose a Social Security benefit based on their spouses' work career rather than their own in order to receive a larger benefit amount. Divorced women, however, must have been married to their ex-spouse for a minimum of 10 years in order to be eligible for a spousal benefit. Moreover, a divorced woman cannot receive payments until her ex-partner (if living) begins to draw his benefits. Even widows, who are often viewed as more deserving than the divorced, may suffer penalties for outliving their spouses and being unattached. For instance, widows whose husbands die prior to their intended retirement (usually age 65) do not have those "lost-income years" computed into their spousal benefit rates and, thus, receive smaller payments. In essence, women of all ages—but especially poor women—who live outside marriage may face negative consequences for their choices or circumstances.

Because women provide most of the caring in the family—caring that has been undervalued and relatively invisible—it would seem at first glance that the concept of a national family policy would be readily embraced by feminists. Would not women have the most to gain from a comprehensive and coherent national family agenda? There is, however, considerable caution among feminists. Dornbusch and Strober (1988) note the following:

> Among proponents of feminism, there are some who are suspicious of the motives of those who have introduced familial language into the national agenda. Is concern for the family only a ruse, a device for transmuting the terms of national debate in ways that result in a vote for stability in the relations between men and women? (p. 4)

Within the family policy debate, the issue that most divides feminists and conservatives is the matter of adult roles—specifically women's autonomy—not children's needs (Cohen & Katzenstein, 1988).

Spakes (1991, p. 23) suggests "the idea of national family policy and what it seems to promise is in ways seductive, particularly to working mothers. However, proposals that have been offered thus far have varied considerably." A number of American feminists have looked toward Sweden, with its national priorities of family welfare and gender equity, as a model for the United States (Acker & Hallock, 1992; Rosenthal, 1994). Sweden's family policy links both family and labor objectives. Concerned with its declining population in the 1930s, Sweden developed policies specifically to boost its birth rate. Similarly faced with a national need for more workers after World War II, Sweden had two choices— either seek immigrants or recruit women. Because of a concern for cultural homogeneity, the former strategy was viewed as undesirable. Instead, policies were instituted to encourage Swedish women into the labor force (Spakes, 1992).

> Thus, what is commonly thought of as the Swedish "family policy" is actually a combination of universal, pro-natalistic and economic goals. These policies include: (1) tax-free children allowances; (2) parental insurance which entitles parents to a leave of absence up to 12 months for childbirth, plus leave to care for a sick child (60 days per year), and 2 days leave per year for daycare or school visits; and (3) day care, subsidized by municipal and national government and provided for an income-based fee. (Spakes, 1992, p. 47)

These policies were viewed as encouraging women both to bear children and to participate in the labor force. It was assumed that by providing women with these public supports for their family responsibilities, they would no longer be disadvantaged in the labor market relative to their male counterparts. Has that occurred—has gender equity in the labor market been achieved in Sweden?

Swedish women have moved into the labor force in slightly greater numbers than their American counterparts. Swedish women represent 48% of their country's entire workforce compared to America's 40% figure. Yet Sweden's labor market is even more gender-segregated than the United States. As in America, Swedish women have primarily transferred their reproductive functions or caring work into the paid labor market and are predominately employed as nurses, teachers, child caretakers, home helpers, kitchen staff, cleaners, secretaries, and shop assistants (Rosenthal, 1994; Spakes, 1989a). Moreover, 43% of Swedish women (as compared to only 6% of Swedish men) work part-time, an average of 26 hours per week. Swedish women who work full-time earn 78% of men's wages, but because so many work part-time, they earn only 37% of total wages (Rosenthal, 1994). Despite women's high level of labor force participation and the presence of universal social welfare benefits, such as the children's allowance, because of their pronounced concentration in low-paying female occupations coupled with part-time employment, 40% of all single-mother families receive means-tested public assistance. Spakes (1992, p. 50) concludes "these supports have not created economic independence for women . . . because many women are now dependent on the public, rather than the private patriarchy."

Still, women and children fare better in Sweden than in the United States. Sweden's poverty rate among children is 5% compared to approximately 20% in the United States (Smeeding, Torrey, & Rein, 1988). This low poverty rate is achieved through a combination of universal programs such as health care, pension rights, children allowances, and state-advanced child support payments (for noncustodial parents) along with means-tested programs such as public assistance and housing subsidies. Single-parent families are more likely to receive public assistance and housing subsidies as well as priority for publicly supported child care, for which they pay lower fees (Rosenthal, 1994). Public assistance in Sweden is required to provide recipients with a "reasonable standard of living"; they do not live in poverty as do their American counterparts on public welfare.

PROMOTING A FEMINIST FAMILY POLICY

Feminists maintain that, contrary to the alarm of conservatives and the New Right, the family is not declining; rather, it is changing (Stacey, 1993). Feminists argue that the family as an institution is resilient, precisely because variation allows it to adjust to changing social conditions (Cohen & Katzenstein, 1988). Social policies must address the needs of all families, recognize the diversity of family forms, and become more flexible in application. The traditional family can no longer be the central model for social policy, nor can the traditional assignment of women to private and unpaid labor in the household go unquestioned. These assumptions have only served to constrain women to marginal, second-class roles in the labor market (Hula, 1991). Feminists caution against the politically popular term "family values," used by conservatives to imply that (a) families should care for their own and can do so best with women doing the unpaid caregiving, (b) the "good family" is a traditional family, and families who do not fit this model are the cause of current social ills, and (c) that upholding family values means maintaining a separation between family and state, private and public (Rosenthal & Hendricks, 1993).

Feminists contend that family policies in the United States should not be based on pronatalistic and patriarchal concepts of the family. Spakes (1989a) emphasizes the following:

> The best family policy for all families would, in fact, be a woman's policy: one that is not paternalistic, patriarchal, or exclusively pro-natalistic, one that is not class biased or preferential, and one that gives all women real choices about their lives. (p. 616)

How do we achieve this? First, as noted earlier, we must acknowledge that the personal is political. It is not possible to separate the public and private spheres of life or of responsibility; the home and the state are intertwined and interdependent (Spakes, 1991). We must, therefore, strive for gender equality both in the family and in broader social institutions.

Scanzoni (1982, 1991) argues that family policy can be used to promote egalitarian relationships in the family and the worth of androgyny in sex roles. He maintains that men should be expected to be efficient householders and effective parents if they choose parenthood.

> The conventional family model relieves men of primary responsibility to households and for children. That model is reflected...in part by child custody awards that generally go to women and also by the difficulties of collecting child support payments from men who sense minimal involvement in, and influence over, the offspring they have sired. (Scanzoni, 1991, p. 21)

He criticizes conservatives who "argue that children are so extraordinarily vital and then fail to assign shared parenting to men by retaining women as primary parenting agents" (Scanzoni, 1991, p. 21).

The pronatalistic values that underlie family policy must be removed to promote gender equality in the family. Family policy must advance women's right to reproductive choice and freedom of sexual expression. Reproductive choice means not only when but also whether they choose to parent. Freedom of sexual expression notes women's right to choose heterosexual or homosexual relationships, and to parent within lesbian relationships (Spakes, 1989b).

A life course perspective must also be incorporated into family policy, recognizing that the caring role extends beyond parenting to include care for such family members as adult children, siblings, spouses, parents, and even grandparents. Children's advocates have successfully argued that children's needs and interests can best be understood within the context of the family or through a family policy approach, but similar gains have not been made by advocates for adults and elders with disabilities. Thus, within the policy arena, younger families continue to be pitted against older families, fueling intergenerational tensions. Feminists note that it is society's extension of the culturally appointed nurturing role of mother that leads women to care for other family members. Moreover, it is women's family obligations that restrict their opportunities in the marketplace and promote their economic dependence across the life span, and in turn, contribute to their poverty in old age.

A key objective of family policy must be promoting women's economic autonomy. "It makes little sense to speak of the well-being of women and children (as well as men) unless and until gender makes no difference with respect to adult economic autonomy" (Scanzoni, 1991, p. 21). The fundamental patriarchal nature of industrial society that promotes gender inequality must be changed. Money and power are distributed through the production system, which is dominated by men, whereas women remain tied to the reproductive system (Spakes, 1989a). Despite the remarkable rise in women's labor force participation, they have primarily transferred their reproductive or caregiving roles into the paid sector. Gender-based occupational segregation and pay inequity continue to dominate the labor market. In order for women to achieve economic autonomy, family policy must encompass the issues of equal opportunity in education and employment, pay equity, and comparable worth.

In conclusion, feminists have been charged by conservatives as being antifamily. Yet, as Cohen and Katzenstein (1988, p. 29) emphasize, "this antifamily charge is basically a slogan that muddles rather than clarifies the true political issue. The real debate is over women's autonomy within and outside the family." Feminism and family policy are not intrinsically incompatible. Rather, gender equality must be an organizing principle of family policy.

9

A Feminist Critique
of Long-Term Care Policies

As emphasized throughout this book, providing long-term care, including mental health care, for dependents with chronic disabilities is a feminist issue because it affects women at their core, constricting their social and economic choices and perpetuating their powerlessness. Using a feminist framework that challenges traditional worldviews, we begin this chapter by critiquing the assumptions and values that undergird contemporary long-term care policies and programs. Because the United States has less a system of long-term care than several ways to pay for it, our analysis focuses on the regulatory and funding mechanisms underlying current policies (Leutz, Capitman, MacAdam, & Abrahams, 1992). Recognizing the interconnections between the personal and political, between private lives and public policy, we then examine how funding for the provision of long-term care interacts with the ideologies of separate spheres and of familism, especially the socially structured assumption that family care is a private issue, producing gender inequities across the life span. These interactions between ideology and policy have negatively affected women's health, social, and economic status. We illustrate how structural factors have served to oppress women: specifically, how the societal devaluation of caregiving interacts with the disproportionate representation of women in the secondary sector of the labor market, wage discrimination, and the gender-based division of paid and unpaid labor.

In addition to these more pervasive factors, recent federal budget cutbacks, particularly in Medicaid and Medicare, and the growing emphasis on cost containment, have disproportionately affected women, especially women of color. Such structural inequities then create and perpetuate gender, class, and racial inequities in caregiving responsibilities; these, in turn, underlie the financial dependency of women on men across the life span, particularly the continued economic vulnerability of many older women. Women are economically penalized both as unpaid family caregivers and underpaid caregivers in nursing homes, mental hospitals, and institutions for the developmentally disabled, as well as in the home care industry. Minkler and Estes (1991) maintain that this economic oppression of women, often under the rubric of family- and community-based care, furthers the government's cost-savings goals: women are essential to fill the nation's growing need for long-term care in ways that do not cost the state and also enable it to reduce the expenses of formal service provision in areas where greater voluntary labor can be extracted. For example, women have stepped in to provide the posthospital care necessitated by changes in Medicare funding through the prospective payment system, in which reimbursement to the provider is limited per diagnosis—changes that were motivated by cost-savings, not by patient or caregiver welfare. Despite the development in the past decade of more support programs for families of the three populations that are the focus of this book, the extent to which these promote gender, racial, and class equity remains subject to question. In many instances, such programs may continue to reinforce the traditional dual role of women as private carers.

The failure of past research to examine how the assumptions and values underlying long-term care policies affect the welfare of caregivers obscures the issue of who is burdened by caring, who is at risk, and who benefits at others' expense (Stober, 1982). Consistent with Hartsock's (1979) definition of feminism as a mode of analysis—a way of asking questions and searching for answers—a feminist critique raises fundamental issues often overlooked in prior analyses: In the development of long-term care policies, why are family caregivers, primarily women, treated as unpaid service providers rather than rewarded and supported by public policies? Why is the informal network preferred over paid care, even though family members, faced with inadequate support options, may have to radically alter their lives to provide care? Why is family care romanticized and institutional care seen as an undesirable last resort, even in instances of caregiver stress, family histories of neglect or abuse, or current abuse of the carer by an adult who is mentally ill? Why are public issues of justice and equity ignored by expecting sacrifice from an individual who simply has the personal misfortune of a relative's becoming chronically disabled? And why is caring within the family seen as costless to individuals and to society whereas caring by society is defined as costly? To begin to answer these questions, we turn now to examine the assumptions and values that underlie current long-term care policies.

UNDERLYING ASSUMPTIONS AND
VALUES OF LONG-TERM CARE POLICIES

The assumptions and values that underlie contemporary long-term care policies are inextricably interconnected, and reflect our overall societal values toward individual dependency and need. These have been briefly described in earlier chapters as follows:

- The individual with chronic disabilities as the target or unit of care rather than the family system as a whole
- The ideology of community care
- The medical definitions of dependency
- The privatization and informalization of care

The Dependent Individual as the Unit of Care

As emphasized in earlier chapters, the organization and distribution of public services has played a key role in reproducing traditional dependencies within the private sphere of the family. A primary reason that gender inequities in caregiving responsibilities persist is because promoting the carer's well-being has not been a policy goal, nor have caregivers' rights to public support been legitimized within long-term care policies. Instead, policies have focused on the dependent individual, not on the interconnections between the disabled person and those who provide care (Osterbusch, Keigher, Miller, & Linsk, 1987). When the individual, not the family system, is viewed as the unit or target of service, the extent and costs of care provided by family caregivers are overlooked. As described in Chapter 5, government intervention with family caregivers is construed as a "last resort."

This "safety net," or residual approach inherent within a public burden model of welfare, has served to penalize family caregivers in a number of ways. Social services have been oriented toward crisis intervention, short-term support, and long-term residential care, rather than toward personal care and in-home maintenance for the long haul. At the extreme, families have been identified as part of the problem, as when families of the chronically mentally ill have been looked on as the source of their relative's illness (Biegel, Song, & Chakravarthy, 1994; Geiser, Hoche, & King, 1988; Hatfield, 1987a; Hugen, 1993; Kane, 1994; Lefley, 1989). Even when families have been defined as causing problems, treatment has tended to focus on the cure of the patient and not on total family needs. Another example of this focus on the individual rather than on the helping system is that eligibility for means-tested benefits, such as Medicaid or Supplemental Security Income, is determined according to the dependent person's financial need, not that of the informal helping system, even though families are expected to deplete their own resources before turning to the government for assistance. Such restrictive definitions of eligibility serve to exclude as many persons as possible and to limit benefits to the minimum required for survival outside an institution, thereby "saving" public costs.

The assumption that disabled individuals with family members as a safety net require fewer services than those without family has penalized families for providing care (Abel, 1987; Lurie, Robinson, & Barbaccia, 1984; Osterbusch et al., 1987). For example, although later repealed, the 1989 catastrophic care legislation stipulated that older people with family caregivers would qualify for fewer hours of respite or homemaker services than those without such family supports. When funds are limited, agencies tend to give priority to providing services to older persons without relatives. Under the Medicaid waiver program, personal care services for the elderly are reimbursable in some states, but not if they are provided by a relative. In other states, a child or grandchild may be reimbursed for care, but not an "able and available" spouse (Estes, Swan, & Associates, 1993). In sum, across all three chronically disabled populations, the presumption that family members, typically women, are both willing and able to care for disabled relatives is, in part, a function of the narrow policy focus on the individual dependent person rather than on the total informal helping system (Abel, 1987).

This focus on the chronically disabled individual has been espoused by policy makers who are concerned with cost containment and who believe that if more services were available, families would abdicate their responsibilities, "come out of the woodwork," and overuse services (Greene, 1983). These fears of substitution and the "woodwork effect" are incongruent with the following facts: (a) most families do not use services and are often reluctant to ask for help, perhaps presuming the disapproval of professionals and others about their need for assistance; (b) when they do so, often at the end of a long process of trying other alternatives, they tend to be selective and modest in their requests for aid, asking primarily for a supplement to and respite from what they continually provide; and (c) as a result, both families and care receivers often "make do," managing their daily lives with important needs unmet. For example, with regard to the care of the disabled elderly, a process of supplementation tends to occur, whereby formal support buttresses the informal network by sharing routine care tasks (Edelman, 1986; Noelker & Bass, 1994). As another example of "making do," individuals with the highest level of need among those with chronic mental illness receive the fewest services (Hollingsworth, 1994). Yet early intervention with both families and individuals with chronic disabilities is likely to prevent the need for more expensive services at the point of a crisis precipitated by the carer's exhaustion; and those who use formal services tend to be those requiring higher levels of family care (Abel, 1987; Bass & Noelker, 1985; Leutz et al., 1992; Montgomery & Borgatta, 1989). When periodic substitution does occur, as in the case of respite care, the effects may be desirable for both the caregiver and care receiver by forestalling caregiver stress and burnout (Hendricks & Rosenthal, 1993b; Noelker & Bass, 1994). Policy makers' fears about overutilization of formal services overlook the fact that paid services frequently complement informal care and need not be qualitatively different. Home care workers, for example, often develop personal ties with their clients (Abel, 1987; Litwak, 1985; Litwak, Jessop, & Moulton, 1994; Walker, 1991).

The traditional focus on the dependent individual sets up false dichotomies between the care receiver and the family, and between the public and private spheres. This polarity is perpetuated by the assumption that if more formal services were provided, informal care would cease or be sharply reduced. When family caregiving is presumed to be primarily a private duty, policies have tended to frame artificially formal services as antithetical to informal supports and to disregard that services often strengthen family's care (Hooyman, 1990). Such dichotomies also minimize the fact that caregiving of disabled individuals occurs across the life course, with interconnections existing among different chronically disabled populations. Interdependency and the need for support are nearly universal within families, the majority of whom face responsibilities of care for dependents at some point in their lives. The need for long-term care across the life span can unite generations. Yet policymakers, influenced by the individual and group-based nature of the pluralistic policy-making process, typically portray long-term care as primarily an aging issue and a basis for intergenerational competition, and overlook the long-term care needs of persons with developmental disabilities and chronic mental illness. This traditional model contrasts with attempts to eliminate artificial boundaries that characterize a feminist approach.

Ideology of Community Care

The ideology of community care is closely related to the presumption that the chronically disabled person is the unit of service. Long-term care in the community by familial providers who keep the individual as independent as possible in his or her own home is assumed to be preferable to institutionalization. Uncompensated care is viewed as more kind, sensitive, attuned to individual needs, and compatible with traditional values than that provided by paid care providers (Briar & Ryan, 1986). Across all three dependent populations an ideology of community care combined with concerns about cost-effectiveness have supported deinstitutionalization.

The rhetoric of community care has moved from an emphasis on deinstitutionalization in the 1960s to strategies for community involvement in the 1970s; in the 1980s and 1990s, care by the community has been conceptualized as a less expensive substitute for government involvement (Pascall, 1988). Currently, the ideology of community care legitimates minimal public activity in the private sphere of the family. Accordingly, the burden of care has been shifted from the state to the community, creating the illusion of cost-effective community care. The reality is that "care by the community" is family care because few publicly funded community-based alternatives to institutionalization have been developed, and a network of community services in support of caring work within the private world of the home does not exist (Gordon & Donald, 1993; Neysmith, 1991; Pascall, 1988). These shifts in the past decade from hospital to community care have occurred in the context of decline in overall funding so that adequate community-based support services have not been available (Hollingsworth, 1994). For example, as responsibility for mental health services has been shifted to below the state level, states have tended to reduce their expenditures even further. In addition, enhanced civil rights for adults with mental illness mean that they are not mandated to use the limited community services that do exist (Biegel et al., 1994). The concept of the "least restrictive environment" for adults with mental illness often translates into the family home because of the lack of adequate community-based alternatives such as halfway houses, therapeutic residential centers, day hospitals, and outpatient services (Abel & Nelson, 1990; Biegel, Song, & Chakravarthy, 1994; Hollingsworth, 1994; Kane, 1994; Neysmith, 1991). The so-called cost-effectiveness of community care thus depends on the presence of an informal care system—usually uncompensated women. When formal interventions in informal networks have been made, they have frequently been justified as preventing caregiver burnout in order to minimize more costly institutionalization (Lewis & Meredith, 1988). Attempts to reduce governmental costs have been largely unsuccessful, however, and in some instances, the utilization of formal, community-based support has been found to increase the likelihood of institutionalization (Callahan, 1989; Fischer & Eustis, 1994; Newman, Stuyk, Wright, & Rice, 1990).

As currently constructed, community care has removed the power of choice from the care receiver and the caregiver, imposing dependency on both of them. In fact, Dalley (1988) maintains that the presumed distinction between "care in" and "care by" the community is meaningless when care by the community—through the provision of public or quasi-public services—is so limited and the physical, emotional, or financial costs for family caregivers are so great. Community care thus becomes essentially a passive, not a proactive entitlement policy in which comprehensive benefits translate the ideology into a continuum of services of care by the community (Qureshi & Walker, 1989). Similarly, Walker (1982) maintains that effective care *by* the community depends, to some extent, on effective care *for* the community, in which public policies strengthen the overall social and economic context, including income and educational resources, within which both formal and informal services provide care (Walker, 1982). The concept of care for the community as a whole—a concept antithetical to residual, individualistic policies—is central to a feminist model of social care.

The Medical Model of Dependency and the Medicalization of Care

We described in Chapter 4 the extent to which governmental funding mechanisms primarily support institutional care. In addition to this institutional bias, the medical model of dependency and the resulting biomedicalization of services underlie the lack of a well-funded and comprehensive system of community-based services (Binney, Estes, & Ingman, 1990). *Medicalization* designates the process by which services are "increasingly brought under the domain and rationality of biomedicine, and elements of the community delivery system are increasingly drawn toward the provision of medically related, medically supportive, and/or medically oriented services" (Binney et al., 1990, p. 762). Long-term care services should be oriented toward meeting custodial care, but instead, they have been shaped by a biomedical model that focuses on high-tech care for acute care needs and preserves the physician as gatekeeper for services, including nonmedical services.

The biomedical model of health and illness, which views ill health as disease-centered, individual, and responsive to medical-technical intervention, has tended to promote the negative aspects of institutional care for the chronically dependent. Medical definitions of dependency have thus produced institutional solutions built around community or psychiatric hospitals or nursing homes, even though the majority of individuals with chronic disabilities are living in the community and prefer to remain there. The domination of medical ideology in nursing homes means that medical tasks, such as checking vital signs, have been emphasized over personal care, such as soothing the dependent person's fears at night. Accounting schemes have been developed based on these tasks; nursing care has been rendered routine and bureaucratic; and illness, specifically mental illness, has been presumed (Diamond, 1990).

The biomedicalization of care—particularly the development of high-tech services—combined with cost-containment measures, such as the implementation of prospective payment systems, have created a paradox, especially for caregivers of the elderly. This paradox is that community-based high-tech services in the home, such as intravenous therapy and ventilation therapy, are increasingly required to respond to the needs of the medically ill who are being discharged earlier from hospitals, yet funds for home care have simultaneously been cut, and eligibility for services made more restrictive. At the same time that funding under the Older Americans Act and the Social Services Block Grant for nonmedical care has decreased, the Health Care Financing Administration has more strictly defined medical necessity, thereby increasing the number of denials for Medicare-financed home health care. As a result, more elderly and their families either have to pay privately for home health care, or do without (Estes et al., 1993). This poses an even greater burden for the caregivers of chronically ill elderly persons who have not been recently hospitalized and thus cannot use the already limited Medicare-reimbursed supports (Binney et al., 1990; Estes et al., 1993).

In summary, the biomedicalization of care, by focusing on individual medical solutions and in instances of the chronically mentally ill, blaming the family for the illness, has limited the choices available both to chronically disabled adults and their family caregivers. This process is most apparent with regard to expensive, high-tech efforts to extend the life expectancy of the chronically disabled elderly, although it occurs for other dependent populations as well. When medical model regimes for cure have been imposed on the lives of chronically ill patients, even though limited outpatient social services may be all that is required for their care, both the disabled person and their families lose the power of choice about the type and extent of care. In contrast, a feminist model of care recognizes the necessity of ongoing, low-tech, but often "high-touch" care.

Professionalization of Care

Medical definitions of dependency are interconnected with the central role of professionals in shaping and delivering services for individuals with disabilities. Professional service providers, in their claims to specialized knowledge and skills, have contributed to the medicalization of long-term care services, in which expensive high-tech care is more likely to be reimbursed by insurance schemes than is custodial care in the community, even though the latter is most often preferred by consumers and their families (Hollingsworth, 1994; Neysmith, 1991). In addition, the more prestigious professions—especially that of physician—are most successful in ensuring that the services they provide are defined as essential and given priority in funding decisions. This has resulted in a system of public funding that preserves a hierarchy in which the physician's role is central to approving or withholding benefits for skilled care. Accordingly, even federally reimbursed social services, as under Medicare, must be medically oriented toward the patient's acute physical condition, not toward their daily nonmedical needs for assistance with personal care, housing, transportation, counseling, or social support.

In the field of chronic mental illness, this process of professionalization has resulted in "guild innovationism" whereby innovations in care are justified under the myth that more and better clinical programs will eventually solve mental health problems. As a result, the professionals end up responding as much to the interests of their "guild" as to the interests of the patient. Accordingly, services are encouraged that are not necessarily effective, and resources are funneled away from nonclinical services that might be more helpful in addressing the chronically mentally ill's real need for housing and income (Lewis, Shadish, & Lurigio, 1989). Inherent in this process, the person with mental illness is defined as the client to be treated, and family caregivers are peripheral. For example, in the past, most treatment programs did not allow families to have access to the mental health system unless they themselves were viewed as clients. This lack of support to the family reinforced the often antagonistic relationships between families and the mental health system (Kelly & Kropf, 1995).

By asserting their legitimate authority to make decisions about the dependent person's care and by distancing themselves both from the people needing care and from their family caregivers, professionals may perpetuate the care receiver's powerlessness. Estes et al. (1993) point to the contradiction that professionals are central to advocating for and planning the support services for the chronically disabled to live independently in the community, yet their decision-making power, inherent in their professionalization, can actually contribute to increased dependency. Similarly, professionals who have developed family support interventions by establishing a distinction between expert and nonexpert may inadvertently undermine family caregiver's confidence and ability to provide daily care (Abel, 1987).

Privatization of Care

Another assumption underlying current policies and funding is that of privatization—the operation of home health care agencies, nursing homes, and hospitals as private business enterprises. As noted in Chapter 4, although the number of home health agencies and volume of visits and services provided increased in the past decade, most of the growth has occurred in for-profit chains that are oriented toward meeting acute-care needs, not toward addressing a continuum of care for chronically ill persons. This growth has occurred in response to the 1980 and 1981 Omnibus Budget Reconciliation Acts, which eliminated the requirement for state licensure as a basis for reimbursing proprietary agencies. These regulatory changes served to stimulate competition, deregulation, and the private provision and contracting out of services to proprietary agencies. The longer-term effect is that the government has begun subsidizing for-profit enterprises in state-contracted and -financed services (Estes et al., 1993). The consequent decline in the proportion of home care provided by public and nonprofit agencies has resulted in the devaluation and delegitimation of such agencies. Consistent with the medicalization of care, the state-financed services that have been reduced are the social and supportive services required for nonmedical needs, such as chore, transportation, and counseling, which are less attractive as business investments; such services are less profitable because of their labor intensity, lower technological content, and general unpredictability (Estes, 1991b). As another example, care of persons with chronic mental illness is increasingly provided by quasi-public agencies (i.e. , private sector agencies carrying out public functions with public funding). Private mental health clinics, sheltered workshops, private nursing homes, and private board-and-care homes are examples of privatization of mental health services (Shaddish, Lurigio, & Lewis, 1989). But these private mental health providers fail to treat individuals with the most severe mental illness at the same time that public funding for persons with such persistent mental illness is decreasing (Hollingsworth, 1994).

Privatization has been associated with agencies emphasizing the criteria of price competition, quick turnover of clientele, maximizing profits by "unbundling" service packages and selling single elements, eliminating unprofitable services regardless of need, and attracting private-pay patients—all emphases consistent with the shift toward managed care (Estes, 1994). There has been a trend toward larger bureaucracies due to extensive organizational restructuring, mergers, and increased management and control strategies oriented toward greater efficiency. An inherent tension exists between caregiving and these trends: the labor-intensive, time-consuming nature of caregiving makes it very expensive so that most forms of care cannot turn a profit or lead to quick results. Long-term care for those with chronic disabilities is, by its very nature, expensive, with most of the costs being absorbed by women in terms of their poorer health and economic status in old age.

Privatization has also served to reduce the services available to lower-income individuals traditionally served by public agencies, most of whom are women and minorities, often perceived as the most difficult and least profitable clients. When government restricts public expenditures on behalf of such individuals, gender and racial inequities are created and sustained (Estes, 1991a). This reflects a shift away from government commitment to a welfare system of collective provision, financing, and regulation of services, to a private system based on the efficient servicing of the least costly client (Bergthold, Estes, Villanueva, 1990).

The effects of privatization on quality of care are unclear. When nursing homes and home health agencies are dedicated to maximizing profit, however, there are built-in pressures to (a) sacrifice their workers' needs for a positive work environment, (b) reduce staff-to-patient ratios, and (c) emphasize easily quantified medical tasks that can be reimbursed but may be counter to supportive personal care (Abel & Nelson, 1990). In order to remain competitive, such agencies are unlikely to raise the salaries and fringe benefits of their workers. This results in high turnover among their staff, which allows the agency to replace higher-paid workers with new lower-paid staff. Such discontinuity undoubtedly reduces the quality of care, negatively affecting women as both care providers and care receivers (Leutz et al., 1992).

Informalization of Care

Privatization's underlying assumption that caring is a private duty, not a societal responsibility, is also reflected in the value placed on informal care. This shift of labor from persons working within the paid labor force to those working outside it, both in voluntary associations and the family, is at the core of our feminist critique. Services of hospitals and community agencies have been transferred out of the formal delivery system into the informal provision arenas of home and community. Care that was once supplied by paid professional providers has shifted to unpaid lay provid-ers, typically women (Binney, Estes, & Humphers, 1989). Government encouragement of the use of volunteers and "natural" helping networks translates into more women providing more care across the life span. The motivation for such a transfer appears to be financial rather than a commitment to building alternative service models (Brody, 1985; Neysmith,

1991). Inherent in this shift is the expectation that both families and lower-skilled, lower-paid workers will perform high-tech tasks previously assumed by higher-skilled, better-paid workers. This has created a process of "deskilling" of tasks (Estes et al., 1993). As a result, both family members and lower-paid workers must perform tasks that require greater skill and must do so without adequate training, supervision, compensation, or back-up services.

The rationale for this shift includes cost containment and prevention of more expensive institutionalization combined with the societal value that care by the informal sector is beneficial for the adult who is disabled. Yet reliance on the informal sector for care appears to be less costly than the public expense of institutional care only because the private costs to family caregivers are not considered (Finch & Groves, 1983; Osterbusch et al., 1987). What is significant from a feminist perspective is that informalization has transferred a large portion of the long-term care provision in this country from paid service providers to unpaid and underpaid women, despite the fact that their caring role is central to the economic stability of the current arrangement of public and private long-term care services. Both underpaid, lower-skilled women in the workplace and unpaid women in the home are economically exploited and penalized by inadequate income, health insurance, and retirement benefits (Estes, 1991a; Estes et al., 1993).

Ideology of Familism

The ideology of familism—the idealization of what a family should embody—also underlies the growing value placed on informalization of care. Revitalizing and strengthening the family and other informal networks became an important economic and political objective in the 1980s. Policies that deliberately shift care to the informal sector are associated with the cult of domesticity described in Chapter 5; by assuming the centrality of women's role in the home, they are based on traditional and outdated models of the family (Hendricks & Hatch, 1993; Osterbusch et al., 1987). Such policies fail to recognize the interconnection between the structural economic conditions of women's lives and a set of social expectations that devalues the care they provide (Osterbusch et al., 1987). The ideology of familism tends to affect most negatively low-income women and women of color, who have been found to use fewer formal support services than higher-income white women. Lower service use means that the responsibility for informal care is disproportionately shouldered by low-income women and women of color who fill the gaps in the long-term care system, whether as unpaid family members or as underpaid workers in home care agencies, nursing homes, or hospitals (Binstock, 1990; Leutz et al., 1992). Women represent over 90% of the paid attendants for the elderly, both in the home and nursing home, and such attendants are disproportionately women of color and of low socioeconomic status (Minkler & Estes, 1991).

THE INSTITUTIONAL BIAS OF FUNDING

Central to a feminist critique is the concept that the personal is political: in this instance, women's private lives in the home are profoundly affected by public policies that finance institutional care rather than home care, implicitly assuming that women will fill the gaps within the home. There is a conflict between the ideology that values noninstitutional care and the reality of public funding mechanisms that provide limited dollars for community care. Under a residual model, individuals are first responsible for the costs of long-term care, until their assets and income are nearly exhausted, at which point the welfare system—through Medicaid—takes over, primarily for nursing home residents. When disabled persons' needs for care exceed the capacities of their informal caregivers, all but the poorest are expected to pay out-of-pocket for formal home care. Families face these dilemmas because most federal funding through Medicare and Medicaid supports institutional care in hospitals and nursing homes.

Medicaid

As we have described in Chapter 4, Medicaid is the primary public source for funding nursing home care for all three focus populations, with nursing home costs accounting for about 45% of the total Medicaid expenditures in contrast to 2% for community-based home health services (Leutz et al., 1992). Although many state Medicaid programs have extended coverage beyond skilled nursing care to intermediate care, those individuals requiring only custodial in-home care remain excluded from Medicaid benefits. Most states still require Medicaid home care to be "skilled." The bias toward skilled care and institutionalization is strengthened by Medicaid's eligibility limits, which are more restrictive for home care than for institutional care. In other words, it is more difficult to spend one's income down to the eligibility ceiling when paying for less expensive home care than when one is institutionalized. As a result of its stringent eligibility criteria and its focus on institutionalization, Medicaid has been described as a policy that promotes both impoverishment and dependency (Wolfe, 1993).

Another example of the institutional bias of public funding mechanisms is the current reimbursement criteria of Medicaid services, which encourage institutional or out-of-home placement for persons with developmental disabilities. Many families who need help with support services or equipment are ineligible for Medicaid because their income level is too high, even though they may be unable to afford the needed services and equipment on their own. But when their developmentally disabled relative is placed outside the home, the family's income is no longer taken into account and Medicaid-reimbursed services become available (Wright & King, 1991). This funding bias toward institutionalization sharply conflicts with the current ideology of community care and with public expectations for families to care for relatives with developmental disabilities. With regard to the care of individuals with chronic mental illness, 80% of the funding comes from the state level. The federal government provides about 15% of the total funding—8% through Medicaid. Although this funding pattern has the potential of financing more home care and community-based options, approximately 62% of funds contributed by state mental health authorities is expended on inpatient care, primarily through state mental hospitals. Despite modest shifts toward community-based care, an overall decrease in government dollars available for persons with chronic mental illness has not resulted in an increase in actual dollars for home care (Hollingsworth, 1994).

Medicaid also creates inequities that negatively affect low-income women who are both the probable recipients of Medicaid support and the caregivers for Medicaid recipients. One way such inequities are created is the discretion of states to determine eligibility, service access and utilization, and reimbursement of providers; this results in wide variations in long-term care expenditures among states. With cuts in federal funds allocated to states since the passage of the Omnibus Budget Reconciliation Act in 1981, states have reduced Medicaid benefits, eligibility, and use, and have increased the required copayments. Because women are more likely than men to have low income, they have been disproportionately hurt by such discretionary Medicaid reductions.

Because only 25% of noninstitutional care is publicly subsidized, most adults with chronic disabilities and their families either pay privately for home care or go without these services. Lack of access to home care is even greater for the 40% of low-income elders who fall just above the eligibility line for Medicaid but who are nonetheless low-income (Leutz et al., 1992). A higher proportion of family caregivers than of the general population have incomes below the poverty line; this may be a function of the higher rates of poor health among low-income and minority elderly, so that those who do survive to old age need the family members' assistance (Abel, 1987). Not surprisingly, those from higher incomes are more likely to be able to purchase privately funded services, and privately paying clients receive more hours of home health care than do those who rely on public funds (Kane, 1989b; Leutz et al., 1992). For example, elders with incomes 300% above the poverty line are nearly 2.5 times more likely to use community services than elders at or below the poverty line (Coughlin, McBride, Perozek, & Liu, 1990). A variety of factors underlie why higher-income elderly use more services than their lower-income peers: educational differences, familiarity with negotiating bureaucratic systems, and access, to name a few. Significant from our feminist perspective is the long-term gender-based outcome of this differential pattern of service use and its negative effects on older women, who comprise over 70% of the elderly poor (Arendell & Estes, 1991).

The affluent are also more likely to rely disproportionately for personal care services on home care aides, companions, and attendants who are not affiliated with established organizations and whom they are able to recruit and pay independently. Because women are more likely to be low-income than men, they are less able to purchase private long-term care home services. A major consequence of the lower rates of formal service use among poor elderly is that informal care responsibilities continue to be disproportionately shouldered by unpaid women, especially by women of color. Not surprisingly, the rates of use of community-based services are lowest among minority elderly. Elders of color face barriers common to all elderly: unavailability of services, stringent eligibility requirements, inadequate transportation, lack of information on specific programs, and complex paperwork. But they also encounter additional obstacles: cultural insensitivity of service providers, discriminatory attitudes and practices, and lack of bilingual or bicultural staff (Leutz et al., 1992).

A more subtle inequity may also result from class differences in service use. Because proprietary agencies that serve private-pay clients increase their business by relieving families of care responsibilities, they tend to encourage relatives to abdicate burdensome tasks. In contrast, publicly funded programs operate under strict spending caps. The more that relatives of clients dependent on Medicaid relinquish their care responsibilities, the more public agencies risk exceeding their funding limits. Hence, publicly funded agencies with limited budgets are unlikely to urge families to reduce their level of care. Instead, they tend to encourage current caregivers to continue their work and attempt to locate relatives who have not been providing care (Abel & Nelson, 1990). Low-income women are therefore more likely than their higher-income counterparts to encounter providers who automatically expect them to provide care and who fail to present them with other viable options (Lurie, 1987; Polansky, 1985).

Although Medicaid does cover nursing home care, the growth of proprietary nursing homes has meant that profit-making considerations tend to govern the admission criteria of many of them. This can put both female caregivers and recipients of care at a disadvantage in locating institutional care. Because the Medicaid rate of reimbursement is substantially below the private-pay rate, proprietary nursing homes usually limit the number of Medicaid beds; thus, publicly funded patients are often relegated to institutions with the poorest quality of care (Rivlin & Wiener, 1988). Publicly funded patients who are very disabled and who require heavy care may face the most difficulty locating nursing home care, creating the paradox that Medicaid recipients with the greatest need for skilled nursing home care are the least likely to receive it.

Medicare

Whereas Medicaid most directly affects low-income women and women of color, regardless of age or type of chronic disability, Medicare affects primarily the elderly and their family caregivers. The major structural limitation of Medicare is its focus on acute care of the elderly, and on younger disabled persons who make up less than 10% of Medicare enrollees. As a result, Medicare reimburses only skilled posthospital home health care of 100 days or less, which has been certified by a physician as necessary to rehabilitation from acute illness. Consistent with the medicalization of care, many community agencies that formerly relied on Title XX funds have sought to recoup their losses under the Block Grant program by reorienting their programs toward the higher-tech medical services reimbursed by Medicare. Because home care agencies are less likely to accept any patients other than those requiring such high-tech, skilled care, the services most likely to be eliminated or reduced are those that could increase the disabled person's self-sufficiency and supplement the work of family caregivers (Abel, 1987; Wolfe, 1993).

Although less than 3% of Medicare expenditures go to home health care (Binstock, 1990), the implementation of Diagnostic Related Groups in 1983 increased the demand for such care and the consequent growth of for-profit home health agencies. The goal of DRGs is to make it most profitable for hospitals to provide services efficiently—that is, at the lowest possible cost—while protecting the quality of service through expanded peer review. A result of this policy has been a drop in hospital length of stay and an increase in the number of early discharges for older patients to a community-service delivery system constrained by federal budget cuts and increasingly stringent Medicare and Medicaid reimbursement policies. Estes and Binney (1988) refer to the "dumping" of elders into the community through shorter hospital stays and from home health agencies—alone or with families—because they cannot pay for their services until another diagnosis and hospital admission is possible (p. 70).

Cost-containment policies combined with technological advances in care have meant that unpaid and underpaid female providers of community-based long-term care are increasingly relied on to assist elderly individuals who leave the hospital "sicker and quicker" (Fischer & Eustis, 1994, p. 289). Ironically, the transfer of responsibility from the hospital to the home through DRGs has not resulted in significant overall Medicare cost savings, but rather has increased federal oversight and regulatory control through hospital rate setting and the regulation of physician behavior. Other Medicare costs have also grown as medical procedures have been shifted to ambulatory settings and doctors' offices, which are not restricted by the prospective payment system. At the same time, beneficiary cost-sharing has risen sharply. Such copayments are disproportionately borne by low- and lower-middle-income elders—many of whom are women and minorities—who have poorer health status and more illness than their middle- and upper-income peers. As an indicator of class-based disparities, the poor and near-poor spend more than 25% of their income on out-of-pocket health costs, compared to only 2.9% for high-income elders (Estes, 1991b). Thus, the costs of care have increased for both formal service providers and family caregivers (Estes et al., 1993).

A fundamental reason that health care costs have continued to rise is that the prospective payment system has not altered Medicare's basic approach nor the structural arrangements that depend on fee-for-service financing, nor did DRGs reduce the incentives for applying costly technologically oriented care (Estes, 1991b). In addition, there is growing recognition that community and home care service a population different from nursing homes; therefore, care in the community is not necessarily an effective way to reduce nursing home expenditures (Raffel & Raffel, 1987). The overall effect may be to increase costs, if another individual, who otherwise might not have been served, fills the nursing home bed vacated by the community-based care recipient.

Even in non-Medicare or Medicaid-funded services—such as Social Health Maintenance (SHMO) demonstration sites, where an established package of services is provided at a single capitated rate—gender inequities persist. Karon (1991) found that following the initial month of receiving community-based services, elders whose primary caregivers were female experienced a decrease in service authorizations over time, whereas those with male caregivers were nearly 2 times as likely to have service authorizations increased. Male caregivers received more services for assistance with intimate activities of daily living, whereas female caregivers were most likely to get services when caring conflicted with employment responsibilities. Because women are less likely to be employed than men, many women participants in such SHMOs would not have equitable access to services.

In summary, most long-term care policies have not had the family caregivers' welfare as a goal; indeed, some policy makers still argue that families should assume even more responsibility as a way to reduce long-term health care costs. The institutional bias of funding mechanisms, combined with the underlying values of community care, cost-effectiveness, privatization, and informalization of care, have perpetuated a two-tier system of health and mental health care, characterized by gender, race, and class inequities in service access and use. With changes in public funding and the structure of health and mental-health care organizations, there has been an increase in fragmentation of service delivery, in providers targeting private-pay clients, and in services that are profitable or can be reimbursed by state or private insurance (Estes, 1991b). The recent development of family support services as a long-term care model represents a modest shift away from this focus on acute care and on the person with chronic disabilities as the unit of service. However, such services are limited in their scope and effect because of inadequate funding and the underlying goal of preserving the family's care capabilities rather than enhancing the family's well-being.

Family Support Services

In the past decade, an increasing number of programs have been initiated at the state level that aim to support families in their caring roles. The definition of *family support services* varies widely among states and by type of chronic disability, but generally includes case management, respite care, education and training for caregivers, home adaptations, special equipment, and transportation. Other services may include information and referral, counseling, peer support groups, homemaker services, attendant care, chore services, and in-home nursing services. We provide a brief feminist critique of three common family support services—education and training, support groups, and respite—and then discuss how they can perpetuate the gender-based expectation of women as natural carers.

Currently, the majority of states provide at least some services or other resources to families who care for a relative who is developmentally disabled, chronically mentally ill, or frail. Our earlier descriptions of funding sources noted that family support services are only a small percentage of the state and federal budgets for services to adults with chronic disabilities. For example, they represent only 1.5% of the public funds allocated for persons with developmental disabilities (Knoll, Covert, O'Connor, Agosta, & Blaney, 1990). For persons with developmental disabilities, support has largely been confined to respite services, limited to fewer than 100 families, in each of 15 states studied (Bradley, Knoll, & Agosta, 1992). Research on mental health services consistently refers to discrepancies between the needs of families and the support services they receive (Bernheim & Lehman, 1985; Intagliata et al., 1986; Zirul et al., 1989). In general, most family support programs offer limited services to relatively few families, restrict the types of services available, fail to use existing community networks optimally, and do not necessarily empower family members (Biegel et al., 1994; Wright & King, 1991).

In critiquing family support programs, it is important to clarify the program's goal and to explore the extent to which it advances a residual or social welfare approach to service delivery and, accordingly, moves toward gender justice. Is the objective only to provide care that the family will not provide? To prevent or delay institutionalization by minimizing caregiver stress and burnout? To reduce costs by maintaining the person with disabilities within the family rather than placement in more expensive institutional care? To provide relief from performance of physical care tasks so that the family can concentrate on emotional support? Is the program oriented toward expecting the family to adapt to the stress of care, or toward developing social policies that achieve a more equitable balance between informal and formal care by men and women? Consistent with a feminist goal of gender justice, do women and people of color, both as caregivers and recipients of care, have equitable access to family support services?

In most instances, the goal of family support programs has been cost-effectiveness through delaying or preventing institutionalization or reinstitutionalization. Home care for persons with developmental disabilities has been found to be generally less expensive than institutional care; it was developed primarily as placement support for individuals being removed from institutions rather than as assistance to those already living at home (Castellani, 1986). As an example of the focus on cost containment, the 1988 average per diem rate at an institution for people with developmental disabilities was $153. 54, or $56,042 per year; on average, Medicaid paid 45% of this rate, with $25,219 in state funds required to support one person in an institution. In contrast, the average annual family subsidy payment was $2,567 in 1988. Although cash assistance to families must be supplemented with family support services—such as case management and other programs—in order to provide a reliable alternative to institutionalization, the total cost to the state for home care for the developmentally disabled, on an individual basis, was less than institutional care and therefore viewed as cost-effective (Bradley et al., 1992; Wright et al., 1991).

Critics of this focus on cost containment maintain that family support services only appear to be less costly than institutional care because they do not take account of the economic, health, and emotional costs to the caregivers (Finch & Groves, 1983; Osterbusch et al., 1987). One reason that such programs may fail to calculate such caregiver costs is that informal care—or the lack of it—has been defined as the problem rather than a structural definition in terms of the long-term economic repercussions for caregivers. Similarly, women's employment, which is presumed to reduce their traditional caregiving availability, is often identified as the problem to be addressed by public policy, not the oppression of women created by current policies and programs (Estes et al., 1993). Consistent with Mills's distinction of the "personal troubles of the milieu" versus the "public issues of social structure" (Mills, 1959, p. 8), family needs for support services are defined as a private trouble, not a public issue requiring a policy response. Such a definition may underlie the growing number of education and support programs intended to enhance the caregivers' daily coping capacities, but that fail to address the larger policy questions about how services are funded, structured, and delivered.

Education and training programs are growing in numbers, in part because they are relatively inexpensive and therefore viewed as a means to contain costs. As noted by Abel (1987), it is far cheaper to establish a ten-week course of lectures for caregivers than to provide them with comprehensive services of visiting nurses, home health aides, or homemakers. The earlier hospital discharge of the elderly under prospective payment systems has meant that families have required more training in the proper methods of administering medical care. This has produced a variety of skills-training programs for caregivers, but has not increased the range of publicly funded services. Consistent with the trend toward professionalization, such programs also provide new roles—and sources of income—for professionals as educators and trainers (Abel, 1987; Estes et al., 1993). But advice by presumed experts can serve to undermine caregivers' faith in their own capacities to solve problems and can threaten their decision-making autonomy (Abel, 1987).

A fundamental limitation of such educational interventions is the definition of individual cause and solution responsibility for caregiver stress—definitions that are consistent with our society's underlying values of independence and personal responsibility. Providing skills or information to enhance caring capacity define both the problem and the solution as being within individual caregivers rather than as connected to broader societal conditions (Estes et al., 1993). Evaluations of such programs have focused on whether they prolong the caring relationship, or in the case of persons with chronic mental illness, reduce relapse rates and prevent institutionalization (Biegel et al., 1994; Hugen, 1993). Such psycho-educational interventions may fail to address the underlying need for services that could enhance the caregiver's well-being. Individual and group interventions that aim to enhance carers' self-efficacy and self-esteem (Gallagher, Lovett, & Zeiss, 1988) may inadvertently imply that caregiver inadequacy is the source of caregiver burden. Such interventions presume that caregiving is stressful only if coping capabilities are insufficient to adapt to the demands of care (Estes et al., 1993). Although skills training and information-support classes may ease stress on a short-term basis, they still assume that caring is primarily the responsibility of individual family members; accordingly, they fail to develop and implement specific programs or services for family caregivers and offer no long-range, collective solutions that address underlying structural inequities (Biegel et al., 1994).

These educational approaches also attempt to impose criteria of efficiency and cost-effectiveness on processes governed by standards of quality. For example, time management training has been used to enhance caregivers' coping abilities under the presumption that increased efficiency at task performance is an antidote to the stresses of multiple demands (Clark & Rakowski, 1983). Efficiency is a misplaced standard for care based on ties of affection, however. Perfecting efficient techniques based on standardized knowledge does not necessarily promote good caring, especially because caregivers' patterns of thought and affective relationships may differ sharply from the most rational way to do things. As a dominant societal value, efficiency implies that caregivers are the cause of their own stress, and that carers can reduce their feelings of burden by better managing their time and multiple demands. Under such conditions, education and training programs may actually increase caregivers' stress by holding up unrealistic standards.

From a feminist perspective, questions of cost-effectiveness are the wrong ones to ask. Instead of asking what are the cheapest ways to keep chronically disabled people alive, we should be determining the best ways to care for them (Sommers & Shields, 1987). To focus on cost containment can overlook the need for increased public funding for services by the formal community-based sector in order to assure quality care (Estes et al., 1993).

Support groups, provided as a way to enhance caregivers' effectiveness, also tend to emphasize individual change through information and emotional support. Short-term evaluations of support groups for families of adults with mental illness have been found to enhance their caregiving abilities and to foster more collaborative relationships with mental health professionals than occurred in the past, when families were blamed for their relative's illness during therapy (Kane, 1994). However, when support groups only let the caregiver ventilate emotions and then return to the same situation, they do not offer long-range policy solutions to the structural causes of carers' stress. In fact, support groups that focus only on individual competence can promote personal adjustment to burdensome situations rather than the system changes necessary to obtain adequately funded in-home services (Abel, 1987). On the other hand, as we will discuss, when support groups adopt consciousness-raising and political organizing techniques, members can be encouraged both to explore the common structural roots of their personal problems and to mobilize to demand collective solutions.

Respite services—to provide temporary relief from care—are one of the needs most frequently identified by caregivers, although whether respite is used for extrafamilial responsibilities or as a method for managing resources may vary with the caregiver's age (Bradley et al., 1992; Caserta, Lund, Wright, & Redburn, 1987; Kropf, 1994b; Lawton, Brody, & Saperstein, 1989; Montgomery & Borgatta, 1989; Montgomery & Prothero, 1986; Salisbury & Intagliata, 1986). Respite care may be designed (a) specifically to give relief to caregivers, or (b) to meet the needs of the person with disabilities, with relief to the caregiver a by-product of service provision (Ziral et al., 1989). When respite care provides tangible relief from the daily burdens of care, such services are invaluable. However, unless caregivers can afford to privately purchase in-home or adult day care on a regular basis, their access to publicly funded respite services, particularly overnight respite, is extremely constrained (Castellani, 1992). For families of individuals with chronic mental illness, respite programs are especially limited (Hollingsworth, 1994; Ziral, Lieberman, & Rapp, 1989). Even when respite is available, the shift of responsibility for care is temporary and minimal. As noted by Abel (1987, p. 39), "the few hours of relief offered by most respite programs may be grossly inadequate," especially for employed caregivers. Respite can provide time for a weekend away, but it does not question why families—typically women—are bearing the primary ongoing responsibility for care. Instead, respite programs assume that family care is natural and do not question the inequities inherent in current caregiving arrangements (Arendell & Estes, 1991; Neysmith, 1991). This is, in part, a reflection of the fact that the need for respite is determined by an assessment of the person with chronic disabilities, not of the familial and situational characteristics that can affect caregiver burden, such as age, family structure, and limitations on access to services, including family income and geographic location (Castellani, 1986).

GENDER AND RACIAL INEQUITIES

As we have suggested, the underlying assumptions and values of current service systems, the gender-based division of paid and unpaid labor, the constrained public funding mechanisms, and the current public policy emphasis on community-based care, privatization, and family supports have all tended to disadvantage women, particularly women of color, in their economic and social choices across the life span. Although the particular constellation of care varies by phase of the life span, the societal denigration of the invisible work of caregiving results in structural economic inequality and powerlessness for most women.

The Economic Consequences Across the Life Span and for Older Women

The average woman spends nearly half her life fulfilling the socially necessary but gender-defined activities of caring for dependents. In order to provide such care, women are more likely than their male counterparts to move in and out of the labor force. As noted earlier, women average 11.5 years out of the paid labor force compared to 1.3 years for men (Older Women's League, 1989, 1990). For most women, employment interruptions generally carry severe economic costs. At least 12% of the gap between men and women's wages, for example, can be attributed to such interruptions (U. S. Bureau of the Census, 1992a). These economic costs are greatest for widowed and divorced women, and increase with age.

Although women are poorer than men at every stage of the life span as evidenced by the growing feminization of poverty, the economic costs of caring are particularly high for women in old age. After devoting her life attending to others' needs, a woman, particularly upon divorce or her husband's death, may face years of living alone on a low income, with inadequate medical care, and with her welfare resting on the presence, willingness, and ability of younger female relatives or underpaid female aides and attendants. Women are 63% of the elderly, but they account for over 73% of those living in poverty, and the poverty rate increases among women of color, with 66% of African American older women living in poverty and forming the poorest group in our society (U. S. Senate Special Committee on Aging, 1992). In addition, the incidence of chronic disease and disability is higher among poor and minority women; they form the largest proportion of the elderly who need care, but are the most likely to lack access to formal services. From a feminist perspective, the reasons for these inequities are structural—the ways in which the devaluation of caregiving work at home and in the marketplace interacts with racism to exploit women's unpaid and underpaid caregiving labor.

For many women, years spent out of the full-time paid labor force to care for others are not compensated by health care and retirement benefits for their old age, even though their caregiving services have been essential to both the family and the economy. In fact, Estes et al. (1993) maintain that "when women are not reimbursed for their caregiving work, their labor time is essentially being donated, often at the expense of paid employment" (pp. 165-166). Interrupted work histories mean that years of lower or no earnings reduce a woman's Social Security benefit, with women's average Social Security benefits comprising only about 75% of a man's. Even though older women form 60% of Social Security beneficiaries, they are 3 times more likely than their male peers to receive only the minimum benefits. It is not surprising that nearly 66% of older female beneficiaries receive benefits that place them below the poverty line (American Association of Retired Persons, 1988b).

As we have noted earlier, discontinuities in employment created by caregiving responsibilities also mean that women are less likely to have an employment history that provides them with vested pension benefits, because the pension system is based on traditional male work patterns of long-term stability that are not interrupted by family care responsibilities. Accordingly, over 40% of men are covered by private pensions compared with less than 20% of women who have been employed. Those women who do have pensions receive approximately 50% of the benefit income of men because of salary differentials during their working years (Older Women's League, 1990). With lower retirement incomes and less access to private insurance, poor older women are at a significant disadvantage to purchase long-term care services beyond those few provided by public programs.

Corporate policies have contributed to the perpetuation of the gender-structured wage and pension systems. Because of interrupted work history, when women have been employed, they are more likely to be concentrated in part-time, short-term, or irregular jobs—in low-status or secondary service, clerical, or retail sales—that are poorly paid and provide few benefits (Arendell & Estes, 1991). Such jobs often do not provide the flexibility or the income to cushion the effects of caregiving demands, such as time to drive an older parent to a doctor's visit or funds to pay for counseling for an adult child with chronic mental illness. As a result, women are more likely than men to reduce their hours or quit their frequently poorly compensated jobs in order to provide care. They do so because of gender-based pay and promotional inequities and because most men simply do not perceive caregiving as their work, not because of psychological or socialization differences (Abel, 1987; Waerness, 1984). In our feminist analysis, the existence of the dual-labor market highlights the structural and ideological bases of different economic opportunities and barriers for women and men (Arendell & Estes, 1991).

Women as Underpaid Caregivers

The role of women as unpaid carers in the home cannot be separated from that of underpaid caregivers in nursing homes, psychiatric hospitals, institutions for adults with developmental disabilities, and others' homes—all places where low-income women are frequently cared for by other low-income women. As noted throughout, when women move into the labor market, they frequently face the double jeopardy of being responsible for caring both at home and at work (Marshall, Barnett, Baruch, & Pleck, 1990). When social policy promotes unpaid care in the family and low-paid care in the public sector, these arrangements constitute "exploitation of one kind of dependency to deal with another" (Pascall, 1988, p. 29).

Of particular relevance to our feminist critique of long-term care is the predominance of women among paraprofessional home care workers—home health aides, chore workers, personal care workers, and home attendants—who provide personal care, assistance with activities of daily living, or both, to disabled adults living in private residences (Leutz et al., 1992). Comprising the least skilled and the most marginally employed workers in the health care industry, 90% to 95% are female, their average age is 45 years, 30% are women of color, and their annual income is less than $9,000—barely above the poverty line for a family of two in 1990. In fact, the average hourly wage of home care workers is about $5.00, usually without fringe benefits, which places them at the bottom of all wage groupings, close to the wage level of janitors (Cantor & Chichin, 1990; Feldman, Sapienza, & Kane, 1990). Not only are paraprofessional home care workers disadvantaged by low salaries, part-time work, and lack of fringe benefits, they also tend to be inadequately supervised and trained and have few opportunities for advancement.

Similar to unpaid family caregivers, home care workers often work in isolation from others, performing tasks that are considered "natural"; it is in part because of this "naturalness" that such tasks are of low status and poorly paid (Holt, 1986-87). Women represent over 90% of the paid attendants in nursing homes. Attendants in institutions are disproportionately women of color and of low socioeconomic class. Low status coupled with low pay and the dead-end nature of the work reinforces their devalued position (Minkler & Estes, 1991). Not surprisingly, the average annual industry-wide turnover rate for home aides is 60% (Feldman et al., 1990). Although workers in nursing homes and hospitals receive 30% to 60% higher wages than home care workers, they also lack autonomy and control over their work. The medicalization of care has adversely affected the working conditions for female aides and nursing assistants in institutions for persons with chronic disabilities. With an increasing emphasis on high-tech skilled care and accountability, hands-on care is relegated to the lowest status and most poorly paid positions (Abel & Nelson, 1990). Low-level employees are also vulnerable to cost-containment policies that entail increased workloads and regulations with accompanying paperwork. Bureaucratic rules limit lower-level workers' sense of autonomy; similar to the people for whom they care, they feel powerless and lacking control over their daily lives in these institutions. They may react to their feelings of powerlessness and devaluation by distancing themselves from their patients, becoming mechanistic in their task performance (Abel & Nelson, 1990).

Although nurse's aides are the primary providers of hands-on care, the emphasis in nursing homes is on medical tasks, such as monitoring and recording vital signs, and the onerous paperwork entailed by bureaucratic regulations, which interferes with nurse's aides forming the type of close personal relationships conducive to quality care. Nonquantifiable and therefore not reimbursable, their caring work remains invisible, unnamed, and may actually result in reprimands rather than rewards (Diamond, 1990). In his participant evaluation in nursing homes, Diamond (1993) observed that nurses aides were penalized for spending time consoling a crying and distraught resident because of the time entailed in such empathic caregiving. When faced with pressures for quantifiable results, "the demands by clients that they demonstrate the warmth and concern traditionally associated with caregiving may appear simply another oppressive feature of their jobs" (Abel & Nelson, 1990, p. 16). Given the expectations for quantifiable results combined with the personal daily strains of poverty, the turnover rate among nurse's aides in institutions is high. In addition, longtime employment is not rewarded because institutions can reduce costs by replacing higher-paid, more experienced workers with newer, cheaper ones (Leutz et al., 1992).

Women predominate as underpaid caregivers in the informal economy of unaffiliated or privately contracted workers as well. Desiring more autonomy or flexibility, some may choose to work independently of a home health agency or institution. Others, particularly recent immigrants with limited education and English, have few options other than piecing together a number of part-time, temporary jobs dependent on individual employers. Their wages remain low because most families of adults with chronic disabilities who resort to hiring unaffiliated workers try to pay as little as possible and may do so "under the table" to avoid taxes. Typically, independent workers receive no fringe benefits nor professional supervision. Hiring unaffiliated workers creates an additional paradox—women who have the economic resources to purchase private care services confront a bind they have always faced: gaining freedom from caregiving chores at the expense of lower-income women of color. Unaffiliated workers face low, unpredictable wages, and working conditions that are subject to personal negotiation in which they have little power to bargain for paid vacations or other benefits. Lacking professional supervision or opportunities for advancement, they may be trapped in dead-end jobs.

In summary, the underpaid women who provide care to persons with chronic disabilities, whether in nursing homes, mental hospitals, other institutions, or within homes, face low salaries, uncertain part-time work, lack of fringe benefits, inadequate supervision and training, and few opportunities for advancement. Similar to unpaid family caregivers, they frequently feel alone and without social or emotional support. Their caregiving work underpins the economy, contributing to the producing sectors' overall efficiency, but remains largely invisible, isolated, misrepresented, and unrewarded by marketplace criteria. Until these conditions are improved, long- term health and mental health care will fail to be a responsive and responsible system and will continue to oppress women, particularly women of color. This is particularly the case for community-based home care, where pay and working conditions are less desirable than in institutions, even though the home is the auspice for care preferred by most chronically disabled individuals and lauded by most policymakers.

In conclusion, by critiquing the values and assumptions underlying current long-term care policies as well as the limits of public funding, we have highlighted their negative repercussions for women. In Chapters 11 through 14, we extend our feminist critique by proposing a feminist model of social care oriented toward gender justice. Fundamental to this model is the societal recognition of the importance of caring work, and the necessity of insuring choices for both the caregiver and the care receiver, components that are sorely lacking under our current long-term care policies. We shift now from the public sector to critiquing private workplace policies that affect the nature and extent of long-term care provided by families as well as the costs of such caring roles for women.

10

A Feminist Critique
of Family-Related
Benefits in the Workplace

Throughout the past decade, families, businesses, communities, and government have been confronted by, and often felt under siege by, a growing number of difficult social and economic problems such as substance abuse, violence, unemployment and underemployment, poverty, inadequate public education, international economic competition, and shrinking public dollars. At the same time, debate has intensified regarding the respective roles of government and business in addressing the economic and social well-being of American families (Starr, 1989). Ushering in the 1980s was newly elected President Reagan's call for reduced government involvement in domestic affairs, the adoption of supply-side economics, and a return to traditional American values. This national mood led to the passage of the Economic Recovery Tax Act and Omnibus Budget and Reconciliation Act of 1981, which resulted in a reduction in federal taxes, shifting of more responsibility to the states, and the subsequent cutback or elimination of many domestic programs, including changes in Medicaid, the primary public funder of long-term care. Many states and localities thus found themselves confronted with new responsibilities and less federal money and also facing citizen tax revolts.

To compensate for the loss of direct government contributions to social welfare on the national level, Ronald Reagan and his successor, George Bush, called for the creation of joint public-private partnerships and stressed the role of corporate philanthropy in addressing contemporary social ills. They also urged employers to assume more responsibility for providing human services programs such as child care (Goodstein, 1994). However, business leaders, facing their own economic woes, generally fought this transfer of responsibility from the public to the private realm. As Kingston (1990, p. 450) states, "Under the impress of foreign competition, take-over frenzies, and industrial transformation, business leaders have increasingly asserted that tending to the business of business is the most socially responsible commitment." Indeed, business leaders such as the Chamber of Commerce and the National Manufacturing Association were two of the strongest opponents of the Family Medical and Leave Act (FMLA) of 1993, arguing that from a business perspective it was expensive, unfair, and anticompetitive (Starrels, 1992).

As discussed earlier, the income disparities between the rich and poor grew wider and more Americans fell out of, rather than rose into, the middle class during the 1980s (Center for Budget & Policy Priorities, 1989). For some American families, the safety net simply disappeared. How did this decline in social protection occur? For a growing number of Americans, it resulted from their loss of jobs in the ever-shrinking core labor sector and their entry into the rapidly expanding secondary or contingent workforce.

Work and family policies, whether provided by government or business, represent the major source of social protection for American families. Receipt of employee benefits is tied to the individual worker, but the protection often extends to the worker's family.

> Health care plans help soften the impact of medical expenses and perhaps, encourage workers and their dependents to seek care that might otherwise be foregone. Retirement plans allow older employees to stop work and maintain certain living standards. Similarly, disability benefits provide income to those unable to work, and survivor benefits protect against loss of earnings resulting from the death of a spouse or other relative. (Wiatrowski, 1990, p. 28)

These work-related benefits are generally tied to employment in the primary or core labor force. As we have noted, the proportion of American workers who have health insurance or pension plans provided through their jobs has declined in recent years. Given the disproportionate representation of women and persons of color in the contingent workforce, the social protection offered by employment has declined more for these groups.

Although the 1980s brought an increasing recognition on the part of both the public and private sectors of the changing nature of the American family and the U.S. labor force (i.e., more single-parent families, dual-earner households), the government and business work-family benefits instituted to date have been fairly minimal. This failure of public and corporate policy has greater negative consequences for women than men. Because care for family members still remains predominately women's responsibility, women suffer more from the inadequacies of work-family policies to support their dependent care roles (Starrels, 1992). We begin this chapter with an overview of the evolution of family-related benefits in the workplace. Then, drawing on a feminist perspective, we criticize the nature and limitations of the benefits currently offered under the rubric of being "family-responsive" or "family-friendly."

HISTORICAL PERSPECTIVES
ON FAMILY-RELATED BENEFITS

Government employment policies have both influenced and responded to changes in American families and the labor force. (For a detailed discussion of the evolution of family-related benefits, see Levitan & Gallo, 1990; and Wiatrowski, 1990.) The 1938 Fair Standards Act, for example, which set a minimum age of 16 for employment and required the pay of time and a half for hours worked in excess of 40 during any week in most fields, profoundly affected family life. The act (coupled with legislation for compulsory education) removed children from the labor force and provided adult wage-earners with more time to spend with their families. Historically, public policy has often discouraged women, especially wives and mothers, from working, often because of concern that these women would displace male breadwinners. "Many school districts did not hire wives, and fired women who married. The 'marriage penalty' in the federal income tax during the 1970s also put working couples at a disadvantage, compared with more traditional family arrangements" (Levitan & Gallo, 1990, p. 36). Yet when women were needed in the labor force, such as during World War II, the federal government instituted (temporarily) a child care program.

Prior to the 1930s, government and business extended workers few social protections. What minimal benefits were offered—a small lump-sum benefit to family survivors upon the death of an employee and short-term disability in the form of small weekly payments to an injured or ill employee—came primarily through worker-financed funds in mutual aid societies or labor unions (Wiatrowski, 1990). It was not until the harsh economic conditions of the Great Depression that the government took a greater role in compensation programs, most significantly creating the Social Security Program. When enacted in 1935, the Social Security Act included a retirement component, Old Age Insurance (OAI), which recognized that, through no fault of their own, persons often had inadequate financial resources for their final years. In 1939, Social Security benefits were expanded to include dependents with a 50% spousal benefit and a widow's benefit (survivor's insurance and now OASI).

Three sets of assumptions about aging, work, and family underlie the creation of Social Security: (a) only a small percentage of Americans would survive to old age, and those who did would collect Social Security benefits only for a short time; (b) Social Security would not be the sole source of financial support for persons in their old age, but would supplement savings, pensions, and other assets; and (c) the family, composed of a wage-earner husband and a homemaker wife in a single lifelong committed marriage, was the "unit" receiving the Social Security benefit (Gonyea, 1994a). The normative standard of referent for this policy was the male-headed nuclear household and male labor force participation patterns of continuous employment.

Employee compensation benefits increased substantially as employment grew rapidly after America's entry into World War II, and benefits continued to expand with the country's economic prosperity in the 1950s. During the war years, the War Labor Board restricted wage increases to stabilize prices. Employers turned to fringe benefits, such as time off with pay and pension plans, as a way to recruit or retain employees in lieu of wage increases (Wiatrowski, 1990). The Taft-Hartley Act of 1947 established that management must negotiate with labor unions elected to represent workers on "wages, hours and other terms and conditions of employment" and also supported the broader adoption of compensation packages.

During the 1950s, responding to growing national expenditures for health care, more employers also began providing their workers with formal health care plans through private insurance vendors such as Blue Cross and Blue Shield. These basic health care plans of the 1960s bear little resemblance to current catastrophic coverage or major medical health care plans. In 1960, slightly fewer than 50% of office workers and only 20% of plant workers had major medical coverage; by 1975 virtually all (94%) office workers and more than 75% of plant workers had catastrophic protection. The aging of the U.S. population brought the issue of pension reform to the forefront of labor issues. The Employee Retirement Security Act of 1974 established standards regarding eligibility requirements, vesting, discrimination rules, and survivor benefits as well as regulations regarding employers' disclosure regarding the soundness of pension funds. Yet reform was incremental. As noted by Wiatrowski (1990, p. 31), "The laws have concentrated in large measure on improving and guaranteeing the provisions of existing benefits, rather than mandating new benefits."

It is important to recognize that although benefit plans continued to expand throughout the 1960s and 1970s, these benefit packages were based on employers' understanding of the "typical American family." Not surprisingly, their perception was the "cultural ideal of the family," with a sole wage-earner father and a full-time homemaker mother caring for children in a lifelong marriage. Despite the growing diversity of American families, the majority of companies' employee compensation benefits remain based on this idealized notion of the family. In addition, most corporate policies viewed the family and workplace as separate spheres, failing to recognize the interaction between the two.

THE CURRENT ERA OF
FAMILY-RELATED WORKPLACE BENEFITS

During the 1970s and early 1980s, businesses began to take notice of the rapidly changing workforce characteristics, especially women's large-scale entry into the workplace and the growing number of dual-earner and single-parent households. Reports such as the Hudson's Institute's Work-force 2000, predicting a shrinking labor pool increasingly female and racially diverse, prompted companies to explore the ramifications of this demographic shift in terms of their own competitiveness (Johnston & Packer, 1987). Kanter's (1977) text, *Work and Family in the United States: A Critical Review and Agenda for Research and Policy,* challenged deeply held cultural beliefs about distinct boundaries between work and family by conceptualizing the two spheres as highly interactive.

Although in the lifestyle (not business) sections of newspapers, popular journals, and news programs, media coverage was increasingly given to the struggles employees, especially female employees, faced with trying to fulfill their family and job responsibilities. Women's difficulties in maintaining a balance between family and work were, to some extent, redefined from a private to a public concern. The popular media as well as professional journals began to debate ways in which business practices and policies shape employees' family lives, and what changes would be necessary if the workplace were to be more responsive (Gonyea & Googins, 1992). The concepts of work-family conflict and job-family strain entered our vocabulary.

The positive economic climate, corporate growth, and labor shortages of the early 1980s prompted several pioneering Fortune 500 companies to respond to these emerging social trends. A number of corporations created work-family task forces and conducted surveys or needs assessments of their employees as a means for carefully feeling their way in these "uncharted waters" (Gonyea & Googins, 1992). These firms most often defined work-family conflict narrowly as a "women's issue" and a "child care problem." Employers gathered statistics regarding the number of workers with dependent children as well as the number of employees living in single-parent and dual-earner households. Data were gathered on how workers perceived their parental responsibilities affecting their work performance, the problems encountered in securing child-care arrangements, the stability of these arrangements, and parental satisfaction with the quality and affordability of this care.

The studies consistently concluded that although the challenge of balancing work and family roles was an issue for both men and women, the "balancing act" still fell predominantly on women (Gonyea, 1993; Rodgers, 1992). Emlen and Koren (1984), in a survey of over 8,000 employees, found that 38% of employed women and 23% of employed men with children under the age of 12 reported difficulties in combining home and job responsibilities. Moreover, 47% of the mothers and 28% of the fathers cited stresses specifically related to securing child care arrangements. The data also reveal that a significant proportion of workers' absences were due to caring for a sick child or a breakdown in care arrangements. Burden and Googins (1987) found that 66% of mothers and 33% of fathers had missed work due to a child's illness. These women averaged 9.23 days' absence each year as compared to the men's 4.10 days absence yearly. Dominion Bank's survey of 152 working parents revealed that approximately 26% had missed one to five days of work in the past year, specifically due to problems or breakdowns with their child care arrangements (Stewart & Burge, 1989).

Impetus for action was also supported by the work of a variety of labor relations and women's organizations such as the Bureau of National Affairs, the Conference Board, Catalyst, and the National Organization for Women. A number of companies created work-family coordinator or work-home-life manager positions within their human resource departments, a specialty unheard of a decade earlier (Johnson & Rose, 1992). A few of the more innovative or socially responsible firms, such as Stride Rite and Campbell's Soup, began to offer on-site or near-site child care programs consistent with women's greater child care responsibilities. Most child care programs were developed on the assumption of benefiting mothers more than fathers. Corporations that ventured into the realm of developing more family-responsive policies generally shared a series of assumptions that family-oriented benefits would assist in recruiting and retaining valued employees, increase corporate loyalty and commitment, reduce absenteeism and turnover, and enhance work performance. As Gonyea and Googins (1992, p. 212) noted, "Although there was little research to buttress these assumptions, at the very least the positive publicity and goodwill generated by these early experiments made it appear this was the right thing for a company to do."

As the 1980s progressed, a growing number of companies provided child care assistance to employees, and the array of corporate work-family initiatives broadened to include such choices as resource and referral services, dependent care subsidies, sick child care, and support groups. In 1985, the landmark Travelers Insurance Company Survey awakened corporate America to the fact that, as a result of the aging of our population and women's entry into the workforce, increasing numbers of employees were also caring for older relatives (Travelers, 1985). Subsequent studies revealed that in some cases, these caregiving responsibilities were causing individuals to experience personal stress and forcing them to make workplace accommodations. Employed caregivers reported more frequent stress in their job (Barr & Warshaw, 1991), excessive fatigue and worry that interfered with job performance (Brody, Johnsen, Hoffman, & Schoonover, 1987; Petty & Friss, 1987), and use of vacation time to provide care (Scharlach & Boyd, 1989). (For a detailed review and critique of this literature, see Tennstedt & Gonyea, 1994.) Elder care programs for employees were soon proclaimed to be the "benefits of the 90s."

In the 1990s work-family conflict is no longer synonymous with child care. Nevertheless, most employers (and researchers) continue to focus only on the two ends of the family life cycle in which dependency is viewed as "normal"—employees caring for children (especially infants and preschoolers) and employees caring for elders (Gonyea, 1994b). Forgotten are employees providing "non-normative" care to young or middle-aged adults, although more individuals under age 65 require such care: approximately 20 million noninstitutionalized persons under age 65 had activity limitations due to chronic health conditions, compared to 11 million noninstitutionalized persons 65 and older (National Center for Health Statistics, 1989). Recent research underscores that workers engaged in adult care experience similar stresses and work interferences as those engaged in elder care (Freedman, Litchfield, & Warfield, 1994; Neal, Chapman, Ingersoll-Dayton, & Emlen, 1993; Scharlach & Fredriksen, 1994).

TYPES AND LIMITS OF
FAMILY-RESPONSIVE WORKPLACE INITIATIVES

Perhaps because most corporations have failed to support the integration of work and family roles, their policies have had relatively limited effect. Shellenbarger (1992) observes the following:

If the river of press releases crossing journalists' desks in the United States were to be taken at face value, the American workplace is becoming a very family-friendly place indeed. . . . [But] only a few major employers have adopted substantively new policies and programs, and an even smaller number are actually trying to change the deep-rooted American management culture that grew out of the white male work force of the 1950s. Most work-family policies primarily benefited skilled professionals. (p. 157)

In fact, corporate family-responsive initiatives have been fairly modest both in the extent of their restructuring of the workplace and in the proportion of the U.S. labor force affected.

In the analysis of family-responsive workplace initiatives, it is important to distinguish between public (government) policy and private (business) policy. (For an examination of public and private interplay in social protection, see Rein & Rainwater, 1986.) The government generally offers social protection to its citizens by either mandating or regulating the provision of a resource by the private sector (e.g., the FMLA), or by providing a resource directly to its citizens and paying (fully or partially) for its provision, or passing the costs (fully or partially) on to the private sector (e.g., Worker's Compensation). Businesses have no such mandating authority. They offer social protection through contracts that may provide either the financing for the resource, cash benefits directly to the families, or services and goods to families.

The underlying rationales for government and business workplace policies are fundamentally different. Starrels (1992) indicates the following:

Although individual firms often create policy on the basis of economic cost-benefit, governmental policy more often cites ideological or moral justifications quite apart from economic costs or benefits. . . . Another advantage of public policies addressing work-family conflict is that government may provide valuable symbolic leadership that can hasten nongovernmental adjustments to workplace policy. (p. 266)

As feminist scholars have noted, however, the federal government has not usually provided such leadership. The United States has failed to provide many of the national policies that Western European countries offer their citizens as an aid to integrating work and family commitments, such as maternity leave, child care subsidies, and part-time job options (Bailyn, 1992; Kamerman & Kahn, 1987; Raabe, 1990). Family-responsive workplace initiatives can be grouped into four general categories: employee benefits, leave policies, flexible work arrangement policies, and dependent care services. Company-based initiatives most often address employees' child care needs, but our analysis will focus on those initiatives that benefit employees caring for adults or elders with disabling conditions. From a feminist perspective, there are a number of limitations, including the extent to which women are still held responsible for most dependent care, and gender, class, and racial inequities in terms of access to such benefits.

EMPLOYEE BENEFITS

Federal Dependent Care Tax Credits

The federal dependent care tax credit represents the largest source of federal assistance to families with employment-related expenses regarding care responsibilities for children, adults with disabilities, frail elders, or a combination of these (Stone & Keigher, 1994). This provision reduces the amount of income tax, but not FICA, the worker owes by a percentage of the dependent care costs. The percentage varies relative to family income, with a maximum of 30% of expenses per dependent up to certain dollar limits. In 1991, the dollar limits were $2,400 for a single dependent and $4,800 for multiple dependents (Neal et al., 1993).

In reality, the dependent care tax credit provides minimal financial help for employed caregivers who must pay someone to provide care while they are at work. Although the credit establishes some principle of equity for the work-related expenses of caregivers based on family income, the maximum credit a wage earner can receive is far too little to make a difference in the basic affordability of paid long-term care. For example, a taxpayer with an adjusted gross income of $10,000 or less could get a credit of $720 for long-term care expenses, whereas a taxpayer with an income of $28,000 could get a maximum credit of $480. Although at first glance the tax credit offers greater benefits to families with lower incomes, these families often do not receive the benefit. Because the tax credit is not refundable, it does not benefit those families who owe no taxes or who do not itemize—disproportionately lower-income families (Osterbusch, Keigher, Miller & Linsk, 1987).

The tax credit is available only if the person is a dependent of the caregiver for tax purposes, which rules out many caregiving situations. In order to be eligible, the taxpayer must have supplied over 50% of the dependent's economic support for the taxable year, and if the taxpayer is married, the spouse must be employed, seeking employment, or a full-time student. Implicit in this federal requirement concerning the spouse (typically the wife) is that a woman "staying at home" has no excuse for not providing this care herself. At the same time, ironically, the federal government does not allow families to place an economic value on the unpaid family (i.e., women's) caregiving and thus receive a tax credit for it.

For the employee to receive the tax credit, the dependent person must spend at least eight hours every day in the employee's household. This co-residence requirement greatly reduces the use of this tax provision for elder care purposes (Scharlach, Lowe, & Schneider, 1991). Approximately 80% of the benefits claimed as federal dependent care tax credits are for child care (Neal et al., 1993). Most adult children with elder care responsibilities do not co-reside with their elderly parent(s). For example, a daughter who respects her mother's wishes to maintain a separate residence (the preference of most elders) and pays someone to provide in-home care for her disabled mother so that she (the daughter) might work, is ineligible for the federal dependent care tax credit. Similarly, the co-residence requirement penalizes families who provide essential support so those adult members with developmental disabilities or serious mental illness can live relatively independently in the community.

Despite the limitations of the Federal Dependent Care Tax Credit, it has two major advantages: because it operates through the federal tax system and is not dependent on employer involvement, it is accessible to all employees; because it does not require the employed caregiver to deposit money into an account in advance of expenditures, it may be more accessible to lower-income employees. In addition to the federal tax credit, approximately 21 states offer a dependent care tax credit and 8 states have a tax deduction for dependent care. There is considerable variation among states in eligibility criteria and scope of coverage (Stone & Keigher, 1994).

Employer-Provided Flexible Benefit Plans or Cafeteria Plans

Flexible benefit plans, also called cafeteria plans, were established in 1978 under federal legislation (Internal Revenue Code Section 125), but did not grow significantly until 1981 when the government issued interpretative guidelines for this legislation. Under flexible benefit plans, employers allocate a specified amount of money to each employee, and he or she then selects from a pool of benefits those that best meet specific family needs or lifestyle and forgoes benefits less important to them. This arrangement departs significantly from traditional benefit programs in which the employer offers all employees a standard package with few individual choices.

Flexible benefit plans may be more responsive to the changing composition of the labor force and the growing diversity in American families. For example, a family with two earners both in the primary labor force may, under traditional benefit plans, have duplicate benefits, such as health insurance. For this couple, child-care assistance may be a highly desired benefit—an option not typically offered in traditional benefit packages based on male labor force participation patterns. A single-parent employee presented with a cafeteria plan might also highly value an employer-provided child care subsidy. Conversely, a childless dual-earner couple may be interested in long-term care insurance as a benefit.

Meisenheimer and Wiatrowski (1989) suggest two additional reasons businesses might be responsive to cafeteria plans. First, companies are searching for ways to control costs. "No longer can employee benefits be considered 'fringes of compensation'; in 1988, benefits accounted for slightly more than 27% of the cost of total compensation" (p. 18). Flexible benefit plans offer employers a possible way to increase workers' satisfaction with their benefit packages without entailing greater costs. Second, given the increase in mergers and acquisitions of U.S. companies, employers may view flexible benefit packages as a successful strategy to integrate the different benefit packages of the previous firms.

The Employee Benefit Research Institute also suggests that the rising cost of health insurance has driven the growth of flexible benefit plans.

> Often a flexible benefit plan is designed to allow employees to choose certain cost-savings provisions that in turn generate extra credits the employee can use to purchase coverage otherwise not obtainable. In addition, when flexible benefits are first implemented, cost control mechanisms are usually added or increased as well, shifting some costs from employer to employee. (Boyce, 1994, p. 28)

Despite dramatic growth, flexible benefit plans are still not widespread. The 1988 Employee Benefits Survey of approximately 2,500 medium or large companies (at least 100 employees) revealed that only 5% of all full-time employees were eligible for these plans. "These plans are more common among white-collar workers than among blue-collar workers. Seven percent of professional and administrative workers were eligible for flexible benefit plans in 1988; only 2% of production and service workers were eligible" (Meisenheimer & Wiatrowski, 1989, p. 18). As 45% of all women are found in the service sector, most women workers do not have access to this benefit arrangement. A 1992 survey conducted by Hewitt Associates of 472 organizations with flexible benefit plans underscores that this benefit option remains more available at large firms. Approximately 33% of females are employed in firms with less than 25 employees. Of the 472 surveyed companies, over 81% employed more than 1,000 employees; the median workforce size was 4,000 employees

(Boyce, 1994). Therefore, these plans are less accessible to low-income women, many of whom are women of color. Moreover, because most employers do not include homosexual couples in their definition of family, relatively few lesbian or gay couples have access to family-related benefits such as cafeteria plans.

Employer-Provided Employee Reimbursement Accounts

Employee reimbursement accounts, regulated through federal legislation (Internal Revenue Code Sections 125 and 129), provide a way for employees to pay for certain expenses—most often health care or dependent care costs—that are not covered by their existing benefits package. With a reimbursement account, an employee may deposit part of his or her wages, before taxes are calculated, into this fund. An employee is then reimbursed from this account for expenses incurred. The health care reimbursement account typically reimburses the employee for costs he or she incurs for the premium contribution, deductibles, and copayments. The dependent care account, also referred to as the dependent care assistance plan or DCAP, reimburses the employee for employment-related expenses for the care of children, disabled adults, and frail elders.

Reimbursement accounts, similar to flexible benefit plans, have been established more commonly at larger companies than smaller firms where women are disproportionately employed. A 1991 U.S. Department of Labor (DOL) survey of full-time employees in medium or large companies (at least 100 employees) found that 27% were eligible for reimbursement accounts (U.S. Department of Labor, 1993), whereas a second 1991 DOL survey of small firms (less than 100 employees) determined that only 7% of employees had the option of a reimbursement account (Barr, Johnson, & Warshaw, 1992). A 1991 DOL study of state and local government employees revealed that almost 33% of full-time employees in the public sector were eligible for reimbursement accounts (Barr et al., 1992). To the extent that women are more likely to be employed part-time in small firms than are men, they have less access to such reimbursement accounts.

Employer-Provided Dependent Care Assistance Plan (DCAP)

DCAP is a type of employee reimbursement account. There are two principal kinds of DCAPs. The most common form is the DCAP funded totally through employee pretax salary reductions deposited to an account set aside to pay for dependent care expenses. The second less common form is the DCAP funded through a combination of employer contribution and employee pretax salary reduction. This second type is generally associated with a flexible benefit plan (Scharlach et al., 1991). The maximum amount of funds an employee may place in a DCAP is $5,000 annually. Based on their survey of 472 companies, Hewitt Associates (1993) report that the average employee contribution to a dependent care account was $2,959 in 1992.

DCAPs offer tax advantages to both employees and employers. Employees' taxable income is reduced by the amount contributed to the DCAP. Employers similarly do not pay payroll tax on the portion of the worker's wages placed in the DCAP. This tax advantage to the employer may offset the related administrative costs. In the case where an employer makes a contribution to the employees' DCAP, the firm can claim this as a business deduction (Neal et al., 1993).

One of the primary disincentives to the use of this option, as is true of the dependent care federal tax credit, is the limiting definition of who qualifies as an adult or elder dependent. Again, the employee must have provided more than half of the dependent's support for the taxable year, the principal residence for the dependent must be in the employee's home, and, if the employed caregiver is married, the spouse must be a full-time student, working, or seeking work. A second disincentive is that the employee must declare at the beginning of the plan year (in advance of actual expenses) the amount he or she will contribute to the account. If the expenses incurred are less than the declared contribution rate, the employee forfeits these unused funds at the end of the calendar year, yet accurately estimating expenses may be quite difficult, given fluctuations in many chronic health conditions as well as changes in the carer's life circumstances. It may also be harder for lower-income employees, who are more likely to be women than men, to set aside funds in advance of expenses. Moreover, in order to get reimbursed from their DCAP account, employees must submit receipts containing the caregiver's name, business address, and social security or identification number (Neal et al., 1993). Some employees may find such record-keeping too burdensome or difficult. The receipt requirement eliminates employment-related caregiving expenses provided by in-home care providers (typically, low-income women and women of color) who, because of the low wages they receive, do not wish to, or are unable to, report their earnings to the Internal Revenue Service.

Employment-Based Long-Term Care Insurance

As we have noted, the costs associated with long-term care can place a severe financial strain on families. Care in a nursing home, for instance, can cost $25,000 or more a year. As one possible way to defray these costs, a growing number of individuals have turned to long-term care insurance. Whereas in 1985 only 815,000 policies of this nature were sold, by 1992, 2.93 million persons had purchased them (Boyce, 1994).

Long-term care insurance policies typically offer indemnity benefits for nursing care. The policies set a fixed payment amount for each day that the policyholder receives care during a specific time period. Policies differ in the degree to which they cover the levels of long-term care generally classified as skilled, intermediate, and custodial. Policies also vary in the types of home health care services covered; they may be defined narrowly as skilled nursing care provided in the home by medical professionals or may include assistance with the activities of daily living (e.g., eating, dressing, bathing).

The most common types of long-term care insurance policies are those purchased on an individual basis or through nonemployment-based groups or associations, such as the American Association of Retired Persons (AARP). These policies are targeted to the elderly and near-elderly— groups for whom the prospect of long-term care is seen as a relevant concern. Employment-based group long-term care policies are new entrants to the insurance market (Boyce, 1994), and only 3% of the policies sold in 1990 were employment-based (Scharlach et al., 1991). Not surprisingly, employment-based long-term care enrollees are younger and healthier than individual and group association plan enrollees.

Currently, a number of disincentives exist for employers to provide a group long-term care policy to their workers. Employers' concerns about liability are a major barrier because the tax implications of long-term care insurance remain unclear.

> For example, if an employer promoted a product and told employees/retirees that they would be covered, the employer was liable if a particular condition was ultimately not covered. In addition, it was not clear whether the premiums could be deducted or whether the benefit was taxable. (Neal et al., 1993, p. 214)

Scharlach et al. (1991, p. 135) argue that "the federal government has lagged in showing support for employer participation (such as by providing tax incentives for both employers and employees)." "Many employers are reluctant to offer long-term care insurance because of fears that the costs of premiums will eventually be shifted from employee to employer" (Neal et al., 1993, p. 214).

Disincentives for employers may also center on the newness of long-term care insurance and general criticisms that it has not, and cannot, provide adequate and affordable coverage for long-term care needs. For most Americans, long-term care insurance remains unaffordable. *Consumer Reports'* survey of 53 long-term care policies found that annual premiums ranged from $2,600 to $4,000. Further, many persons who could most benefit from long-term care insurance are excluded from purchasing these policies because of preexisting physical conditions or mental disorders. Typically, these policies do an inadequate job of covering home care services—the type of care most often desired by families.

The federal government has provided little direction in the issue of long-term care insurance. Traditionally, states have had the primary responsibility for regulating the insurance industry. The National Association of Insurance Commissioners (NAIC) suggests minimum standards, but they are not mandatory. The U.S. General Accounting Office's (GAO) 1991 report, *Long-Term Care Insurance: Risks To Consumers Should Be Reduced,* notes that state standards for long-term care insurance policies have improved, but suggests that a number of additional standards are necessary. Indeed, businesses' fears of offering employment-based long-term care insurance because of liability concerns would not be allayed by the GAO's conclusion to their report:

> New standards alone would not ensure adequate consumer protection. Despite substantial progress in recent years, many states have not adopted key NAIC standards, and when they will do so is uncertain. Therefore, if states do not adopt the NAIC standards, the Congress may wish to consider enacting legislation that sets minimum federal standards for long-term care insurance. (U.S. General Accounting Office, 1991, p. 15)

EMPLOYEE LEAVE POLICIES

The Federal Family and Medical Leave Act (FMLA)

The Federal Family and Medical Leave Act, (FMLA) (U.S. Public Law 103-3) was one of the first acts signed into law by newly elected President Bill Clinton, and became effective August 5, 1993. It requires employers with 50 or more employees to grant up to 12 weeks of unpaid leave annually when a child is born or adopted, when an immediate family member with a serious health condition needs care, or when the employee is unable to work because of a serious health condition. Employers must maintain any preexisting health coverage during the leave period and, once the leave is completed, reinstate the employee to the same or equivalent job. In order to be eligible to take a leave under the FMLA, the employee must have worked for the particular employer for at least 12 months, and for a minimum of 1,250 hours during that period. The employer is allowed to exclude the highest-paid 10% of the workers who live within a 75-mile radius of the facility.

The FMLA was enacted after a long political battle. Businesses generally perceived it as costly and not beneficial to their organizations. Rather than viewing the FMLA as protecting the jobs of valued, competent employees (and thus aiding companies), businesses felt the act burdened them with the costs of maintaining health insurance coverage for employees on leave, and also the expenses of recruiting and training replacement workers whose productivity would be lower. The act ultimately signed into law is a product of political compromise and, as such, it leaves out significant numbers of employed caregivers.

Employees not covered under the FMLA include workers in small firms, part-time workers, and contingent or temporary workers. A significant portion of the workforce is therefore omitted because more than 50% of all employees in the private sector (and a disproportionately larger number of women) work for businesses with 50 or fewer employees. Moreover, because women and persons of color are overrepresented in the contingent workforce, a greater proportion of these persons are denied access to family and medical leave. These part-time and temporary workers often face greater economic vulnerability and job insecurity than full-time or permanent staff, and could most benefit from this protective legislation.

Also, employed caregivers who are not spouses, parents, or adult children or children-in-law are not covered. The legislation designates only "immediate family members" (as defined by the majority culture) as appropriate beneficiaries and does not allow families to determine for themselves who is best able or available to deliver this care. Families cannot substitute siblings or grandchildren for parents or children. Neither are the rights of gay or lesbian partners recognized. Finally, because the FMLA mandates only unpaid leave, many workers who are economically vulnerable—especially women and persons of color—are unable to use this benefit.

State Family and Medical Leave Legislation

The first attempt to pass a federal Family and Medical Leave Act, was vetoed in 1985 by President Bush. After this failure, 31 states and the District of Columbia passed legislation concerning family and medical leave. Although some states laws are more restrictive than the FMLA that eventually passed, other states offer more generous provisions. For example, whereas the FMLA grants up to 12 weeks annually of unpaid leave, Connecticut allows employees to take up to 16 weeks of unpaid leave in a 2-year period (Stone & Keigher, 1994). Some states extended worker coverage farther than the federal legislation by mandating that employers with less than 50 employees (the FMLA criterion) offer employees unpaid leaves. In Maine, businesses with 25 or more employees are required to allow employees up to 10 weeks of unpaid leave in a 2-year period (Stone & Keigher, 1994). However, most of these state policies have restrictions similar to the federal policy that particularly limit the access of low-income women, women of color, and gays and lesbians to this benefit.

Employer-Provided Family and Medical Leave

Prior to the passage of FMLA, a number of businesses had instituted their own family and medical leave policies. In their review of workplace programs for employed caregivers, Barr et al. (1992) cite two national surveys—Bureau of National Affairs, 1989; and Hewett Associates, 1990—that found that 15% of firms allowed their workers to take unpaid leaves to care for elderly relatives. A number of companies offer benefits that are more generous than the minimum standards established by FMLA: Bristol-Myers Squibb Company extends its family leave policy to all full- and part-time employees (other than temporary and supplemental employees) who have completed 1 full year of service of at least 1,000 hours, versus FMLA's 1,250 hours. These employees have the opportunity to take an unpaid leave for 16 weeks versus FMLA's 12 weeks (Boston University Center on Work and Family, 1994).

Employer-Provided Family Illness Days or Hours and Personal Days

Surveys of employed caregivers consistently find that a significant proportion of work absences are caused by adult or elder care responsibilities. For example, Scharlach and Boyd's (1989) study of 341 caregiving employees reveal that, because of elder care responsibilities, 33% had taken at least 1 day off with pay, 33% left work early, and 15% had an extended break. To respond to workers' needs to tend to family responsibilities, a number of employers have expanded their definition of sick leave to include care for ill family members and thus have instituted *family illness days*. These days (usually 3 or 4 per year) may be included in employees' normal sick leave allotments or they may represent additional days off (Neal et al., 1993, p. 196). Some companies have gone further and introduced *family illness hours*, which allow employees the flexibility to use smaller segments of time and thereby extend the annually allotted 3 or 4 family illness days over a longer period of time. With family illness hours, an employee might choose to take 2 hours off each month to accompany her mother to regularly scheduled medical appointments, or an employed spouse may take an extra hour or two off from work to get a back-up system in place when a care arrangement breaks down. A growing number of companies have eliminated designated absences, such as personal illness days and family illness days, and instead instituted a broader category of *personal days*. With personal days, the employer designates a set number of days per year that employees can use based on their own judgment of need.

Employer-Provided Flexible Work Arrangements

Americans' notion of a typical work week has long been to "put in 40 hours" at the office, the shop, or the plant on a fixed shift or schedule. A growing number of companies are offering employees greater flexibility both in the scheduling of work hours and where the work is done. Companies often prefer flexible work arrangement options over direct services or subsidies to employed caregivers because these arrangements are both less expensive and seem more equitable because they are available to all employees. A 1987 Bureau of Labor Statistics survey of 10,000 organizations employing at least 10 persons revealed that only 2% had child care centers, 3% subsidized child care expenses, and 6% offered relevant information and referral. In contrast, 61% offered flexibility in work schedules or leave policies (Hayghe, 1988).

Flexibility in Work Schedule

Businesses have several ways to increase flexibility in employees' work schedules. These are flextime or compressed work week, part-time employment and job sharing, and gradual return to work or phased retirement. Approximately 25 years since its introduction, it is estimated that flextime is currently offered by approximately 33% of companies and is used by over 5 million workers. In a flextime arrangement, employees work a 40-hour week, but have some freedom to set their own schedule. Often there is a core band of hours—usually in the middle of the day or shift—when everyone must be present. Beyond that, employees can vary their starting time, lunch or dinner break, and quitting time to meet their specific needs. Compressed work weeks allow the employee to work 40 hours in the week but in fewer than the standard 5 days. Typically, the employee works four 10-hour days, or slightly longer hours 4 days a week and shorter hours on the 5th day, or takes a day off every other week.

Although flextime is an increasingly popular arrangement, Christensen and Staines (1990) come to this conclusion, based on their review of the research:

> No compelling case can be made for flextime solely on the grounds of employers' conventional concerns with organizational effectiveness, organizational membership, or job attitudes. Research reveals, further, that flextime is beneficial in resolving work/family conflicts, but not as beneficial as often hoped. (p. 455)

Christensen and Staines note, however, that the lack of stronger positive effects may be due to the fact that most flextime programs offer only a modest level of flexibility (i.e., employees have only 1 or 2 hours in which they can modify starting and quitting times). From the perspective of a caregiver trying to juggle the equivalent of two jobs, flextime does not, in itself, reduce the number of hours of work and therefore may not mitigate stress. In addition, some studies may confuse access to flextime with use of flextime, thereby diluting the positive effects. Finally, they note that these flexibility programs are not necessarily available to all employees, and that professionals and administrators are more often the beneficiaries (Christensen & Staines, 1990). As a result, low-income women in lower-status positions, who often have less discretionary time during the workday, cannot rearrange their work schedules.

In their evaluation of a New York City pilot flexible schedule program, Rothman and Marks found that the option met different expectations for men and women.

> Women employees often requested a specific schedule to resolve a particular family obligation. Most often they used the schedule to coordinate child care or transportation with their husbands. . . . [Men] often reported a release from the rigidity of the time clock that made them feel "more professional"; . . . the new schedules gave them an increased sense of autonomy. (Rothman & Marks, 1987, p. 474)

In such instances, flextime perpetuates traditional sex roles related to dependent care responsibilities, with women still carrying most of the domestic burden.

Another form of flexible work scheduling is options to work part-time, voluntary reduced time (also called V-time), or job-sharing (Christensen & Staines, 1990). Employees whose prescribed work schedules are less than a standard 40-hour work week are generally regarded as part-time employees. In contrast, *voluntary reduced time* employees agree annually to reduce their work by some percentage (usually 10% to 50%) for a specified period of time (usually from 3 months to 12 months). *Job-sharing* is when two individuals share a full-time position designated by a single budget line.

Part-time employment offers some employees more flexibility in balancing work and family responsibilities, but it comes with disadvantages. A major drawback is the lack of employee compensation benefits, particularly health care and pension plan contributions, especially true for women who are more likely to be employed in part-time or temporary positions. Although some businesses do prorate benefit coverage based on hours worked, the vast majority of part-time workers receive no coverage. A second disadvantage is the lack of a career path in part-time employment. Companies are less likely to offer managers or professionals the opportunity to work part-time, or develop higher-level jobs that are part-time. In contrast to part-time work, persons in V-time employment or job-sharing arrangements often receive employee benefits and accrue seniority on a pro-rated basis. However, questions exist about career path opportunities in these flexible work arrangements.

Gradual return to work and *phased retirement* represent two important flexibility options. Gradual return to work allows an employee who has had a family or medical leave to ease back into the work environment. This allows a working parent of an adult child with a developmental disability who has just returned home from medical surgery to gradually increase his or her work hours back to a standard 40-hour week. Phased retirement allows individuals to slow down the pace of their transition from full-time employee to full-time retiree. For many older employees with caregiving responsibilities, phased retirement allows them to remain at work and continue to receive an income and other employee benefits such as health care coverage as well as the psychological benefits of doing a craft, skill, or job they enjoy. Especially during the current period of corporate downsizing and restructuring, phased retirement can be a valuable option for older workers.

Flexibility in Work Location

For many businesses, changes in technology have reduced the need for all employees to be physically present at the office or plant in order to perform their job assignments. Options in employee flexibility in the location of work are commonly referred to as *telecommuting* or *flexplace*. It is estimated that the number of telecommuters (defined as persons who work at home via computer modem or fax for a single employer on a full- or part-time basis) is now 4.5 million Americans and will surpass 7 million by 1996. The inclusion of employees who do any work at home on a regular basis would increase this current estimate to 39 million people ("Number of telecommuters pegged," 1993). The benefits of telecommuting are often promoted, such as flexibility in caring for children and adults with disabilities and the elimination of commuting time. For some employees, however, there may be disadvantages in working at home. These may include an increase in work-family conflict, burnout due to the lack of clear physical or time boundaries between the two domains, a self-perception or a perception by other family members that what they are doing is not "valued work" because it occurs at home, and the loss of social contact and camaraderie with co-workers. In addition, some work conducted at home may not have benefits.

Again, gender differences exist in the reasons for choosing home employment. Olson (1983) found that for young mothers, home-based employment was the result of a work-family tradeoff, but the same was not true for young fathers who work at home. Women view their lack of credibility as wage-earners as one of the most serious disadvantages of home-based employment. "Women report that because they are home, friends, family members and institutions think of them first as wife and mother and second as wage-earner. They do not believe that they or their efforts are taken as seriously as they were taken when they were employed outside the home" (Christensen, 1987b, p. 486).

Employer-Provided Adult and Elder Care Services and Programs

As with other family-related employee benefits, employer-provided adult and elder care services are more likely to be available at large businesses. Because women are overrepresented among the workforces of small businesses, their access to these services and programs is more limited. Companies offering adult or elder care services generally target these programs to the employed caregiver rather than directly providing services to the care recipient. Rare exceptions do exist. The Stride Rite Corporation created an on-site intergenerational program linking a child care center and an adult day care center, and Remington Products, Inc. instituted a respite care benefit that paid 50% of the fee for services provided by a local Visiting Nurses' Association, up to a maximum of 95 hours annually (Barr et al., 1992; Scharlach et al., 1991). Most companies, however, have chosen to focus on less costly options such as education, resource and referral, and counseling. Although some companies offer this assistance in-house, a growing number of companies are purchasing these services from a rapidly expanding market of vendors.

Informational programs and materials offered by employers may include adult or elder care seminars, articles in company newsletters, adult or elder care handbooks, and caregiving fairs (Scharlach et al., 1991). In 1993, the consulting firm of Work/Family Directions, Inc. gave 575 company-based elder care seminars on such diverse topics as paying for elder care, legal issues, and choosing a nursing home (Shellenbarger, 1994). Resource and referral programs are offered by a growing number of companies. IBM, AT&T, Travelers, Prudential, and Aetna, for example, all have contracts with Work/Family Directions, Inc., which provides their employees with a toll-free telephone number so that they can speak to a counselor and get information on services available in particular geographic areas (U.S. General Accounting Office, 1992b). After reviewing the records of the 24,500 employees and retirees who had used their elder care consultation and referral service since its establishment in 1988, IBM found that 52% of these older relatives lived at least 100 miles away from the employee (U.S. General Accounting Office, 1992b).

Another service option some companies have established is short-term counseling. If offered in-house (as opposed to being contracted), the counseling is most often provided by the company's Employee Assistance Program (EAP). Rooted in the Occupational Alcoholism Movement of the 1940s, EAPs now number over 10,000 in the United States and about 75% of America's 500 largest firms have established EAPs (Luthans & Waldersee, 1989). EAPs have great potential as a resource for employees coping with dependent care responsibilities, but unfortunately, most EAP counselors lack knowledge of chronic disabilities and aging. Brice and Gorey's (1989) survey of 180 EAP coordinators revealed that the majority had little understanding of the basic disorders of aging. Similarly, Scharlach and Boyd (1989) found that 40% of the employees at Transamerica Life Companies who had used the EAP for their elder care problems rated it as "not at all helpful." These informational and counseling programs, although they may be useful to caregivers in the short run, usually offer individual solutions to work-family conflict and fail to address structurally based inequities in care responsibilities.

To conclude, despite media publicity of the growth of "family-friendly" businesses, most employees still face inadequate support from the public (government) and private (business) sectors. Kingston (1990) suggests the following:

> The fact that a family-friendly initiative becomes front-page news underscores a significant social change. . . . At the same time, the fact that this initiative was news, labeled an ambitious experiment, indicates that the social definition of the issue (from private to public concern) has changed far more than has institutional practice. (p. 438)

Corporate family-responsive initiatives have been fairly minimal in terms of the degree to which the workplace has been restructured as well as the number of American workers, especially women, who have been affected. Because caregiving remains predominantly a woman's role, the inadequacy of both the public and private sectors' responses to employees' struggles to balance work and family responsibilities continues to fall more heavily on the shoulders of women than men in American society.

In part, the limited changes in the American workplace are the result of decisions by business leaders, policy makers, and scholars to define "family responsive" narrowly. As Kingston (1990) notes, family-responsive policies have come to be viewed as either additions to the corporate welfare system as designated through fringe benefits (e.g., DCAPs, cafeteria or flexible benefit plans) or modifications in work schedules (e.g., flextime, compressed work week).

> This operational definition has two significant implications: it obscures the full breadth of the ways business practices shape family lives, and it constricts policy debates to a fairly narrow range of modest reforms. . . . [The failure] to link wages and job security to family welfare narrows the contours of the policy debate. (Kingston, 1990, p. 441)

By limiting the definition of family responsive policies, business and government leaders have avoided confronting broader issues such as gender-based occupational segregation and wage inequity. The American labor market, as we have noted, is bifurcated into jobs with high wages and good benefits and jobs with low wages and poor benefits, and gender and race are clearly related to this bifurcation. Employees with higher wages, those in higher status occupations or in jobs with greater autonomy, and those in industries characterized by large firms, are more likely to have access to benefits. Miller (1992) notes the following:

> One result of this distribution variation is a gender gap in benefit receipt. Women, who are disproportionately represented in lower wage jobs and in the highly competitive service industries, are less likely to be offered health insurance, pensions, and most other types of benefits. (p. 3)

Although little national data exist specifically on the distribution and use of adult or elder care benefits (given the relative newness of these initiatives), some insights may be gleaned from the 1990 National Child Care Survey (NCCS), a nationally representative sample of 2,608 employed mothers with children under age 13. This data revealed that, even among women, access to employee child care benefits and flexible work arrangements varied by occupational status, income level, education level, labor force status, and industry (Miller, 1992). For example, women in professional occupations were the most likely to be offered at least one child care benefit, whereas women in service, production, and agricultural occupations were least likely to receive them; women in more highly paid jobs had greater access to unpaid leave and flextime, whereas women earning less than $10 per hour were more likely to have the option of part-time work; and mothers in dual-earner families, mothers who had higher educational attainment, and mothers with higher wages were most likely to use pretax spending accounts or DCAPs (Miller, 1992). Thus, the data suggest that employers most often make these benefits and flexible arrangements available to employees who are "highly valued" by the company and that women with higher incomes and occupational status are more likely to use these resources.

Because of the gendered nature of the bifurcation of the labor market, although a number of these family-responsive policies may be gender-neutral in intent, they clearly are not in their effect. For example, family leave is intended as a gender-neutral policy, but as long as women continue to receive lower wages than men, making the loss of the wife's salary versus the husband's less costly, and as long as society continues to define caring as a woman's role and penalize men who choose this option, then many more women than men will continue to pursue this option. Similarly, although flexible work arrangements such as part-time work, home-based employment, and job sharing may allow women the opportunity to attempt to balance work and family responsibilities, if these options remain associated with lower wages, fewer opportunities for career advancement, and less access to other employee benefits, their use will continue to penalize women economically.

PART IV

Toward a Feminist Agenda for Family Caregivers

In setting forth a feminist agenda, the authors are proposing a profound rethinking of how the problem of caregiving is defined and policy solutions are formulated, or as Dalley (1988) notes, "to contemplate alternatives to today's accepted wisdom" (p. 149). The reader may initially react that such an agenda is impractical at best and impossible at worst, given limited public resources; underlying cultural values of familism, individualism, and independence; and human beings' general tendency to resist change. The authors contend, however, that thinking about something in a different way is a necessary first step to action in what is undoubtedly a long-range undertaking. It is acknowledged that the gender-based division of caregiving labor in the home and in the workplace will change very slowly. Accordingly, the suggested strategies have not necessarily been conceived in terms of what is realistic within the framework of a given system—although some are more feasible than others—but rather what is possible in terms of human needs and demands. By proposing what may initially be viewed as a radical or impossible agenda, we aim to stimulate different ways of thinking about the relationship between the family, state, and labor market and how the interaction among these three spheres affects the social construction of caring and women's social and economic status throughout the life span. We emphasize again that a feminist argument against familial and individualistic models of caring is not against those who are in need of care nor those who choose freely to provide care, but against the socially structured assumption that women will automatically and willingly care. It aims to recognize the worth of both those cared for and those providing the care.

The following principles are proposed as integral to a feminist agenda for caregiving of dependents:

1. The goal of change is gender justice to provide caregiver choice and empowerment for both men and women.
2. Changes are structural, not just individual. This involves a stronger public or governmental presence than currently exists to assure a comprehensive range of social, economic, medical, and workplace services and supports for caregivers.
3. The interconnections between the public and private, the formal and informal, the medical and social spheres are recognized rather than set up as artificial dichotomies. Similarly, generational interdependence is strengthened.
4. Along with the universality of women's experiences as caregivers, the diversity of experiences by race, ethnicity, class, and sexual orientation are taken into account.
5. Organizing strategies are built upon women's historical role in community politics as collective agents of structural changes.

The overall goal of a feminist agenda for caregiving of dependents is gender justice through the development and support of gender, race, and class equity regarding the performance of care responsibilities. Fundamental to gender justice is that caregivers have the information, access to comprehensive resources, and social and economic supports that empower them to choose whether to provide care or not. Gender justice is not the same as gender neutrality (Osterbusch et al., 1987), which assumes that society and the government are neutral in their treatment of women; our feminist critique of current policies and our documentation of the greater care burdens born by women show that gender neutrality does not exist in reality. Gender-neutral language has no relation to the different realities of men and women's lives and does not necessarily imply fairness. For example, as noted earlier, the Family and Medical Leave Act is gender-neutral in language by allowing all employees to take time off to care for sick or newborn relatives; however, women are more likely than men to take the allowed time off for a variety of structural reasons, including their predominance in lower-paying and temporary or part-time positions. Women's use of the presumed benefit of the leave may, however, penalize them in terms of their current income as well as their economic security in old age. By presuming gender neutrality, the different experiences of men and women in the home and in the labor market can be distorted. The goal of a feminist agenda is not one of social protection of women as nurturers, which is to invoke a 19th-century image of the female as moral gatekeeper of society or a notion of female superiority. As shown in our critique of the ideology of separate spheres, women's moral sanctity within the home served to limit their economic opportunities in the marketplace.

As noted throughout this book, the current gender-based division of caregiving labor is unfair because care tasks are undervalued, less is asked and expected of men, and government support for family caregivers is minimal. It is unfair because women and the dependent persons they care for are cast as victims or victimizers when they are neither (Neysmith, 1991). Men are now viewed as choosing to care, with those who are primary caregivers of dependents rewarded and praised for their exceptional behavior, while women typically have no such choice. Because men's contributions are defined by society as more valuable, their management of financial support for a relative, for example, may be perceived as an equitable contribution, even if it takes less actual time than women's hands-on care. While public policy cannot change how men and women define their roles in society and family, it can reduce the barriers to such changes by modifying the societal evaluation of men's contributions (Finley, 1989). Fundamental to the feminist principle of the personal as political, the very act of questioning and challenging the assumptions upon which the business of daily living and caring are based can have profound repercussions at other levels of society, including individual and public attitudes (Dalley, 1988).

Gender justice demands that both men and women have positive choices about how to care for dependent family members as well as choices in the marketplace and that the needs of carers and care receivers be equally considered. The roles of men and women, carer and care receiver, must be rebalanced in a way that recognizes the worth of both the cared for and the caregiver. For those who choose to assume the primary role of providing care, public resources must support them. Callahan (1988) has argued that even with adequate social supports, we are still faced with moral claims that confront caregivers with imperative duties that are often impossible demands. If we must ask caregivers to meet those demands and if they agree, then it becomes essential that we reward and sustain them through new social forms more fitting to current demographic, economic, and social conditions. Such forms imply (a) a reordering of the family, in which the roles of men and women are balanced so that neither gender is obliged to be the primary caregiver but both are free to choose between caring and other roles; (b) economic policies to improve women's position in the labor market, insure workplace equity in terms of salary and benefits, and increase the adequacy and fairness of the retirement system (Allen & Pifer, 1993); and (c) long-term care policies that integrate comprehensive economic, social, mental health, and medical supports, in which government assumes more responsibility for who will be helped, the types of provisions made, the organization of service delivery, and the distribution and management of the financial resources involved (Linsk et al., 1992; Osterbusch et al., 1987).

Current policies have tended to support the model of the traditional nuclear family, with the men being the breadwinners and women dependent in the home, even though this form no longer fits demographic and economic realities, as shown in Chapter 2. Closely related to the assumption of women as the "natural" caregivers are efforts to preserve the norm of family privacy. From a feminist perspective, the state, rather than focus on the family's freedom from intrusion, should assume a strong public presence to assure freedom for family members to choose whether to provide care by making available adequate resources.

Given the structural basis of gender inequities and the magnitude of the change required, *structural,* rather than individual, modifications are essential. The medicalization of care has supported a focus on individual stress and burden, with incremental interventions to strengthen caregivers' problem-solving and coping capacities. Policy changes must address the larger social and economic forces in the marketplace and in the home that have subordinated women as a class. From a feminist perspective, increasing public concern about the "problem" of caregiving is not just a problem for individual families to resolve as a private trouble, but a public issue that demands a collective response for protecting the welfare of vulnerable groups. Such a response conflicts with current assumptions about the privacy of the family, the naturalness of women as nurturers within the family, values of individualism and independence, a market-based economy, and noninterventionist government. In Chapters 8 through 10, these underlying premises of current family long-term care and workplace policies have been questioned. As Neysmith (1991) notes, comprehending the relationships among government, the family, and the labor market is central to understanding our social construction of caring because government participates as an actor, arbitrator, and definer of the emotional and physical work conducted within both the private and public spheres.

Inherent to such structural changes is a *holistic perspective that articulates the interconnections between the public and private, formal and informal spheres, medical and social aspects of care.* A feminist perspective acknowledges how caring work cuts across the boundaries of family and employment (Pascall, 1986). As we have seen in our analyses of how policies affect women's personal experiences, private life is not private from public and corporate policy, and public life reflects the division of labor in the home. To break down the rigid demarcation between the breadwinner-dependent model of the family and the mindset that caring is a private duty, economic and social strategies are needed to integrate women into the public sphere (i.e., to move women into the labor force at wages comparable to their male counterparts) and to extend the imperative of caring to men as well as to women (i.e., to increase the number of men who are primary caregivers). Our proposals for change also attempt to cross the micro-macro, medical-social-economic splits that characterize many interventions, since the realities of women's lives do not fit into the professional boxes of policy and clinical practice nor the categories of paid work versus family care (Neysmith, 1991). Instead, the inextricable interconnections between policy and practice and across a wide range of service systems present us with new and more holistic models for approaching the problem of caring for dependents.

Feminist strategies build on the *interconnections between young and old,* recognizing that, with increased life expectancy, there will be no substantial life stages for average adult women that are empty of potential caregiving demands. The following was noted by Neysmith (1991):

> Although the particular persons women care for may change over time, caring itself is a constant. The continuity of caring in women's lives is obscured by academic disciplines that delineate areas of interest for detailed examination and/or social programs restricted to specific population groups. (p. 273)

Rather than framing competition among different age groups, a feminist approach acknowledges that women are often the critical links between the interests of the young and the old, to ensure that policies benefit caregivers of dependents of all ages. We would argue that the apparent intergenerational war is actually a conflict between the public and private spheres, with government not assuring the basic needs of either young or old. When public policy ensures that women of all ages receive higher earnings and improved benefits and are not penalized for their caregiving, then they will be able to provide both young and old dependents with better care (Allen & Pifer, 1993). Accordingly, a feminist approach avoids conceptualizing different caregiving issues as belonging to separate categories of need, but builds coalitions to address their issues comprehensively.

Throughout this book, we have attempted to balance the universality of women's experiences as carers of dependents across the life span with recognition of the *diversity* of their experiences by race, ethnicity, class, and sexual orientation. Caregiving cuts across lines of income, race, and class, with nearly every family affected in some way. A feminist approach recognizes the multiplicity of truths and realities, and that efforts to reduce caregiving inequities must encompass class, race, and sexual orientation as well as gender. In a feminist model, a wide range of familial arrangements are supported without any assumption about normative family structures. Reconstructing the missing voices of women, particularly women of color, is essential to advancing a feminist agenda on caregiving.

To give women's individual concerns public voice and visibility is to propose strategies in which women are *collective agents of structural changes*. Historically, women have been more involved than men in community politics with much of their activity centered on health, education, and housing, but their activities within the traditional electoral arena have been relatively invisible. Many women's organizations have challenged traditional bureaucratic forms of service delivery as well as their dominant ideologies. To achieve gender justice, women must be involved at the grass roots level in defining needs and identifying strategies.

Using these criteria—gender justice; caregiver choice and empowerment; structural change; linking the spheres of public and private as well as medical, social, and economic support across generations; attention to diversity; and community-based advocacy—the authors propose changes in the following areas: economic supports for caregivers, social services and social support, long-term care within national health care reform, and workplace supports. Underlying the changes proposed in each of these domains is what feminists have defined as an alternative model of social or community care in which public provision for vulnerable groups in our society is the basic foundation of care (Dalley, 1988; Neysmith, 1991; Osterbusch et al., 1987). Under this model, the social welfare system bears greater responsibility for alleviating suffering than is the case under our residual individualized approach. A social care model acknowledges the normality of dependence and interdependence across the life course and the network of reciprocal relationships that bind society together. In a collective approach to caring, responsibility for care is shared by family and government, with government care as an addition to, not a substitute for, family care, and community care is available to all in accordance with a broadened definition of need. This public provision assures families flexibility and freedom of choice regarding care. The normative issue of family privacy is dealt with by viewing family care as the "social good." Spending on caregiving is viewed as a long-term and preventive investment, with the benefits of a social model of care measured in terms of family and community welfare rather than only the short-term costs saved (Allen & Pifer, 1993; Dalley, 1988; Linsk et al., 1992; Neysmith, 1991; Osterbusch et al., 1987).

We turn now to an examination of the policy issues and implications of a social-collective approach to care in each of the areas of economic, social, long-term care, and workplace supports.

11

Economic Supports

A Feminist Approach

Increasing attention has been directed in recent years to the role of economic supports for families providing care for dependent relatives with chronic disabilities. It is occurring within the overall context of a stagnant national economy, growing concerns about the escalating costs of long-term care, and a widespread public policy bias toward services and in-kind benefits rather than cash (Axinn & Levin, 1992; DiNitto, 1991). This attention may reflect increasing understanding of the replacement costs of care: It has been estimated that if families were not providing care, as much as $54 billion annually would be added to the cost of long-term care nationally (McConnell & Riggs, 1994). As examples of the recognition of the need for economic supports, financial incentives for family caregivers of the elderly have been debated in Congress since 1965, often as a cost-effective alternative to institutionalization. Frequently conceptualized as an inducement to families to sustain their care responsibilities, 50% of state family support programs for the developmentally disabled include some type of financial assistance (Bradley, Kroll, & Agosta, 1992). Most recently, the Family Caregiver Support Act has been introduced in Congress, which would provide an entitlement of $2,400 a year for a person with functional disabilities either to purchase supportive services or to compensate a family caregiver. Most policy debates regarding economic supports have focused on care of the elderly or younger adults with chronic disabilities, not on adults who are mentally ill, as reflected in the examples cited in this chapter.

Even though flexible and individualized social supports appear to be more important than economic ones for most families' willingness and ability to provide care, there are significant economic costs for those providers, particularly for women (Arling & McAuley, 1983; Black, Coh,

241

Smull, & Crites, 1985; Engelhardt, Brubaker, & Lutzer, 1988; Grassi, 1988; Horowitz & Shindleman, 1983; Keefe & Fancey, 1994; Lewis & Meredith, 1988; Linsk, Keigher, Simon-Rusinowitz, & England, 1992). These economic costs encompass not only reduced or lost wages and retirement income, but the costs of special diets, home modifications, and equipment (Abel, 1990). We have emphasized the long-term financial costs for women and the structural economic inequality that accrues when women move in and out of the labor force to provide care for dependent relatives with chronic disabilities. Because caregiving is both unpaid and underpaid, women who leave paid employment, even temporarily, to assume family care roles, are then often locked into lower socioeconomic status and socially powerless positions throughout their lives. In order to address these economic consequences for women, fundamental structural changes are needed in how caring work is valued and rewarded in our society. Modifications in the Social Security system to recognize the economic value of years spent out of the labor market to provide care as well as direct economic supports in the form of a caregiver wage or attendant allowance are ways to recognize the importance of the work of caring for dependents.

This chapter begins with a brief review of the role of financial motivations and incentives for family caregivers; identifies the economic costs of caring, especially for women; and then examines the extent of public policies to financially compensate family caregivers, care receivers, or both in other industrialized countries and the United States. Drawing on the social, political, and economic contexts identified in Chapter 5, we highlight the structural factors that underlie the limited role of financial supports for caregivers in the United States. We recognize the paradox of financial compensation for tasks based on affective ties as well as some feminists' criticisms of wages for care. Nevertheless, we suggest a model for economic supports that incorporates feminist principles intended to address the structural economic inequities experienced by many women who have provided care for dependent relatives across the life span.

FINANCIAL MOTIVATIONS FOR CARE

For most families, finances are not the primary consideration in their initial decision to provide care, although for low-income families, financial support can make a difference in their ability to sustain care. Accordingly, financial problems are seldom the major reason for institutionalizing adults with chronic disabilities (Arling & McAuley, 1983; Black et al., 1985; Linsk et al., 1992). As an illustration, a comprehensive review of the literature on the needs of families of adults who are mentally ill, which identifies the importance of information, skills, and support, does not allude to any economic factors, even though a sample of 409 older parents of adults with mental illness was estimated to spend an aggregate of more than $4 million in time and money on caregiving expenses (Franks, 1987; Marsh, 1992a). Nor do economic incentives appear necessary to induce most families to assume their care responsibilities, or to continue their caregiving work.

Although finances do not appear to be the primary barrier to care, nor the precipitant to abdicating or assuming care responsibilities, the unpaid and gendered-nature of care nevertheless has negative economic consequences for women, as manifested in their lower retirement benefits through Social Security and private pensions in old age and resultant higher rates of poverty. From a feminist perspective, we question whether families fail to cite finances as either a short-term barrier or incentive to care simply because caregiving is assumed to be women's natural role and is not viewed as real work deserving of pay. Another explanation may be that financial compensation is not perceived as even meriting attention, because rates of reimbursement have been low and relatively insignificant in the past. Even if not articulated by family members, however, long-range financial considerations are paramount for women. It is precisely the poverty of women throughout life that makes it essential that a feminist policy perspective address the issue of economic supports for their caregiving roles. Before turning to an analysis of the current types of economic supports, we first examine the central role of Social Security in women's socioeconomic status. Although women are less likely to be covered by pensions in old age than are their male counterparts, a detailed examination of private pensions and their negative effects on caregivers of dependents is beyond this book's focus on the gender inequities of public policies.

SOCIAL SECURITY TYPES OF
ECONOMIC SUPPORTS FOR CAREGIVERS

Social Security—a family protection program that provides benefits to covered workers, their families, or both in the event of the worker's disability, death, or retirement—covers approximately 93% of American workers (Ball, 1988; Beedon, 1992). As a social insurance program, it has no means test, which partially explains its universal appeal to most Americans. More than other social and health policies, it depends on a traditional notion of the idealized nuclear family and deals explicitly with gender roles, with married women defined as homemakers dependent on husbands as breadwinners (Miller, 1994). From a feminist perspective, this codification of the family ideology has served to marginalize women's incomes, paid and unpaid work, and women themselves (Pascall, 1986; Ungerson, 1987).

Designed around a traditional male lifetime employment pattern, Social Security is characterized by the following assumptions:

- Couples consist of one full-time worker (usually male) and one "housewife" whose work outside the home is insignificant.
- Women are available to perform housework and dependent care, which are not "real" work, are not valued, and therefore are performed without pay or disability benefits.
- Women's relationship to marriage is a key factor in their Social Security benefits in old age. Because homemakers have neither income nor employers, married women look to men for financial support. Their benefit rights depend on their relationship to a particular man and on his contributions record.
- Although women's position as dependents is central to the plan, women who are employed outside the home can count as contributors in their own right, and single women are treated like single men.

Although employed women contribute to the system, in reality, most married women are financially better off at retirement if they depend on their husband's insurance record rather than their own; in effect, women who have been employed have gained "independence" as contributors but not as beneficiaries (Pascall, 1986). This painful paradox for women in retirement results from structural inequities in the workplace and the division of labor in households, whereby women, as a whole, are paid less than men and are more likely to interrupt their employment, move in and out of the labor force, work fewer hours, or take unpaid leave across the life span to provide care to dependent relatives (Neal, Chapman, Ingersoll-Dayton, & Emlen, 1993; Stone & Short, 1990). Such disruptions typically occur first in the child-rearing years. A 1982 study found that only 20% of African American and white women had worked fairly continuously from the time they first returned to work after the birth of their eldest child until the date of the interview (Mott & Shaw, 1986). As noted earlier, women are out of the labor force for close to 33% of their potential work lives compared to only 3% for men (Salvo & McNeil, 1984). An average woman who has two children is out of the labor force for an estimated 4.5 years, and her lifetime earnings are substantially lower than those of women who do not have children (Smith, 1989).

With the growth of populations with chronic disabilities, especially the oldest-old, more women will be faced with the expectation to leave employment in order to provide care. In the 1982 National Survey of caregivers of the elderly, 14% of wives caring for disabled husbands and 12% of daughters caring for elderly parents quit their jobs to assume caring responsibilities. Among employed caregiving daughters, almost 40% reported rearranging schedules, 23% cut back on hours, and 25% took time off without pay (Stone, Cafferata, & Sangl, 1987). In a 1983 study, 20% of the never-married women in the sample left the labor force for the first time because of the health status of a parent; 25% of married women left for this reason, but this was the second interruption in their work history (Keating & Jeffrey, 1983). Other studies have found that as many as 25% of female caregivers have left employment to care for older family members, thereby increasing the probability of being poor at some point in their lives (Seccombe, 1992).

Accordingly, at least 12% of the gap between men and women's wages can be attributed to interruptions in women's employment. Despite income gains, women still earn only 72% of what their male counterparts earn, with the majority segregated into services and wholesale and retail trade positions (U.S. Bureau of Labor Statistics, 1991, January). In addition, women are more likely to be employed in part-time or temporary jobs than their male counterparts, which may allow them the flexibility to perform their care responsibilities, but rarely provides adequate wages or pensions (Fuchs, 1989). Others are concentrated in the "invisible" world of housecleaning and child care, where, as the Zoe Baird situation made public, employers often do not pay into Social Security nor provide other benefits. Given women's employment discontinuities and concentration in lower-paying and part-time, temporary positions, it is not surprising that the mean income for year-round, full-time women workers aged 15 to 65 was $13,722 as compared to $26,870 for men; the median income in 1989 was $10,470 for women and $21,275 for men (U.S. Bureau of the Census, 1990). These gender inequities persist into old age, with the median income for women over 65 at $7,103 as compared to $12,471 for men (Moon, 1990). The opportunity costs of caregiving include not only lost wages, but also losses in pensions and other work-related benefits (Stone & Kemper, 1989). As an example, the opportunity costs of caring for disabled elderly women with cancer in 1989 were $61.3 billion with $92 billion in wage equivalent (substitution) costs (Manton & Stallard, 1992). The opportunity costs of caring for disabled males with cancer was $72.1 billion with $108.1 billion in substitution costs. These income inequities and opportunity costs are magnified for women of color.

Interruptions in employment to assume dependent care responsibilities directly affect women's current and future income as well as their Social Security benefits or primary insurance amount (PIA) in old age because of the way benefits are calculated. Assuming a 40-year base of earnings, the 5 lowest-earning or zero-earning years are dropped, leaving 35 years on which to compute the worker's lifetime average earnings and determine the benefit amount. A woman who moves in and out of the paid labor force because she is providing dependent care has her benefit calculated using the same number of base years (35) as a lifetime earner. If she spends more than five years out of the paid labor force, those nonearning years are counted as zeros in the averaging of her lifetime benefits. This means that the years in excess of five that she spends in caregiving negatively affect the benefit amount that she can receive based on her own employment record, even though the value of women's unpaid family work in the home is estimated at $33,147 per year (Stoller & Gibson, 1994).

As a consequence of combining employment and family roles, women are more likely than men to have years of no earnings and of lowered earnings. Low wages combined with more years out of the labor force resulted in an average monthly PIA or benefit for retirement-aged women workers of $426 in 1988, compared with an average for men of $654.90, which put women approximately $260 below the poverty threshold for single Americans aged 65 and over (Lingg, 1990; U.S. Bureau of the Census, 1988). In a study that examined the effects of both child care and parent care, the PIAs of women who raised children were lower than the PIAs of women who did not raise children, and the PIAs of women who left work to care for other relatives were lower than the PIAs of women who retired for other reasons. Not surprisingly, leaving paid work to care for relatives other than children was found to be even more costly for low-income women (Kingson & O'Grady-LeShane, 1993). For women who have provided essential care to dependent relatives, particularly those with disabilities that entail considerable expense, such limited Social Security benefits in no way compensate them for the lost earnings combined with the daily costs of care, such as expenditures for health care, special equipment or diets, and modifications to the home. As noted by Hendricks (1994), benefits tied to work histories are based on a market mentality related to narrowly defined contributions, rather than to need. These lower benefits serve to perpetuate income inequities in old age because for most women, Social Security is their main source of retirement income. In 1988, 69% of unmarried women (widowed, divorced, or never-married) aged 65 and over depended on Social Security for 50% or more of their income; for 33% of these women, Social Security represented 90% or more of their income. And because women live longer than men, their comparatively smaller benefits must last longer (Rodeheaver, 1987; Stone, 1989). In summary, because Social Security is predicated on differential opportunity structures for men and women, income irregularities throughout the first half of life are replicated in the second (Hendricks, 1994; Quadagno & Meyer, 1990).

For married women who have trusted that their husband's contribution would benefit them in old age, the experience of divorce, widowhood, or disability can significantly alter their expectations. As illustrations of how women remain "one man away from poverty," a widow under age 60 who has no children under age 16 is ineligible to receive Social Security benefits. If she chooses to receive her widow's benefit on turning 60, her benefit is actually reduced to 71.5% of the amount she would have received at full retirement. A divorced woman must have been married at least 10 years to receive 50% of her former spouse's benefit. And a woman who is a homemaker and who becomes disabled is not eligible for disability benefits under Social Security unless she has an employment record of her own and has been in the paid labor force for 5 of the last 10 years before the onset of the disability (Beedon, 1992).

A number of changes in Social Security to address inequities have been debated in Congress in recent years. A *Modified Earnings Sharing Plan* was devised by the Technical Committee on Earnings Sharing, a Washington-based feminist group (Miller, 1994). It has been advanced by the national organization the Older Women's League and studied by Congress as a way to protect those who provide unpaid labor in the home and to recognize the economic value of homemaking. Under earnings sharing, marriage is treated as an economic partnership, acknowledging that women's work at home is work: a married couple would share equally any earnings credited for Social Security benefits during the years of marriage; a separate earnings record would be maintained for each spouse so that a woman who does not have earnings would nevertheless have a Social Security record in her name based on half of her husband's Social Security contributions. The plan also includes adequate disability benefits for both spouses, including homemaker and caretaker benefits for survivors caring for children or for disabled spouses, and child care credits for low earners (Miller, 1994). Implementation of earnings sharing, however, would require a total overhaul of the Social Security system, a change unlikely to happen because of the costs involved and the strong support among senior organizations, such as the American Association for Retired Persons, for the concept of "earned" benefits through contributions into the system. From a feminist critique, a major limitation of earnings shares is that it further supports traditional marriage and women's roles within it, ignoring the large number of never-married women and gay and lesbian families.

A basic issue underlying these proposals, which is not always made explicit, is whether the definition of *work* in covered employment should be extended beyond paid labor to include unpaid work in the home and community. From a feminist perspective, women deserve an adequate retirement income whether their work life was spent in the home, in the paid workforce, or a combination of the two. Although an overhaul of the system entailed by a change like earnings sharing is unlikely, this goal could be achieved through a number of other incremental changes in Social Security that are more feasible than earnings sharing: for example, providing for 66% of a couple's combined benefits to go to a surviving spouse, removing limitations on disabled widow benefits, and removing actuarial reductions and delayed retirement credits for employed widows.

Another incremental proposal garnering some Congressional support is to credit years of lost wages resulting from caregiving toward the Special Minimum Benefit currently available for workers who have worked for many years at low wages. This would increase the benefits of those with long employment histories who drop out of the workforce to provide family care. The major obstacle to this change is that the Special Minimum Benefit is being phased out and would therefore need to be extended. Another option is to allow credit for drop-out years associated with child-rearing. This would mean excluding up to 10 years (as compared to the current 5 years) in which the worker had both a child under age 7 and no paid work, from computation of benefits. In fact, a 1980 provision of current Social Security law allows 3 dropout years associated with child care. This approach would potentially increase the PIA of a caregiver whose benefit was based only on her own work record, but recognizes only care of young children, not of dependent adults with chronic disabilities (Beedon, 1992). In contrast, care responsibilities for dependent adults are recognized under the 1993 Social Security Caregiver Act sponsored by the U.S. House Select Committee on Aging and supported by the Older Women's League. Under this act, workers could drop up to 5 years of either zero or low earnings in the calculation of average annual earnings on which benefit amounts are based, if those years are devoted to raising children or providing care to a chronically dependent relative, including a spouse (Kingson & O'Grady-LeShane, 1993).

Another approach is to finance paid caregiving over the family life cycle through a social insurance approach: investments in caring during particular phases of the life cycle would be financed by savings during the "productive" (i.e., paid employment) years. This approach is based on the assumption that some caregiving expenditures, such as child care, occur in the early years, whereas others, such as home health care for the elderly, occur later. Recognizing that the family's needs peak at certain periods and recede at others, the savings and spending patterns of families could be spread out through a social insurance scheme that works at both ends of the age spectrum. For example, a single mother may need paid child care in her 20s, but may not require other kinds of caregiving assistance until she is in her late 40s and a parent becomes ill. Caregiving accounts would allow this woman to contribute toward those needs during her peak earnings years of say 30 to 45 years of age. Such caregiving accounts could be financed through a combination of payroll tax and designation of fringe benefits to this purpose (Allen & Pifer, 1993). This direction argues for public support to meet paid caregiving needs, such as purchasing adult day care, but it does not take account of women who leave the workforce to provide "unpaid" care on a daily basis to their dependent relatives, and therefore does not address fully the gendered nature of care.

In summary, although changes to the Social Security law would be highly useful, there are obstacles to using Social Security as the primary vehicle through which to correct gender-based inequities in the labor market. The strongest obstacles are the contributory nature of Social Security and the fact that Social Security is based on the assumption that caring work in the home is not of value to the marketplace, despite the female caregiver's innumerable contributions to societal well-being (Hess, 1990). Given the difficulties of fundamentally altering Social Security, we turn now to examining other types of compensation, such as wages paid directly to the caregivers or allowances to the care receivers, as ways to benefit caregivers of dependent relatives and to accord economic value to the unpaid work of caring.

Other Industrialized Countries

In contrast to the limited direct financial supports for caregivers in the United States, models for financial support exist in at least 59 other industrialized countries, allocated through any of the following branches of their social security systems: (a) old-age, invalidism, death and survivorship, long-term risk, and pensions as income replacement; (b) sickness and maternity, encompassing short-term wage replacement, medical benefits, or both; (c) work injury, providing wage replacement, compensation, and medical benefits; (d) unemployment, providing partial wage replacement, training, and job placement; and (e) family allowances that provide additional income for raising children. In practice, allowances for either the caregiver or the care receiver are most often included under old-age and invalidism (Linsk et al., 1992). Economic supports in these other countries fall into three main categories: (a) *constant attendant allowances* in which cash payments are made directly to the person who requires either full- or part-time care in a noninstitutional setting; (b) *invalid care allowances* in which some type of wage is paid directly to the caregiver; and (c) *family allowances,* which are less common and typically focus on provisions related to children, not adults across the life span.

Of other industrialized countries with social security systems, 70% include constant attendant allowance benefits, most often as a benefit under old age and invalid insurance, sometimes under sickness or work injury protection, and occasionally under family allowances (Linsk et al., 1992). Cash payments are made directly to individuals who require assistance with activities of daily living, household tasks, or personal care or supervision, and are intended to provide consumers with the discretion to purchase what services best meet their needs. Such cash payments are viewed as an efficient type of social spending because they can encourage consumer spending.

In general, care allowances that are made directly to the caregiver are less common—when they are provided, they are intended to give special protection, either directly or indirectly, for nonemployed carers. The care allowance is viewed as a compensatory provision (or earnings replacement) for wages and payments into the social security system that have been given up in order to assume caregiving responsibilities and, therefore, differs from a family allowance. Benefits are generally proscribed for certain types of caregivers. For example, under the Great Britain model of invalid care allowances, a caregiver may also receive an allowance if he or she has given up all gainful employment and can meet the means-test (Keigher, 1991). This contrasts with the more straightforward wage systems of the Scandinavian countries, where no distinction is made between family and other caregivers who may be hired, and families need not fully leave the marketplace to receive a caregiver benefit (Keigher, 1991; Linsk et al., 1992). Under the payment programs of Scandinavian countries, carers of older relatives are given actual wages for their services with regular employment benefits of vacation days and pensions. If an older person is assessed to need 20 hours or more care per week, the family caregiver receives a wage (not an allowance) comparable to that of a homemaker or nurse's aid (Hokenstad & Johansson, 1990). Relevant to our feminist critique of the residual, individualistic context of U.S. public policy (see Chapter 5), it is important to note that the Swedish program occurs within the societal context that publicly provided care is every person's right.

United States

In the United States, despite the societal context that emphasizes individual and family responsibility, financial support for caregivers, care receivers, or both, ranges from direct payment to tax allowances, dependent care tax credits, and unpaid leave. As we have discussed earlier, the primary way that the federal government provides benefits to family caregivers is through the Dependent Care Tax Credit for the purchase of care to allow family members to remain fully employed. An extension of the child care credit for working parents, this tax credit is a form of "inconspicuous" government intervention. From the perspective of removing gender inequities related to care of adult dependents, it has a number of limitations: families are not directly compensated for care; the credit does not take account of the care receiver's degree of functional impairment, which can affect the costs of care; it tends to benefit higher income households who can afford to hire caregivers and other outside services; and, because this credit is not refundable, it is valueless to the very poor who do not owe taxes. Perhaps the greatest limitation is that the large proportion of caregivers who have left the labor force to look after chronically disabled relatives receive no benefit because families are eligible only if all taxpayers in the household are employed (Abel & Nelson, 1990; England, Linsk, Simon-Rusinowitz, & Keigher, 1990).

From our feminist viewpoint, *direct financial support* is a more appropriate method to help alleviate the costs of caring, even though it conflicts with our cultural values of individual responsibility (Rivlin & Wiener, 1988). Historically, mothers' pensions were the first example of a home care allowance system in the United States that paid poor mothers for caring for their children in order to save the costs of institutional care (Abramovitz, 1988). Another precedent for cash support exists in the form of the Veterans Administration (VA) Universal Aid and Attendance Allowance, which provides grants to 220,000 veterans with which to purchase homemaker, personal care, and other services at their discretion, but is not part of the Social Security system. The VA does not require that payments actually be spent on services, or even that the patient be receiving services. By allowing veterans to employ relatives, including surviving spouses, the program gives eligible families discretion regarding distribution of the benefit, which is set according to the disability level (Osterbusch, Keigher, Miller, & Linsk, 1987). California was the first state to compensate low-income families through a home care allowance in 1959. Under the California system, families are paid directly for personal care services, which are defined as noninstitutional, medically oriented tasks necessitated by the recipients' physical or mental impairment. The primary function of the personal care attendant is to provide direct patient care and to perform incidental household or chore services to prevent or postpone institutionalization.

Despite the lack of federal policy and direction, approximately 70% of the states (35 of the 50) have developed some form of financial payment to relatives, such as an unrestricted cash grant or vouchers for specific services for the provision of homemaker, chore, personal, or attendant care. Cash allowances may be given directly to the care receiver, family members may be hired as employees, or families provided with a voucher or cash. Compensation may be given for work done through wage programs or only for out-of-pocket expenses through allowance programs. However, the goal of such programs is more often economic—to reduce or delay institutionalization—than to provide social support to families per se. In addition, restrictions on eligibility are numerous, with at least 15 states explicitly disallowing, by state law or regulation, the payment of relatives for their caring roles, and instead relying on home care agency employees (Keigher, Simon-Rusinowitz, Linsk, & Osterbusch, 1988; Stone & Keigher, 1993). Fearing that families would abuse the programs or "emerge from the woodwork" to claim such payments, most state programs are narrow in terms of eligibility, scope, and means of payment. States vary the most on criteria for paying a spouse as a caregiver, depending on whether a state determines that the spouse's care and the provision of an incentive to sustain it "produces a marginal benefit." States also differ on whether the caregiver and the care receiver must live together to receive any type of allowance (Linsk, Keigher, & Osterbusch, 1988).

A primary reason for the variability among states regarding restrictions on who can be compensated is the federal Medicaid regulations, although 7% of the 15 states that do not allow payments to relatives cite state rules and state concerns with cost containment (Linsk et al., 1988). A major constraint on the freedom of states to compensate family members is the prohibition against using Medicaid funds to pay family members, particularly spouses and adult children, for personal care services. These Medicaid restrictions have been criticized for promoting a medical model of care by restricting personal care to medically oriented tasks performed only by medically certified providers (Estes, Swan, & Associates, 1993). As noted in the discussion of the medicalization of care in Chapter 9, this may create a gap between people needing personal care services to remain independent in the least restrictive environment and those whose medical condition requires the skilled services of professional, medically trained personnel. These restrictions may also serve to promote professionalism at the expense of consumer choice and family welfare. Despite the goal of cost-savings, these restrictions can result in the utilization of overly qualified and unnecessarily expensive care (Keigher & Murphy, 1992). Nevertheless, some states (Michigan, California) are able to pay family caregivers of the elderly, including children, siblings, and nieces, by using the flexibility of the 2176 Medicaid waiver option for home and community-based care (i.e., Medicaid Personal Care Program), or funds from other sources, such as the Older Americans Act, Social Services Block Grants, or state general funds, but only if costs can be kept within "allowable ranges" (Linsk et al., 1992; Stone & Keigher, 1993).

States have been less restrictive regarding financial assistance to families of the developmentally disabled, particularly for children; at least 25 states with family support programs provide some type of financial assistance (Stone & Keigher, 1993). In fact, some states use financial assistance as the essence of their approach to family supports for the developmentally disabled because it is assumed that cash is a critical component in a system where services are, to some extent, to be determined by the family and responsive to individual needs. Financial assistance for families of persons with developmental disabilities takes the forms of (a) *discretionary cash subsidies* through a monthly payment to families, equivalent to the state's SSI payment for an adult with a disability, that families can spend on whatever they define as necessary to assist them in providing care; (b) *cash reimbursement or allowance* necessary to assist them in providing care for specific goods and services, such as respite, medication, food, clothing, and transportation; (c) *vouchers* that are given to the provider who is paid by the state agency and allocated for specific services, thereby limiting families' discretion; or (d) in the state of Texas, a *line of credit* where families are issued a bank card with a monthly credit limit, which they can use to cover the cost of services or supports with participating providers, who then bill against the balance remaining in the family's account (Bradley et al., 1992; Stone & Keigher, 1993).

As is true of cash benefits to caregivers of the elderly, there is wide variability among states regarding financial assistance to families of individuals with developmental disabilities, with the majority viewing financial assistance as a supplement to available services rather than a stand-alone benefit (Stone & Keigher, 1993). States with few publicly subsidized services tend to impose few restrictions on the use of funds, except that families must use them to purchase the services most needed. States that are richer in services provide service vouchers. Some states use financial aid to allow families to obtain supports beyond those the state offers, but restrict what families are allowed to purchase. A few states, which have an extensive array of publicly subsidized services, have an open-ended approach, allowing families to determine their own needs (Bradley et al., 1992). An evaluation of four family support pilot projects in Pennsylvania found positive results when families could decide how to use the cash component and programs were flexibly administered (Ellison et al., 1991). A number of proposals to benefit family caregivers of children with developmental disabilities include allowing an additional exemption within the federal income tax structure, paying for extra medical expenses, and raising income eligibility levels for local social services provided by Title XX funds.

Families of adults with developmental disabilities no longer receive any direct cash or voucher assistance, but rather a payment through Supplemental Security Income to cover basic living expenses. For many families, loss of a cash subsidy represents a significant hardship because the extra costs of living with a person with developmental disabilities do not diminish after age 18. In fact, costs may increase because many programs available to children, such as special education and child health specialty clinics, are not open to adults. In addition, the parents' capability to provide care may diminish due to their own advancing age and reduced earning capacity (Bradley et al., 1992; Smith & Tobin, 1989). There are, however, some promising model programs that can benefit caregivers of developmentally disabled adults, including reimbursement for respite services and consumable supplies and one-time grants for home modifications and assistive devices (McConnell & Riggs, 1994). Few financial supports exist for families of adults with chronic mental illness, although there are services in some states for families of children with mental impairments. As we have noted, the policy direction in mental health is for prompt release from hospitalization to community-based care, but this thrust is not supported by either appropriate long-term care facilities and rehabilitative services in the community or by supplemental financial aid for either the person with mental illness or the family. In fact, programs, resources, and access to services are least developed for persons with chronic mental illness compared to those for the frail elderly and those who are homebound and under age 65 (Hollingsworth & Hollingsworth, 1994). When their relative with mental illness is not hospitalized, families are typically left with the obligation of providing appropriate living arrangements as well as financial and social supports (Marsh, 1992).

SOCIETAL CONTEXT

Restrictions on the use of financial supports in the United States are rooted in the larger social and political context that emphasizes personal rights and freedoms over entitlements or economic assurances (Keigher & Stone, 1993). The United States' residual approach to welfare and government intervention as a last resort manifests in policymakers' suspiciousness about family compensation policies—specifically, fears that families would abuse such policies and require extensive government monitoring to prevent reimbursement of services that families would otherwise provide. Despite the fact that economists have long documented that cash payments are the most efficient type of social spending, our cultural distrust of the individual's ability to make proper choices with his or her money is a primary barrier to more widespread use of payments to assist people with disabilities to purchase needed care and services.

As is true of governmental resistance to funding other kinds of in-home supports for caregivers, it is feared that if families were compensated for care, the number of families providing care and seeking such compensation would escalate (i.e., the woodwork effect); or, alternatively, that families would provide care only if reimbursed for such services, with reimbursement considered an entitlement (i.e., the substitution effect). These concerns are rooted in cultural attitudes, not data. For example, under the Michigan Adult Home Help Payment, which is targeted for highly disabled low-income clients who are nursing-home eligible, caregivers are paid approximately $250 a month, which must be spent specifically to purchase services. This contrasts with approximately $1,800 a month for institutionalization of comparable clients (Health Care Reform Week, 1993). Even though the maximum payment is only equivalent to about 50% of the minimum wage, caregivers may not take on other employment while receiving the benefit. In an evaluation of the Michigan program, most families clearly stated that despite these restrictions, they appreciated the payment and felt that it had strengthened their sense of obligation to older relatives. The majority performed their caregiver roles for personal reasons and did not view the extra money as an incentive to care for someone outside their family as well. They also emphasized that they would continue to provide care if the payment was eliminated, albeit at financial hardship to themselves. Without the payment, most of the low-income families would have to find another job, decrease the amount of care provided, have someone else provide the care while they worked elsewhere, or get public assistance (Keigher, 1991; Keigher & Murphy, 1992).

Resistance to compensating family caregivers is also rooted in our societal idealization of the family—the ideology of familism described in Chapters 1 and 5. When women are perceived as natural caregivers performing a labor of love, it is assumed that they would lose their moral virtue and that their care would be less loving if they were paid for their care work (Abramovitz, 1988; Linsk et al., 1992; Neysmith, 1991). Closely related to the ideology of familism is the presumption that earlier generations carried the responsibility of family caregiving without external help. Such a view overlooks the fact that earlier generations were less likely to face competing demands from dependent care and employment.

Our societal tendency to dichotomize formal versus informal, paid versus unpaid care also underlies resistance to caregiver compensation. Critics of family compensation draw on the classical sociological distinction between the family and the state, believing that money has a destructive effect on family relationships and that by financially rewarding nonmonetary, nonrational motives, intimate caring relations are replaced by instrumental or more businesslike ones. Deeply ambivalent about introducing government payments into familial affairs, critics fear that the quality of care will decline if it is paid for, or that a caregiver wage will attract the "wrong kind of people" (Neysmith, 1991); yet this fear is never voiced regarding the work of physicians and other professionals where higher pay is equated with greater skill, expertise, and higher quality care (Dalley, 1988; Abramovitz, 1988). Payment and care are not antithetical; payment does not negate caring just as nonpayment does not guarantee it (Neysmith, 1991). This fear also overlooks the fact that altruism in the family is often compelled both economically and normatively, and that women, as the less powerful family members, have based their relationships on financial considerations simply to survive (Sipila & Simon, 1993). Central to a feminist perspective is the recognition that love and money are not mutually exclusive elements that ruin each other, but are cohabitants of both the public and private domains.

Given the pervasiveness of such underlying values and attitudes against the compensation of family caregivers, cost-effectiveness has become the primary justification for the limited financial assistance that does exist. Under a market ideology, family care is viewed as a way to reduce costs, not a social good. In other words, the goal is cost reduction and efficiency rather than caregiver welfare or support for a socially valuable function (Keigher, 1991). Accordingly, family care compensation tends to be evaluated by state policy makers by whether state monies are saved, or if federal matching funds can be captured (Linsk et al., 1992). From this perspective, family caregiving labor is assumed to be without cost; keeping it free to the state becomes an economic rationale for keeping it unwaged. When the state is faced with the cost of institutionalization, however, then the government can save costs by paying caregivers at the minimum wage level in order to defer or avoid institutional costs or to extend less costly alternative services. In some instances, family payments may be justified as the states' getting more for their money by generating more care provision than what is specifically purchased, or as opposed to agency care (Linsk et al., 1992).

This emphasis on cost efficiency overlooks the psychological benefits that both caregivers and care receivers often experience when some type of cash payment is involved. Transfer payments have been found to be more efficient and satisfying mechanisms for alleviating hardship than in-kind benefits. One reason for this degree of satisfaction is that the care receiver often feels that he or she has the ability to choose the conditions of care, thereby enhancing their sense of personal autonomy. In addition, family care often provides for greater familiarity, reliability, and availability of care by those who know the care receiver's personal preferences and idiosyncrasies, and eliminates the care receiver's apprehensions about accepting help from strangers. From the care receivers' point of view, knowing that their caregiver has been compensated may make it easier for them to ask for help because they perceive the caring relationship as more balanced. Payment is viewed as a way for the caregiver and care receiver to help each other. Consistent with the concept of intergenerational interdependence across the life span, the client receives the services needed to stay at home and the caregiver earns an income. In some situations, caregivers may gain independence from public assistance on which they would depend if the family compensation program did not exist (Keigher & Murphy, 1992).

TOWARD A FEMINIST MODEL OF ECONOMIC SUPPORTS FOR CAREGIVERS

Feminists disagree on whether to compensate family caregivers. Some argue that an economic approach overlooks the complexity of factors affecting caregiving decisions, including feelings of love and responsibility, and leaves untouched the emotional and physical strains of care (Abel, 1990). Others contend that attaching a financial value to caregiving transforms it into a commodity (Horowitz & Shindleman, 1983b). Even when there is agreement on the value of financial supports, disagreement persists about the approach: whether to offset the expenses involved in caring, enable family members to purchase outside help, or compensate carers for the services they render. If families are reimbursed for their care, it is unclear how to assign a value to their services and what distributive principle should be followed, including means-testing. We do not attempt to resolve all these issues in our proposed model, but take the approach advocated by Abel (1990, p. 77): "to delineate these difficulties is not to argue that the project should be abandoned. Because a significant fraction of caregivers need economic relief, some method of rewarding their efforts must be found." It is in that spirit that we provide the broad parameters of a feminist model of economic supports for caregivers.

Such a model has gender justice as its goal, achieved through structural change. Rather than setting up artificial dichotomies, it builds on the interconnections between the public and private, the formal and informal spheres and takes account of the diversity of women's experiences, including women's role as collective agents of structural changes. A fundamental criterion of any feminist model is that any changes in economic supports must operate to women's advantage because the exclusive assignment of caring responsibilities to women is the issue, not simply the level of payment accorded for this caring (Baines, Evans & Neysmith, 1991).

Ensuring equity, adequacy of services, and choice for both familial and nonfamilial caregivers regarding performance of the carer role are all central to a feminist model of economic supports. Such a model begins with the recognition that current gendered inequities in caregiving are a social problem, not a "private trouble" (Mills, 1959). Addressing this problem requires a combination of public responsibility and gender equity within the confines of the family. Accordingly, a feminist model assumes that care of dependent relatives is socially important and hard work that must be supported with public resources and shared by both men and women (Sipila & Simon, 1993). A first step toward gender justice is to make visible and attach market value to the socially necessary work of caring for dependents. All caring work should be paid work, whether by women and men in the home; outside the family in public, voluntary, or for-profit residential homes, day centers, and nursing homes; or inside the family through home help or home care nurses (Dale & Foster, 1986; Holter, 1984). In developing economic support policies, it is useful to distinguish between caring about and caring for someone. As mentioned earlier, *caring about* implies ties of affection, whereas *caring for* can be seen as an obligation that can be performed by nonfamily members as attendants as well as by family members (Aronson, 1986; Jarrett, 1985). In both instances, adequately reimbursing the caregiver, whether family, neighbor, or public employee, accords societal recognition that caring performed in the home is a service to society that is just as important as the manufacture of sports cars or the generation of electricity.

To address the structural inequities of Social Security and private pensions, the provision of benefits to family carers, including health care, retirement, and worker's compensation for caregivers, is essential. Payment levels should also be indexed relative to inflation in order to insure integrity and incentive value for family members who choose to be paid for their caregiving. Given marketplace conditions, class inequities would be reinforced unless payment levels are adequate, as only caregivers with restricted earning potential would give up paid employment in order to receive a caregiver allowance (Stoller & Gibson, 1994). A true market test would make compensation and benefits for family carers commensurate with those provided to other caregivers providing comparable assistance in nonfamily settings; as in the Scandinavian countries, no distinction should be made in the payment for care provided by relatives or by others (Hokenstad & Johansson, 1990). Payment should be geared to the needs and level of disability of the care receiver and the number of individuals for whom care is provided, not to whether the provider is a family member or not. In addition to a standard payment that takes account of level of disability, special discretionary funds should be available for families with unique or pressing needs so that services can be responsive to individual needs.

Choice about whether to assume the caregiver role is essential. As Osterbusch et al. (1987) have noted, government's responsibility is to ensure that those who contribute to society by providing care to dependents have full opportunity to choose that role free from coercion. The rights and expectations of those who provide the care must be guaranteed along with the rights and expectations of those persons with disabilities (Dalley, 1988). Family caregivers must also have the right to opt for gainful employment outside the home. This option is particularly important to prevent class and racial inequities whereby low-income women and women of color feel that their only chance for employment is through paid caregiving in the home (Ungerson, 1987). Family carers should have the opportunity to accept better-paying employment by asking the care receiver or the state to hire another caregiver or by subcontracting the work. The caregiver's right to seek other employment is essential to avoid their feeling coerced into their care roles, or trapped, exploited, or isolated by the situation (Baldwin & Glendinning, 1983). To ensure that carers have such choices requires attention to the flexibility of jobs in the labor market (e.g., shared jobs, flextime), and the development of supportive services, such as substitute care facilities during the day (see Chapter 12). Pay equity and comparable worth in the marketplace must continue to be addressed through federal legislation.

To attach an economic value to caregiving might also include abandoning the term *caregiver* itself, which can be disempowering to both the provider and receiver of care: by implying "caring" and "giving" are free, caregiving always leaves the receiver in debt. From this perspective, the concept of caregiving itself is a trap, because it is an attempt to empower one group by praise through implied self-sacrifice and disempower the other, who is in debt of the "caring" and the "giving" (MacDonald, 1988). The concept of *attendant* for both family and nonfamily providers may be more empowering, by "attending" to those aspects of living that cannot be accomplished by the care recipient because of long-term disability. Under the concept of attendant care, one party to the exchange gets a service as well as preserving autonomy in meeting his or her needs, and the other receives an income through an attendant allowance (Dale & Foster, 1986; Holter, 1984).

Fundamental to the concept of an attendant allowance is autonomy and choice regarding how the allowance is used, whether on services to benefit specifically the care receiver or to support the family as a whole. In states that currently provide some type of allowance to caregivers, most carers spend it in ways that directly benefit the care receivers and, contrary to fears of abuse or misuse, make purchases within appropriate boundaries (Bradley et al., 1992; Linsk et al., 1992). Making the family a partner in formal care can disabuse the agency of any negative view of the family as cheating the system. Compensation of family members moves the decision-making and financial authority closer to the family and con-sumer and farther away from agencies and government. Family carers should not be required to report how they spend their attendant wage nor submit to handing in receipts or using a voucher system. This degree of choice and autonomy builds on reciprocity and empowerment, whereby the care receiver obtains the services needed to stay at home and the caregiver earns an income for his or her socially important work. Know-ing that their relatives are paid may make it easier for some care receivers, particularly the elderly, to ask for their assistance. Such an approach builds on the concept of interdependence and the role of intergenerational exchanges across the life span (Keigher & Murphy, 1992).

In contrast to most current policies, the goal of our feminist model of economic support is not cost containment, but rather, society's enhanced capacity to meet the social dependency needs of its citizens (Linsk et al., 1992). Effects should be measured in terms of caregivers' welfare as well as improvements in the quality of care and quality of life for the care receivers and in the quality of the communities in which we all live. England et al. (1990) argue for a shift in how agencies view programmatic success, so that it is not equated only with saving money. Keigher and Murphy (1992) note that the option to compensate family caregivers becomes more viable if total home care costs are monitored to stay within some proportion of institutional long-term costs.

A feminist approach recognizes that although financial compensation is a necessary first step in legitimizing the important work of caring, it is not sufficient to relieve the burdens experienced by family caregivers over time. Consistent with a feminist perspective that attempts to break down the distinction between informal and formal care, interconnections must be built with other aspects of the service system. Therefore, an attendant allowance must be one part of a broad-based family approach that includes support services such as counseling, homemaker services, respite, day care services, flexible residential care, transportation, and assistance with economic expenditures like household alterations, supplies, and high-tech equipment (Cantor, 1994b; Keefe & Fancey, 1994; Keigher & Murphy, 1992; Ungerson, 1987). No matter how adequate the rate of pay, caregivers inevitably experience the emotional burdens of isolation and feelings of unending care and therefore require other types of comprehensive support services to help their performance of specific tasks (described more fully in Chapters 12 and 14). In fact, one study of financial compensation in Canada found that caregivers who reported the most positive changes in most areas of their lives were those who received both financial compensation and home care services (Keefe & Fancey, 1994).

Payment of caregivers is an essential first step, but it does not necessarily challenge the traditional division of labor between the public and private spheres, which has served to ensure that women are doing more caring work than men. Strategies are needed to move women into the paid labor force, to compensate them for their caregiving work within the home, to extend the imperative of caring to men as well as to women, and to acknowledge explicitly women's "complex allegiances and claims, and offer them more choice" (Lewis, 1986, p. 97; Ungerson, 1987). Achieving a more equitable division of labor of informal care between men and women requires fundamental changes in how men and women perceive their roles in family and society, and therefore necessitates long-term alterations in attitudinal and behavioral socialization. Public policy cannot in itself cause this profound rethinking, but it can question underlying assumptions about gender-based inequities and reduce some of the barriers to change. Strategies such as assuring comparable worth for women's work in the marketplace and family-responsive workplace policies can enable and encourage men to take on more of the caregiving responsibilities (Allen & Pifer, 1993). As a number of feminists have cautioned, the short-term gains for individual women from societal recognition of their unpaid work must not undermine longer-term efforts to produce a society in which housework and caring are no longer seen only as women's work (Finch & Groves, 1983; Neysmith, 1991; Ungerson, 1987). Attention to choice, the use of criteria other than gender to allocate care tasks, and coordinated services to ensure tangible relief from caregiving chores will help prevent further solidification of the traditional division of labor between men and women.

The fundamental gender imbalance of caregiving responsibilities will not be addressed, however, without attention given to the rate of pay and the quality of the work environment for employed caregivers, such as nurse's aides and home care aides, whether within institutional or home settings. As noted earlier, among home health aides, whose wages and benefits are lower than nursing home or hospital aides, the main reason for high rates of turnover is low wages. In addition, in-home care workers are often part-time or temporary and receive few fringe benefits. Because wages are low, social security contributions earn no pension gain in the long run, whereas the foregone benefits have immediate cash value to the employee (Keigher & Stone, 1993). Typically, in-home workers who are on contracts negotiated privately face even less desirable conditions because of the lack of any formalized monitoring of such arrangements; privately contracted workers generally do not receive either Social Security or workers compensation. High rates of turnover and unreliability among home health aides inevitably have negative effects on both family caregivers and care receivers (MacAdam, 1993). Such underpaid caregivers are frequently women of color, who return home from performing the personal care and household tasks of more affluent, often white women to their "second shift" of unpaid domestic work (Stoller & Gibson, 1994). Therefore, any strategy to reimburse family caregivers should be coupled with attention to the work conditions of paid care providers, most of whom are low-income women of color.

Although adequate pay, benefits, and training are the crucial first steps in improving such employment conditions, there is also growing recognition of the need to address less tangible factors that influence work satisfaction—feelings of support, the quality of the personal relationship between the caregiver and care receiver, and the perception of opportunities for increased responsibility and advancement. All of these factors have been found to influence the degree of staff commitment to their work and to the care receivers (Kane, 1989b). Tellis-Nayak and Tellis-Nayak (1989) emphasize the importance of change strategies that take account of workers' social, psychological, and organizational needs; nurture their idealism; and value their central role. Without attention to such factors, nursing homes and home health agencies will continue to experience high staff turnover, which, in turn, can negatively affect both the care receiver and the family caregiver. As is the case with family caregivers, wages and benefits must reflect the importance of home care services so that attendants feel that their work and abilities are respected. The long-range goal of a feminist model of social care is that the informal economy of household production and maintenance, caregiving work, volunteer community service, and all other cooperative activities that permit the marketplace to be successful and that meet public policy goals would be appropriately valued and rewarded. In this model, the role of full-time caregiver is abolished in favor of a variety of forms of collective care performed by both men and women.

As discussed more fully in Chapter 14, caregiver organizations, similar to the Carers National Association in Great Britain, are needed to campaign and litigate for adequate financial support, both for family members and for those employed in nursing homes and home health care agencies. Ensuring adequate wages and benefits for chronic care workers as part of a national caregiver agenda can serve, in the long run, to help break the cycle of the feminization of poverty across the life span (Older Women's League & American Federation of State, County, & Municipal Employees, 1988).

In conclusion, to develop policies that reduce gender inequities in caregiving, it is important to recognize the interrelationships among the oppression of women, the devaluation of caring in our society, and the ways in which caring relationships in the home underlie economic security. A just and equal society—a caring society that can meet the needs of all individuals who require long-term assistance—is not possible as long as inequality between men and women persists in the marketplace and in the home. An underlying theme of this book is that a long-range challenge for public policy is how to integrate caregiving values into the mainstream as a central force in shaping society. Ultimately, caregiving values must become public values, rather than divided along economic, racial, and gender lines. From a feminist perspective, an overriding imperative for creating a more caring society is to redefine the boundaries of the private and public spheres, the personal and the political, family and work. A long-range solution to the inequity of women bearing the burdens of care is to rebalance the roles of men and women through the reintegration of women's and men's private and work lives (Ehrenreich & English, 1979). A public policy goal is not only the integration of women into the public sphere (i.e., to move women into the labor force) but also to move men into the private sphere and to extend the imperative of caring to men as well as women. For women to achieve their economic aspirations, not only a substantial increase in their income-earning capacity is required, but also societal support for the functions generally performed by women on an unpaid basis. Such reintegration would enable women to pursue their own career goals, and a more equitable distribution of domestic and interpersonal care would be achieved.

The authors recognize, however, that in order to overcome the normative designation of women as carers and the moral imperative for them to care, changes in fundamental social institutions—the family and the workplace—will be required (Walker, 1985). Such changes will come slowly, if at all, given the larger cultural, historical, and political context. One step in that direction, albeit incremental, is financial compensation for caregiving. Compensation at an appropriate and equitable level serves to recognize caregiving work as a legitimate economic category, with its own criteria of value and rewards for both men and women; under such conditions, caregiving would be more likely to be experienced as a choice for both men and women than is currently the case. Without such choice, impossible and costly demands will be placed on families, particularly women. With such choice, gender justice in caregiving roles may ultimately be possible.

12

Social Services and Social Supports

Economic supports to family caregivers of dependents with chronic disabilities must be part of a larger integrated system of long-term care that combines social, health, and mental health services because long-term care is, by definition, a hybrid of such services. This chapter focuses on services typically conceptualized as community social services—case management, adult day and respite care, support groups, and education—needed to improve functioning or to compensate for functional impairments. Such services, albeit limited, are provided to people of all ages who need assistance with everyday activities of life. This constellation of services, combined with care by families, has been expected to fill the gaps created by deinstitutionalization of adults with chronic mental illness and developmental disabilities, and earlier hospital discharge of the frail elderly.

We begin by describing the types of social service needs most frequently identified by caregivers of the three focus populations, the importance of such formal services in sustaining the care ability of the informal sector, and reasons for low rates of service use despite growing needs. We differentiate between two types of social services: those oriented primarily to changing the care receiver's environment—specifically, case management and adult day care—and those intended to support the caregiver's physical and mental well-being—specifically, respite care, psychoeducational interventions of education and training, and support groups. The line between these types of services becomes blurred, however, because some interventions, such as respite care, can benefit both the caregiver and the care receiver. We critique the limitations of these services in altering the gender-based nature of care, drawing on the feminist criteria of structural change oriented toward the goal of gender justice. We then propose a feminist model for community support systems organized around caregiver choice, empowerment, and adequate resources to insure care capability. Although supportive long-term and transitional housing, particularly for adults with chronic mental illness or developmental disabilities, is a need frequently mentioned by families (Petch, 1994), it is beyond the scope of this chapter to cover the wide range of housing options for dependent populations.

SERVICE NEEDS

Caregivers and their dependent relatives cite needs requiring social care more frequently than those requiring medical care. The unmet needs of the elderly most often reported as necessary to avoid institutionalization are supportive and basic, not medical (Wallace, 1990). Adults with chronic mental illness have great need for community-based social services, some need for home social services, and very little need for home medical services (Hollingsworth & Hollingsworth, 1994). Despite differences in the extent of need for medical and nonmedical care across the three groups of caregivers, there is overlap among the services identified as necessary to support the carers and to maintain the dependent person in the home: an adequate system of community-based care, including aides to provide personal care, housekeeping, home repair, companionship, and transportation; information about the dependent person's illness and available resources; skills to cope with the care receiver's behaviors and to manage the caregivers' own process of adaptation; financial and legal planning; social contacts with people who have similar experiences; and substitute or respite care to relieve the caregiver (Bernheim, 1989; Caserta, Connelly, Lund, & Poulton, 1987; Marsh, 1992; McConnell & Riggs, 1994; Smith & Tobin, 1989).

In addition, parents caring for adult children with developmental disabilities or chronic mental illness face unique challenges in their interactions with service systems at a time when the normative expectation is to "launch" one's adult children to be more independent. Faced with limited service options and their own age-related declines in health and energy, families are frequently unsure of appropriate goals and programs for their adult children (Black, Cohn, Smull, & Crites, 1985; Cohler, Pickett, & Cook, 1991). Reductions in SSI payments, for example, have created problems in affording alternative residences for adults with chronic mental illness (Cohler et al., 1991). As a result, many families confront the options of institutionalizing their relative or trying to maintain him or her in the home without an adequate system of community-based services (Smith & Tobin, 1989). For older families, during their children's lives, developmental disabilities services have moved from an institutional system to a community-based paradigm so that families have to think about and use services differently than in the past (Rowitz, 1987). For families of individuals with developmental disabilities, a crucial turning point occurs when their children are no longer eligible for mandatory educational services. Concurrently, many of these caregivers are facing their own age-related health changes, which can limit their ability to provide care. Not surprisingly, aging caregivers of adults with developmental disabilities express the need for legal and financial planning, case management, and advocacy that will allow them to provide for their child's care after their own death or illness (Kelly & Kropf, 1995). Family caregivers also need resources from the network of aging services for themselves, not just for their adult child. This need was recognized, if only in part, by the 1992 amendments to the Older Americans Act, which contained a provision calling for the funding of demonstration projects expanding supports for older individuals with caregiving responsibilities for adult developmentally disabled family members. On the whole, however, both the aging and developmentally disabled service networks have tended to be unresponsive to the needs of older parents (Smith & Tobin, 1989). In a 1992 study of families aged 55 and over who care for adult children with developmental disabilities, only 33% had even met with provider agencies (Wood & Skiles, 1992).

Family caregivers of individuals with chronic mental illness particularly face the stigma of mental illness, which can isolate them from the rest of society and has, at times, reduced their ability to influence the care and treatment systems (Anthony & Blanch, 1989; Hollingsworth, 1994). As noted earlier, caregivers, especially mothers, have often felt that they have been held responsible for their adult child's maladaptive behavior (Geiser, Hoche, & King, 1988; Kane, 1994; Marsh, 1992). In such instances, interaction with the social service system can become another source of stress, particularly when carers feel demoralized and blamed during interventions like family therapy, and services do not meet family's needs (Grunebaum & Friedman, 1988; Hollingsworth, 1994). One consistent finding in the mental health literature has been families' complaints about their relationships with and inefficient help from mental health professionals (Biegel, Sales, & Schulz, 1991; Biegel & Yamatani, 1986; Fisher, Benson, & Tessler, 1990; Hatfield & Lefley, 1987; Tessler, Gamache, & Fisher, 1991).

LOW RATES OF SERVICE USE

The extent to which service use is related to reducing caregiver stress and sustaining the family's ability for care is unclear. The number of perceived unmet formal needs is a key factor influencing the well-being of parents of adults with developmental disabilities, with increases in unmet formal service needs associated with greater caregiver burden (Heller & Factor, 1991). Similarly, assessments of caregivers of adults with developmental disabilities regarding their current and future ability to provide care have been found to be significantly related to their use of services (Englehardt, Brubaker, & Lutzer, 1988). On the other hand, some innovative community-based programs that improve outcomes among individuals with chronic mental illness do not appear to reduce family burden substantially (Bernheim, 1989). Nor do respite, social support, and psychoeducational services necessarily minimize the burden of caring for frail relatives; one reason for this may be that many families of the elderly do not use services until late in the course of caregiving, when they are already exhausted and, in some cases, ill (Gwyther, 1989; Montgomery & Borgatta, 1989).

In addition to mixed findings regarding the long-term benefits of social services, rates of service use are low among family caregivers. In a study of adults with developmental disabilities referred for institutionalization, only 31% were involved in any type of day programming and 14% in activity centers; less than 5% used supportive services, such as behavior management, psychotherapy, or socialization programs; and only 5% of the families used respite (Black et al., 1985). Many families of individuals with developmental disabilities attempt to provide care on their own until they reach a crisis point of needing emergency residential placement (Wood, 1993). It has been estimated that more than 50% of the severely mentally ill do not receive adequate specialty care (Torrey, 1988), with only 20% of persons with recent mental disorders of any type reporting mental health visits in the past six months (Hollingsworth, 1994). Similarly, services for the elderly are not heavily used, and many families turn to them only at a crisis point of rapidly escalating care needs (Chappell, 1990; Lawton, Brody, & Saperstein, 1989; Montgomery & Borgatta, 1989; Noelker & Bass, 1994). In fact, only 10% of all caregivers of the elderly draw on formal services (Stone, Cafferata, & Sangl, 1987), and only 2% of families of relatives with Alzheimer's—a population with presumed higher service needs—receive any supportive services (McConnell & Riggs, 1994). A longitudinal study of care networks for the elderly found that informal support networks do not tend to expand when persons become more disabled and in need of higher levels of care. Instead, it appears that a small number of caregivers provide more services as needs increase (Stoller & Pugliosi, 1991). This suggests that formal services are an essential supplement to the care provided by informal networks when the networks' capacity is exceeded (Fischer & Eustis, 1994).

When families of the elderly do use formal services, they selectively choose them, rather than seeking total relief from caring, and the primary caregiver does not substantially reduce her level of care as a result (Christianson, 1988; Fischer & Eustis, 1994; Horowitz, 1985; Moscovice, Davidson, & McCaffrey, 1988). Higher levels of need among caregivers of the elderly have been found to correlate with use of community services. Even when elder need was controlled, caregiver need explained a significant portion of the variance in the elders' use of community services (Leutz, Capitman, MacAdam, & Abrahams, 1992). These findings contradict the assumptions underlying current public policies, which determine need based on the dependent person, not their caregivers; these findings also recognize that services can supplement, complement, and strengthen caregiving capacities rather than encourage an abdication of care (Noelker & Bass, 1994, 1989). When there are effective partnerships between the formal and informal sectors, caregivers of the elderly are able to focus their attention on other care needs, especially socioemotional tasks, that they are better equipped to handle than are professionals.

Community-based social services are often justified on the basis of deterring institutionalization, but this is not necessarily the outcome. As we have seen, many of the elderly who use community services differ in levels of need from their peers who live in nursing homes; and familiarity with services, perhaps acquired through support group participation, may make it more likely that some families will consider nursing home care as an option (Montgomery & Borgatta, 1989). In some instances, formal community-based support has been found to increase the likelihood of institutionalization (Newman, Stuyk, Wright, & Rice, 1990). And information about the use of formal services increases the probability that family caregivers of adults with developmental disabilities will prefer a residential program placement for their relative. However, most families who place their developmentally disabled relative in residential care or their older relative in a nursing home still remain involved in their care (Heller & Factor, 1991; Montgomery & Borgatta, 1989). In most instances, institutionalization of a dependent relative does not mean that family care totally ceases.

There are many reasons for the overall low rates of service use by caregivers of chronically disabled relatives. The most fundamental is the residual, incremental nature of U.S. social policy and the biomedicalization of care described in earlier chapters. Although there may be a slowly increasing acceptance of health care as a right, our country has never had a strong tradition of guaranteeing social support services to dependent populations, and certainly not to those who provide their informal care. Personal services, such as home repair, tend to be viewed by many policymakers as a luxury to which only the wealthy (who can pay for them) are entitled. As we have emphasized, existing policies are not oriented to the well-being of the caregiver, and although a Family Caregiver Support Act has been introduced in Congress, it has not passed. In fact, some programs for the elderly reduce the availability of services when family caregivers are available to provide assistance (Stone, 1991). Direct federal support for social services to benefit family caregivers has been limited primarily to research and demonstration programs. No unified approach, or even philosophy, exists for supporting families who are primary caregivers for relatives who are developmentally disabled or chronically mentally ill (Hollingsworth, 1994; Hollingsworth & Hollingsworth, 1994; Singer & Irvine, 1989).

Accordingly, as noted in earlier chapters, there is little federal funding for social services. In-home care and other services are not usually funded under Medicare; and even when they are financed, the extent of funding varies greatly from state to state. Other federal sources of funding are the Social Services Block Grant, the Veterans Administration, and the Older Americans Act programs. Federal support for such community-based services declined dramatically during the 1980s, with funding for social services reduced more than 20% during the first 2 years of the Reagan presidency through policies designed to promote cuts in domestic programs, minimize federal responsibility, and increase family care. These policy shifts had the greatest negative effect on low-income and racial and ethnic minority families and care receivers. Under block grant funding, federal discretion for targeting social service funding was transferred to the state and local levels, with cuts in federal entitlement programs at the state level ranging from 10% to 50% (Estes, Swan, & Associates, 1993). With regard to the elderly, for example, the 1992 Amendments to the Older Americans Act specifically authorized support services for caregivers of the elderly under a new Title IIIG program, but authorization levels are low and no funds have been earmarked for the new program (McConnell & Riggs, 1994).

Services to the chronically mentally ill have been especially hard hit by changes at the federal level. Federal funds for alcohol, drug abuse, and mental health programs were consolidated into a block grant funded at a level well below previous appropriations; the Omnibus Budget Reconciliation Act (OBRA) repealed major provisions of the Mental Health Systems Act and further decentralized systems of care to the substate level. The overall effect of decentralization of state mental health programming to the local level—making local units the locus of legal responsibility for providing programming to individuals with chronic mental illness—has been the reduction of state expenditures for mental health services. As a result, government funding for persons with chronic mental illness has been decreasing in terms of constant dollars (Hollingsworth, 1994). In addition, Medicaid funds were capped under OBRA, limiting the availability of federal funds for mental health services to the poor.

With restricted federal funding, most social services to populations with chronic disabilities are provided through the voluntary sector, with nonprofits contributing more than 50% of all services delivered (Estes et al., 1993). At the same time, nonprofits are increasingly concerned with providing the greatest amount of service at the lowest cost. Competing effectively often involves serving clients who can pay for services and those with a quick turnover, along with cutting nonprofitable services. This has had the effect of eliminating or reducing services to the low-income and the most severely disabled, many of whom are racial and ethnic minorities (Estes & Woods, 1990). Accordingly, neither public nor nonprofit agencies are likely to encourage families to reduce the amount of their care and utilize formal services; instead, both nonprofits and for-profits market to families who can afford to purchase services (Abel, 1987). Proponents of cost-effectiveness would argue that the United States cannot afford to equalize access by expanding either voluntary or public services to low-income people.

Even when services exist, families may not be aware of them, particularly information and referral, respite, and in-home helping programs, or they may encounter long waiting lists (Black et al., 1985; Caserta, Lund, Wright, & Redburn, 1987; Wallace, 1990). For example, in a 45-state study of residential options for people with developmental disabilities, it was reported that 63,000 persons were on waiting lists for community-based residential facilities (Davis, 1987). In some instances, dependent persons and their caregivers may decline to use services due to their personal belief systems or cultural values (Noelker & Bass, 1989). This is often the case with elderly women caregivers who believe that no one can provide care as well as they do, or who feel guilt or a sense of failure over abdicating care (Roberto, 1993a). In many instances, there is a discrepancy between the caregiver's perception of need and what policy makers or service providers view as important (Wallace, 1990). Services may not be available when and where families need them or through providers that families prefer and feel most comfortable with, consider most appropriate, and find congruent with their culture's values and beliefs. Other factors that reduce service availability are geographic distance, lack of flexibility, inadequate outreach and transportation, psychological and attitudinal barriers, and lack of sensitivity to ethnic and cultural differences (Stone, 1991; Whitlach, Zarit, & von Eye, 1991). Because services are limited, they often focus on crisis intervention, occurring too late in the process to sustain family caregivers; they also tend to be short-term when the complexity of the problems may require long-term involvement (McConnell & Riggs, 1994).

This mismatch of services with needs is particularly evident in services to caregivers of individuals with chronic mental illness (Marsh, 1992). In many areas, even crisis services to assure client safety are inadequate, let alone more specialized programs such as family respite (Mechanic & Rochefort, 1990). Families interacting with the mental health service system have often felt excluded, neglected, blamed, and frustrated by the emphasis on therapy when their needs were for concrete services, and have been dissatisfied with the amount of help they received (Kelly & Kropf, 1995; Lefley, 1989, 1987; Posner, Wilson, Kral, Lander, & McIlwraith, 1992; Ziral, Lieberman, & Rapp, 1989). Early studies of therapy with families of chronically mentally ill individuals determined that for 45% of these families, individual therapy was of no value and for 58%, family therapy was not useful (Hatfield & Lefley, 1987). Families experienced professionals' tendency to offer insight therapy as a guilt-inducing burden and a failure to respond to their immediate needs for clear explanations of their relatives' illness, practical help with handling behavior problems, and referrals to appropriate community resources (Biegel & Yamatani, 1987; Hatfield & Lefley, 1987). Recognition of the limits of traditional therapeutic approaches led to the development of psychoeducational family interventions more oriented to supporting families than blaming them, and are based on family's strengths, resources, and adaptive capacities (Hatfield & Lefley, 1987; Hugen, 1993; Marsh, 1992). Despite this change in emphasis, families have had to become their relatives' advocates and case managers because of gaps in services and reductions in state funding, and they have typically done so without adequate community-based supports for their efforts (Francell, Conn, & Gray, 1988).

SERVICES TO ALTER THE
CARE RECEIVERS' ENVIRONMENT

From the perspective of families who provide long-term care, a fundamental limitation of most public policies and programs is that they are oriented to the dependent person's well-being, not to that of the informal carers. The majority of services have focused on what is needed to maintain the chronically disabled person functioning in the community and in the home rather than on how the caregiver is affected by these care responsibilities. As such, they are of value to the care recipient and may indirectly benefit the carer, but caregiver welfare is not their primary goal.

Case/Care Management

System-wide case management, now often called care management, is increasingly considered the cornerstone of most community-based long-term care programs; it is oriented to reducing fragmentation of services from numerous providers; insuring continuity of care, accessibility, and accountability; and keeping the dependent person in the home (Challis, 1994; Gallagher-Thompson, 1994; Hollingsworth, 1994; Intagliata, 1982). Central components of case management include a thorough assessment of the care receiver; planning, obtaining, and coordinating or "brokering" comprehensive services; effectively communicating resources to families to ensure acceptability; and monitoring continuity, efficiency, effectiveness, and accountability. In addition to these concrete tasks, effective case management also involves advocacy for individual clients, efforts to change the service delivery system, and integration of formal and informal care (Challis, 1994). Case management of frail elders has grown over the past 2 decades as a result of Medicare's prospective payment system, "quicker and sicker" discharges from hospitals, and the lack of coordination between and within acute and long-term care organizations. Current health care reform plans as well as systems of managed mental health care rely on case managers for assessment, service plan design, and follow-up monitoring (Noelker, 1994).

Efforts to reduce the fragmentation of services to the chronically mentally ill have also increased in recent years. The Community Support Program (CSP), funded through the National Institute of Mental Health (NIMH), is a coordinated system of services and draws on the case management principles of continuity of care among the hospital, mental health center, and caregiver for accessibility of services and facilitating independence. However, funding for CSP was greatly reduced in the 1980s, and most care programming for persons with chronic mental illness cannot be termed a coordinated system (Hollingsworth, 1994; Thorncroft, Ward, & James, 1993). Another approach for community-based care to adults with chronic mental illness is the Assertive Community Treatment (ACT) model in which all care is to be provided by the same team of people, but the family is not always included as part of the team (Hollingsworth, 1994). In contrast, the family's role in planning services for developmentally disabled relatives is emphasized in the federal legislation (P.L. 99-457) (Rinck & Calkins, 1993), and over 40 states have some type of family support program that involves case management for individuals with developmental disabilities.

Most case or care management programs have resulted in the increased use of community-based services, and in some instances, have supported individuals who otherwise would probably have entered an institution (Challis, 1994; Hollingsworth, 1994). Case management has not necessarily benefited family caregivers, perhaps because an underlying rationale has been cost containment (Christianson, 1988; Corson, Grannemann, & Holden, 1988; Thornton, Dunstan, & Kemper, 1988). In fact, concerns have been raised that case management puts individuals with mental illness at risk for reduced access when it is used as an excuse for cost containment (Caserta et al., 1990; Goldberg, 1994). Although case management is oriented toward the care receiver, it has been found to increase the satisfaction of families of the chronically mentally ill in some instances through providing information and support via "supportive interactions with system representatives" (Grella & Grusky, 1989). Despite these findings of satisfaction, there are times when the needs and interests of family caregivers, the service systems, and the care receiver differ from one another, and when both the caregiver and the care receiver lack any means to participate in or challenge the decisions of the case manager. In some instances, professional case managers of the chronically mentally ill, who maintain that they are "working allies" with families, develop elaborate decision-making models that have no provision for involving the family and that create an additional layer of bureaucracy and cadre of professionals (Goldberg, 1994; Hatfield & Lefley, 1987).

Evidence is limited regarding whether case managers actually serve to improve access, limit costs, coordinate services, and advocate effectively, or whether they instead promote rationing of services (Estes et al., 1993; Noelker, 1994). Case management has also been criticized for being misleading and demeaning to the care receiver and further limiting his or her sense of control by implying that he or she is a case that must be managed (Thorncroft et al., 1993). Despite these limitations, comprehensive case management programs have the potential to improve service delivery to individuals with chronic disabilities and perhaps to reduce care demands on family members.

Adult Day Care

Adult day care has developed as a way to promote the functioning of the frail elderly, adults with chronic mental illness, and adults with developmental disabilities. Although attendance at an adult day care center can provide relief for families, the caregivers' well-being has not been a primary goal. Historically, adult day care was associated with psychiatry patients, with its roots in the day treatment centers and day hospitals for geriatric mental patients in England (Goldstein, 1982). The concept was expanded to include physically impaired and chronically ill aged, with the first program in the United States beginning in 1947 under the auspices of the Menninger Clinic (Kaye & Kirwin, 1990). The National Institute on Adult Day Care (NIAD), organized in 1979 as a unit of the National Council on the Aging, aims to promote the concept of adult day care as a viable community-based option for disabled older people within the larger continuum of long-term care. It is intended to reach older people who would not otherwise participate in traditional community clubs, senior centers, and church groups. The growing popularity of adult day care—with over 2,000 centers serving more than 70,000 older adults in 1989—emerged from the need to explore alternatives to institutionalization and to contain costs, despite the absence of any national policy or a permanent funding base. Day treatment for adults with mental retardation was encouraged by the 1975 Developmentally Disabled Assistance and Bill of Rights Acts and the Accreditation Council for Ambulatory Care's focus on community treatment.

There are three types of adult day care, determined by their affiliation with (a) a hospital or nursing home, (b) a social service or housing agency, and (c) a special purpose center, such as one serving veterans. Services are usually offered on a means-tested basis, and include rehabilitation, nursing, social services, recreation, nutrition, socializing, education, personal care, and transportation (Hollingsworth & Hollingsworth, 1994). Arising in local communities, services are funded through a wide variety of sources, primarily Medicaid, Social Services Block Grants, and private funds. Findings are mixed regarding the effectiveness and costs of adult day care, especially in light of a lack of clarity of program goals and criteria for effectiveness. Some studies of the elderly have found a reduction in mortality, increased cognitive functioning, heightened social activity, and high levels of client satisfaction (Arling, Harkins, & Romaniuk, 1984; Bilitski, 1985).

Although adult day care is less expensive than some types of home care, such as visits from a home health nurse (Weissert, Elson, Bolda, Cready, Zelman, Sloane, Kalsbeek, Mutran, Rice, & Koch, 1989), use of adult day care may not reduce institutionalization and may actually increase the total cost of care (Kaye & Kirwin, 1990). One reason that the rate of institutionalization is not necessarily altered is that the populations served by day care are not necessarily the same as those in institutions. Elderly participants in day care are more likely to be younger, married, less dependent, and less frequently mentally impaired than their counterparts in nursing homes. For adult day care to be an appropriate alternative for the elderly, the disabled person must be ambulatory, have a relatively stable health condition that allows for participation in day care programming, possess adequate communication skills, and have a supportive caregiver in the community who is willing to take major responsibility for his/her care during the evening or on weekends. Therefore, it remains unclear if adult day care can be a substitute for nursing home care (Arling et al., 1984). The effect of adult day care on the caregiver is also unclear, although studies of developmentally disabled adults and their families have found that day programs are often a crucial factor in maintaining what otherwise might be an intolerable situation (Smith and Tobin, 1989). As a secondary benefit, most caregivers reported reduced stress through gains realized in personal time, opportunities to return to the workplace, and relief from worry (Kaye & Kirwin, 1990). In such instances, many adult day care centers serve the dual function of providing care and socialization for the dependent person and short-term respite to the family caregiver.

SERVICES TO SUPPORT CAREGIVERS

Services to support caregivers—*respite, education and training,* and *mutual support groups*—have grown in the past decade. In general, however, these have been motivated by the goals of prolonging the family's ability to provide care, reducing institutionalization and therefore saving costs, not by the goal of enhancing the caregiver's quality of life.

Respite Care

Respite can be defined as a temporary period of rest provided at intervals for family caregivers of dependents with chronic disabilities (Geiser, Hoche, & King, 1988). Respite as an intervention for family caregivers has been evolving since the 1960s, when it was used for elderly and developmentally disabled populations. It has more recently become available to families of the chronically mentally ill, although rates of participation are low because of care recipients' general unwillingness to return voluntarily to a hospital, even for a short time. As described earlier, respite programs aim to give the family relief, reduce the stress of long-term care, decrease the duration of hospital or nursing home stays, and develop an effective partnership between the family and professionals.

Caregivers of all three dependent populations often identify respite as their greatest need (Horowitz & Schindelman, 1983a; Jennings, 1987; Montgomery & Borgatta, 1989; Scheyett, 1990; Wallace, 1990). Such relief may be even more important for caregivers who are elderly—an increasing number among the developmentally disabled and chronically mentally ill population—than for younger parents who have relief during the day when children with disabilities are in school programs (Kelly & Kropf, 1995). The types of respite vary from nursing home and hospital beds for short-term stays, to day care, to in-home respite in the dependent person's home. Some type of respite care is now provided by nearly every state, although the numbers of disabled persons served and the amounts of available funding vary widely.

From a policy-maker's point of view, the underlying rationale for most respite programs is to avoid or delay institutionalization and therefore to save costs by prolonging the family's ability to provide care. The effects of respite on both the care receiver and caregiver are unclear. In one study of a program that provided respite over a 12-month period, families with respite care maintained their impaired older relative 22 days longer in the community than those without respite. They did so by using relatively small amounts of respite—on average, just under 1 day of day care or 4 hours of in-home respite care a month. This low amount of time may explain why respite had no measurable effect on caregiver burden and mental health. Nevertheless, caregivers expressed satisfaction with the service, prompting debates about whether consumer satisfaction justifies funding of services that are not necessarily cost-effective (Callahan, 1989; Lawton, Brody, & Saperstein, 1989). With regard to the care of individuals with chronic mental illness, respite has been found to decrease social isolation for both the caregiver and the care receiver (Scheyett, 1990) and to reduce the number of days that the ill family member is hospitalized (Geiser et al., 1988).

One reason for limited effect is that respite services may not be flexible enough to meet a family's diverse needs. For example, some caregivers may prefer an extended period of time for a vacation, whereas others need regularly scheduled short breaks to attend to standing appointments and household errands. Older parents of adult children with disabilities may require respite as a method for managing the family resources rather than for extrafamilial activities (Kropf, 1994a). Unless caregivers can afford to purchase respite and have transportation to the site, their access to it is necessarily limited. As a consequence, low-income families and families of color have less access to respite. In addition, respite hours, if less than a full day, often do not meet the needs of employed caregivers who paradoxically may be the ones most able to purchase respite care.

A fundamental limitation is that respite services alone do not guarantee that a caregiver will have the opportunity to evaluate her circumstances and make conscious choices about providing care. Although day care and respite can provide some relief, they nevertheless build on and reinforce family-based care because they presume that a family member is available to provide care during the hours when their relative is not at the day center or respite program (Baines, Evans, & Neysmith, 1991). Although there is temporary relief from stress, the conditions that gave rise to it remain unchanged because the service is provided within the overall assumption that women will perform the unpaid caregiving work during the "non-respite" time. Assuming that a caregiver can find trustworthy care providers to give her a break, it may take her months or even years to experience relaxation with their temporary presence. When the shift of responsibility for care is temporary and minimal, respite services may inadvertently imply that family caregivers, presumably refreshed by their short breaks, will continue to be primarily responsible. Whether caring work is organized in a just and equitable manner in our society is not questioned.

Psychoeducational Interventions

In the past decade, short-term psychoeducational interventions of education and training for caregivers have proliferated. Such self-help techniques are consistent with our society's values of individualism, independence, and personal responsibility. An underlying assumption, which is faulty from a feminist perspective of social care and gender justice, is that if caregivers learn more, operate more efficiently, and become more skilled at coping, their stress will be reduced. Admittedly, such educational and group methods can (a) address cognitive and behavioral issues and increase carers' knowledge of problems facing their relatives, (b) teach coping strategies, (c) improve their knowledge about resources and care alternatives, (d) produce feelings of being connected to and supported by other group members, and (e) provide ways to address secondary strains in the workplace and other areas of their lives. Yet most educational interventions have had little long-term effect on reducing the family's overall stress of caring for an older disabled relative (Abel, 1991; Callahan, 1989; Cazzallo et al., 1989; Haley, 1989, 1991; Hugen, 1993; Montgomery & Borgatta, 1989; Smith, Smith, & Toseland, 1991; Toseland & Rossiter, 1989; Toseland, Rossiter, & Labrecque, 1989a, 1989b; Whitlach, Zarit, & von Eye, 1991).

From a feminist critique, these short-term interventions have numerous limitations, primarily because their underlying rationale is to inform caregivers about ways to operate more effectively within the constraints of existing service systems. The cost-effectiveness of such interventions is often measured by whether they reduce relapse and prolong the caring relationship, rather than by the caregivers' well-being. By focusing on effective ways to live with and manage a relative's illness, education and training can reinforce traditional gender-based inequities in care responsibilities. Similar to counseling interventions with caregivers, the focus on individual attitudes and behaviors, on cognitive restructuring of the caregiver experience, and on personal change may obscure the underlying gender-based structures that cause caregiver burden and inequities (Dellman-Jenkins, Hofer, & Chebra, 1994). Stress management techniques can reinforce the belief that the priority should be to help caregivers adjust to unavoidable burdens. Interventions that aim to enhance carers' efficacy and self-esteem may inadvertently imply that personal inadequacy is the source of caregiver burnout. Training programs that rely on a lecture format may, in fact, reduce families' sense of efficacy by emphasizing the expertise of the professional educator (Pfeiffer & Mostek, 1991). Although such interventions may ease stress on a short-term basis, they still assume that caring is primarily the responsibility of individual family members and offer no long-range, collective solutions that address underlying structural factors (Abel, 1991).

Educational groups and training are a relatively inexpensive means to inform caregivers of community resources, but they cannot address insufficient program funding, lack of needed policies, or problems of inadequate health or long-term care insurance. They cannot resolve structural causes of caregiver stress, such as insufficient program funding. It is much less costly to set up a 10-week training course of lectures for families than to provide home health aides or homemakers to supplement their care (Abel & Nelson, 1990). As noted by Montgomery and Borgatta (1989), the level of work required by a caregiver can be relieved only by assistance over an extended time period; education may help families in terms of their perceived stress, but the level of impairment of their older relative still dictates the extent of care necessary and the cost of such care in time, energy, and money. Abel (1991) contends that the critical question for evaluating such interventions is not whether programs make caregivers feel better about themselves, but whether they improve the quality of the carers' lives and minimize the sacrifice required.

Such educational approaches also attempt to impose criteria of efficiency and cost-effectiveness on processes governed by standards of quality. Time management training has been used to enhance caregivers' coping ability, under the presumption that increased efficiency at task performance is an antidote to the stresses of multiple demands (Clark & Rokowski, 1983). Yet increased efficiency cannot in itself mitigate the fatigue from being wakened several times a night to prevent a parent with dementia from wandering or to change an incontinent partner's bedding; whether it takes 5 or 15 minutes to change the bedding is of little consequence when one's sleep is disturbed night after night. Efficiency is a misplaced standard for caregiving, and questions related to cost-effectiveness are the wrong ones to ask. Feminists argue that we should be determining the best ways to care for older persons, instead of asking what is the cheapest way to keep them alive (Sommers & Shields, 1987).

From a professional and policymakers' point of view, such programs (a) provide an expanded role for professionals such as counselors, for whom providing care is the raison d'etre; and (b) create a new cadre of trainers and a plethora of how-to books (Baines, Evans, & Neysmith, 1991). Even so, low-income, immigrant, and minority women tend to be left doing the routine, lower-paid maintenance tasks of home care that are critical to a chronically disabled person's functioning (Tellis-Nayak & Tellis-Nayak, 1989). Although sharing information and enhancing coping skills are valuable, these interventions can serve as a means to shift responsibility from formal services to the informal sphere of the family and to underpaid female caregivers of color. For example, instructing families on how to administer more medically oriented, high-tech care enables hospitals to discharge patients to their families prematurely (Abel & Nelson, 1990; Wood & Estes, 1983). In some cases, the type of technical skills taught in educational programs for caregivers of the elderly may serve to undermine carers' own problem-solving capacity and sense of autonomy and control over the situation (Abel & Nelson, 1990). As caregivers learn more about bureaucratic requirements and the low levels of service availability, this information in itself can become an added stressor (Zarit, 1994). Perfecting techniques of care based on standardized knowledge does not necessarily promote good caring, which is founded on intimate, personal, and individualized knowledge and requires a different thought process than finding the most rational way to perform tasks (Waerness, 1983).

With regard to individuals with chronic mental illness, psychoeducational interventions have been useful in providing caregivers with ways to respond constructively to disturbing patient behavior, especially conflict management techniques (Abramowitz & Coursey, 1989), and with increased understanding of mental illness (Posner, Wilson, Kral, Lander, & McIlwraith, 1992). However, they have often been oriented more toward altering the family's behavior toward their relative in order to prevent relapse and hospitalization than to supporting families per se (Hugen, 1993). For example, families are taught ways to reduce the amount of "expressed emotion"— hostility toward and overinvolvement with their relative with chronic mental illness. Although this may be an important therapeutic goal, it does not necessarily address the emotional needs of family caregivers (Scheyett, 1990). The success or failure of the psychoeducational family intervention is typically defined by the relapse rate of the chronically ill relative, not by the reduced levels of burden within the family (Grunebaum & Friedman, 1988). Such training may subtly blame the family member for exacerbating their relative's illness (Scheyett, 1990). Not surprisingly, studies of psychoeducational interventions have found that they did not diminish parents' negative feelings toward their adult children with mental illness nor change their coping behavior, level of family satisfaction, or psychological well-being (Posner et al., 1992).

Support Groups

The number and types of support and mutual help groups have grown in recent years for reasons similar to those underlying the popularity of education and training. Support groups are presumed to strengthen the caregivers' motivation to continue to provide care, to compensate for the carers' decreased social involvement, and to provide opportunities to vent their negative feelings and receive the acceptance of these by others who are in similar situations (Greene & Monahan, 1989; Stone et al., 1987; Toseland & Rossiter, 1989). Findings regarding the extent of these presumed benefits are mixed. With regard to support groups for caregivers of the frail elderly, participants do experience improvements in their relationships with care receivers, increased informal supports and knowledge of resources, improved self-appraisal in managing the demands of caring, increased competence in handling interpersonal concerns related to care, and decreases in the severity of psychological problems (Toseland, Rossiter, & Labrecque, 1989b). Statistically significant reductions in caregiver anxiety and depression have also been found, although these benefits are reduced over time (Greene & Monahan, 1989). Gonyea (1989) documented the benefits of information and peer support for caregivers of Alzheimer's patients. But support groups have only modest benefits as measured by global ratings of well-being, mood, stress, psychological status, and burden (Zarit & Toseland, 1989).

Although an underlying rationale for support groups is often to prolong the caregivers' ability to keep their dependent relative in the home and therefore to save costs, support groups have not necessarily deterred institutional placement (Callahan, 1989). However, avoidance of institutional placement should not always be viewed as the primary goal. Although nursing home placement is unattractive from an economic perspective, it may reflect an appropriate use of services and a desirable clinical outcome from the caregivers' point of view; in such instances, a support group's expression of psychological support can be aimed at reducing guilt or remorse experienced regarding the institutionalization decision (Haley, 1989; Montgomery & Borgatta, 1989).

Early group treatment in the late 1970s for parents of adults with mental illness aimed to change the parents' behavior, making them less overprotective, critical, and hostile toward their relatives in order to prevent relapse and rehospitalization (McLean, Greer, Scott, & Beck, 1982). Since then, the focus has shifted toward supporting caregivers, helping them to separate from their adult child and function more effectively as a family. Accordingly, support groups for carers of relatives who are mentally ill—such as those sponsored by the National Alliance of the Mentally Ill (NAMI)—emphasize emotional support, reciprocity, referrals to service, education, and advocacy (Battaglino, 1987). Support group participants may gain some sense of control over chronic problems and issues; in addition, the support of an intimate trusted group can make it possible for families to discuss problems in coping with chronic conditions that they would not feel comfortable discussing elsewhere, which can, in some instances, lower feelings of burden (Anthony & Blanch, 1989; Marsh, 1992; Potasznik & Nelson, 1984). Families' satisfaction with support groups has been found to be correlated with their perception of the group as empathic, nonjudgmental, and nonthreatening. But support groups, especially those that are short-term, cannot necessarily assist families in altering patterns of behavior with their relatives nor learning specific skills (Biegel & Yamatani, 1987).

An unexpected negative finding regarding support groups for caregivers of individuals who are chronically mentally ill is that participants in one study reported greater burden and conflict and less gratification than nonparticipants (Bulger, Wandersman, & Goldman, 1993). This may be because group discussions make caregivers more aware of, and freer to express, their unhappiness, and less likely to use stoicism as a coping mechanism. Other studies have found that being able to talk with those who understood the situation provided relief, reduced their sense of isolation, and encouraged advocacy rather than feelings of victimization and ineffectiveness in dealing with the mental health system (Potasznik & Nelson, 1984).

From a feminist perspective, support groups for caregivers have limitations similar to those of education and training techniques. Mixed findings regarding the effectiveness of support groups may result from the fact that they do not address what caregivers perceive to be the problems and needs, nor are they necessarily congruent with carers' goals for the group (Smith et al., 1991). Well-meaning practitioners may be too eager to focus on the caregivers' symptoms of stress and depression when the carer wants assistance with specific tasks, such as arranging community services or residential placement (Smith et al., 1991). Given the range, complexity, and chronicity of issues facing families, it is unrealistic to expect that 6 to 10 group sessions will have a profound effect on caregivers' lives (Whitlach et al., 1991). Families are often referred to support groups after they have provided extensive care and may be experiencing high levels of stress, rather than using groups early in the caring process as a preventive measure. For some caregivers, support groups may be experienced as yet another burden, particularly if they are faced with locating transportation and respite or attendant care in order to be able to attend. Support groups may not be integrated with other services, so that participation becomes still another demand on their time and energy, which may explain difficulties encountered in recruiting caregivers to such groups (Montgomery & Borgatta, 1989).

When support groups function as a safety valve to let the caregiver blow off emotional steam and then return to the same situation, they do not offer long-run solutions to stress. From a feminist critique, support groups may serve to promote individual competence, coping, and personal adjustment skills—for example, cognitive restructuring techniques to alter how they think about the caring experience—rather than the structural change required for the development and funding of new community-based services (Abel & Nelson, 1990; Hooyman, 1992). As noted by Hatfield and Lefley (1987) in their review of services for individuals who are mentally ill, the popularity of support groups is due, in large part, to the failure of the mental health system to meet families' needs through other types of services. Support groups can provide an immediate and visible response to families, but they do not alter gender inequities in care responsibilities nor necessarily increase the accessibility of culturally appropriate and affordable services.

A FEMINIST MODEL FOR COMMUNITY SUPPORT SYSTEMS

The overall goal of a feminist model of social care is to assure gender justice in terms of caring responsibilities. Our objective in describing this model is to present a framework for conceptualizing community support services within long-term care, not to give a blueprint for specific services nor resolve the question of funding. This model is organized around several key elements: the opportunity for both men and women to choose roles, information and advocacy as a basis for caregiver empowerment, and caregivers' capability to provide quality care, which includes their rights to a comprehensive range of available, accessible, and acceptable services (Kirp, Yudof, & Franks, 1986; Marsh, 1992; Wallace, 1990). We recognize that this model conflicts with current prevailing assumptions about the roles and responsibilities of family and government for providing care for dependents. Given the current economic and political climate, changes of the magnitude suggested by this model may seem impossible.

On the other hand, social invention on a grand scale occurred in the face of economic crises in the 1930s, and Social Security and public education now exist as entitlement for all citizens. The crises facing families today are no less severe than the economic ones of the Great Depression. The problems facing family caregivers of the chronically dependent are so complex, multifaceted, and long-term that it is essential to think creatively and comprehensively about alternatives beyond simple, short-term solutions. It is a question of political resolve to reallocate societal resources over the long run, not a matter of insufficient resources in the aggregate.

Opportunity to Choose

A feminist model is built around the concept of choice for the caregiver, and oriented to enhancing the quality of life for both the caregiver and the care receiver. Choice for both men and women about care and workplace roles is a necessary condition for gender justice (Kirp et al., 1986). In addition to the freedom not to provide care, the government should assure the freedom to give quality care by making support resources available to both the caregiver and the care recipient, including assistance with the most basic care tasks (England, Keigher, Miller, & Linsk, 1990). In a feminist model, care management (not management of a case) is conceptualized as a way to facilitate consumer preference by assessing need and insuring the existence of alternative modes of services that are culturally appropriate (Kane & Kane, 1985). The centrality of choice in this model also recognizes that supporting families to enable them to care is not always in the best interests of the caregiver or the care receiver, and therefore ensures that institutional and other types of residential placements are available when the choice is not to care (McConnell & Riggs, 1994). In order to assure choices regarding the degree of caregiver involvement, community social service approaches must be integrated with the comprehensive development of housing alternatives, encompassing nursing homes, group homes, shared housing, surrogate families, and independent living.

Education for Empowerment

Closely interconnected with the concept of choice is that of empowerment: caregiver control or autonomy over the selection of community supports. Autonomy in the field of developmental disabilities, for example, is conceived as a negotiated or assisted process leading to an enhanced sense of worth or dignity (Ansello & Roberto, 1993). In the area of mental health, empowerment programs give the family full treatment authority with the understanding that they will make decisions and learn from their mistakes (Pfeiffer & Mostek, 1991). The professional then assists the family in implementing their decisions. The emphasis on empowerment contrasts dramatically with the traditional medical model that has dominated mental health, in which family members have been only tangentially involved in the treatment process (Biegel, Song, & Chakravarthy, 1994).

As a first step toward such autonomy, caregivers need to be educated about what their options are: to have adequate information on which to base their preferences (Kirp et al., 1986). The goal of caregiver education should be empowerment, not increased efficiency nor cost savings. Because the meaning of caregiving varies among ethnic and racial groups, education needs to occur within the cultural context of the caregiver's beliefs and values and, where possible, to use natural helping systems rather than rely on professionals.

In contrast to current short-term psychoeducational interventions, education about care options needs to be ongoing and available to families before they assume the full-time caregiver role as well as during their caring career. Such programs would have a preventive emphasis, and information would be presented early enough in the caring cycle before options are closed off. Too often, families have been informed of services too late, after a crisis has occurred or they have reached the breaking point and are seeking institutionalization for their relative. In order for education to be an effective means of early intervention, information must be provided to both current and potential caregivers in natural settings, such as employee assistance programs in the workplace, family resource centers and parent associations in the schools, family life programs and adult education in the churches, and neighborhood programs of community centers. By providing education within such natural contexts, all family members, not just the individual most likely to be the primary carer (e.g., mother, daughter, wife, or sister), can be included. This more inclusive approach has the potential to promote the development of a larger supportive and helping social network involving both men and women than when only the primary caregivers are targeted for education or support after they have assumed the role of carer (Abramowitz & Coursey, 1989).

Education could be structured to be longer-term than many current training or workshop programs by building in follow-up sessions. For example, after a general educational program informs current and potential caregivers of the range of care options available to them and the individual has chosen his or her primary role, specialized training could be provided at the point when a greater need for more technical skills is identified by the carers. Opportunities to explore issues more in depth, perhaps through counseling, could be provided. Recognizing that those who choose the caring role may not have the time nor the respite care to allow them to attend ongoing workshops, specialized educational programs could be made available through videotapes, satellite programming, and computers. The possibility of ongoing education through information technology is particularly salient for future generations of caregivers, who are likely to be technologically sophisticated and have access to the necessary resources. For some caregivers, however, cultural values may be more conducive to face-to-face interaction as a basis for learning care techniques. In such instances, volunteers or peer helpers from a similar cultural background and from the local community can be effective educators. For example, peer consultants—family members who model collaboration with mental health professionals—have been effectively used in education groups with families of the chronically mentally ill (Pfeiffer & Mostek, 1991).

Education is necessary not only for the caregiver but also for the general public through awareness campaigns that are integrated into the natural settings of workplace, school, church, and community club as well as disseminated through the media. As part of a national caregiver agenda, such an approach can inform the public of caregivers' needs for support, and also of the invaluable and extraordinary work performed by carers (Ansello & Roberto, 1993). Public education about the caring role, its importance, and its consequences can, over time, begin to change the societal evaluation of the role. If both men and women are informed of the supports available, caregiving may become more highly valued in our society than currently, when many women feel compelled to provide care because their time is viewed as less valuable in the marketplace.

Capability to Provide Quality Care

In a feminist model of social care, community care must be a social utility, like public education, available according to a broader definition of need than currently exists under federal funding (England et al., 1990). The goal of such a model is not just to save money or to prevent nursing home or hospital admissions. Rather than defining services as a gift or charity, caregivers of dependents are entitled to services across the life course (Estes & Binney, 1988; Estes et al., 1993; Kane & Kane, 1985). If families choose to provide care and are to be capable providers, they must be supported by a comprehensive range of accessible, integrated, and culturally appropriate services that provide a strengthened infrastructure of support (Ansello & Roberto, 1993). Public services are therefore available to people who need them as part of a social security system based on the rights of citizenship (Neysmith, 1993). As reviews of the Canadian system illustrate, affordable long-term care can be offered as an entitlement rather than as a welfare benefit (Kane & Kane, 1985). Consistent with the goal of empowerment, policies that provide the right or entitlement to services and some type of payment or allowance are requisite to the preservation of personal control. The uniform provision of services ensured by entitlement provides for predictability and equity in access (Collins, 1991). Organizational and clinical principles would be linked with the norms and incentives of daily practice in a feminist model of care (Stein, Diamond, & Factor, 1989).

In a feminist model, the family is recognized as a legitimate consumer of services (Heagerty & Eskenazi, 1994). Accordingly, mechanisms are provided for families' input into decisions about the development, funding, distribution, and evaluation of services (Neysmith, 1993). Partnerships between families and formal service providers recognize the rights of families to be involved in care planning as well as the particular strengths and expertise that both families and service providers can bring to the process (Kropf, 1994a). As noted by Marsh (1992), it is not simply that family members rightfully belong on the mental health treatment team in light of their caregiving responsibilities, expertise, resources, and commitment, but the expansion of the team to include family members can enhance the overall effectiveness of treatment (Rosenson, Kasten, & Kennedy, 1988). When families are involved, services are less likely to become overprofessionalized, rigid, or obfuscated in bureaucratic rules (Jennings, 1987; Zarit, 1994).

In such a model, the care manager would work closely with the family as team partners or collaborators in order to tailor services to the needs and goals of families and patients (Ziral et al., 1989). The care manager in a family-centered system would not just be a broker and administrator of services for a case, but an advocate for mobilizing and changing services to better meet individual client needs and to support family members. Efforts would be made to influence care at the individual client level, and also to advocate at the system level to change the patterns of services themselves and how they affect family caregivers (Challis, 1994; Kane, 1990). In mental health, for example, effective care management would be systematic and include assertive outreach and individually tailored programs of care across the life course. It would include respite, ongoing monitoring, titration of levels of support according to needs, training and support of families as members of the team, and building on the strengths of patients and families treated as responsible citizens, rather than focusing on deficits.

With regard to carers of the chronically mentally ill, consumer choice and voice may represent the fourth cycle of mental health reform, where comprehensive systems of care involve the family and the care recipient in treatment planning encompassing case management, community outreach, grievance procedures, support groups, advocacy organizations, and systematic evaluation of services (Marsh, 1992; Torrey, Wolfe, & Flynn, 1988). The principles specified by Bernheim (1989) for family-professional relationships in the area of mental health are applicable to all three of the populations that are the focus of this book. These guidelines for professionals are to (a) view relatives who desire to participate as empowered members of the caring network, (b) provide adequate orientation, (c) create multiple channels for access and communication, (d) aim services toward reducing family burden, (e) develop individualized service plans that take account of cultural differences, (f) respond flexibly to changing needs over time, and (g) involve family representatives in systemic planning and oversight. As caregivers become better informed about options through the educational process and feel some ownership in the process, a bottom-up approach to policy development to support families can occur.

As a result of federal legislation (P.L. 99-457) in the field of developmental disabilities, family-oriented care management is conceptualized as a way to involve families in the process of initiating, monitoring, reassessing, and terminating services (Rinck & Calkins, 1993). Bradley and Knoll (1990) describe a new paradigm for delivery of services to persons with developmental disabilities, composed of four elements: commitment to the community and families, emphasis on human relationships, person-centered programming, and real choice and control for consumers. Operationally, such a paradigm brings together consumers, family caregivers, and professionals in developing, evaluating, and managing services, resulting in a strengthened infrastructure of support. This paradigm has been implemented through demonstration projects at the local level, such as a Vermont project in which citizens and policymakers are redesigning the entire long-term care system, through grassroots planning, into one more oriented to community-assisted independent living (Ansello & Roberto, 1993).

With regard to caregivers of frail elderly, Estes et al. (1993) have advocated for community gerontology teams encompassing both formal and informal caregivers, including representatives from senior, children's, and other social action groups, to discuss issues affecting the elderly from an intergenerational perspective and to develop experimental projects and initiatives to empower both the older person and their caregivers. The role of the care manager, identified earlier with regard to the chronically mentally ill, would also apply to working effectively with carers of the elderly.

Closely related to the concepts of capacity-building and consumer involvement is the development of support groups as a means to promote social change (Abel & Nelson, 1990). Through open discussion, including consciousness-raising and politicizing techniques, support group members have the opportunity to explore the common systemic roots of their personal problems. Women caregivers can begin to understand the structural factors that underlie the devaluation of their caring role and can be encouraged to seek common solutions to problems they previously viewed as private, moving from individual coping and mutual sharing to advocacy and finding a collective voice (Hooyman & Ryan, 1985; Sommers & Shields, 1987). For example, caregivers of the elderly in the California-based support group *Women Who Care* moved from being victims of circumstances to "healers of social wrongs" (Sommers & Shields, 1987). The National Alliance for the Mentally Ill (NAMI) is an example of a caregiver group embracing advocacy and social change. However, caregiver welfare has not been the explicit goal of many of NAMI's advocacy activities, which have focused on improving the quality of life of the person who is mentally ill. Perhaps one reason that NAMI has not directly focused on caregiver well-being is that it is not feminist in its orientation; it therefore has not addressed the issue of gender and the interconnections between women's oppression and that of persons with mental illness (Battaglino, 1987; Scheyett, 1990). Nor has NAMI effectively involved low-income and ethnic minority families. Nevertheless, it does illustrate what can be achieved by the strength of grassroots organizations to influence the allocation of resources.

Given the large numbers of families who are caring for dependent relatives—a number that will escalate in the next 20 years with the aging of the baby boomers and their parents—organizations of carers who are also voters can profoundly influence the development of public policy. Networks could be developed among the diverse range of support groups for caregivers of dependents, building intergenerational alliances across the life span to affect the political process. In addition to facilitating such cross-group organization, professionals can insure that families have the services that they need—transportation and attendant care, for example—to be able to participate in the political process.

An essential component of the infrastructure of support for caregiver capacity-building is to recognize the interconnections between social and economic aspects of care. As emphasized earlier, community-based social services cannot be separated from the concept of a caregiver allowance or stipend, or from assistance with the expenditures that are often involved in caring such as housing alterations and high-tech equipment, the tax structure and vouchers for such services, and reimbursement for the care provided (Cantor, 1994; McConnell & Riggs, 1994). Because stipends and vouchers have the effect of providing income to the family, they are also part of an overall comprehensive service approach in which the family is the consumer (McConnell & Riggs, 1994). The development of community support services also cannot be separated from employment or workplace policies and practices, which must be structured in ways that will not penalize those who assume caregiving responsibilities. In summary, a policy approach to providing services to caregivers must be comprehensive and coherent, insuring access through economic and emotional supports as well as accessible services.

This discussion of social service needs sets the context for the absolute necessity of a comprehensive long-term care policy that includes community-based social, health, and mental health services and is integral to national health care reform (Kane & Kane, 1985). McConnell and Riggs (1994) contend that policy makers cannot be left believing that they can "get off the hook" on long-term care just by initiatives to support family caregivers (p. 28). The fundamental shift needed in our society is to move beyond defining issues related to long-term care of dependents as an individual or family problem to that of a societal problem requiring a comprehensive universal long-term care policy. The ideal of such a national policy that protects against disease and disability is the focus of Chapter 14.

13

Gender Justice

Achieving a More Family-Responsive Workplace

Gender inequality in the home and market dramatically influences how men and women experience both family and work activities. The ideology of separate spheres spawned during the Industrial Revolution continues to shape American family life and the U.S. work economy. Feminists argue that government and business policies have continued to reinforce this ideology of the gender stratification of the two spheres. They emphasize the following:

> The net effect is to maintain a primary identification of women with domestic and family concerns that all too often hamper them when they move into the labor force. . . . In addition, these policies propel men to concentrate on jobs while they depend on their wives for creating and maintaining a home. (Gerstel & Gross, 1987, p. 463)

Historically, a central underpinning of the U.S. work economy has been business's reliance on the presence of women at home so that men can enter the workplace unencumbered by family responsibilities that might restrict their time or distract their attention from the job. Now that more women are in the labor force, this ideology works against their equality in the workplace. By arguing that, unlike men, their primary and natural orientation is toward their family, women's second-class status in the labor market continues to be justified, and their efforts to combine family and work responsibilities are not adequately supported.

In this chapter, we explore strategies by which society can help promote a healthy balance between family and work roles for both women and men. In proposing policy directions, we employ a feminist framework of gender justice. We discuss the U.S. cultural and business ideologies concerning the interconnectedness of family, work, and gender roles as well as current social and economic conditions that form the context for advancing this feminist agenda. The respective roles of government and business in promoting healthy families and workplaces will also be addressed.

FAMILY-RESPONSIVE WORKPLACE POLICIES AND A GENDER JUSTICE FRAMEWORK

Lambert (1993, p. 253) suggests that the term "family-responsive policies in the workplace" may be a misnomer in that "many of these policies function as work supports to help ensure that workers continue to give priority to work over personal responsibilities." The growing diversification of the workforce and family structures (e.g., dual-earner households and single-parent families) has resulted in some businesses implementing family-responsive policies (e.g., child care or elder care supports, employee assistance programs), but few businesses have restructured the traditional male work environment to support an integration of home and work roles.

> Women are welcome, indeed desired, in influential organizational positions as long as they follow the existing rules, rules established when gender roles clearly differentiated the two spheres. . . . The family, according to traditional U.S. career rules, needs to be invisible at work, to be dealt with only at the margins. (Bailyn, 1992, p. 203)

It should not, then, be surprising that many of the family-responsive policies function more as "work supports" rather than "family supports" and, in turn, serve to keep caring work relatively invisible (Lambert, 1993). To convince business to adopt family-responsive measures, proponents of these initiatives often have emphasized the benefits for business, not for families or women. These initiatives are "sold" to business through a "win-win" argument that meeting the needs of workers ultimately makes a business more productive and competitive. Kingston (1990, p. 447) urges, however, that a skeptical view be taken regarding the "proverbial win/win situation whereby business self-interest dovetails with the family interests of the new workforce." He maintains that although part-time employment is viewed as especially appealing to women with children, it can have negative economic consequences for women; because most of these jobs offer few benefits, they provide mutual benefits only under "a very strained sense of mutuality" (Kingston, 1990, p. 447).

Family-oriented benefits are often championed as assisting business in the recruitment and retention of valued employees, the strengthening of company loyalty and commitment, the reduction of absenteeism, and the enhancement of work performance. Thus, these policies are designed to help employees find ways to cope with family problems that interfere with their job performance (work supports) rather than to restructure the male-model organizational structure to accommodate workers' personal or family responsibilities (family supports).

Focusing on the recent U.S. debate concerning family leave, England (1990, p. 21) suggests that "arguing what is best for business is of little substantive or political value to most caregivers." Proponents of family leave have framed the debate narrowly in response to business opponents; England (1990) contends thusly:

> Despite its centrality to the problem, the question of where responsibility for the care of health-impaired dependent citizens should lie is not addressed. . . . By reframing the issue as one of gender justice, the discourse can be broadened to include the health and social policy context that leaves so many women with the stark choice between caregiving and employment. (p. 10)

A gender justice framework asserts that women and men should have the same rights, obligations, and opportunities in both the family and work spheres. Just as a woman should have the right to choose employment, so should a man have the right to choose to care. A central tenet of a gender justice ideology is that every individual—woman or man—should have the right to a secure job with favorable wages that allow an adequate standard of living for a family. "This (an adequate family wage) is the essential foundation for a sustaining, stable family life. If private businesses fail to deliver on this count, all other concerns about 'responsiveness' are moot" (Kingston, 1990, p. 441). This philosophy then moves the gender equity debate regarding the family-responsive workplace from a fairly narrow discussion of fringe benefits, such as flextime and dependent care tax credits, to a much broader discourse of gender equity in terms of job security, wages, work conditions, and career opportunities.

This broader discourse is critical, given women's disadvantaged status in the marketplace and the devaluation of their work in the home. As we have seen, the U.S. workforce is still characterized by gender-based occupational segregation and a female-male earnings gap. More than 66% of all employed women are still found in just two sectors of the labor market—services (45%) and wholesale and retail trade (22%). Women still continue to earn only $.72 for every $1.00 of men's wages (U.S. Bureau of Labor Statistics, 1991), and women are almost twice as likely to work for minimum wage than their male counterparts (Reis & Stone, 1992). Women are also disadvantaged in unemployment. Unemployment compensation programs (originally named Workmen's Compensation) were designed to respond to the needs of regularly employed male heads of households. Women constitute a disproportionate share of the unemployed, but they are disqualified as claimants or are allotted reduced unemployment benefits more often than men. A woman who quits her job because of the demands of her caregiving responsibilities (e.g., unavailability of child care, lack of elder care, or inappropriate hours relative to family responsibilities) is unlikely to qualify for compensation (Gerstel & Gross, 1987). Finally, as noted earlier, the trivialization of housework and the invisibility of many caregiving activities have led to a devaluation of women's unpaid work in the home. Indeed, feminists have criticized the assumption that "work" and "worth" are linked to performance in the marketplace or formal economy and therefore the value of endeavors in the home go unrecognized (Gerstel & Gross, 1987).

WOMEN'S "SPECIAL" STATUS IN THE WORKFORCE

Despite the fact that over 66% of American women now work for a living and more than 40% of all U.S. workers are female, women are still considered a special group within the workforce. Why is this so? Kessler-Harris (1987) argues that women's special status in the marketplace derives in part from society's historical failure to come to terms with whether, in fact, women are different from men. The perceived difference, feminists argue, is largely based on men's and women's dissimilar relationships to their families. For example, men in the workplace are generally referred to as simply "workers," but women in the workforce typically bear labels that connote their family roles as well as their work status, such as "working mother" and "working wife." Kessler-Harris (1987) notes the following:

> To say that women have historically remained a special group, then, is to say that in the past they did not act like male workers, choose the same responsibilities, make the same commitments, compete as effectively, or expect the same rewards. (p. 521)

U.S. policy has historically been based on the assumption that a woman's place was in the home and that women who did work for pay did so only because of economic necessity. A woman who was "forced" to enter the labor force was primarily oriented toward her family's well-being, not toward individual achievement, self-fulfillment, or success. Protective legislation was created to safeguard those women who had to enter the marketplace. For example, the 1908 decision of the Supreme Court upheld maximum work hours legislation for women (Muller v. Oregon, 1908, p.422) on the following basis:

> [A woman's] physical structure and proper discharge of her maternal functions—having in view not merely her own health, but the well-being of the race—justify legislation to protect her from the greed as well as the passion of men. (Spakes, 1992)

In promoting women's position in the labor force, feminists have continually debated whether to emphasize women's differences from men and the unique set of talents, skills, and perspectives that they bring to the marketplace—a "gynocentric, or women-centered, view of feminism"—or to stress that women and men share a common set of human rights that transcend biology—"a humanistic view" (Fuller, 1971). (For a historical analysis of this debate, see Kessler-Harris, 1987). The humanistic view is reflected in the work of the National Women's Party during the 1920s, which sponsored the first Equal Rights Amendment and promoted workplace equality for women, through slogans such as "Give a woman a man's chance industrially" (Kessler-Harris, 1987). In contrast, the women's rights advocates who held a women-centered view sought as their goal the opportunity for women to bring their own moral influence into the public sphere, not equality. Eleanor Roosevelt, for instance, opposed the Equal Rights Amendment, fearing it would eliminate all special protection for women in the workforce and overlook women's particular needs. Kessler-Harris (1987) notes the following:

> Their [women-centered feminists'] position achieved public support because it did not explicitly violate commonly held views of men's and women's separate spheres and partly because it seemed to offer some moderate and sensible solutions to the social and economic problems produced by women's increasing wage-earner roles. (p. 524)

Women were designated a special class within the workforce that required protection, given their weaker physical constitution, their childbearing (and rearing) roles, as well as their greater emotional, moral, and spiritual sensitivities.

The designation of women as a special population in the labor force brought short-term positive gains for women (e.g., better working conditions, shorter working hours), but in the long run, resulted in discrimination (e.g., the restriction of women from certain occupations, obstacles to career advancement). And the debate regarding how women can best achieve equality in the workplace continues. Kessler-Harris (1987, p. 523) suggests that a central question to this debate remains whether women can achieve workplace equality "without either negating family roles or reifying them."

The recent debate is best captured in the controversy surrounding Felice Schwartz's (1989) article in *Harvard Business Review*, "Management Women and the New Facts of Life," in which she identifies the existence of a "mommy track." Schwartz distinguishes between two types of corporate women: "career primary" women, who put their careers first and are willing to forfeit their personal and family lives, and "career-and-family" women who are willing to sacrifice some degree of career growth and compensation for release from some job pressures. She argues that it is time for society (and businesses) to acknowledge that women, primarily due to maternity issues, are more costly to firms than are men, and that corporations have a responsibility to offer greater flexibility in employment arrangements for women attempting to pursue both career and family. A feminist, Schwartz suggests that a significant proportion of those women in the workplace who are trying to "have it all" (the so-called "superwomen") are, in fact, suffering the costs of this decision, and that business has an obligation to make some accommodations to those women who choose to combine career and family roles.

Schwartz's objective was to help promote women's position in the workplace, but her "mommy-track" article produced a great deal of anger from a number of feminists. Newspaper columnist Ellen Goodman strongly criticized Schwartz for identifying only a two-track system and for her failure to incorporate a life-span perspective that recognizes that family and career interests may shift in priority over time. Schwartz does not address the fact that women now spend many years free from child care obligations, nor does she raise the phenomenon of caring for aging parents or other adults with chronic disabilities. Hall (1990, p. 7) asked the question of "Why just a mommy track?" Although the evidence is mounting that men also make career accommodations based on family need, he argued that the "daddy track" remains invisible. He suggested that one outcome of the acceptance of the mommy track is that work-family balance will continue to be defined by business as a woman's concern rather than a universal employee concern.

Underlying Schwartz's argument is the assumption that women—in either of the two tracks—must ultimately be willing or prepared to make sacrifices. Although Schwartz does suggest that firms need to offer more flexible work arrangements to women who choose to combine career and family, it remains clear that she believes that these women will also need to make accommodations—that is, trade career advancement as well as wage and nonwage compensation for a less pressured work environment. Schwartz lacks a class perspective (reflected by her primary interest in management women) and ignores the reality that many working women simply cannot afford to sacrifice wages or benefits. This perspective also overlooks the limited options of many women of color who are disproportionately represented in low-income jobs. Nor does Schwartz seem to be concerned with the experiences of the women in the "career-priority track." Although a significant proportion of these women have forgone marriage or children in order to advance in the male corporate environment—choices made by many fewer of their "career priority" male colleagues—their sacrifices receive little attention from Schwartz, perhaps because these choices are viewed as self-imposed or having only personal costs and few corporate costs.

Schwartz invokes a women-centered view of feminism that emphasizes women's need for special status in the workforce because of their unique childbearing and rearing roles. Although intended to advance women's position in the workforce, Schwartz's designation of women as special is viewed by most feminists as increasing their second-class status by providing corporations with ready excuses for failing to hire these "more costly" women and denying women promotional opportunities (Hall, 1990). Although Schwartz argues that corporations have a social responsibility to respond to these "career and family" women's needs with more flexible work arrangements, her recommendations are modest, and she fails to question the male model of the work organization.

THE LIMITATIONS OF GENDER-NEUTRAL FAMILY-RESPONSIVE POLICIES

A number of feminists also caution against the rhetoric of "integrating work and family" and the adoption of gender-neutral family-responsive policies. As Spakes (1992, p. 58) argues, "When people are differentially situated in the economic situation, equal treatment policies do not and cannot produce equal results." As we have emphasized, women and men are not operating on a "level playing field" within the marketplace. Both the designation of women as caregivers in our society and the existence of the female-male earnings gap suggest that, although alternative work arrangements are intended as gender neutral policies, women will be more likely than men to "choose" these options. One of the most frequently cited reasons given by mothers (but not by fathers) for home-based employment was "to take care of my family" (Christensen, 1987b). A growing number of feminists warn that too often these family-responsive programs mean that women do more work in less time, get paid lower wages, and receive little or no benefits (Spakes, 1989). In fact, Christensen's (1987b) analysis of home-based employment reveals that a number of corporations assign a different status to clerical and professional persons who pursue this option. Moreover, full-time employees who switch to independent contractor status often lose benefits, receive lower wages, and forfeit the right to a guaranteed number of work hours. Christensen (1987b) comes to this conclusion:

> Such arrangements threaten to turn home-based independent contractors into second-class corporate citizens, denied the rights and benefits for full-time employees. Insofar as more women than men accept this arrangement, and the evidence is that more women do, then they run the further risk of becoming a disadvantaged corporate community, denied access to pools for advancement or skill upgrading. (p. 487)

Citing evidence that alternative work schedules (or flextime) increases men's satisfaction with a particular job whereas they allow women to concentrate more on family obligations, Gerstel and Gross (1987, p. 460) also warn that these policies may actually serve to reinforce gender inequality rather than reduce it. The recently passed U.S. Family Medical and Leave Act is yet another example of a policy that is gender-neutral in its intent, but not so in its effect. Surveys of U.S. companies reveal that few men take advantage of this benefit because they are fearful of being viewed by supervisors or colleagues as "not serious about their careers," "female-dominated in their home" or "eccentric." Even in Sweden, where paternity leave policy offers both job protection and 90% of salary for the leave period, men generally remain reluctant to use this option (Hall, 1990). Men's low use of family leave supports England's contention that gender-neutral policies may influence choices already shaped by sex-role stereotypes and thereby act to reinforce gender inequities (England, 1990, p. 10). Thus, traditional gender-stereotyped patterns not only restrict women's options in the marketplace, but also deprive men of opportunities for family interaction (Gerstel & Gross, 1987).

WORK-FAMILY BALANCE AND GENDER EQUALITY: BUSINESS POLICY

If society is to promote "equality of opportunity" and "equality of results" to maximize the choices available for women, what is needed are *gender-equality* policies—as opposed to gender-neutral policies—in the workplace (Spakes, 1992). To advance gender equity effectively, work-family policy must be viewed in the context of a labor market that is being radically reshaped by forces such as global competition and technological advances. Company downsizing and reengineering, the emergence of the virtual corporation, and an increased reliance on contingent workers represent only some of the techniques that corporations are increasingly employing to guide them into the 21st century. The workplace is being rapidly transformed with little attention paid to the effect of these changes on employees and their dependent care responsibilities.

For many women, the recent restructuring of the labor market has not resulted in positive gains.

High paying jobs for men have been "deskilled" and given to women at lower pay. Jobs have moved to depressed areas inside and outside the United States in a deliberate attempt to depress wages. The growth of the lower-paying service economy has depended upon the availability of women for work. (Spakes, 1992, p. 55)

Politically conservative *Newsweek* columnist Robert J. Samuelson (1993) makes this suggestion:

What is also wounded is our idea of the welfare state. Since World War II this has always been an unofficial blend of private and government benefits. As more firms became "good companies" we thought more workers would receive welfare benefits (health insurance, pensions). Government would protect only the poor, disabled and aged. Companies had become spontaneous instruments of social policy; for a citizenry suspicious of government, this seemed fine. (p. 41)

Job security and universal benefits, however, are eroding. As we have discussed, fewer workers now have employer-paid pensions or health insurance, and employers who provide health coverage expect workers to pay a larger share of their premium. Gaps in the social safety net have widened, particularly for women, who are disproportionately found in the low-paying service sector, in part-time employment, and in the contingent workforce. It is within this economic and social context, then, that we examine strategies to advance work-family balance and workplace equality for women.

As we have noted, work-family corporate initiatives were originally launched in the 1970s to respond to a rather narrow set of employer-employee concerns—the need of employed parents for child care. The scope of corporate family-responsive initiatives has continued to expand, both in terms of the extension of benefits for dependent care across the life span (i.e., care for chronically ill or disabled adults and elders), and in terms of the types of benefits (i.e., information and referral, flexible benefit plans, or cafeteria plans). For the most part, these benefits have been well-received by both employees and employers. Increasingly concerned about skyrocketing health insurance costs, employers have found most of these family-related benefits relatively inexpensive to implement. Flexible benefit plans, as we have seen, offer employers a way to increase workers' satisfaction with their benefit packages without entailing greater cost. When cafeteria plans are introduced, cost control mechanisms are typically added or increased in order to shift some costs from employer to employee (Boyce, 1994). Further, family-related benefits are generally viewed as nondisruptive to operations and as not challenging the status quo of the male work organization.

A growing number of professionals, however, have urged a rethinking of the work-family field from a narrow focus on employee benefits to a broader view of work-family as a key human resource strategy for promoting a healthy workplace in the 21st century (Lobel & Googins, 1994). Suggesting that at the heart of the work-family problem is the issue of corporate values, Hall (1990) urges a more fundamental organization-change approach to fostering work-family balance. He argues that framing this balance as a "parent problem" versus a "corporate problem" allows corporate executives "to look progressive by working on family issues without confronting important issues of discrimination—based not just on gender, but also on race, ethnicity, and other kinds of differences" (Hall, 1990, p. 13). Hall suggests that corporate leaders need to explore their values regarding women reaching top-level positions along with their assumptions about what is a "good" executive, parent, and career. He advises that with an organization-change approach, corporate management should broaden their work-family analysis to encompass not only the issues of dependent care and benefits, but also the issues of work restructuring, management training opportunities, and career paths.

Bailyn (1992) argues that rethinking career rules and success is central to promoting gender equality in the workplace and also to increasing the perceived value of work in the domestic sphere. Although American women have entered the marketplace, "the expectations for careers have not changed; career success is still dependent on primary priority to family. Nor has there been a significant shift in male roles in the domestic sphere" (Bailyn, p. 207). Bailyn maintains that the prevalent assumption that long hours equal productivity is an outmoded holdover from assembly line work; with the increase in "knowledge work," the goal should be to "work smart, not to work long" (p. 207). She maintains that we should shift thinking about careers from "life-long continuity to discontinuity" recognizing that individuals' needs and priorities change across the life course (p. 207). If discontinuities were viewed as the norm, perhaps the economic costs that currently exist from movement in and out of the workforce would be reduced. Central to Bailyn's thesis is the belief that the equalizing of gender roles within both the family and marketplace is necessary. She concludes that without gender equality in domestic and public spheres, either family care or women—who have been designated as the ones to balance this conflict—will continue to suffer.

Promoting gender equality in the workplace—the ability of both women and men to achieve a healthy balance between their work and family roles—is an extremely complex issue. Mounting evidence suggests that simply creating alternative family arrangements, which are used primarily by female workers may, in fact, further contribute to workplace gender inequity. Rather, from a feminist perspective, what is truly needed is an exploration of how the corporate culture, the work organization, and company policies shape male and female workers' experiences.

To achieve gender justice in the workplace, we offer the following recommendations in terms of corporate policy:

The Redefinition of Work-Family Balance From
a "Benefits Issue" to a "Strategic Human Resource Issue"

Although the current business trend is for companies to become "lean and mean" in order to increase productivity, a growing number of management experts suggest that this strategy may, in the long run, prove to be counterproductive. Experts such as O'Toole (1985), Kanter (1983), and Bailyn (1992) argue that, for the United States to regain its competitive edge, American companies must produce high-quality and innovative products that will increasingly require employees who are willing to "think" about their jobs rather than just "do" them. An expanding body of literature suggests that, in fact, workers are more likely to think about their jobs in innovative ways and make contributions to the company when they perceive that the organization is supportive of them personally (Eisenberger, Fasolo, & Davis-LaMastro, 1990). Nevertheless, by most accounts, the social contract between employer and employee has been badly fractured in the past decade by factors such as company downsizing. Policies that promote a healthy work-family balance for employees may represent an important component in rebuilding the employer-employee social contract (Lobel & Googins, 1994). This process may also strengthen the concept of work-family balance as a strategic human resource issue and solidify the link of work-family to other organizational efforts such as employee productivity and career development, leadership training, health promotion, and workforce diversity programs.

Adoption of Strategies That Promote the Advancement
of Women, Persons of Color, and Homosexuals to
Senior Management as well as Strategies to Eliminate
Gender-Segregation and Gender-Based Wage
Discrimination in all Job and Occupational Categories

The America of the 21st century will be a very different place in terms of demographics. By the year 2050, an estimated 48% of the population will be persons of color; 21% Hispanic; 16% African American, and 11% Asian American (U.S. Bureau of the Census, 1992e). Although persons of color, as well as women, gays, and lesbians, are well-represented among the ranks of the American worker, they are underrepresented in management, especially at the senior level. U.S. corporate senior management remains a white male bastion. Despite the promotion of women, persons of color, and homosexuals to middle management positions, a "glass ceiling" of subtle gender and racial discrimination as well as homophobia have effectively kept them out of top management. Hall (1990) suggests that a primary reason organizations have not made much real progress on work-family issues is a deep belief by top managers, mostly white males in their 50s and 60s, that the woman's role really is at home and not in the boardroom.

> When top management's basic values and experiences are very much those of the traditional one-earner family with the enabling spouse (wife) at home—and as long as those values remain unexamined—top management will block true progress on the advance of women and on work/family issues. (Hall, 1990, p. 12)

To achieve gender justice in the workplace, barriers preventing the recruitment and promotion of women, persons of color, and homosexuals to leadership positions within organizations must be removed. The entry of women, persons of color, and homosexuals into senior management will bring new perspectives and new voices to the work-family issue.

Achieving diversification is not only a management issue. Gender segregation unfortunately occurs within many job and occupational categories. As we noted in Chapter 3, the extent of such segregation is reflected in the survey of California companies that found that almost 50% were completely gender-segregated by job category—that is, not a single man or women within the same company shared the same job title (Baron

& Bielby, 1984). A restaurant hires only men as waiters or chefs and only women as cocktail servers or hostesses; a hotel hires only women as maids and only men as groundskeepers. To allow each person to reach their full potential and to maximize choice in their job selection, companies must evaluate whether their hiring, training, and promotion practices promote gender equality across all positions. Without a serious commitment—and subsequent actions—to reduce occupational segregation, the majority of employed women will continue to hold clerical and service jobs in the future. Occupational segregation creates a situation in which employers have greater freedom to pay women lower wages. Recognizing the existence of gender-based *occupational* segregation within their company is not sufficient; employers must also take responsibility to identify and eliminate gender-based *wage* discrimination. Companies should undertake studies to determine whether salaries are objectively based on the skills, effort, and responsibilities required to perform a job effectively. Without such changes, women's paid jobs will still be viewed as lower in status and more expendable than men's.

Rethinking the Concepts of "Family," "Boundaries Between Work and Family," "Employer-Employee Partnerships," and "Employer-Community Partnerships" in Order to Promote Healthy Families, Workplaces, and Communities

As American families have become more diverse, the boundaries as to what comprises a family are less clearly demarcated, and the definition of who is a family member has become increasingly complex. Corporate America needs to recognize these changes in family structure and embrace a philosophy of equity in developing benefits and policies that support employees with diverse lifestyles, family structures, and dependent care responsibilities. The adoption of employer-provided flexible benefit plans, or cafeteria plans (described in Chapter 10) represents one type of corporate initiative that respects some forms of family diversity (e.g., dual-earner households, single-parent families, employees with young children, childless couples, single individuals, older couples). Cafeteria plans allow employees to select those benefits that meet their particular family or lifestyle needs from a pool of benefits, and forgo benefits that are less important to them.

However, corporate America also needs to broaden its definition of family to include persons who are emotionally and financially connected but not related by blood or legal ties. Although approximately 5.2 million heterosexual persons and 3.2 million homosexual persons are currently cohabiting (Issacson, 1989), few companies extend benefits to these individuals. Thus, employees in informal domestic partnerships (either by choice, or, in the case of some homosexual partners, the inability to marry legally) are generally unable to secure protection for their families. Although a small number of forward-thinking companies such as Levi Strauss, and a small number of communities such as San Francisco and Seattle, have extended employees' family-related benefits to homosexual and heterosexual domestic partners, these organizations remain the exception. In explaining the New England Medical Center's recent decision to extend health benefits to the domestic partners of homosexual workers, the vice president for human resources stressed the issues of diversity and equity:

> The New England Medical Center community is diverse. . . . It is important that all members of the community have access to important benefits that support them, their partners and dependents. Gay and lesbian employees have been excluded from important benefits because they can not legally marry. . . . Our new policy is designed to address that inequality. ("Medical center adds benefits," 1993, p. 8)

Although it is generally accepted that the worlds of work and family are interrelated and not separate domains, the boundaries between them remain murky. Thus, corporations now need to thoughtfully examine questions of the extent of their involvement with their employees' personal and family lives. In exploring "where to draw the line," Parker and Hall (1993) raise important questions:

> Can organizations use what they learn about personal lives in unfair ways? [and] does the provision of programs such as sick child care create the expectation that employees will be able to work no matter how sick their children are? (p. 149)

Potential problems with corporate efforts to integrate work and private lives are just beginning to be identified. Careful study needs to be undertaken concerning the roles of employers in helping employees cope with difficult social and economic problems such as substance abuse, violence, inadequate public education, and the lack of community-based long-term care services.

Clearly, the paternalistic model of the past, in which the company "took care of employees and their families," is undesirable. Companies need to develop new models that emphasize employee choice and empowerment, employer-employee partnerships, and employer-community partnerships to generate resources (Lobel & Googins, 1994). In some instances, these partnerships may bring together companies that are fierce competitors in the marketplace. An encouraging model is the team effort of four electronics firms (IBM, Amdahl, Southware Publishing, and Scitor) who pooled resources to create two child care centers in Silicon Valley ("Silicon firms develop child care centers," 1993). Although the centers give enrollment preference and discounts to employees of the four firms, they are open to all families in the surrounding communities. Such collaborative models—between companies or between employer and community—may be especially relevant for smaller firms who lack sufficient resources to develop services on their own.

Reframing the Concepts of "Productivity" and "Career." Adoption of a strategy of promoting "mutual flexibility" for employer and employee. Elimination of the second class status, and promotion of career paths for individuals choosing flexible or alternative work arrangements.

Despite women's large-scale entry into the workforce, the deep-rooted white male work culture and organization has changed little. Women and people of color are still expected to adapt to the existing organizational culture, rather than seek to change it. Lambert (1993) suggests the following:

> The business world's continued devotion to the male model of job structures is based primarily on the belief that intense and sustained involvement in work ensures high productivity and profitability . . . [and on] a belief that jobs based on a male model are good for workers—they tend to pay well and to offer opportunities for advancement. (p. 240)

A growing body of evidence challenges the veracity of these benefits for both employees and employers. For instance, men experience a higher rate of certain stress-related diseases that have been linked to occupational conditions, and, on average, they die at an earlier age than do women. A significant proportion of men at midlife or old age express remorse or regret for their earlier single-mindedness about their careers and the resultant lack of involvement with family members (Lambert, 1993). Women who deviate from the male model of an intense and relentless job focus, or who are assumed by management to depart from this model simply by virtue of their gender, often pay a price through restricted job or career opportunities and lower wages. In addition, there is little evidence to support the belief that working longer means working better. Lambert (1993, p. 241) concludes that "if anything, the research suggests that overinvolvement in work leads to inefficiency and, in extreme cases, may even result in physical and emotional exhaustion, increased absenteeism, and poor-quality work." Despite mounting evidence to the contrary, the business world remains unwilling to give up the myth that workers must spend large amounts of time and energy on their jobs in order to do them well and has yet to embrace the concept of "quality time" for the workplace (Lambert, 1993).

Corporate America must rethink both the concepts of *productive work time* and *career* if women are to achieve equality in the public economic sphere. Many supervisors continue to believe that work performed in the workplace is more productive and valuable than work done off-site. A related assumption is that the more time one is seen in the workplace, the more "face time" one puts in, the more one is regarded as valuable to the company.

> Employees frequently report . . . that work performed after 5:00 p.m. counts more. For many employees with families who strive to be as productive as possible in the hours they have at work, nothing is more frustrating than to be told that their contribution is not, by itself, enough—that extra hours at the office (face time) are also essential in order to advance a career. (Rodgers, 1992, p. 189)

Adherence to the traditional male model of career, which assumes a consistent upward trajectory of intense and focused work commitment, will continue to reinforce the glass ceiling for women. Based on their 7 years of company research, Rodgers & Associates Research found that, although almost all women in the workforce were either single or part of a family in which the partner-spouse was employed full-time, nearly 66% of the men in professional or managerial roles had a wife at home. Rogers (1992) draws this conclusion:

> The support system that makes it possible to devote the long hours to the job and meet the expectations for advancement are lacking for women. They are at a serious disadvantage compared to their male peers. . . . Getting more women "into the pipeline" will not by itself solve the problem. (p. 189)

What is also needed is business leaders' adoption of a view of careers as "life-long discontinuities" in which individuals' priorities shift over time (Bailyn, 1992). Thus, persons who choose to modulate their work efforts at various points in their life cycle are not labeled "stalled" or "unmotivated" and at risk of jeopardizing all future career advancement as well as reduced pensions and Social Security in old age. Alternative work arrangements that offer career opportunities and do not connote a second-class status are also required.

Mahoney (1988, p. 13) suggests that "every age has its slogans and energizing concepts." If so, it could be argued that "maintaining competitiveness through flexibility" represents the current banner of American business. Much of the discussion regarding flexibility has focused on two issues: (a) company downsizing and restructuring to respond swiftly to market changes, and (b) the institution of flexible work arrangements to enable employees to balance their work and nonwork lives. Yet, for many American workers, flexibility in the workplace has negative connotations. Although many business leaders praise the concept of a flexible workforce, saying that global competition forces them to be "lean and mean," many workers have become modern-day nomads, moving from one company to another without health insurance and pensions; as noted earlier, the past decade has witnessed a rapid growth of the contingent workforce. Other workers, however, have welcomed companies' introduction of alternative work arrangements that may offer flexibility in time (i.e., compressed work week); in space (i.e, telecommuting); and in style (i.e., job sharing, phased retirement). It is imperative, however, that companies develop policies to ensure that individuals who choose these alternative arrangements do not become second-class workers who earn lower wages and lack the benefits, training, and career advancement opportunities of permanent full-time employees. Senior management has a special responsibility to use these flexible work options to demonstrate that their use does not jeopardize one's career opportunities.

Companies must adopt an orientation of "mutual flexibility," recognizing that both employers and employees have need for flexible arrangements. As Lambert (1993, p. 243) asserts, "the interests of employers and employees are not always compatible, but neither are they always at odds." Productive workers obviously benefit the company, but productive workers always find their jobs more rewarding and view their home lives more positively than nonproductive workers (Lambert, 1993). A framework of mutual flexibility is proposed by Parker and Hall (1993) that recognizes the importance of both human capital and flexibility to corporate productivity and success. Broadening the concept of flexibility beyond the typical dimensions of time, space, or style, they suggest that flexibility can also be a means of promoting *psychological availability:* "A flexible workplace enables employees to bring their 'full' selves to work and to be psychologically engaged in the tasks, activities, and relationships that make up their jobs" (Parker & Hall, 1993, p. 124). They argue that: (a) individuals have personal identities (as women, as African Americans, as lesbians, etc.) and nonwork roles (as caregivers for disabled adult relatives, spouses, parents, community volunteers) beyond their employment roles (data entry, secretary, sales); (b) people carry these identities and nonwork roles into the workplace every day; and (c) people are more engaged in the work organization and their employment role when they can express, rather than suppress, these identities in the workplace. Based on this philosophy, flexibility becomes an approach of valuing differences and a means of transforming the male work structure and organizational culture. Consistent with our feminist framework, diversity is then viewed as a strength within the organization.

WORK-FAMILY BALANCE AND GENDER EQUALITY: PUBLIC POLICY

Although a small but influential group of forward-thinking companies, typically larger corporations, have instituted a rather extensive array of family-responsive initiatives, the vast majority of American companies have not. Even within companies that offer some family-oriented initiatives, employers often make these benefits and flexible work arrangements more available to employees who are highly valued by the company, and women who have higher occupational status and incomes are more likely to use these corporate resources (Miller, 1992). Moreover, the rapid expansion of the contingent workforce means that fewer American families find themselves protected by the corporate welfare safety net.

Employers generally create policies based on perceived economic gain for the company, not from a sense of social responsibility. Companies who have implemented family-oriented benefits believe that these initiatives will pay off on the bottom-line (Gonyea & Googins, 1992; Lambert, 1993).

> Altruism, whether pure or otherwise, has never prompted much business policy, nor are there signs that it will do so. . . . Rhetoric avowing a broad concern for the social ramifications of business operations is standard fare as corporate leaders promote their contribution to American life, but the public attention these statements receive far exceeds their impact in corporate suites. (Kingston, 1990, p. 451)

The business community historically has raised strong opposition to each attempt at raising the minimum wage standard, fought vigorously against the passage of the Family Medical and Leave Act, and now is waging a battle against National Health Care Reform. In each case, business leaders have argued these policies would hurt workers through the loss of jobs.

America's heritage, reflecting our cultural ideology of individual choice, autonomy, and personal liberty, clearly favors private over public solutions to resolving social problems (Clark, 1993). Lack of a greater U.S. response to issues of work-family balance can be attributed to cultural beliefs that families constitute a private domain and any kind of government help in this area is a stigma, or a sign of personal failure; nurturance of children or elders is rightfully the province of women because it is their job or they do it better; and we are an individualistic, achievement-oriented society. Thus, rather than a balance between work and personal life, career is the high priority goal (Bailyn, 1992).

However, government does have a long history of protecting citizens' rights as workers, even if at times it has played this role reluctantly. For example, the 1938 Fair Standards Act established 16 as the minimum age for employment and the payment of overtime for work in excess of 40 hours for most fields. In fact, public policy has an important and necessary role to play in achieving gender justice in the workplace. First, unlike corporate policy, which is primarily created on the basis of economic benefits or gains, government policy more often identifies ideological or moral justifications for the proposed legislation (Starrels, 1992). Second, as long as there is a reliance on private-sector initiatives to support families' need for dependent care, the inequities between those employed in primary-sector jobs and those found in the secondary labor market will continue to increase. Third, the public sector has two attributes that make it strikingly different from the private sector: government has responsibility for collective well-being and has the legal right to use coercion to get its way. The reality is that businesses have generally addressed discrimination in the workplace, extended employee benefits, or improved working conditions only when either mandated to do so by law or through collective bargaining (Kingston, 1990).

Recognizing the critical role of government, we suggest the following public policy strategies to advance gender equality and work-family balance in the workplace:

The Extension of Family-Oriented Benefits to Lower Income Workers

Because higher-wage, higher-level employees represent a larger investment on the part of companies, it is not surprising that many employers target benefits specifically toward this group of valued workers. As Miller (1992, p. 17) notes, "In a profit-making system, the benefits of personnel policy must outweigh the costs. . . . Employers provide family benefits when it is in their interest to do so." Many business leaders can see no clear economic gain from the extension of benefit coverage to lower-wage, lower-level employees.

Government can promote a fairer distribution of benefits through two very different approaches. In the first, government can offer employers a tax incentive for employment-based benefits specifically targeted to low-income workers. These benefits might include subsidies to local child care providers, adult day care centers, or homemaker services. In the second, government can mandate employer provision of dependent care benefits. The tax incentive approach offers employers a carrot, whereas the mandatory benefits approach uses a stick. Although the tax incentive strategy prompts some employers who were previously reluctant to offer dependent care benefits, it does not assure equal access for all lower-income workers. This approach permits major differences in benefit provision across employers, industries, and geographic regions. Also, the tax incentive results in the loss of some public revenue (Miller, 1992). In contrast, the mandatory benefits approach, which requires all employers to provide some minimum level of dependent care benefits, has a more progressive distribution than voluntary benefits (Miller, 1992; Smeeding, 1983).

The difference between the two approaches is perhaps best illustrated by the debate surrounding the passage of the U.S. Family and Medical Leave Act (FMLA). President Bush opposed mandatory requirements and vetoed the FMLA of 1992. He offered instead alternative tax incentive legislation, the Family Leave Tax Credit Act. This legislation proposed to provide a 20% refundable tax credit to businesses with fewer than 500 employees that offer them up to 12 weeks of leave. Employers would be eligible for a maximum tax credit of $1,200 per year per employee. The FMLA of 1993, signed into law by President Clinton, mandates business's provision of leave and is more progressive than Bush's proposed tax credit. However, a number of compromises in the legislation, to ensure its passage in Congress, have severely restricted leave access to lower-income workers. The most glaring restriction is that small businesses employing 50 or fewer employees are exempt from the FMLA. Over half of all employees in the private sector—including a disproportionately larger number of women—work for businesses with 50 or fewer employees.

Extension of family-oriented benefits to low-income workers also means ensuring that the benefits are economically viable options. The FMLA is less accessible to lower-income workers because it addresses only one need of caregivers—job protection—and does not confront workers' need for an income during the leave period. Most workers who depend on an hourly wage simply cannot afford to take an unpaid leave (England, 1990). Although most Western European and Scandinavian countries offer workers a percentage of their income during the leave period, U.S. employers vigorously fought this provision in the FMLA, arguing that such a requirement would limit their ability to compete globally.

The dependent care assistance plan (DCAP) also comes with limitations that effectively exclude most low-income workers. Like the family and medical leave, DCAPs are more likely to be found at larger firms than at small companies. And similar to the FMLA, DCAP requirements present some economic disincentives for lower-income workers. DCAPs offer workers the opportunity, through pretax salary reductions, to set aside monies for dependent care expenses. Yet the requirement that these funds be set aside in advances creates a significant barrier for many lower-income workers. Further, if the expenses incurred are less than the contribution rate, the employee forfeits the remaining monies in the DCAP—a potential cost too great for many wage earners.

Extension of Social Protection to Contingent Workers

We offer separate policy recommendations regarding contingent workers, given both their rapid expansion in the workforce and the special vulnerabilities they face. Contingent workers now represent 30% of the total workforce. Between 1980 and 1992, part-timers increased by 39%, contracted services rose by 61% and temporary workers increased 250%. The Bureau of National Affairs estimates that, by 1995, 1,060,000 Americans will be employed by temporary help firms (Christensen, 1987a).

The contingent workforce represents a radical transformation of the American work economy. Karen Nussbaum, director of the Women's Division at the U.S. Department of Labor, suggests that "the shift toward contingent work may be as profound as the change society underwent from farms to factories" (Shao, 1994a). From employers' perspective, one of the primary advantages of contingent work is cost containment. Employers only have to pay for work done; rarely do they pay any discretionary benefits such as health insurance, paid leave, job retraining, or pensions (Christensen, 1987a). This becomes a feminist issue because so many women are contingent workers.

Critics of employers who increasingly turn to the use of contingent workers suggest that these labor practices will result in an even larger underclass. U.S. Senator Howard Metzenbaum argues that employers who choose contingent workers "are cutting the heart out of the American workforce [and that] this insidious trend is tearing at the social fabric of our country"(Shao, 1994a). Others, such as Richard Belous, the chief economist of the National Planning Association, argue that the trend toward the use of contingent workers cannot be reversed and the challenge is to "humanize" contingent work.

One temporary help firm that stands apart from the others in offering benefits to its employees is MacTemps, Inc., a firm employing 5,500 employees as temporary computer specialists skilled in word processing, desktop publishing, and graphic and database techniques. At MacTemps, 1,500 hours of work qualifies an employee for health insurance, with the company paying 50% of the premium; after 1,200 hours of work, the temp gets a 1-week paid vacation; and after 1,000 hours, the temp is eligible for a 401K pension plan with a 25% company match (Shao, 1994b). Interestingly, the MacTemps CEO argues (much like employers of per-manent workers) that offering benefits helps them make money in that they attract and retain good employees and thus have lower turnover and recruitment costs.

Unfortunately, temporary help firms such as MacTemps, Inc., are the exception. Most contingent workers receive few social protections. For too many, contingent work means lower wages, few or no benefits, and no job security. Critical issues for the contingent workers that government must address are (a) laws and regulations requiring pay equity between contingent workers and permanent, full-time workers; (b) revision of federal regulations on unemployment compensation to address program gaps in the coverage of contingent workers; and (c) legislation mandating that contingent workers have access, on a prorated basis, to the same employer-provided fringe benefits available to regular workers.

Broadening the Government's
Definition of "Family" and "Dependent"

As we have seen, the majority of contemporary American families differ significantly from the idealized form of a nuclear, heterosexual family in which a prescribed sexual division of labor limits the wife's role to the private domestic sphere. Today, gay parents, grandparent-headed households, stepfamilies, dual-earner couples, and commuter marriages challenge the idealized form of family. Nevertheless, nontraditional fami-lies have consistently been viewed as a threat to survival of the family, and also to the state. Legislation and the courts have striven to design policies that promote the traditional family (Wisensale & Heckart, 1993). Consequently, nontraditional families have fewer rights and less protec-tion than do traditional families.

Despite the tremendous growth in cohabiting couples and greater acceptance of cohabitation by society throughout the past several decades, domestic partners still have few rights. Policies on domestic partnerships are limited to municipalities, corporations, and organizations. For the most part, the extension of rights to heterosexual and homosexual "spousal equivalents" has proceeded primarily through the courts. (For a detailed discussion of family law and domestic partnerships, see Krause, 1990.) Although the courts have historically denounced homosexual marriages, they have begun to move forward on this issue, as evidenced in the Braschi v. Stahl Associates Co. ruling (Krause, 1990; Wisensale & Heckart, 1993). In this case, the New York Court of Appeals concluded that a gay couple's relationship went beyond that of roommates and could be considered a family under New York rent-control regulations. Thus, the rent-controlled apartment could be held by the survivor after his partner died of AIDS. Although the ruling was narrowly focused on rent-control laws, the court did state that "the definition of family should not rest on fictitious legal distinctions or genetic history, but instead should find its foundation in the reality of family life" (Kraus, 1990, p. 160). Although some successes have been won in the judicial system, we argue that federal and state legislation should specifically extend family rights to heterosexual and homosexual domestic partners who choose to make this commitment. The definition of family should be derived from the realities of family life, not from a cultural ideal. Individuals who make a commitment to each other's care and who view themselves as a family should have the same access to social and economic entitlements that we offer traditional families.

Similarly, many informal caregivers for disabled adults and elders are denied access to indirect financial assistance through tax relief because they fail to meet the Federal Internal Revenue Service's (IRS) definitions of "family" and "dependent." In order to be eligible for the Federal Dependent Care Tax Credit or to participate in employer-provided benefits (such as DCAP) based on federal tax codes, not only must the taxpayer supply over 50% of the dependent's economic support for the taxable year, but the dependent person must spend at least 8 hours every day in the employee's household. It is this co-residence requirement, as previously noted, that greatly restricts employees' access to the federal tax credit or DCAP for purposes of caring for disabled adults. Eighty percent of Federal Dependent Care Tax credit claims are for child care. The government's decision to narrowly limit "family" to "household members" and "dependent" to "co-residency status" reflects neither the desires nor the realities of most families' dependent care situations. Most adult children and most aging parents prefer to live near, but not with, each other. Substantial levels of care, however, may be provided by relatives who live close to adults or elders with chronic health impairments. If the Federal Dependent Care Tax Credit (and other employer-provided benefits based on the IRS code) are to be used by families assisting adults or elders with disabling health conditions, it is imperative that the co-residence requirement be eliminated.

*Commitment to Economic Equity for Women Workers
Through the Elimination of Gender-Based Occupational
Segregation and Wage Inequity, and the Promotion
of Affirmative Action, Equal Education Opportunity,
and Comparable Worth*

Of primary importance to employees with family responsibilities is the ability to obtain a secure job that offers an adequate wage to support a stable family life. Yet, for many women, such a job is unattainable. Nearly 40% of women who work full-time earn less than $15,000 per year, compared to 20% of full-time male workers (U.S. Bureau of Labor Statistics, 1988). Despite the fact that an increasing number of women have found themselves solely responsible for the financial support of their children (often through fathers' failure to pay court-mandated child support), the low wages most women earn are inadequate to maintain a family in today's economy. Fifty-five percent of the children living in female-headed households are in poverty, compared to only 11% of children in other families (Chadwick & Heaton, 1992).

The Women Employed Institute (WEI) argues that "occupational segregation is a major contributor to the wage gap and a major barrier to economic self-sufficiency for the majority of working women" (WEI, 1988, p. 6). Between 1975 and 1990, 20 million women were added to the U.S. labor force; however, most entered traditionally female occupations—e.g., clerical workers, salespersons, waitresses, and hairdressers (Ries & Stone, 1992). Although women have made significant gains in entering certain fields—e.g., law, medicine, journalism—overall, the workforce remains as segregated by gender today as it was twenty-five years ago (WEI, 1988).

National legislation to promote economic equity, and the will to enforce the legislation, are the keys to advancing economic equity for women. In many cases, federal and state laws prohibiting discrimination already exist. What is lacking is a strong national commitment to enforce these laws. Drawing largely from WEI's (1988) study of occupational segregation, we present the following recommendations for strengthening the federal government's role in promotion of economic equity.

Affirmative action in the recruitment, hiring, and promotion of women must be used in order to end gender-based occupational segregation. The WEI argues that two federal offices—the Department of Labor's Office of Federal Contract Compliance Program (OFCCP) and the Equal Employment Opportunity Commission (EEOC)—have the potential to play a significant role in combating discrimination and enforcing affirmative action. The OFCCP enforces Executive Order 11246, which requires federal contractors to undertake affirmative action in hiring, promotion, pay, and training for women and minorities. Because federal contractors employ 33% of the labor force and receive over 1 billion federal dollars in contracts, OFCCP's influence is potentially far-reaching. Under the Carter administration, the OFCCP focused on industrywide targeting, negotiated settlements, and imposition of sanctions to bring substantial changes to a number of industries (e.g., construction, financing, educational institutions). Unfortunately, Reagan weakened OFCCP's regulatory policies and enforcement strategies (WEI, 1988). WEI maintain that the OFCCP must be restrengthened by executive order to target structurally based industry practices of occupational segregation, both through the establishment of timetables for occupational integration and the imposition of sanctions to those contractors who do not comply.

EEOC enforces Title VII of the Civil Rights Act of 1964, which prohibits discrimination in the private and public sectors in hiring, pay, and promotion. Yet EEOC under both Reagan and Bush has focused on individual complaints versus cases of structural patterns of discrimination, engaged in lengthy case-processing discouraging to claimants, and narrowed the interpretation of Title VII rights (WEI, 1988). As WEI notes, the federal administration must reestablish the importance of Title VII rights, charge the EEOC with the broadest application of these rights, make the combating of systemic discrimination a priority, and provide EEOC with sufficient resources to promptly investigate individual charges.

Equal education and job training opportunities for women are key to reducing occupational segregation. America's public education systems, along with federally funded job training programs, continue to channel girls and women into traditionally female occupations. Moreover, educational institutions historically have devoted fewer funds and resources to girls' or young women's activities. Vigorous enforcement is required of Title IX of the Educational Act Amendments of 1972, which prohibits institutions receiving federal funds to engage in discriminatory practices. The Job Training Partnership Act (JTPA) enacted in 1982 provides states with monies to prepare the economically disadvantaged and long-term unemployed with job training; WEI (1988) charges that JTPA has inadequately served women by channeling them into training for low-paying clerical jobs and by not requiring programs to set aside a percentage of funds for child care. Moreover, the Department of Labor's Bureau of Apprenticeship and Training (BAT), which oversees the certification of apprenticeship programs, presides over programs that have historically excluded women and minorities from training and higher-pay skilled craft jobs. We strongly support WEI's recommendation that all federally funded job training programs, such as JTPA, BAT, and welfare-to-family programs, set up stronger affirmative action and enforcement procedures to promote women's entry into nontraditional fields.

Elimination of gender-based wage discrimination is key to women achieving economic self-sufficiency. As we have noted, despite passage of the Pay Equity Act in 1963, a significant wage gap continues to exist between female and male earnings. One important reason that women still generally earn only $.72 for every $1 men earn (U.S. Bureau of Labor Statistics, 1991) is that the Equity Pay Act does not affect wages for people in different occupations. Although the pay equity movement for women is based on the assumption that discrimination by gender in work and pay is illegal, "comparable worth rests on additional assumptions that work traditionally labeled 'women's work' or associated with supposed special talents of women, ought to be valued equally with those labors traditionally associated with men" (Kelly & Bayes, 1988, p. 4). Comparable worth advocates assert that gender segregation in the workplace has unjustly depressed wages in female-dominated jobs and that comparable worth policy is designed to eliminate pay differentials between male and female-dominated jobs for which skill, effort, responsibility, and risk are equivalent (Wittig & Lowe, 1989). In contrast, opponents of comparable worth argue that the market provides the appropriate valuation of labor and that government involvement is undesirable. Proponents counter this argument by citing other instances in which the government has intervened in the market, such as in antitrust cases.

The comparable worth movement grew rapidly during the late 1970s and early 1980s. By September 1986, 10 states had written pay equity or comparable worth policy, and 27 states had completed studies to determine if sex-based wage differences or occupational segregation existed (Kelly & Bayes, 1988, p. 239). Although several local municipalities have successfully implemented comparable worth policies on a statewide level, Minnesota is still the only one requiring all localities to develop and implement a comparable worth-pay equity plan for their employees. One of the greatest difficulties the comparable worth movement has faced in the late 1980s and 1990s is the scarcity of public funds. Based on four case studies, Kelly and Bayes (1988, p. 244) conclude that several conditions must exist before implementation is likely: "an adequate resource base to fund the pay adjustments; political support of the chief executive who is responsible for implementing the effort; and, good-faith bargaining among unions, workers, and managers." Despite the difficulties of advancing this agenda in the economic climate of the 1990s, comparable worth as a public policy should continue to be pursued. From our feminist perspective, it remains a central means to achieve "wage justice" for women in a labor market that remains gender-segregated.

In conclusion, the assumptions that women's first responsibility (unlike men's) is to their families and that low-wage "women's work" is most compatible to their role as caregiver are integral elements of gender discrimination in the workplace, which penalizes women economically across the life span. Although women now represent 40% of all workers, they remain second-class citizens in the labor market. Within our feminist model, achieving gender justice in the workplace will require a strong national commitment to the principles of both economic equality for women and a healthy work-family balance.

14

National Health Care Reform and Long-Term Care

A Feminist Perspective

Even as we write, the health care arena is rapidly changing, as numerous proposals for health care reform have been debated and defeated before the 103rd Congress and as some state governments have attempted to implement changes despite the lack of federal direction. Since the 1992 elections, health care reform quickly moved from an academic debate to a legislative process, but one that ended in gridlock and raised questions of whether substantial change is possible. In spite of escalating costs, growing numbers of uninsured citizens and restrictive insurance policies, attempts to change the health care system create a clash of ideologies between egalitarianism versus the belief that health care is not a universal right and between the goals of cost containment versus guaranteed access for all. Another fundamental barrier is the disproportionate influence of powerful special interest lobbies, particularly insurance companies and small business, who, in the 1994 debates, spent approximately $85 million to protect their financial interests and ways of doing business. As noted earlier, health insurance in America, with the exception of Medicaid for the poor, is basically a private commodity, with only about 40% of health care expenditures coming from public sources (Keigher & Stone, 1993). Given our culture's emphasis on privatization, personal rights, and freedoms, over public entitlements or economic assurances, the majority of Americans, although they support health care reform in the abstract, are unwilling to accept less personal choice of doctors or hospitals, even if doing so would reduce health care costs or make universal coverage possible (Gill & Ingman, 1994). Resistance to large-scale change in the health care system is even greater after the gridlock of the 103rd Congress and the Republican sweep in the November 1994 local and national elections. Not surprisingly, health care reform is visibly absent in the Republican National Committee's 10-point program in its "Contract with America," and any alterations within the next 2 years are likely to be incremental.

Nevertheless, given the number of Americans who lack access to adequate health care, the debate will undoubtedly continue, particularly at the state level, although perhaps in less visible forms and arenas. Central to such debate is whether long-term care will be included in any health care package. The current dichotomy between long-term care and acute care is not functional for either the disabled person or the formal and informal care providers. As noted throughout, acute and chronic disease and disability are experienced concurrently. And disability is not confined to small groups of permanently disabled individuals, but affects many persons for short periods. What is needed is a health care system that eliminates artificial boundaries through an integrated approach to acute and long-term care over the course of each individual's lifetime.

The potential for national health care reform to insure access to health coverage for all Americans is particularly salient to people with chronic disabilities and their families because they are the population often not covered by insurance companies. Although over 37 million Americans have no insurance for hospital and doctor costs, over 200 million have no insurance for long-term care (Corry, 1994). Obviously, passage of a national long-term care insurance program could reduce both the financial and the emotional risks to families of the chronically disabled. Despite some public misperceptions that long-term care benefits only the elderly, findings from four national surveys conducted between April 1993 and January 1994 show that bipartisan public support for health care reform increases dramatically when long-term care coverage is included. Such support may signal recognition that the absence of a viable long-term care policy affects persons of all ages, classes, and racial and ethnic groups, because long-term care is the health crisis for which virtually every American is uninsured (Riley & Mollica, 1994). The integration of long-term care into national health care reform is of societal concern because persons with serious and persistent chronic conditions are the fastest-growing, highest-cost, and most complex segment in the health care area (National Chronic Care Consortium, 1994). The passage of long-term care reform particularly affects women as the primary providers of care and as the major residents of nursing homes and congregate care facilities. Accordingly, any delays or incremental phasing in of long-term care into health care reform will negatively affect women disproportionately.

This chapter begins by briefly reviewing the history and status of long-term care legislation at the national level. We then present a model of long-term care that attempts to build on feminist values. Because the health care arena is changing so rapidly, we do not attempt to address all the detailed issues of funding and service delivery surrounding the development of long-term care policy. Rather, we provide a framework for conceptualizing long-term care services, and feminist criteria by which to measure current proposals for reform. In doing so, we acknowledge that many of the current health care proposals, including that of President Clinton, contain some components that correspond to what we view as central to a feminist model. A feminist model of long-term care differs from other proposals, however, by its underlying recognition of the burdens faced by women as underpaid and unpaid caregivers of persons with chronic disabilities and by its overall goal of gender justice in the allocation of services. In the short run, our proposed approach is not feasible, given the current political climate, the Republican Party's dominance, and public resistance to universal access; although we are realistic, we nevertheless present a feminist model as an ideal toward which to move, however slowly. As noted by Neysmith (1991), fundamental changes in how our society views and provides care have to be defined as long-term endeavors that will inevitably be riddled with compromises. Given that the system changes necessitated by large-scale health care reform constitute a paradigm shift, deeply ingrained but outdated assumptions about the family, the state, and the economy must be set aside—an extremely difficult undertaking. A feminist framework, however, allows us to think about these things in a different way, which is a necessary first step to action and in itself a change (Neysmith, 1991). Therefore, our feminist model is intended to advance the dialogue over time about a paradigm shift in health and long-term care.

OVERVIEW OF LONG-TERM CARE LEGISLATION

The rapid changes in the health care arena make predictions about future directions difficult, but health care is clearly moving from a system oriented toward acute care, treatment of illness, independent providers, and fee for service insurance to one oriented toward chronic care, disability prevention, provider networks, and managed care. Because of market changes and the growth of managed care, these patterns of consolidation and cost savings in the delivery of health care will continue at the local level even without the passage of national legislation. The limitations of private insurance are also increasingly apparent. For example, about 50% of severely disabled individuals aged 15 to 64 had private health insurance in 1991 to 1992, compared to 80% for those without disabilities. Approximately 15% of disabled and nondisabled people—including individuals who are employed—lack any type of health insurance coverage; 36% of people with a severe disability and 5% of people with no disability are covered by either Medicare or Medicaid ("News analysis," 1994). An estimated 58.5% of employed Americans do get health insurance through their employers, but this percentage is declining (Shalala, 1994). For those fortunate to have comprehensive health insurance, premiums continue to escalate, in part because of the 23% administrative cost that insurance companies use for commissions on the sale of their plans (Goldstein, 1994). Private long-term care insurance remains beyond the financial reach of most persons with chronic disabilities, with high-quality policies costing as much as $7,700 for individuals aged 79 (Wiener & Illston, 1994b). Accordingly, private insurance covers only about 2% of the nation's long-term care expenditures (National Committee to Preserve Social Security and Medicare, 1993; Riley & Mollica, 1994).

The first comprehensive long-term care legislation was introduced by Claude Pepper, who tied an initiative to fund long-term care in the home to the ill-fated catastrophic health care legislation in 1988. In 1990, the Pepper Commission recommended public funding of home, community, and nursing home care for seriously disabled Americans. In 1992, the Democratic leadership in the House and the Senate introduced bills for long-term care known as the Long Term Care Family Security Act. During the 1992 campaign, Bill Clinton was the first Presidential candidate to call for expanded public funding for home care services provided on a nonmeans-tested basis. In contrast, President Bush's health care reform proposal did not even mention long-term care. Major national organizations concerned about long-term care, such as the National Committee to Preserve Social Security and Medicare and the Leadership Council of Aging Organizations, favor universal and comprehensive long-term care plans for disabled individuals of all ages, with services encompassing institutional, home, and community-based care and personal assistance. Of the major proposals that have been debated by Congress, only two offer any new long-term care benefits (President Clinton's National Health Security Act and the Wellstone-McDermott American Health Security Act).

President Clinton's National Health Security Act of 1993 (introduced by Senator Mitchell and Congressman Gephardt) made a significant commitment to dependent populations. It assured universal coverage by 1998; provided premium discounts on a sliding scale for those living in up to 250% of poverty; included some mental health and substance abuse services in the standard benefit package with a commitment to increase and integrate these benefits over time; provided tax credits for employees with disabilities who pay for personal care; established financial incentives for health plans to enroll vulnerable populations; covered prescription drugs;

and expanded long-term care coverage, especially home care. The president's original plan mandated businesses to provide 80% of the cost of health insurance for employees, a provision that created strong resistance from the small business lobby, mounted with the insurance companies, through a costly television ad campaign. Under the president's proposal, Medicare remained intact, although premiums were increased to cover more managed-care options and prescription medications (Riley & Mollica, 1994; Wiener & Illston, 1994a). In recognition that a federal program cannot address all long-term care health needs, the president's proposal provided for favorable tax treatment for private long-term care insurance plans that meet federal consumer protection requirements. Acknowledging the fiscal realities of the national debt, public fears of an uncertain national economic future, and resistance to new taxes, the president's plan was a complex mix of social insurance, private insurance, and Medicaid reform. Nevertheless, through its design to provide consumer choice and prevent unnecessary institutionalization, it represented a significant shift from the Reagan and Bush focus on private long-term care insurance as the primary basis for reform (Wiener & Illston, 1994a; 1994b).

In terms of the issues raised throughout this book, most significant in the president's plan is the proposal for Home and Community-based Services for Individuals with Disabilities—a new nonmeans-tested program providing additional federal money for long-term care of people at home without regard to income. This program for community-based services carried an estimated price tag of $38 billion per year if it had been fully implemented in 2003 (Wiener & Illston, 1994b). Eligibility would have been determined regardless of age on the basis of impairments in three or more of five activities of daily living due to physical, cognitive, or mental conditions or other defined limitations in capacity. Although eligibility was based primarily on ADL measures, the Clinton plan took account of the wide-ranging differences within the total population of those with disabilities. For example, a person with serious cognitive disability (Alzheimer's disease or mental retardation, for example) may be able to perform activities of daily living but still require significant ongoing help and supervision. Language in the legislation clarified that people with Alzheimer's Disease, mental illness, mental retardation, or physical impairments were eligible as well as the frail elderly (Riley & Mollica, 1994). With such definitions, it was projected that 3 million individuals with disabilities would be eligible, 1 million of them under age 65 (Lumsdon, 1993; Riley & Mollica, 1994; Wiener & Illston, 1994a). On the other hand, some groups have criticized the eligibility criteria of three ADLs for being too restrictive and excluding many chronically ill and low-income persons (Massachusetts Women's Health Care Coalition, 1993).

Although the benefits under the president's proposal were broad and somewhat ambiguous, it made clear that consumer-directed personal care had to be included in any state plans. In addition, each category of recipient must be assured services appropriate to their needs and that encompass home and community-based long-term care, adult day care, assisted living, case management, cash payments to purchase assistance, habilitation and rehabilitation, home modifications, personal care, respite care, supportive employment, and supportive services in residential care settings. If it had passed, however, this legislation would not have guaranteed that all states would provide community-based long-term care because states would have had flexibility on how to structure programs to tailor individual service packages to fit the recipient's needs; accordingly, they could have chosen what to provide from a menu of services and could capitate benefits to a range of providers. States would have been required to submit plans to integrate mental health and substance abuse services, a significant recognition of the complex physical and mental health needs of the populations that are the focus of this book (Wiener & Illston, 1994b). Even though state participation would have been optional, it was assumed that the generous grants to states—from 75% to 95% of the cost of the plan—might have been sufficient incentive to insure wide participation. But the flexibility allowed states made it difficult to describe what benefits families would actually have received, because the answer depended on what the state decided to provide and on whether funding was available (Wiener & Illston, 1994a).

Copayments from 20% to 40% were proposed, with exemptions for the poor. A funding limit or cap would have been established so that expenditures could not exceed the budgeted levels. This limit, indexed to population growth and inflation, was based on the best estimate of what would be required to provide the services needed by the eligible population. Although Medicare was not included as part of this health care reorganization, caps on the growth of Medicaid and Medicare were to pay for the program over the first 5 years. These limits differentiated the president's proposal from open-ended entitlement programs such as Social Security. As a capped entitlement program, people were to be entitled to an assessment and plan of care, but government-financed services were to be provided on a funds-available basis only (Wiener & Illston, 1994a).

Although most proposed models of long-term care reform do not explicitly address the needs of family caregivers, President Clinton's proposal took initial steps toward supporting families by offering a broad array of services and encouraging greater consumer choice and autonomy than under current policy; states could offer cash or vouchers directly to consumers or family caregivers as part of a flexible benefits package

(Stone & Keigher, 1993). However, in contrast to a feminist model, there was no explicit recognition given to the gender-based care and economic inequities facing women, and therefore no overall goal of gender justice in terms of the economic, social, or health supports available to family caregivers.

Although the president's proposal would have mandated that all states provide programs for the medically needy through Medicaid (currently, only 36 states provide such programs), this requirement was only for institutional long-term care. His proposal thus perpetuated the institutional bias inherent in the current Medicaid program. Class-based inequities would also have continued because nursing homes and intermediate care facilities for the mentally retarded would have remained the only service with open-ended funding to which the poor were entitled. Although spousal impoverishment protection was assured for those who were in nursing homes, a Medicaid recipient at home would qualify for protection of spousal income only through a waiver, and, should medically needy coverage be available, a homebound recipient could receive coverage for services only, not for room and board. Although room and board costs would continue to be paid in a nursing home by Medicaid, they would not be paid for home care, even if the individual's resources were exhausted. In summary, even if the Clinton plan or a variation of it were to be enacted in the future and even though it began to recognize the importance of funding for home care, it perpetuated larger federal expenditures for institutional, specifically nursing home, care to which all who become poor are entitled; yet no such entitlement exists for home care (Riley & Mollica, 1994).

Another major health care reform proposal, that addressed many of the issues identified throughout this book, is the American Health Security Act, introduced by Senator Paul Wellstone and Congressman Jim McDermott and consistent with the model proposed by the National Association of Social Workers. This single-payer plan was strongly resisted by many in Congress as well as by insurance lobbyists; in fact, it has been argued that single-payer plans may be so strongly opposed, in part, because they offer better coverage and lower costs (Goldstein, 1994). Insurance would have been replaced by a single payer, thereby eliminating insurance practices that have left many people with disabilities without coverage, and universal access would have been financed through progressive taxation. Similarly, affordability would be assured through the progressive financing, thereby removing the need for premium subsidies. Of the proposals before Congress, the Wellstone-McDermott plan provided the largest voice to the concerns of chronically disabled populations through consumer participation on the oversight board. The standard benefit would have provided for more comprehensive coverage for all in need than did the president's proposal, particularly in mental health and substance abuse services. A Home and Community Care program would have been funded for adults unable to perform two to five ADLs or with cognitive or mental impairment that poses a threat to themselves or others. Similar to the president's plan, this would not restrain the growth of institutional facilities that would be covered in the standard benefit. In contrast to the president's proposal, the Wellstone-McDermott plan would have phased out Medicare and Medicaid and integrated all needed services into one system, eliminating some of the fragmentation that exists for adults with chronic disabilities, particularly those who try to coordinate care among multiple payment sources (Riley & Mollica, 1994).

A full description of all the other proposals that were introduced in Congress is beyond the scope of this chapter, which aims we present an alternative model for long-term care reform. However, we briefly mention the other major bills: the House leadership bill would have provided universal coverage by 1999 through an "employer mandate" and expansion of Medicare. It provided for equitable coverage for mental health and substance abuse treatment and an option for states to implement single-payer systems. The Senate leadership bill sought to cover 95% of the population by the year 2000 through voluntary measures, insurance reforms, and subsidies, thereby lacking the vital criteria of universal coverage and a firm employer mandate. For sources of funding, both bills relied on higher taxes on tobacco and ammunition, Medicare and Medicaid savings, and a tax on health insurance premiums. Much of the activity on health care reform in the second session of the 103rd Congress took place within the five primary committees exercising jurisdiction—the House Committees on Education and Labor, Energy and Commerce, and Ways and Means, and the Senate Committees on Finance and Labor and Human Resources. Four of these committees reported health care reform bills, three of which maintained the underlying principles of the Clinton plan: universal coverage, an employer mandate, a comprehensive benefit package with a strong mental health and substance abuse benefit, measures to ensure quality, and a state single-payer option. Of relevance to the populations that are the focus of this book, the 103rd Congress's treatment of mental health and substance abuse services through health care reform represented a significant step forward. The three committee bills that included a defined benefit package also contained mental health and substance abuse benefits. The importance of outpatient case management services was recognized, with unlimited coverage and no copayment.

While long-term care was debated at the national level, 35 states, most visibly Washington, Oregon, Wisconsin, Hawaii, Florida, Minnesota, and

Vermont, moved ahead to develop their own long-term care packages. The primary goals of most state reforms have been to improve access to private health insurance and to assure universal access to coverage for people who are uninsured, without focusing on the chronically disabled per se among the insured. Nevertheless, many of the state reforms have set the stage for improved access to vulnerable populations (Mollica, Riley, & Rydell, 1994).

Model demonstration projects that seek to develop a continuum of care across systems and also test capitated managed care continue to emerge locally. These include replications of On Lok, a social model of care begun in San Francisco that aims to provide comprehensive care in community settings; Social Health Maintenance Organizations (Social HMOs), which are prepaid health plans that provide both acute medical and custodial care, and seek to reduce costs by keeping Medicaid recipients out of nursing homes; and coordinated health care networks across systems through the National Chronic Care Consortium. For example, as part of the consortium, the Lutheran General Health System's Chicagoland Continuum of Care seeks to accommodate all traditional levels of care from prevention to chronic long-term care through a "seamless continuum" of health, medical, and social services spanning all levels and sites of care (National Chronic Care Consortium, 1994). Despite ongoing resistance to health care reform, particularly by people representing business and insurance interests, a positive sign is that some policy makers, primarily local Democratic elected officials, have been ready to consider profound and proactive solutions to these problems, rather than continue tinkering. In addition, local groups, often by securing private funding, have moved ahead and implemented such solutions without waiting for government leadership. However, the recent political party changes at both the state and national levels may considerably slow these more decentralized processes.

A FEMINIST MODEL OF LONG-TERM CARE

Drawing on plans currently before Congress as well as those being implemented at the state level, we turn now to propose the key components of a feminist model of long-term care within the overall context of health care reform. These components include *family support, empowerment, and choice as a centerpiece of the system,* along with a partnership between families and formal service providers; a strong public presence to guarantee *universal access to comprehensive community-based care,* which integrates a wide array of social and health services for physical and mental health care; a *life span approach* that builds on connectedness rather than individualism and insures access throughout life; *a redefinition of health that integrates social and health services, physical and mental health care, and prevention as well as treatment;* and, as we discussed in Chapter 11, *adequate compensation of women as the primary formal and informal providers of care.* A feminist discourse on caring addresses how the current system, with its reliance on competition, high-tech medicine, out-of-control capital expenses, and employee-based premiums, has ill served women, both as frequent users of health and long-term care and as the primary providers and arrangers of care. It contrasts an individualistic orientation, which emphasizes the duties and responsibilities of individuals to provide for their health care, to a collective orientation, in which society is responsible for providing health care for all and citizens are empowered to be active participants of the care team (Gill & Ingman, 1994). As noted by Neysmith (1991, p. 296), a feminist discourse on caring offers a "vision of community based on connectedness rather than one based on the possessive individualism that underlies familism." Central to such a vision is recognition of women as providing the connectedness within and across generations.

FAMILY SUPPORT AND CHOICE AS THE CENTERPIECE OF THE LONG-TERM CARE SYSTEM

The underlying assumption of a feminist approach to long-term care is that women's caregiving is integral to the current system; therefore, women must have their needs met and must have a significant voice in determining how that is accomplished. Whereas it is recognized that approximately 20% of primary caregivers are men, a feminist model of long-term care moves beyond gender-neutral services, in which it is assumed that men and women are affected in similar ways by services, to gender justice, in which the long-term care service system explicitly takes account of the additional burdens that women as family caregivers have disproportionately borne across the life span. It empowers women and men to be able to choose whether to provide care. Recognizing the lifelong demands that caring makes on women and the commitments of women to care, support for families as consumers of long-term care would be the centerpiece of a feminist system of coordinated care, rather than an addition that could be eliminated under tight fiscal conditions. A feminist approach sets the stage for a national caregiver agenda by acknowledging that the caregivers' well-being is inextricably connected to that of the chronically disabled person and to the larger societal good.

Supportive nonmedical services would thus be built around the functional needs of the dependent person and also those of the caregiver, with the family considered part of the unit for receiving services (Bradley, Kroll, & Agosta, 1992; Cameron, 1994). By providing real choice and flexibility, a feminist approach focused on caregiver support would encourage new and innovative ways of providing care. Consistent with the overall paradigm shift represented by a feminist approach, a wide range of familial arrangements would be supported, without any assumptions as to what constitutes the normative family, thus moving away from the nuclear family norm, heterosexist models, and the ideology of familism that have undergirded most current policies and programs.

Supporting and empowering families to make informed decisions about care is thus the centerpiece of a feminist approach to long-term care. One way to accomplish this is to provide opportunities for families and their disabled relatives to be involved in planning and shaping programs. Consumers of all ages, income levels, and racial and cultural backgrounds should be included on relevant long-term care decision-making boards, commissions, and other advisory and regulatory bodies, reflecting the diversity of the populations served. A model for this partnership between consumers and formal service providers is the California-based Public Interest Center on Long Term Care that uses regional advisory groups around the state to bring together older people, adults with disabilities, advocates, and researchers to engage in decision making, problem solving, and advocacy around a collective vision (Loring & Porter, 1994). Such consumer involvement on a local and regional level would ensure that programs and services are sensitive to cultural and linguistic diversity and to the unique characteristics of urban and rural communities.

Under a feminist model, the institutional bias of the current long-term care system would be altered. Services would be psychologically accessible—that is, provided in a manner and setting to optimize individual choice about the mix of informal and formal care and to enhance independence, well-being, and personal dignity for both the family caregivers and the adult who is chronically disabled. Choice would also be encouraged through culturally relevant, geographically accessible outreach and education so that people know how to obtain care through local service systems that are perceived as welcoming and relevant. Culturally and linguistically competent care would be accessible in a wide range of community-based settings, including hospitals, physician's offices, other outpatient settings, neighborhood health centers, clinics, skilled nursing centers, long-term care facilities, and hospices. This more localized approach recognizes that health care costs have been driven up by unnecessary procedures ordered by physicians, inappropriate use of high-tech care, and out-of-control capital expenses. Yet much of long-term care does not demand complex technology nor sophisticated medical settings at high cost, but can be provided in low-cost environments by a range of providers. In other words, as Callahan has argued for nearly a decade, the emphasis should be on care, not on cure (Callahan, 1988; 1994).

A feminist model would also aim to insure consumer choice regarding the type of health provider from among a wide array of nonphysician or midlevel providers. Contrary to the biomedicalization of care described in earlier chapters, providers would include nurse practitioners, clinical nurse specialists, social workers, physical therapists, other allied health practitioners, chiropractors, and non-Western or holistic providers of care, such as acupuncturists. The physician would no longer be the primary gatekeeper to access services. By reducing the medical dominance of care, both the person with disabilities and his or her caregiver would have more choice among providers; this approach contrasts markedly with the professionalization of services, described earlier, whereby professionals determine the organization of services as well as consumer options in the use of services (Gill & Ingman, 1994). Optimizing consumers' choice of providers encourages a more egalitarian and collective approach to caring for others than the professional turf-guarding that has not served women well. Another way to optimize choice for both caregivers and their dependent relatives and to support women would be through vouchers or cash payments as part of a flexible benefit package, as discussed at length in Chapter 11. Consumers could pay a family member to provide care, or could hire their own attendant, or buy other services.

As noted in Chapter 13, both families and their dependent relatives must be supported by offering a broad array of services and by encouraging consumer involvement in decisions about the kinds of supports they require (Cameron, 1994; Massachusetts Women's Health Coalition, 1993). Supporting families to make informed choices about a broader range of services does not mean giving them complete autonomy and control in the decision-making process, however. Instead, such processes must involve collaboration among the family caregivers, the adult with chronic disabilities, and formal service providers. For example, although family caregivers should be involved in developing and reviewing care plans, adults with chronic disabilities should have as much discretion as is reasonable in determining the appropriate mix of services to meet their needs.

PUBLICLY FUNDED UNIVERSAL ACCESS

As noted in earlier chapters, women, especially women of color, have typically had less access to health insurance because of their domestic caregiving roles, their disproportionate employment in part-time, temporary or contingent jobs, and their lower incomes, which preclude their purchase of costly private insurance. Central to a feminist approach is that long-term care is defined as a public responsibility to guarantee a minimal level of services to all citizens as a public good in which all citizens should participate without undue burden. It recognizes that the need for long-term care is a normal risk of life. Therefore, there should be a financing system that people are confident will offer a way of paying for services when they need them, without any connotation of welfare (Rivlin & Wiener, 1988). Under a feminist model of long-term care—as was true in single-payer models introduced in the 103rd Congress—universal coverage and equitable access would be provided regardless of employment, health, income status, marital status, geographic location, preexisting health conditions, or actual health care needs. In other words, long-term care services are structured in such a way that no one is barred from access to them and people are protected against catastrophic, out-of-pocket costs. Accordingly, the two-class system of care—those who can afford to pay for care versus those who cannot—would be minimized (Wiener, Illston, & Henley, 1994). This model of universal access contrasts markedly with current managed care models that depend on employer-based insurance mechanisms and emphasize primarily outcomes, and have not developed methods for appropriate risk adjustments for chronically dependent populations with disabilities (e.g., methods to pay more for certain enrollees who are viewed as more risky or costly) (Riley & Mollica, 1994).

The issue of universal care, hotly debated at state and national levels, vividly represents the clash between private wants and the public good. A universal approach, which represents collective responsibility for protecting the welfare of vulnerable groups, is at odds with the current market-based economy, noninterventionist government, and the individualistic ideology of family privacy—values further supported by the 1994 national and state elections. Accordingly, opinion polls about support for universal health care have found resistance primarily from the middle class, who are more likely to have health care coverage and who, as a whole, do not feel responsible for those without health insurance; not surprisingly, they interpret universal access as a giveaway to the poor at their expense (Corry, 1994; Riley & Mollica, 1994). Such resistance is especially great when middle class voters become aware of the actual costs that would be involved.

From a feminist perspective, health is so integral to both individual happiness and a person's ability to contribute to society that government must assure access to quality care for all. As defined by Estes and Binney (1988, p. 76), "the health of the population is in the national interest" and cannot be assured by differential state responses under a pluralistic model. Instead, it requires a national (federal) response. Therefore, in a feminist model, health is not just an individual personal problem, but also the responsibility of community and government, acting at the local level under national direction, similar to public services of police, fire, and public schools (Massachusetts Women's Health Care Coalition, 1994). It presumes that citizens who are structurally disadvantaged by class, race, or gender must nonetheless be treated equitably by the health care system (Neysmith, 1993). It thus requires a strong public sector presence that takes leadership in defining policy directions to insure entitlement to health care based on rights of citizenship, even at the risk of bureaucratization. The policy focus is therefore on determining how much community-based long-term care, including life care housing and respite care services, our society is willing to purchase, not on how much money can be saved (Estes & Binney, 1988; Lumsdon, 1993). Wiener et al. (1994c) suggest that such a focus is possible, because increasing taxes for long-term care would not necessarily consume the taxing capacity that might otherwise be used for other purposes.

The policy approaches of universal access and treating long-term care as a normal risk of life suggest a social insurance model for financing, in which a basic package of services is available to people who need them as part of a social security system based on the rights of citizenship and regardless of individual financial or employment status (Leutz, Capitman, MacAdam, & Abrahams, 1992; Wiener & Illston, 1994a). As noted by Leutz et al. (1992, p. 191), "only a national social insurance approach to providing long-term care can guarantee the same basic dignity and protection against the disasters of disease that motivated our creation of the Social Security and Medicare programs." A social insurance approach recognizes that many women, especially low-income and minority women, currently lack access to health care through either full-time employment or high cost individual insurance policies. Long-term care, including community care coverage, is therefore viewed to be as essential as the Medicare benefit for acute care for the elderly or Social Security's income protection for the elderly and disabled. As noted by Wiener and Illston (1994a, p. 407), "coverage of long-term care on a nonmeans-tested basis will go a long way toward treating disability as normal risk of life rather than the failure of the individual deserving of public charity through welfare." In contrast with Medicaid, a feminist approach avoids the stigma of means testing.

Admittedly, a social insurance system is costly. As noted by Wiener et al. (1994c), "the primary disadvantage of all the social insurance approaches to long-term care is their expense" (p. 136). Our goal in this discussion is not to resolve financing details, but a social insurance system, although costly, could be financed through an employer payroll tax (which would replace the costs employers are now paying for insurance), personal and corporate income taxes on the wealthiest, state and local resources, and modest copayments by consumers, with the exception of those who are low-income. Because copayments at a flat rate disproportionately affect women's already fragile economic status, given their histories of part-time and low paid employment, cost-sharing mechanisms for total out-of-pocket expenses and premiums would be set on a sliding scale and capped at a reasonable percentage of income. In fact, some evidence suggests that home care should not involve any cost-sharing mechanisms, because copayments for home care can keep individuals from seeking necessary care in less expensive settings, eventually resulting in use of higher level, more costly services (Leutz et al., 1992).

Admittedly, the goal of maximizing consumer choice would need to be balanced with that of cost containment, and some type of cap on expenditures, premiums, and profits would be required to control costs (Wiener & Illston, 1994a; Massachusetts Women's Health Care Coalition, 1993). Yet as Sommers and Shields (1987) note, "arguments based on cost-effectiveness fail because providing some help is always more expensive than doing nothing. And nothing is what most caregivers now receive" (p. 183). In addition, a disability index to determine those to receive services would be desirable as a way to equitably address the issue of social efficiency (Hollingsworth & Hollingsworth, 1994). Funds would be targeted on those who most need care, whereas those with less than a threshold amount of disability would not receive publicly financed services. Because a social insurance approach does mean high public costs, we recognize that it is unlikely to be approved in the near future, given the current political economic context. In fact, Wiener et al. (1994c, p. 186) maintain that "given the public cost of comprehensive social insurance, . . . a hybrid system consisting of a combination of private insurance, Medicaid, and social insurance is inevitable." Yet, consistent with our goal of a new paradigm, we contend that social insurance is the method of equitable and adequate financing most congruent with the overall goal of gender justice of a feminist model, and a standard by which to assess other methods of financing.

A LIFE SPAN APPROACH

A feminist approach recognizes the interdependence across age groups and the vulnerability of each of us to the personal and economic cost of chronic illness. An examination of how well health care reform treats the most vulnerable citizens is more than a test of how policies affect a subpopulation: "It is a test to determine if coverage will truly be there when the most serious illness or disability occurs for any of us and for our families" (Riley & Mollica, 1994). The interconnection across age groups was clearly articulated by Robert Ball, former Commissioner of Social Security, as he spoke about the future of health care reform:

> Only a plan that anticipates the needs of society as a whole and spreads the risk as broadly as possible can meet the need at a cost that is bearable for each us. It's not just a matter of the elderly (or the disabled) wanting more protection for themselves. Those who are really at risk most are middle-aged people. (p. 6)

As we have documented, such at-risk middle-aged people are typically women who are juggling multiple responsibilities.

A financing system that relies on determining "categories of people" to establish different levels of eligibility for services or subsidies should be avoided. Under a feminist model—and under most long-term care reform proposals debated by the 103rd Congress—services would be geared to disability, functional ability, and need instead of age. Rather than pitting age groups against one another, as has happened with categorical approaches to policy, a nonage-based long-term care policy can appeal to different constituencies of caregivers of all ages who provide assistance to persons with disabilities across the life span (Hollingsworth & Hollingsworth, 1994; Stone & Keigher, 1993). Efforts would then be made to build on shared interests and needs for health care and long-term care across generations, in order to insure equity across age lines. The competition among generations for resources would be replaced by the question of how best to allocate resources in order to insure well-being throughout life and avoid inequitable access to basic necessities within generations (Callahan, 1994; Hendricks & Leedham, 1992). Indeed, one of the positive developments with regard to lobbying for national health care reform has been the new coalitions formed between groups representing younger age groups with disabilities and senior organizations, particularly AARP. Although the first priority under this model is for home care—the greatest need faced by adults with chronic disabilities and their caregivers—it recognizes that, as the oldest-old population grows, the need for institutional care will increase, necessitating comprehensive nursing home protection on a phased-in basis as part of the overall long-term care system. Institutionalized care would be coordinated with care provided in the community, thus building on shared generational interests.

The difficulties in developing long-term care policies based on inter-dependence, however, are readily apparent; they include differences across disability groups in terms of eligibility criteria, breadth of services needed, and desire to control or direct the services (Wiener & Illston, 1994a). One reason that age-based interest group struggles have persisted is that each group has different definitions and conceptualizations of the problems, which complicate the development of agreements and consensus on broad goals (Torres-Gil & Pynoos, 1986). For example, the elderly are themselves often split between the needs of the frail elderly, which typically require new and often institutional services, and traditional community-based programs, such as senior centers and congregate meals for the "well elderly." In contrast, advocates for adults with disabilities tend to focus on rehabilitation and independent living. Use of ADLs to determine services has limitations for adults who are mentally retarded and who may not be able to perform socially oriented instrumental activities of daily living, but have the physical capacity to perform ADLs (Wiener & Illston, 1994a). The shared interest among these groups, however, is to minimize unnecessary institutionalization, which provides a commonality for developing new models of community-based care as well as coalitions across groups.

A REDEFINITION OF HEALTH

When health has been defined by the marketplace and the medical model of care, the emphasis has been on productivity and economic returns. A feminist model would instead define health more broadly, in terms of the type of life it makes possible for adults with disabilities and their family caregivers. Mechanic (1987) states the following:

> The quality of a health care system is truly measured not by what it spends or the number of sophisticated procedures that it performs, but how it enhances the potential of the population to fulfill its personal and social choices and the extent to which it limits suffering. (p. 22)

If the long-range goal is social justice, then health and long-term care are evaluated in terms of adequacy of results obtained with available resources and what it takes to make possible a decent minimum standard of life, rather than quantitatively equal benefits for all and cost-efficiency as a way to minimize dollar expenditures (Hendricks & Leedham, 1992; Lumsdon, 1993; Stone & Keigher, 1994).

The goal of long-term care should be to help people achieve a maximum state of health within their reach, whether this means managing a chronic illness, living a full life with a disability, maintaining independence while aging, or other ways of achieving the highest level of health possible. The multidimensional and changing nature of chronic conditions must be recognized in order to avoid the functional decline that can result from unmet needs, as well as the unnecessary costs of providing care at too high a level. Therefore, health is not merely the absence of disease or impairment, but includes the prevention and management of chronic conditions. Under a feminist approach, maintenance (e.g., supportive assistance) and prevention or health promotion services, not just services to improve function, would be covered, because for some disabled individuals, improvement of function is not a realistic goal. Instead, what is necessary is coverage to minimize limitations, acquire skills, sustain function, or prevent deterioration. Required are primary, preventive, acute, rehabilitation, and chronic care services for ongoing periods of time to assure good health and maintenance or restoration of functioning. As an example, health promotion services for older adults might be offered in neighborhood-based centers integrating exercise, health education, nutrition, counseling and support groups, and a system for accessing transportation.

A feminist approach to care avoids a dichotomy between acute and chronic care, recognizing the interconnections between short- and long-term care. The beneficiaries of long-term care reform cross the boundary between episodic acute care and long-term care hundreds of thousands of times a day. A goal under a feminist approach—which is shared by other advocates of fundamental changes in health care—would be an integrated continuum of disability prevention, medically necessary acute care, rehabilitation, and chronic care management over the course of an individual's lifetime; this has been described by health researchers as an "integrated and seamless" continuum of services to respond to the multidimensional, ongoing, and costly nature of chronic conditions (Cameron, 1994; NCCC Update, 1994; Wiener & Illston, 1994b).

Home care based on patient and caregiver needs would be the centerpiece of this integrated delivery model that incorporates clinical and social services and coordinates providers across home, community, and institutional settings. Community care networks would cover individuals with a comprehensive continuum of social and community services to support both the adult who is chronically disabled and his or her family caregiver. Unencumbered by the medical orientation of traditional health care coverage, prior hospitalization would not be required as a prerequisite to home care nor would home care be allowed only in lieu of hospitalization. One approach to financing such home care would be to price out the benefit of 100 days of skilled nursing care and allow certified health plans to work with consumers and their caregivers in developing less expensive, community-based care, e.g., 100 days of skilled nursing care or the substitution of noninstitutional services at lesser cost.

In order to ensure access, responsiveness, and flexibility, integrated case management by care providers who are separate from service providers and familiar with the needs of each population, would link the management and development of care across time, place, and profession (Cameron, 1994). Care management, involving more than the brokering of services, would be closely tied to clinical practice across organizational settings. In addition to assessing the most appropriate services to address patient and caregiver needs at every phase of care, these care managers would share information across settings and over time. Information-sharing with the chronically disabled and their families would empower them to make better informed decisions about care. This would differ from more medically oriented case management, which is provided on an episodic basis and typically requires a physician to sign off for home health services (Leutz et al., 1992). Care managers would be involved not only in managing individual care but also in advocating for services and for changes within the larger systems and patterns of service (Challis, 1994; Marsh, 1992). Mechanisms would be developed to increase access and public accountability, including community outreach, grievance procedures, self-help and support groups, advocacy organizations, and systematic evaluation of services (Leutz et al., 1992). The kinds of programs in different areas would develop and grow, not simply because a funding pool was available, but because they met the needs of adults with chronic disabilities and their caregivers.

Given the diversity of needs of long-term care populations and the broadened definition of health, services would be comprehensive, integrating medical with social services. They would include home care, home health, hospice, adult day care, therapy, attendant care, homemaker services, meal preparation, assistive technology or home medical equipment, respite care, chore services, assistance with transportation, rehabilitative services for maximum independent functioning, along with more medically oriented benefits such as drugs; dental, vision, speech, and hearing care; and mental health services beyond prevention and assessment. For example, for many adults with serious mental illness, hospitalization, counseling, and medications should be coordinated with services for activities of daily living, income maintenance, housing, and social and recreational programs. As noted by Hollingsworth and Hollingsworth (1994), providing psychotherapy to someone with serious mental illness is not very useful if the person lacks a home.

The interconnectedness of social and health care services, of both physical and mental health, would be fully recognized in a feminist model, with attainment of optimal mental health as a national priority. Mental health services would be treated on the same terms and conditions that exist for physical health services, without restrictions in scope or duration other than medical necessity. A comprehensive system of services for adults who are chronically mentally ill would include prevention, emergency care through adequate crisis stabilization services, inpatient care, and outpatient case management to insure access to an array of residential and treatment settings, including social and vocational rehabilitation services, psychotherapy, medication, physical health services, outreach, supportive social networks, and transportation. Consistent with access to physical health services, consumers of mental health care should have the choice to select their care provider. Because of the nature of mental illness, services must be made available to adults with chronic mental illness and their caregivers for long periods of time, often for life, in ways that assure both geographical and psychological access and that address the differential needs of individuals throughout the life cycle (Bachrach, 1986). As articulated by the National Association of Social Workers, services should be age-appropriate, family-focused, and community-based and fit into the cultural heritage of the family and community (NASW, 1994). This also means establishing intersystem linkages with public programs related to education, employment, housing, and the justice system that critically affect adults with mental illness.

COMPENSATION FOR WOMEN CAREGIVERS

As described more fully in Chapter 12, inherent in a feminist approach is the recognition that women have been economically penalized by their caring roles, whether as unpaid carers in the home or as underpaid caregivers within institutions or community-based services. The complex interaction among the family, the state, and the employment histories of women is thus explicitly articulated (Hendricks & Rosenthal, 1993b). Although well-trained volunteers can provide intermittent care to those with chronic disabilities, ongoing care should not be provided by volunteers, who are disproportionately women. Adequate and equitable compensation for women caregivers, both in the home and long-term care facilities, is fundamental to health and long-term care reform that advances gender justice. Under a feminist model, such compensation would be oriented toward the caregiver's well-being, not toward decreasing costs through avoiding institutionalization. Stone and Keigher (1994) propose that financial supports for women caregivers should meet the criteria of adequacy (i.e., sufficient to achieve and maintain a decent standard of living); equity (i.e., how fairly and impartially benefits are distributed among caregivers who meet a certain standard of need); and appropriateness (i.e., compensation suited to or compatible with caregivers' needs). To these we would add the criterion of reasonableness of eligibility criteria because currently, stringent criteria have excluded women whose extensive caring is not recognized by society (Keefe & Fancey, 1992; Keigher & Stone, 1993). Under a feminist model, financial compensation would be only one part of a multifaceted approach that combines financial support with in-home services, especially homemaker services (Keefe & Fancey, 1992). Such an approach provides recognition of the economic value of women's caring as well as tangible relief for caregivers.

In conclusion, given the outcome of the health care reform debate before the 103rd Congress and the 1994 election shift to the right, the federal reform agenda for health care will undoubtedly be more limited. Probable incremental changes include insurance reforms, managed care expansion, encouragement of voluntary purchasing alliances or paperwork simplification, cost-centered accounting, and growing attempts to cut Medicare and Medicaid to reduce the deficit. The main theme will be cost containment, not access and equity, which over time will solidify a three-tiered system of health care for rich, middle-class, and poor citizens. Yet the failure to enact comprehensive health care reform that includes long-term care and guarantees universal coverage, cost containment, and good quality care will ultimately be very costly to our society for a number of reasons. One is that incremental changes will, of necessity, force future Congresses to "tinker" in order to correct the imbalances created by the previous ones. Another is the dramatic demographic changes and the growth of populations with chronic disabilities, which have been documented throughout this book.

The stark reality is that long-term care in the next decade will become an issue that Congress and the president cannot ignore because of the aging of the baby boomers and the continued growth of populations with developmental disabilities and chronic mental illness. Given these demographic changes, new visions of integrated health and long-term care must evolve in the United States by the turn of the century. We have provided a feminist approach as one vision. Although critics will contend that a feminist model is unrealistic, we maintain that citizens and their elected representatives must come to grips with the fundamental issue about how much care will be provided to every citizen. As the current disagreements about health care reform indicate, the most critical challenge is not in devising the particulars, but in organizing the political will to intervene publicly in areas where a collectivist structure is wanting. This suggests the importance of broad-based, multigenerational coalitions for change, to insure that caregivers will be included in the national health agenda, which is the focus of the next chapter.

15

Feminist Strategies for Change

Toward a National Caregiver Coalition

Fundamental changes in policies related to long-term care, social and economic supports, and the workplace will require the political involvement of family caregivers and their disabled relatives in the policy development process. In the long run, as Abel (1990) notes, the allocation of societal resources for persons who are chronically disabled will be determined not by the cogency of the arguments that policy analysts can muster, but by the strength of caregiver organizations. In this chapter we review (a) the diverse forms of community activity traditionally performed by women, and (b) political advocacy and organizing efforts typically undertaken within a pluralistic model of politics by or on behalf of individuals who are chronically mentally ill, persons who are developmentally disabled, and the frail elderly. We then present the underlying values, assumptions, principles, and processes of a feminist strategy toward the development of grassroots, local caregiver organizations that could, over time, form a national coalition.

CURRENT POLITICAL ADVOCACY

Under our current pluralistic and individualistic political system, interest groups compete for limited resources. With politics essentially an expression of individual interests, policy makers serve as referees, seeking tradeoffs in decisions that balance or compromise contending individual or group perspectives (Hahn, 1994). Because priority issues tend to be those that draw bipartisan support, such a system is not oriented toward making fundamental changes. Feminists have criticized that our pluralistic system "allows for minor skirmishes among the players, but basic power relationships remain in place" (Bonepart & Stoper, 1988; Neysmith, 1993,

p. 151). By itself, participation in traditional political activity, such as lobbying, promotes neither a redistribution of resources nor social change. In fact, under the interest group approach, citizens tend to perceive politics as dominated by special interests and to lack confidence in the political process to solve problems (Hahn, 1994). This pluralistic approach is nevertheless consistent with our society's underlying values of individualism and self-determination as well as the importance of the marketplace; it contrasts with a more collective approach that articulates what community or society can accomplish in enhancing the well-being of all citizens.

A more basic limitation of the pluralistic model is that women have been relatively invisible as political actors; this is because politics has been conventionally understood as the activities of elected officials and the workings of government through lobbying, litigation, and coalition-building. Because politics has remained within the bounds of conventional two-party politics—an essentially male domain—and has been dominated by jostling among interest groups, male definitions of society and its institutions become normative standards against which all other behaviors are judged (Minnick, 1990). In this traditional model, women have been marginalized and viewed as deficient, or as not good enough to participate in the political arena (Davis, 1994). As long as this pluralistic model was viewed as the only way to participate politically, women's status could not fundamentally change, and underlying values about women's roles and responsibilities were neither questioned nor altered (Bonepart & Stoper, 1988; Reeser, 1988). Although women have recently made more inroads into the legislative arena, politics has overlooked the extensive political activities women carry out in the workplace, schools, neighborhoods, and churches, which are enmeshed in the social and economic institutions that embody the basic power relations in our society. Older women have been even less visible in the traditional political arena than women generally, even though they provide leadership for complex endeavors in churches, senior centers, and public housing and were the founders of major national organizations for the elderly, including the Gray Panthers, the American Association of Retired Persons, and the Older Women's League. The relative invisibility of women in the conventional political arena has meant that the issues of greatest concern to women—safe neighborhoods, decent jobs, education and day care for their children, paid dependent care leaves, and availability of health and long-term care—have often been treated as irrelevant or of secondary significance in the formal political arena (Bookman & Morgen, 1988; Susser, 1988).

Women's success in working for political change at the grassroots level, by merging their public and private roles, has been overlooked, in part, because the traditional political model has tended to dichotomize the public and private spheres of activities, defining women as isolated or protected within the private sphere. Nevertheless, women have found ways to participate in collective neighborhood activities in the daily round of their domestic responsibilities. Historically, women's sense of their responsibilities at home and in the wider world has formed the core of their shared social conscience.

Women of color, especially, have traditionally combined paid work, volunteering in the community, and family life (Kaminer, 1993). Studies of grassroots organizations among low-income and minority women have documented women's conscious and collective ways of expressing and acting on their interests as wives and mothers, residents of neighborhoods and communities, and members of particular racial, ethnic, and class groups (Morgen & Bookman, 1988). Historically, women have acted as leaders and activists in "bread riots" and tenants' organizations, have participated actively in factory-based strikes, and have led struggles for better schools and safer neighborhoods. In her study of working-class women in a New York City neighborhood, Susser (1988) describes how they moved from localized self-help grassroots activities to demanding that the government take action to ameliorate bad conditions and to fund a broad range of services as a right:

> Although the movements have focused on what are now regarded as women's "traditional concerns,"—the care of the young and the disabled, for example— they demonstrate women's ability to build on their collective experience for organizing purposes and to demand collective goods and services from that state. Women are demanding that the state take over caretaking activities that are commonly thought to be women's responsibility. (p. 268)

The very conditions that foster women's oppression—their multiple responsibilities as workers, wives, and mothers—are also the conditions that enable them to be effective as leaders. In her research on working-class women organizing for quality desegregated education, Luttrell (1988) identified how women transferred the skills of interpersonal communication and organization from the private realm of family and community into public leadership abilities.

Within the conventional pluralistic model, advocacy organizations involving both men and women and built around the interests of separate populations have been effective to some extent. The best known organization in the field of mental illness is the National Alliance for the Mentally Ill (NAMI), which was formed in 1979 in response to problems resulting from deinstitutionalization. The organization came together in the context of greater awareness of the biological basis of many mental illnesses, which reduced the shame and stigma that families of the mentally ill had previously experienced (Howe & Howe, 1987). NAMI represented a shift away from excluding families from active involvement in the treatment of relatives' illness, to families advocating to change the mental health system to better meet their relatives' needs. As a group developed by people facing a particular problem, NAMI exemplifies a philosophy of self-help, mutual support, public awareness, and advocacy for improved services. NAMI has focused on obtaining better care for persons with chronic mental illness in the community, not on enhancing mental health among the general population.

Although NAMI has grown rapidly, with approximately 60,000 members in 900 chapters, only about 1% of families with a member who is chronically mentally ill are involved with the organization (Hollingsworth, 1994; Howe & Howe, 1987). From the family caregivers' perspective, a limitation of NAMI is that most of the advocacy has focused on influencing appropriations to obtain better services for the severely mentally ill, not on the caregivers' well-being. Nevertheless, to the extent that NAMI succeeds in improving and expanding community-based services, it has the potential to reduce demands on caregivers of adults with chronic mental illness.

The National Association for Retarded Citizens, founded as the Association for Help to Retarded Children, began in the 1950s when a few distressed parents banded together to seek help and support. It has evolved from small local units providing emotional support to its members to a large, well-known national organization substantially influencing the delivery of services (Hatfield, 1987b). Since the early 1970s, a wider range of self-advocacy groups for persons who are developmentally disabled have formed, which seek to improve their members' self-esteem, train them to advocate effectively on their own behalf, and alter public attitudes and service provision (Herr, 1983). The movement that spawned the passage of the American Disabilities Act in 1992 has not focused on the developmentally disabled or chronically mentally ill, but defines disability broadly, and represents one of the most successful civil rights efforts in recent decades (Hollingsworth, 1994; Shapiro, 1993). It has effectively cut across traditional boundaries by passing legislation that can benefit all three dependent populations that are the focus of this book.

The best known and largest organization advocating on behalf of the elderly in general is the American Association of Retired Persons (AARP), with over 33 million members, nearly 50 lobbyists, and over 400,000 active volunteers. In fact, over 13% of the American public belongs to AARP. Members usually join for the benefits of lower-cost health insurance, credit cards, travel discounts, mail order drugs, and myriad programs related to retirement planning, crime prevention, housing, and widowhood—not out of a desire to influence the public policy-making process (Jacobs, 1990). In recent years, however, AARP has become increasingly active politically. The organization was instrumental in ending mandatory retirement based on age, and in the initial passage of catastrophic health care legislation (that was later repealed) (Montgomery, 1989). AARP has launched a caregiver initiative oriented primarily toward caregiver education and support. It has been criticized for being concerned only with advancing the interests of its primarily middle-class membership and for being reformist, using fairly conventional lobbying methods toward noncontroversial piecemeal adjustments, rather than advocating major new policies to redistribute income and health care benefits to large numbers of individuals across age groups (Jacobs, 1990). To the extent that this conservatism is the case, it is consistent with the U.S. pluralistic interest group system, which is structured toward the most advantaged who are best able to organize to press their claims.

In the past two decades, caregivers of the elderly have begun to organize. One of the earliest and best-known organizations is Women Who Care in Marin County, California, which began in 1977 as a support group for women caring for disabled husbands, and focused on providing mutual support and encouragement. As women exchanged stories about the dilemmas they faced due to the dearth of services, they recognized the need to take collective action on their own behalf. According to founder Clemmie Barry, "we collectively found our voice and made it heard," moving on to attain significant relief (Sommers & Shields, 1987, p. 171). They developed a program of overnight respite care, home care, and community education, and joined with the Older Women's League to launch a national campaign to increase public awareness of caregiver needs (Abel, 1990; Sommers & Shields, 1987). Many of the women participants were transformed from "victims of circumstances to healers of social wrongs" (Sommers & Shields, 1987, p. 172).

The national organization, the Older Women's League (OWL), whose slogan is "Don't agonize—organize," has grown rapidly, and advocates on behalf of middle-aged and older women on issues of health care, long-term care financing, economic security, retirement, violence, and caregiving. Tish Sommers, the primary force behind OWL, recognized that "as a feminist, I see the problems of aging in America as women's issues" and effectively linked gender, politics, and aging (Huckle, 1991, p. 237). OWL has skillfully utilized the feminist principle of turning the personal into the political, with women telling their life stories as a way to mobilize others to action and influence policy makers. Recognizing that the poverty, loneliness, and neglect of many women in old age is the "payoff" for performing traditional roles, OWL encourages caregivers to tell their stories firsthand, as a way to develop a collective voice. Successfully developing a model bill on respite care that has passed in several states, OWL has long advocated for a national caregiver movement that would open the problems of caregivers to public scrutiny.

Despite efforts to reach diverse groups of older women, OWL remains primarily an organization of relatively well-educated, white women who live alone. Many enjoyed a middle-class lifestyle until the death or divorce of their husbands. OWL has struggled with the tension between social and political action to influence legislation versus the primary need of many older women for emotional support and social contacts (Huckle, 1991; Sommers & Shields, 1987).

A wide range of organizations have developed nationally that focus on advocacy around the development of more disease-specific services and programs (Biegel, Sales, & Schulz, 1991). The largest is the Alzheimer's Disease and Related Disorder Association, which has served to bring Alzheimer's to national attention. Other groups have formed around issues raised by stroke, cancer, heart disease, or Parkinson's disease. However, these organizations tend to emphasize the illness and those who suffer from it, and may neglect how the family, specifically women, are affected by caregiving demands.

Each of these organizations has aimed to have their voices included in policy deliberations to insure that services are available to their constituent populations. As noted by Biegel, such a categorical direction can lead to unproductive competition for limited resources, and is appropriate only if it is assumed that there are greater differences than similarities among the needs of caregivers across diseases. Nor do organizations exist that cross-cut chronic illness, disabilities, and the life span in order to foster a comprehensive and holistic approach to care (Biegel, Sales, & Schulz, 1991; Kahana, Biegel, & Wykle, 1994a). Yet advocating for public policy to support research into possible common etiology of Alzheimer's Disease and Down's Syndrome, for example, could result in recognition of commonalities between the Alzheimer's Association and the American Association for Mental Retardation (Ansello & Roberto, 1993).

Throughout, we have highlighted the similarity of needs across caregivers of these three adult populations with chronic disabilities. Currently, there is no broad-based organization that collectively addresses the interests of such caregivers or that has their welfare as its overall goal. We turn now to defining the underlying assumptions of a feminist organization that would encompass the three populations of focus, consider the temporal dimensions of caring across the life span, develop a broader sense of community responsibility, and have gender justice and caregiver well-being as primary goals.

CHARACTERISTICS OF A
FEMINIST ORGANIZATION FOR CAREGIVERS

Central to such an organization would be the recognition that gender has structured women's political experiences and that race, ethnicity, and class intersect with gender in shaping political action and consciousness. The enactment of gender justice policies, which involve the redistribution of status and social power, depends on women becoming actors in the political process, rather than objects of policies made largely by men (Quadagno, 1990).

Because the majority of women are caregivers for dependent relatives at some point in their lives, we assume that caregiver organizations, begun at the local level with the potential to form a national coalition, would have broad appeal in mobilizing women to self-help support and to action toward social change. However, many women caregivers do not identify themselves as feminists, in part because there are so many misconceptions in our society about what feminism means. The extent to which the women's movement alienated homemakers and mothers illustrates the importance of language and symbols, because women in traditional caregiver roles felt attacked by younger women's rhetoric that focused on careers and upward mobility. If a caregiver's organization is to be effective, it will have to overcome the obstacles faced by many women when confronted with membership in feminist organizations: women do not usually focus their concerns or cast their votes on the basis of "women's issues" per se. This is because their lives and concerns are interconnected with the interests of their partners, children, colleagues, and the larger community (Simon & Danziger, 1991). Bringing to bear a feminist perspective, however, does not mean that the majority of members have to define themselves as feminists. Feminism is not dependent on ideological purity, but has always been a mixture of conflicting ideologies without formal organizational structure (Kaminer, 1993). In fact, the women's movement has been characterized by great diversity in organizational structures (Buechler, 1990). As noted by Cott (1987) and as illustrated in models proposed throughout this book, ideas with ideological origins in feminism have found their way into numerous institutional and cultural niches where they modify social organization and inform social practices without being labeled feminist. What is important to the development of a caregiver organization is that the process, values, and principles are feminist.

The feminist values that should underlie caregiver organizations include validation of women's experiences as caregivers of chronically dependent individuals, interconnections among women's multiple roles, the importance and legitimacy of caregiving work, the personal as political, and empowerment as both the goal and means to attain the goal.

Validating Women's Experiences as Caregivers

Validating, listening to, understanding, and building on women's individual and collective experiences as caregivers—experiences that have been traditionally hidden, devalued, and unacknowledged—is the first step in breaking the silence that surrounds the issue of caregiving and is a basis for changing the prevailing pattern of care (Aronson, 1991; Wedenoja, Sommers, & Shields, 1991). According to Kaplan (1982), "female consciousness" is shared by all women and is rooted in the expectation that women take primary responsibility for the protection and nurturance of human life and the meeting of basic needs. "Breaking the silence" enables the discovery of a common ground and establishes publicly the uniqueness and diversity of women's experiences (Bricker-Jenkins & Hooyman, 1986, p. 29). In their analysis of African American women organizing for quality education, Nicola-McLaughlin and Chandler (1988, p. 192) portray women finding their voices through initial collective action, and then moving to a wide range of other forms of political action. Pharr (1988, p.1) notes that "each of us has the right to speak one's own truth in one's own voice and have a part in making decisions that affect one's life." Creating the conditions in which women can speak about their experiences is crucial to their ability to make claims on their own behalf. For example, with regard to caring for elderly parents, Aronson (1991) urges that within service structures, the policy-making process, and research conceptualizations of care, it is important to seize opportunities to challenge prevailing images of dutiful daughters and undemanding mothers. Questioning taken-for-granted service patterns and advocating for women who do not conform to traditional expectations can make small but incremental contributions to resisting care arrangements that have systematically constrained women. Dominant explanations and solutions of caregivers' situations can be challenged.

The validating of women's stories underlies the success of both the Displaced Homemaker Movement and the Older Women's League. As women like Tish Sommers and Laurie Shields—the primary organizers in the Displaced Homemakers movement—told their personal stories of pain and discrimination, they mobilized other women who had made "traditional marriage bargains and then been abandoned" (Huckle, 1991,

p. 193). In fact, central to their founding of the Older Women's League was their belief that "if every woman were to tell her story, there would be a sudden and dramatic change in policy on aging" (Sommers & Shields, 1987, p.170). By naming and identifying what was previously silent and invisible through collective social processes, women in these organizations were able to influence government and corporations to provide more resources in support of caring. The failure of established services to respond to carers' needs were made apparent, and new practice and policy issues for community services, previously invisible, were put on the public policy agenda.

Interconnections Among Women's Multiple Roles

Women's political activity is profoundly shaped by the interconnections among their social relationships and daily experiences in the family, the workplace, and the community. The interconnections among women's roles in the public and private spheres are central to a feminist approach. Public policy has promoted thinking that separates the home, the workplace, and the provision of child care, and as a result, has addressed inadequately the issues of family care that are of most concern to women. Yet women's traditional caring roles may lead them into activities that challenge the very assumption of a dichotomy between public and private, community and workplace (Susser, 1988). In doing so, women cross the boundaries between the so-called public and domestic arenas and draw on their social relationships to create networks through which they engage in public activity (Bookman & Morgen, 1988). For many women activists, the spheres of family, work, and political action are linked, and individual action is interconnected with group identification (Weeks, 1994).

In contrast to the individualistic model of interest group politics, women's networks and community associations develop from their responses to issues that confront them—not as isolated individuals, but as members of households and of communities in which these households are embedded (Morgen & Bookman, 1988). In a feminist model, such human connectedness in communities and networks is essential to politics (Ackelsberg, 1988) and would be validated within caregiver organizations. Accordingly, middle-aged and older women caregivers can be a powerful voice for social change on behalf of people of all ages, because they are "critical links between the interests of the young and those of the old" (Pifer, 1993, p. 251). Building on interconnections also requires starting from the caregiver's needs and issues viewed as a whole rather than fragmenting her experience by different funding streams or a professionalized concept of the issues faced (Weeks, 1994).

The Importance and Legitimacy of Caregiving Work

A feminist caregiving organization would explicitly recognize the importance of caregiving work to society. Such acknowledgment is contrary to the low value and marginal status assigned to caring and nurturing under patriarchal marketplace arrangements (Bricker-Jenkins & Hooyman, 1986). In a feminist organization, these values of nurturance and care are central organizing principles for a "new social order" (Berlin, 1981, p. 11). Explicit attempts to protect and preserve these values would lead, over time, to challenging the current neglect of social responsibility and to fundamental changes in how caring relationships are structured (Bricker-Jenkins & Hooyman, 1986). As occurred in the Displaced Homemakers movement, where divorced and widowed women who did not yet qualify for Social Security received counseling and educational opportunities, caregiving efforts that have been taken for granted would be explicitly valued and acknowledged, challenging the current neglect of social responsibility. Public education about the importance of caregiving work would be one of the primary functions of organizations of carers. This approach is based on the belief that attitudes and knowledge must change if caregivers are to be more personally powerful and if community life is to be organized to meet carers' needs (Weeks, 1994).

The Personal as Political

The concept of the personal as political is basic to feminism. The personal and the political, an individual's experience and the broader social structure, private troubles and public issues, a person's everyday life and sociopolitical change, are inextricably interconnected. This concept challenges the conventional definition of political activity and, as noted earlier, subverts the distinction between the public and private worlds. As described by Luttrell (1988) in her study of white women activists involved in a community struggle for quality desegregated education, these women did not separate their roles as public leaders from those as private mothers, but saw both as intimately related. Rather than dichotomizing the separate spheres of their lives, they found success by merging their public and private roles. As another example, a recurring theme in the activities of older women's organizations has been their capacity to translate personal difficulties into a political agenda (Barusch, 1994). Maggie Kuhn's personal experience with forced retirement motivated her to found the Gray Panthers when she was aged 65: "Something clicked in my mind and I saw that my problem was not mine alone" (Kuhn, 1991, p. 129). AARP was started by Ethel Percy Andrus, who recognized that her problems securing health insurance after retirement were shared by others (Barusch, 1994). Such connectedness is central to a feminist perspective: The way that we view reality determines the way that we try to change it.

In a feminist organization for caregivers, the societal, political, and cultural origins of an individual caregiver's pain and stress are fully recognized; women's experiences with powerlessness in their personal everyday lives are linked to the social, political, and economic structures that more broadly determine community and family life. Accordingly, the focus of political and grassroots activity is less on reducing an individual caregiver's burden and more on the development of policies and programs to support caregivers as a group. Just as there are no private realities apart from political processes, there are no private solutions to collective problems (Bricker-Jenkins & Hooyman, 1986, p. 14). Recognizing the need for widespread change in existing structures of power and privilege, the concept of politics in a feminist organization is not narrowly construed to refer only to formal public processes, but rather to the distribution of power in all social systems, from the family to the society at large. Politics involves not only conventional electoral or legislative activity, but any attempt to change the social and economic institutions that embody the entrenched power relationships in our society (Morgan & Bookman, 1988). Different forms of political action, both individual and systems advocacy, are intertwined in a search for a common ground among caregivers of diverse populations and their particular issues. In seeking to change the larger social context, we also change ourselves: "We change ourselves as we change the world as we change ourselves" (Bricker-Jenkins, 1991).

Closely related to the recognition of the interactions between the personal and the political, between the individual caregiver's situation and the larger societal context, is awareness of the links between sexism, racism, classism, homophobia, and other forms of oppression and discrimination. As noted in Chapter 1, the political activity of the second wave of feminists (of the late 60s and early 70s) too often emerged from the personal issues of white middle-class women, with the resulting women's organizations failing to represent all women. Members of women's movement groups in the 1970s were predominantly white, middle-class, and well educated (Bonepart & Stoper, 1988).

A feminist approach recognizes how social class and racial background affect women's political and personal concerns and shape their political involvement. According to Morgan and Bookman (1988, p. 11), "the triple oppression suffered by many women of color has fostered innovative methods and approaches to political organizing." Low-income African

American women, concentrated among domestic and service workers, have long sought to change the systems that have oppressed them through individual acts of resistance. Even when isolated in private homes, they have shared their work experiences with friends and other domestic workers in community-based social clubs, and have received information and support from their communities. These contacts have allowed them to develop cultures of resistance to prevailing arrangements (Dill, 1988; Gilkes, 1988; Sacks, 1988). In her examination of Black activism in a hospital union organizing drive, Sacks (1988) found grassroots leadership among working-class African American women to be a "collective and dynamic process, a complex set of relationships and negotiations rather than a mobilization of parallel but individual actors" (p. 77).

A feminist caregiver organization seeks to understand and eliminate all forms of oppression; it offers a means for analyzing the dynamics of the process of oppression as well as a vision of personal and social relationships rooted in equality (Wedenoja et al., 1991). Diversity is actively valued as a strength, not merely tolerated. Rather than the traditional model of building organizations on the basis of similarities, the collective social processes of a feminist caregiver organization are founded on differences. Despite the conflicts inherent in such an approach, it seeks to identify common ground while preserving uniqueness and maximizing freedom and self-actualization (Buechler, 1990; Cott, 1987). In her research on women working for quality desegregated education, Luttrell (1988) found that in waging a struggle against middle-class and male-dominated institutions, a new women's self-concept emerged that challenged gender, race, and class relationships and broke down divisions among the women.

> The new self-concept, built on a female consciousness, which values affiliation and nurturance, became a vehicle for action. These women came together as women and challenged racial distinctions. As an outgrowth of their female relationships and activities, and their embeddedness in working class community life, they realized their power and developed distinctive leadership styles. (p. 151)

A feminist strategy to build unity through diversity contrasts markedly with our current categorical, interest group approach that fosters separateness and false dichotomies of competitiveness among groups, especially along the lines of age, race, and income.

Empowerment as Both a Goal and Means to Attain the Goal

Empowerment is a process aimed at consolidating, maintaining, or changing the nature and distribution of power (Bookman & Morgen,

1988). Gutierrez's (1990) definition of empowerment is particularly relevant to organizing caregivers: empowerment includes maximizing a sense of personal control over one's own decisions combined with the ability to affect the behavior of others, a focus on enhancing existing strengths in individuals and communities, a goal of establishing equity in the distribution of resources, and a structural rather than individual or victim-blaming form of analysis for understanding problems. The process of empowerment occurs on the individual, interpersonal, and institutional levels through developing a sense of personal power, an ability to affect others, and a capacity to work with others to change social institutions.

For women whose access to economic resources and political power has been constrained by gender, race, and class, the empowerment process begins when they change their ideas about the causes of their powerlessness, recognize how systemic forces oppress them, and act to modify the conditions of their lives (Bookman & Morgen, 1988). Under this definition of empowerment, everyday acts that assert personal dignity and stand up to authority are themselves empowering. For example, a low-income nurse's aide's interactions with her boss can challenge and alter the effect of power relations in her work (Dill, 1988). Similarly, individual strategies of resistance employed by minority domestic workers have been found to be linked to collective forms of action (Sacks, 1988). The empowerment process builds on women's strengths that have emerged from their attempts to deal with oppressive conditions; as part of the process, efforts are first made to increase women's sense of self-efficacy, develop a group consciousness, reduce self-blame, and assume responsibility for restructuring oppressive conditions (Gutierrez, 1991).

Although personal and interpersonal power may be enhanced through the cognitive and skill development typical of education and training interventions (as discussed in Chapter 12), a feminist model of empowerment reaches for political power to change oppressive conditions through collaboration and collective action. It is important that a sense of empowerment among caregivers be fostered not only in relation to the caregiving role, but also in relation to the role of advocate within the broader policy arena (Cantor, 1994b). As women caregivers participate in decisions that affect their lives, they move from dependence to a sense of power and control over their lives.

A sense of group consciousness and collective identity is essential to mobilize others to challenge traditional gender relations. However, group identity and consciousness do not lead to mobilization unless that identity and consciousness are politicized (Buechler, 1990). The process of politicization, whereby women reframe their individual difficulties as grievances, become aware of their powerlessness, and then seek change through collective action, can occur through mutual aid and support groups that have a consciousness-raising focus or through active involvement in organizing in the workplace. Through politicization, women act collectively out of a shared sense of grievance, anger, and oppression. Support groups for caregivers have the potential—although rarely attained as currently structured—to facilitate empowerment by creating a basis of social support within the change process. They can provide a format for giving concrete assistance, an opportunity to learn new skills, and a potential power base for future action. As noted by Gottlieb, Burden, McCormack, and Nicarthy (1983), support groups "counteract the special isolation that has kept women from valuing each other and understanding their common experience" (pp. 83-84), emphasize social and political factors, and serve to clarify realistic goals for individual responsibility. They can provide the context for developing group consciousness by involving caregivers in dialogue with others who share their problems (Gutierrez, 1990). Given the growing numbers of employed caregivers, the workplace may well be a fertile site for organizing them to advocate for family-responsive workplace policies. Historically, when women in the workplace have taken action against injustices, such as lack of child care, their sense of empowerment has increased (Almeleh, Soifer, Gottlieb, & Gutierrez, 1993). As an example, Zavella (1988) describes cannery workers who became politicized through close relationships—social activities and informal discussions—with their co-workers.

Regardless of the specific site for organizing caregivers, consciousness-raising techniques are essential to developing their awareness of how economic and political structures affect their individual and collective experiences as carers. Buechler (1990) notes that consciousness-raising gives meaning to the slogan that "the personal is political" (p. 113) by validating individual experiences and revealing commonalities with other women that provide a collective identity in power. Consciousness-raising unmasks the societal origins of caregiver stress and burden so that carers can focus their actions on the causes of their problems, not on changing their internal subjective states. Closely tied to the process of consciousness-raising is organizing to change structural factors, rather than holding oneself responsible (Gutierrez, 1990). Developing group consciousness can enhance a sense of belonging, along with the supportive bonds and skills needed to claim the sense of power that develops. Networking and coalitions with other groups are important to this consciousness-raising process. As caregivers come together in small groups, as they did in Women Who Care, they become more cognizant of shared concerns. They see that others have similar experiences and similar views about providing care for persons with chronic disabilities. At the same time, they recognize how gender, race, class, and sexual orientation affect such experiences.

Women's awareness of choices and their connections with others who are experiencing similar challenges provide a foundation for political action and advocacy. Through a politicization process, their focus shifts from "Who am I?" which is inherent in traditional educational and support groups, to who benefits from how caring arrangements are currently structured and what must change and how (Bricker-Jenkins, 1991). Thus, they begin to formulate a vision of the possible in concrete terms and to experience themselves as active in the world. As Weick (1987, p. 226) states, "to even imagine that one has the capacity to create a new definition of oneself is in itself a radical act." They develop their own analyses regarding what they can do and what the sources of power are to effect change, rather than depend on others' analyses. Through the consciousness-raising process, women caregivers can confront the reality of their conditions by examining their experience and then taking this analysis as the starting point for individual and social change, to translate things that "aren't right" into visions of policies or conditions that they believe would be better.

The politics of relationship are central to the politicization process and resultant political action among women. Women workers have been found to develop work culture and work-related networks whose family-like support and family-rooted values sustain them both in the workplace and outside it (Ackelsberg, p. 304). In her research on hospital union organizing, Sacks (1988) described the intense social networks that sustained women during difficult actions such as walkouts.

> As networks in the kitchen, in outpatient areas, and in other areas mobilized politically in the course of the drive, the social density and political intensity of each increased, particularly where key people were members of the organizing committee. Center women in such work-based networks exemplified family values and reinforced them by their actions. Their initiatives in setting up social groups and activities were important parts of the process by which coworkers "become family" and were able to teach and enforce familistic values in the workplace. (p. 89)

For many women, the process of coming to political consciousness seems to be a process of building relationships and making connections— between their own lives and those of others, between issues that affect them and their families in the neighborhood or community and those that influence them in the workplace, and between the so-called separate spheres of their lives (Susser, 1988).

As noted earlier, women act not as isolated individuals, but as people rooted in networks and communities (Morgen & Bookman, 1988). These networks provide the resources and opportunity for them to be able to take action (Buechler, 1990). In her study of a hospital union drive, Sacks (1988) identified African American women who, although not public leaders, had the ability to connect with people who had mutual concerns and to understand and utilize existing networks both inside and outside the workplace for social change. She found that the particular skills that women learn in their families and communities are translated into effective political leadership. Similarly, the working-class women who organized for quality desegregated schools developed a notion of rights that is more relational then men's because their political activity emerged from their embeddedness in the community. Luttrell (1988, p. 153) writes that, because "women must juggle conflicting needs and interests within families and communities, their concept of 'rights' must somehow accommodate conflicts and facilitate affiliation and connection between people." Their social networks become a means for affirming positive values about women, their work and family roles, and their rights. They oppose negative messages that women have traditionally received about their roles and become a shared context for political activity (Sacks, 1988). This emphasis on relationship and connectedness contrasts dramatically with the individual interests of traditional electoral politics and makes women's leadership visible. Their ongoing commitment to community also contrasts with political action as a means to individual autonomy.

The concept of connectedness and mutual support would also mean that caregivers' organizations would include care receivers as well as givers. By recognizing the reciprocity of caregiving transactions, it aims to avoid further marginalizing and disempowering disabled women (Lloyd, 1992). Likewise, it would not be restricted to women only, acknowledging that a small but growing number of men share caregiving concerns and thus the similarities between women's interests and those of society at large. The interconnections between local grassroots activity and national initiatives would also be articulated, with local chapters coming together into a loose national coalition or conglomeration of groups to attempt to influence federal legislation. In other words, the basis for organizing would be at a local level, building on the connections that exist among women in their neighborhoods, communities, churches, and other locality-based organizations and thereby making it easier for caregivers to become involved. Similar to the Older Women's League, a national office could mobilize the time, expertise, and energy of diverse local groups around federal policy issues. Such a model of alliance building and coalition policies can take account of diversity by race and class (Buechler, 1990).

CONCLUSION

A feminist analysis begins with recognition that women's place in the social structure is fundamentally different from men's because of women's daily experiences with oppression. Feminism has profound implications for ensuring equitable choices for male and female caregivers, for changing existing institutions and policies, and for the absolute necessity of taking collective action to improve women's lives. As noted by Bricker-Jenkins (1991), a feminist perspective is unashamedly political. All caring activities entail the political dimensions of power and conflict and raise questions about justice and equality. Therefore, in a feminist model, women are collective agents and full actors in the political process who are organizing for structural changes, not passive victims of circumstance.

Throughout this book, we have argued for mobilizing caregivers and for formulating new policies and practices in the long-term care system and in the workplace. To do so, however, requires a profound rethinking of how problems facing caregivers are defined and how solutions are formulated. It requires, as feminist policy analyst Gillian Dalley (1988) writes, contemplating alternatives to today's accepted wisdom. We have emphasized that a feminist framework is one way to question accepted wisdom, specifically to challenge how the relations between the family, government, and labor market affect the social construction of caring. It provides a framework for analysis and action to begin to change the larger economic, political, and social environment that has defined caregiving as women's natural life work. Ultimately, a reexamination and transformation of all gender-based relationships of domination and subordination in society, a redistribution of resources, and a rearrangement of work and social relationships are necessary if fundamental changes in caregiving work are to occur. We hope that our evolving analysis has provided some beginning guidelines and criteria for rethinking economic and social policies and programs in the arenas of work and long-term care. As noted by Miller (1994), clarity about what is ultimately desirable and what is an acceptable but limited incremental change is essential to a vision for the future; "the vision of a world as we would like it to be is essential to progress toward that world" (p. 30). Our model of social care and gender justice may not yet be feasible, but the very act of questioning and challenging the assumptions on which the basis of daily living and care are based can have profound repercussions on societal values, attitudes, and policies. The contradictions and tensions within our analysis can, in fact, be a source of strength, inviting reflection, dialogue, and criticism, which all seek to clarify both the differences and commonalities among caregivers. As noted by Buechler (1990, p. 179), social change always occurs in a series of short runs in which agenda are partially and unevenly implemented. It is our belief that in the long run, both men and women caregivers could benefit from implementation of a feminist critique and model of care that bridges home and work and that ensures choice in both.

References

Abbott, P., & Wallace, C. (1992). *The family and the new right.* Boulder, CO: Pluto Press.

Abel, E. K. (1986). Adult daughters and care for the elderly. *Feminist Studies, 12,* 479-497.

Abel, E. K. (1987). *Love is not enough: Family care of the frail elderly.* Washington, DC: American Public Health Association.

Abel, E. K. (1990). Family care of the frail elderly. In E. K. Abel & M. K. Nelson (Eds.), *Circles of care: Work and identity in women's lives* (pp. 65-91). Albany: State University of New York Press.

Abel, E. K. (1991). *Who cares for the elderly? Public policy and the experiences of adult daughters.* Philadelphia: Temple University Press.

Abel, E. K., & Nelson, M. K. (1990). *Circles of care: Work and identity in women's lives.* Albany: State University of New York Press.

Abramovitz, M. (1988). *Regulating the lives of women: Social welfare policy from colonial times to the present.* Boston: South End Press.

Abramovitz, M. (1991). Social policy in disarray: The beleaguered American family. *Families in Society, 72,* 483-495.

Abramowitz, I. A., & Coursey, R. D. (1989). Impact of an educational support group on family participants who take care of their schizophrenic relatives. *Journal of Consulting and Clinical Psychology, 57,* 232-236.

Ackelsberg, M., & Diamond, I. (1987). Gender and political life: New directions in political science. In B. B. Hess & M. M. Ferree (Eds.), *Analyzing gender: A handbook of social science research* (pp. 504-525). Newbury Park, CA: Sage.

Ackelsberg, M. (1988). Communities, resistance, and women's activism: Some implications for a democratic policy. In A. Bookman & S. Morgen (Eds.), *Women and the politics of empowerment* (pp. 297-314). Philadelphia: Temple University Press.

Acker, J. (1988). Class, gender, and the relations of distribution. *Signs: Journal of Women in Culture and Society, 13*(3), 473-497.

Acker, J. (1989). The problem with patriarchy. *Sociology, 23,* 235-240.

Acker, J., & Hallock, M. (1992, March). *Economic restructuring and women's wages: Equity issues in the U.S. and Sweden.* Paper presented at the Women, Power and Strategies for Change Seminar, New York University, NY.

Aday, L. A. (1993). *At risk in America: The health and health care needs of vulnerable populations in the United States.* San Francisco: Jossey-Bass.

Adlin, M. (1993). Health care issues. In E. Sutton, A. Factor, B. Hawkins, T. Heller, & G. Seltzer (Eds.), *Older adults with developmental disabilities* (pp. 49-60). Baltimore: Brookes.

357

Aldous, J. (1980). Introduction. In J. Aldous & W. Dumon (Eds.), *The politics and programs of family policy* (pp. ix-xix). Notre Dame, IN: University of Notre Dame Press.

Allen, J. (1993). Caring, work and gender: Equity in an aging society. In J. Allen & A. Pifer (Eds.), *Women on the front lines: Meeting the challenge of an aging America* (pp. 221-240). Washington, DC: The Urban Institute.

Allen, J., & Pifer, A. (Eds.) (1993). *Women on the front lines: Meeting the challenge of an aging America.* Washington, DC: The Urban Institute.

Almeleh, N., Soifer, S., Gottlieb, N., & Gutierrez, L. (1993). Women's achievement of empowerment through activism in the workplace. *Affilia: Journal of Women and Social Work, 8*(1), 26-40.

Amado, A. N., Lakin, K. C., & Menke, J. M. (1990). *Chartbook on services for people with developmental disabilities.* Minneapolis: University of Minnesota, Center for Residential and Community Services.

American Association of Retired Persons (1988a). *America: Changing work force.* Washington, DC: Author.

American Association of Retired Persons (1988b). *Roundtable on older women in the workforce.* Washington, DC: Author.

American Association of Retired Persons. (1990). *Understanding senior housing.* Washington, DC: Author.

American Association of Retired Persons. (1992). *Fact sheet: The role of the Older Americans Act in providing long-term care.* Washington, DC: Author, Public Policy Institute.

American Association of Retired Persons. (1993a). *A profile of older Americans.* Washington, DC: Author.

American Association of Retired Persons. (1993b). *Pollings on long-term care.* Washington, DC: Author.

American Society on Aging. (1988). *Long term care: Who's responsible? Critical debates in an aging society* (Report No. 2). San Francisco: Author.

Anastas, J. W., Gibeau, J. L., & Larson, P. J. (1990). Working families and eldercare: A national perspective in an aging America. *Social Work, 35,* 405-411.

Andersen, M. (1983). *Thinking about women and rethinking sociology.* Working paper No. 113. Wellesley, MA: Wellesley College, Center for Research on Women.

Anderson, M. (1978). *Welfare: The political economy of welfare reforms in the United States.* Stanford, CA: Hoover Institute.

Anderson, M. L. (1991). Feminism and the American family ideal. *Journal of Comparative Family Studies, 22,* 235-246.

Ansello, E. F., & Eustis, N. N. (1992). Aging and disabilities: Seeking common ground. *Generations, 16*(1).

Ansello, E. F., & Roberto, K. A. (1993). Empowering elderly caregivers: Practice, research and policy directions. In K. A. Roberto (Ed.), *The elderly caregiver: Caring for adults with developmental disabilities* (pp. 173-189). Newbury Park, CA: Sage.

Anthony, W., & Blanch, A. (1989). Research on community support services: What have we learned? *Psychosocial Rehabilitation Journal, 12*(3), 55-81.

Antonucci, T. (1985). Personal characteristics, social support and social behavior. In R. Binstock & E. Shanas (Eds.), *Handbook of aging and the social sciences* (pp. 94-128). New York: Van Nostrand Reinhold.

Arendell, T., & Estes, C. (1991). Older women in the post-Reagan era. In M. Minkler & C. Estes (Eds.), *Critical perspectives on aging: The political and moral economy of growing old* (pp. 209-226). Amityville, NY: Baywood.

Arling, G., Harkins, E. B., & Romaniuk, M. (1984). Adult day care and the nursing home: The appropriateness of care in alternative settings. *Research on Aging, 6*(2), 225-242.

Arling, G., & McAuley, W. (1983). The feasibility of public payments for family caregivers. *The Gerontologist, 23,* 300-306.

Aronson, J. (1985). Family Care of the elderly: Underlying assumptions and their consequences. *Canadian Journal on Aging, 4*(3), 115-125.

Aronson, J. (1991). Dutiful daughters and undemanding mothers: Contrasting images of giving and receiving care in middle and later life. In C. Baines, P. Evans, & S. Neysmith (Eds.), *Women's caring: Feminist perspectives on social welfare* (pp. 138-168). Toronto, Canada: McClelland & Stewart.

Aronson, J. (1992). Women's sense of responsibility for the care of old people: "But who else is going to do it?" *Gender & Society, 6,* 8-29.

Ascher-Svanum, H., & Careguy, S. T. (1989). Mentally ill adults: A woman's agenda. *Hospital and Community Psychiatry, 40*(8), 843-845.

Ashbaugh, J. W., Leaf, P., Manderscheid, R., & Eaton, W. (1983). Estimates of the size and selected characteristics of the adult chronically mentally ill population living in U.S. households. *Research in Community and Mental Health, 3,* 3-24.

Axinn, J., & Levin, H. (1992). *Social welfare: A history of American response to need* (3rd ed.). New York: Longman

Baca Zinn, M., & Eitzen, S. (1987). *Diversity in American families.* New York: Harper & Row.

Bachman, S., & Drainoni, M. (1992). *Issues in state mental policy.* Waltham, MA: Brandeis University, Heller School, Health Policy Institute Center on Vulnerable Populations.

Bachrach, L. L. (1986). The challenge of service planning for chronic mental patients. *Community Mental Health Journal, 22*(3), 170-174.

Bailyn, L. (1992). Issues of work and family in different national contexts: How the United States, Britain, and Sweden respond. *Human Resource Management, 31,* 201-208.

Baines, C. T., Evans, P. M., & Neysmith, S. M. (1991). Caring: Its impact on the lives of women. In C. T. Baines, P. M. Evans, & S. M. Neysmith (Eds.), *Women's caring: Feminist perspectives on social welfare* (pp. 11-35). Toronto, Canada: McClelland & Stewart.

Baines, C., Evans, P., & Neysmith, S. (Eds.). (1991). *Women's caring: Feminist perspectives on social welfare.* Toronto, Canada: McClelland & Stuart.

Balbo, L. (1982). The servicing work of women and the capitalist state. *Political Power and Social Theory, 3,* 251-270.

Baldwin, S., & Glendinning, C. (1983). Employment, women and their disabled children. In J. Finch & D. Groves (Eds.), *A labour of love: Women, work and caring* (pp. 53-71). London: Routledge & Kegan Paul.

Ball, R. M. (1988). Social security across the generations. In J. R. Gist (Ed.), *Social security and economic well-being across generations* (pp. 11-38). Washington, DC: American Association of Retired Persons.

Bane, M. J., & Jargowsky, P. A. (1988). The links between government policy and family structure: What matters and what doesn't. In A. J. Cherlin (Ed.), *The changing American family and public policy* (pp. 219-261). Washington, DC: Urban Institute.

Baron, J. N., & Bielby, W. T. (1984). A women's place is with other women: Sex segregation in the workplace. In B. F. Reskin (Ed.), *Sex segregation in the workplace* (pp. 27-52). Washington, DC: National Academy Press.

Barr, J. K., Johnson, K. W., & Warshaw, L. J. (1992). Supporting the elderly: Workplace programs for employed caregivers. *Milbank Quarterly, 70,* 509-534.

Barr, J. K., & Warshaw, L. J. (1991). *Working women and stress: Summary results.* New York: New York Business Group on Health.

Baruch, G. K., & Barnett, R. C. (1986). *Role quality, multiple role involvement, and psychological well-being in midlife women.* Working Paper No. 149. Wellesley, MA: Wellesley College Center for Research on Women.

Barusch, A. S. (1994). *Older women in poverty.* New York: Springer.

Barusch, A. S., & Spaid, W. M. (1989). Gender differences in caregiving: Why do wives report greater burden? *The Gerontologist, 29,* 667-676.

Bass, D., & Noelker, L. (1985). The influence of family caregivers on elders' use of in-home services: An expanded conceptual framework. *Journal of Health & Social Behavior, 28,* 184-196.

Battaglino, L. (1987). Family empowerment through self-help groups: NAMI. In A. Hatfield & H. Lefley (Eds.), *Families of the mentally ill: Meeting the challenges* (pp. 43-51). San Francisco: Jossey-Bass.

Baxter, C. (1989). Investigating stigma as stress in social interactions of parents. *Journal of Mental Deficiency Research, 33,* 455-466.

Beck, R. W., & Beck, S. H. (1989). The incidence of extended households among middle-aged black and white women: Estimates from a 15-year panel study. *Journal of Family Issues, 10,* 147-168.

Beedon, L. E. (1992). *Women and social security: Challenges facing the American system of social insurance* (Issue Brief No. 2). Washington, DC: American Association of Retired Persons, Public Policy Institute.

Belcher, J. R. (1988). Mothers alone and supporting chronically mentally ill children: A greater vulnerability to illness. *Women and Health, 14,* 61-80.

Bell, A. P., & Weinberg, M. S. (1978). *Homosexualities: A study of diversity among men and women.* New York: Simon & Schuster.

Bengtson, V. L., Rosenthal, C., & Burton, L. (1990). Families and aging: Diversity and heterogeneity. In R. H. Binstock & L. K. George (Eds.), *Handbook of aging and the social sciences* (3rd ed., pp. 263-287). New York: Academic Press.

Berger, B., & Berger, P. L. (1983). *The war over the family: Capturing the middle ground.* New York: Anchor/Doubleday.

Bergthold, L. (1987). The impact of public policy on home health services for the elderly. *Pride Institute Journal of Long Term Home Health Care, 6,* 12-26.

Bergthold, L., Estes, C., & Villanueva, A. (1990). Public light and private dark: The privatization of home health services for the elderly in the U.S. *Home Health Care Services Quarterly, 11*(3/4), 7-33.

Berk, S. (1985). *The gender factory: The apportionment of work in American households.* New York: Plenum.

Berlin, S. (1981, November). *Feminist practices.* Paper presented at the Institute on Social Work Practice of Women, NASW Professional Symposium, Philadelphia, PA.

Bernard, J. (1971). *Women and the public interest.* Chicago: Aldine.

Bernard, J. (1983). The good provider role: Its rise and fall. In A. Skolnich & J. Skolnich (Eds.), *Family in transition* (4th ed., pp. 155-175). Boston: Little, Brown.

Bernheim, K. F. (1989). Psychologists and families of the severely mentally ill: The role of family consultation. *American Psychologist, 43*(3), 561-564.

Bernheim, K. F., & Lehman, A. F. (1985). *Working with families of the mentally ill.* New York: Norton.

Bernstein, A. (1994, June 15). A troubling picture of gender equity in academe. *Chronicle of Higher Education,* pp. U1, B1-B3.

Biegel, D., Sales, E. & Schulz, R. (1991). *Family caregiving in chronic illness: Alzheimer's disease, cancer, heart disease, mental illness, and stroke.* Newbury Park, CA: Sage.

Biegel, D., Song, L., & Chakravarthy, V. (1994). Predictors of caregiver burden among support group members of persons with chronic mental illness. In E. Kahana, D.

Biegel, & M. Wykle (Eds.), *Family caregiving across the lifespan* (pp. 178-215). Thousand Oaks, CA: Sage.

Biegel, D. E., & Yamatani, H. (1987). Self-help groups for families of the mentally ill: Roles and benefits. *International Journal of Family Psychiatry, 8,* 151-173.

Bilitski, J. S. (1985). *Assessment of adult day care programs and client health characteristics in U.S. Region III.* Disseminated by West Virginia University.

Binney, E., & Estes, C. (1988). The retreat of the state and its transfer of responsibility: The intergenerational war. *International Journal of Health Services, 18*(1), 83-96.

Binney, E., Estes, C., & Humphers, S. (1989). Information and community care for the elderly. In C. L. Estes, J. B. Wood, et al. (Eds.), *Organization and community responses to Medicare policy: Consequences for health and social services for the elderly* (Vol. 1, pp. 204-229). Final Report. San Francisco: University of California, Institute for Health and Aging.

Binney, E., Estes, C., & Ingman, S. (1990). Medicalization, public policy, and the elderly: Social services in jeopardy? *Social Science and Medicine, 30,* 761-771.

Binstock, R. (1990). The politics and economics of aging and diversity. In S. Bass, E. Kutza, & F. M. Torres-Gil (Eds.), *Diversity in aging* (pp. 73-98). Glenview, IL: Scott, Foresman.

Birenbaum, A., Guyot, D., & Cohen, H. (1990). *Health care financing for severe developmental disabilities.* Washington, DC: American Association on Mental Retardation.

Black, M., Cohn, J., Smull, M., & Crites, L. (1985). Individual and family factors associated with risk of institutionalization of mentally retarded adults. *American Journal of Mental Deficiency, 90*(3), 271-276.

Black, M. M., Cohn, J. F., Smull, M. W. & Crites, L. S. (1985). Individual and family factors associated with risk of institutionalization of mentally retarded adults. *American Journal of Mental Deficiency, 90*(3), 251-276.

Blau, F. D., & Ferber, M. A. (1986). *The economics of women, men, and work.* Englewood Cliffs, NJ: Prentice Hall.

Bonepart, E., & Stoper, E. (1988). *Women, power, and policy: Toward the year 2000.* New York: Pergamon.

Bookman, A., & Morgen, S. (1988). Carry it on: Continuing the discussion and the struggle. In A. Bookman & S. Morgen (Eds.), *Women and the politics of empowerment* (pp. 314-321). Philadelphia, PA: Temple University Press.

Boston University Center on Work and Family. (1994). *Work & family roundtable member survey: FMLA.* Boston, MA: Author.

Bould, S., Sanborn, B., & Reif, L. (1989). *Eighty-five plus: The oldest old.* Belmont, CA: Wadsworth.

Boyce, S. (1994). *Questions and answers on employee benefit issues.* (Brief Number 150). Washington, DC: Employee Benefit Research Institute.

Bozett, F. (1989). Gay fathers: A review of the literature. *Journal of Homosexuality, 18,* 137-162.

Bradley, V., & Knoll, J. (1990). *Family support services in the United States: An end of decade status report.* (Final report prepared by the Human Services Research Institute for the Administration on Developmental Disabilities). Washington, DC: U.S. Department of Health and Human Services.

Bradley, V., Knoll, J., & Agosta, J. (1992). *Emerging issues in family support.* Washington, DC: American Association on Mental Retardation.

Braithwaite, V. (1992). Caregiver burden: Making the concept scientifically useful and policy relevant. *Research on Aging, 14,* 3-27.

Briar, K., & Ryan, R. (1986). The anti-institution movement and women caregivers. *Affilia: Journal of Women and Social Work, 1,* 20-31.

Brice, G. C., & Gorey, K. M. (1989, July/August). Eldercare as an EAP concern. *EAP Digest,* 31-34.

Bricker-Jenkins, M. (1991). The propositions and assumptions of feminist social work practice. In M. Bricker-Jenkins, N. Hooyman, & N. Gottlieb (Eds.), *Feminist social work practice in clinical settings* (pp. 271-303). Newbury Park, CA: Sage.

Bricker-Jenkins, M., & Hooyman, N. (1986). *Not for women only: Social work practice for a feminist future.* Silver Spring, MD: National Association of Social Workers.

Bricker-Jenkins, M., Hooyman, N., & Gottlieb, N. (Eds.). (1991). *Feminist social work practice in clinical settings.* Newbury Park, CA: Sage.

Brickman, J. (1984). Feminist, nonsexist and traditional models of therapy: Implications of working with incest. *Women and Therapy, 3*(1), 49-67.

Briggs, A., & Oliver, J. (1985). *Caring: Experiences of looking after disabled relatives.* London: Rutledge & Kegan Paul.

Brody, E. M. (1985). Parent care as a normative family stress. *The Gerontologist, 25,* 19-30.

Brody, E. M. (1990). *Women in the middle: Their parent-care years.* New York: Springer.

Brody, E. M., Johnsen, P. T., Fulcomer, M. C., & Lang, A. (1983). Women's changing roles and help to elderly parents: Attitudes of three generations of women. *Journal of Gerontology, 38,* 597-607.

Brody, E. M., Johnsen, P. T., Hoffman, C., & Schoonover, C. B. (1987). Work status and parent care: A comparison of four groups of women. *The Gerontologist, 27,* 201-208.

Brody, E. M., & Schoonover, C. B. (1986). Patterns of parent-care when adult daughters work and when they do not. *The Gerontologist, 26,* 372-381.

Brown, G., Bone, M., Dalison, B., & Wing, J. (1966). *Schizophrenia and social care.* London: Oxford University Press.

Brubaker, E., & Brubaker, T. H. (1993). Caring for adult children with mental retardation. In K. A. Roberto (Ed.), *The elderly caregiver: Caring for adults with developmental disabilities* (pp. 51-60). Newbury Park, CA: Sage.

Brubaker, T. H., Englehardt, J. L., Brubaker, E., & Lutzer, V. D. (1989). Gender differences of older caregivers of adults with mental retardation. *Journal of Applied Gerontology, 8,* 183-189.

Bryant Quinn, J. (1991, September 23). Living from job to job. *Newsweek,* p. 41.

Buechler, S. (1990). *Women's movements in the United States: Women suffrage, equal rights, and beyond.* New Brunswick, NJ: Rutgers University Press.

Bulcroft, K., Leynseele, J. V., & Borgotta, E. F. (1989). Filial responsibility laws. *Research on Aging, 7,* 374-393.

Bulger, M. W., Wandersman, A., & Goldman, C. R. (1993). Burdens and satisfactions of caregiving: Appraisal of parental care of adults with schizophrenia. *American Journal of Orthopsychiatry, 63*(2), 255-265).

Burden, D. S., & Googins, B. K. (1987). *Balancing job and homelife study: Managing work and family stress in corporations.* Boston: Boston University, School of Social Work.

Burr, J. A., & Mutchler, J. E. (1993). Nativity, acculturation, and economic status: Explanations of Asian American living arrangements in later life. *Journal of Gerontology, 48,* S55-S63.

Burton, L. M., & Bengston, V. L. (1985). Black grandmothers: Issues of timing and continuity of roles. In V. L. Bengston & J. Robertson (Eds.), *Grandparenthood* (pp. 61-77). Newbury Park, CA: Sage.

Burton, L. M., & Dilworth-Anderson, P. (1991). The intergenerational family roles of aged black Americans. *Marriage and Family Review, 17,* 311-329.

Calasanti, T. M., & Bailey, C. A. (1991). Gender inequality and the division of household labor in the United States and Sweden: A socialist-feminist approach. *Social Problems, 38*(1), 34-53.

Callahan, D. (1988). Families as caregivers: The limits of morality. *Archives of Physical Medicine and Rehabilitation, 69,* 323-328.

Callahan, D. (1994). Setting limits: A response. *The Gerontologist, 34*(3), 393-398.

Callahan, J. (1989). Play it again Sam—There is no impact. *The Gerontologist, 29*(1), 5-6.

Cameron, K. (1994). *Health and long-term care reform in Washington state.* Olympia, WA: Department of Social and Health Services.

Cancian, F. M. (1987). *Love in America: Gender and self-development.* New York: Cambridge Unversity Press.

Cantor, M. H. (1983). Strain among caregivers: A study of experience in the United States. *The Gerontologist, 23,* 597-604.

Cantor, M. H. (1991). Family and community: Changing roles in an aging society. *The Gerontologist, 31,* 337-346.

Cantor, M. H. (1994a). Family caregiving and social care. In M. H. Cantor (Ed.), *Family caregiving: Agenda for the future* (pp. 2-8). San Francisco: American Society on Aging.

Cantor, M. H. (1994b). Reflections and recommendations. In M. H. Cantor (Ed.), *Family caregiving: Agenda for the future* (pp. 145-149). San Francisco: American Society on Aging.

Cantor, M. H., & Chichin, E. (1990). *Stress and strain among home care workers of the frail elderly.* New York: Fordham University, Brookdale Third Age Center.

Capitman, J. A. (1988). Case management for long-term and acute medical care. *Health Care Financing Review, Annual Supplement, 10,* 53-55.

Caserta, M., Connelly, J., Lund, D., & Poulson, J. C. (1987). Older adult caregivers of developmentally disabled household members: Service needs and fulfillment. *Journal of Gerontological Social Work, 10,* 35-50.

Caserta, M., Lund, D., Wright, S., & Redburn, P. (1987). Caregivers to dementia patients: Use of community services. *The Gerontologist, 27,* 209-213.

Caserta, M., Lund, D., Wright, S., & Redburn, P. (1990). Case management and home care. *Caring, 9,* 7-8.

Castellani, P. U. (1986). Development of respite services: Policy issues and options. In C. L. Salisbury & J. Intagliata (Eds.), *Respite care: Support for persons with developmental disabilities and their families.* Baltimore: Brookes.

Cazzallo, C., Bertrando, C., Clerici, C., Bressi, C., Da Ponte, C., & Albertini, E. (1989). The efficacy of an information group intervention on relatives of schizophrenics. *The International Journal of Social Psychiatry, 35*(4), 313-323.

Center for Vulnerable Populations. (1992). *Familiar faces: The status of America's vulnerable populations: A chartbook.* Portland, ME: Center for Health Policy Development.

Center for Vulnerable Populations. (1993). *Families focus: The status of America's vulnerable populations: A chartbook.* Waltham, MA: Brandeis University Press.

Center on Budget and Policy Priorities. (1989, October 18). *Poverty rate and income stagnate as rich-poor gap hits postwar high.* Washington, DC: Author.

Chadwick, B. A., & Heaton, T. B. (1992). *Statistical handbook on the American family.* Phoenix, AZ: Oryx.

Chafetz, J. S. (1988). *Feminist sociology: An overview of contemporary theories.* Istasca, IL: F. E. Peacock.

Challis, D. (1994). Case management: A review of UK developments and issues. In M. Titterton (Ed.), *Caring for people in the community: The new welfare* (pp. 91-112). London: Jessica Kingsley Publisher.

Chan, Yung-Ding. (1992). *A three-legged stool for long-term care.* Unpublished paper. Amherst: University of Massachusetts.

Chappell, N. C. (1990). Aging and social care. In R. B. Binstock & L. K. George (Eds.), *The handbook of aging and the social sciences* (3rd ed., pp. 438-454). New York: Academic Press.

Chavetz, J. S. (1988). *Feminist sociology: An overview of contemporary theories.* Istasca, IL: F. E. Peacock.

Chodorow, N. (1978). *The reproduction of mothering: Psychoanalysis and the sociology of gender.* Berkeley: University of California Press.

Christensen, K. E. (1987a). Women and contingent work. *Social Policy, 17,* 15-21.

Christensen, K. E. (1987b). Women, families, and home-based employment. In N. Gerstel & H. E. Gross (Eds.), *Families and work* (pp. 478-490). Philadelphia: Temple University Press.

Christensen, K. E. (1990, June 15). The invisible workforce: Transforming American businesses with outside and home-based workers. *Science, 248,* 1428-1429.

Christensen, K. E., & Staines, G. L. (1990). Flextime: A variable solution to work/family conflict? *Journal of Family Issues, 11,* 455-476.

Christianson, J. B. (1988). The evaluation of the national long term care demonstration: The effect of channeling on informal caregiving. *Health Services Research, 23*(1), 99-117.

Cicirelli, V. G. (1985). The role of siblings as family caregivers. In W. J. Sauer & R. T. Coward (Eds.), *Social support networks and the care of the elderly* (pp. 93-107). New York: Springer.

Clark, C. (1992, September 3). Housework needs more men's hands, study says. *Star Tribune,* p. 11E.

Clark, N., & Rakowski, W. (1983). Family caregivers of older adults: Improving helping skills. *The Gerontologist, 23,* 637-642.

Clark, P. (1993). Public policy in the United States and Canada: Individualism, familial obligation and collective responsibility in the care of the elderly. In J. Hendricks & C. Rosenthal (Eds.), *The remainder of their days: Domestic policy and older families in the United States and Canada* (pp. 13-49). New York: Garland.

Cohen, G. (1994). Journalistic elder abuse: It's time to get rid of fictions, down to facts. *The Gerontologist, 34*(3), 399-401.

Cohen, S., & Katzenstein, M. F. (1988). The war over the family is not over the family. In S. M. Dornbusch & M. H. Strober (Eds.), *Feminism, children, and the new families* (pp. 25-46). New York: Guilford.

Cohler, B., Pickett, S. A., & Cook, J. A. (1991). The psychiatric patient grows older: Issues in family care. In E. Light & B. D Leibowitz (Eds.), *The elderly with chronic mental illness* (pp. 82-110). New York: Springer.

Coleman, M. T. (1988). The division of household labor: Suggestions for future empirical consideration and theoretical development. *Journal of Family Issues, 9,* 132-148.

Colerick, E. J., & George, L. K. (1986). Predictors of institutionalization among caregivers of patients with Alzheimer's disease. *Journal of American Geriatrics Society, 34,* 493-498.

Collins, J. (1991). Power and local community activity. *Journal of Aging Studies, 5,* 209-218.

Collins, P. H. (1990). *Black feminist thought: Knowledge, consciousness, and the policies of empowerment.* Boston: Unwin Hyman.

Cook, J. A. (1988). Who "mothers" the chronically mentally ill? *Family Relations, 37,* 42-49.

Cook, J. A., Hoffschmidt, B. A., Cohler, B., & Pickett, S. (1992). Marital satisfaction among parents of the severely mentally ill living in the community. *American Journal of Orthopsychiatry, 62,* 552-563.

Copper, B. (1986). Older, not other. *Women's Review of Books, 3*(17), 14-15.

Corry, M. (1994). *Statement of the American Association of Retired Persons on Medicare and health care reform.* Washington, DC: American Association of Retired Persons.

Corson, W., Grannemann, T., & Holden, N. (1988). The evaluation of the national long term care demonstration: Formal community services under channeling. *Health Services Research, 23*(1), 83-98.

Cott, N. (1977). *The bonds of womanhood: Women's sphere in New England, 1780-1835.* New Haven, CT: Yale University Press.

Cott, N. (1987). *The grounding of modern feminism.* New Haven, CT: Yale University Press.

Coughlin, T. A., McBride, T. D., Perozek, M., & Liu, K. (1990). *Home care for the disabled elderly: Predictors and expected costs.* Washington, DC: Urban Institute.

Coverman, S. (1983). Gender, domestic labor time, and wage inequality. *American Sociological Review, 48,* 623-637.

Coward, R. T., & Dwyer, J. W. (1990). The association of gender, sibling network composition and patterns of parent care of adult children. *Research on Aging, 14,* 331-350.

Cowin, P. A. (1993). The sky is falling, but Popenoe's analysis won't help us do anything about it. *Journal of Marriage and the Family, 55,* 548-553.

Crawford, M., & Maracek, J. (1989). Psychology reconstructs the female: 1968-1988. *Psychology of Women Quarterly, 13,* 147-165.

Curtis, R. F. (1986). Household and family in theory on inequality. *American Sociological Review, 51,* 168-183.

Dale, J., & Foster, P. (1986). *Feminists and state welfare.* London: Routledge & Kegan Paul.

Dalley, G. (1988). *Ideologies of caring: Rethinking community and collectivism.* London: Macmillan.

Daniels, E. (1987). Invisible work. *Social Problems, 34,* 403-415.

Daniels, N. (1982). *Am I my parent's keeper?* New York: Oxford University Press.

Davis, K., & Rowland, D. (1991). Old and poor: Policy challenges in the 1990s. *Journal of Aging and Social Policy, 2,* 37-59.

Davis, L. V. (Ed.). (1994). *Building on women's strengths.* New York: Haworth.

Davis, L. V. (1994). Why we still need a women's agenda for social work. In L. V. Davis (Ed.), *Building on women's strengths* (pp. 1-26). New York: Haworth.

Davis, S. (1987). *A national status report on waiting lists of people with mental retardation for community services.* Arlington, TX: Association for Retarded Citizens.

de Beauvoir, S. (1968). *The second sex.* New York: Modern Library.

DeVault, M. (1991). *Feeding the family: The social organization of caring as gendered work.* Chicago: University of Chicago Press.

Degler, C. (1980). *At odds: Women and the family in America from the revolution to the present.* New York: Oxford University Press.

Dellman-Jenkins, M., Hofer, K. V., & Chebra, J. (1992). Eldercare in the 1990s: Challenges and supports for educating families. *Educational Gerontology, 18,* 775-784.

Developmental Disabilities Services and Facilities, Construction Ammendments 1970, Pub. L. No. 91-507, 84 Stat. 1316.

Diamond, T. (1990). Nursing homes in trouble. In E. Abel & M. Nelson (Eds.), *Circles of care: Work and identity in women's lives* (pp. 173-188). Albany: State University of New York.

Diamond, T. (1993). *Making gray gold: Narratives of nursing home care.* Chicago: University of Chicago Press.

Dickey, B., & Goldman, H. (1986). Public health care for the chronically mentally ill: Financing operating costs. *Administration in Mental Health, 14*(2), 63-77.

Dill, B. T. (1988). Domestic service and the construction of personal dignity. In A. Bookman & S. Morgen (Eds.), *Women and the politics of empowerment* (pp. 33-53). Philadelphia: Temple University Press.

DiNitto, D. (1991). *Social welfare: Politics and public policy* (3rd ed.). Englewood Cliffs, NJ: Prentice Hall

Dolinsky, A. L., & Rosenwaike, I. (1988). The role of demographic factors in the institutionalization of the elderly. *Research on Aging, 10,* 235-257.

Dornbusch, S. M., & Strober, M. H. (1988). Our perspective. In S. M. Dornbusch & M. H. Strober (Eds.), *Feminism, children, and the new families* (pp. 3-24). New York: Guilford.

Dressel, P. L., & Clark, A. (1990). A critical look at family care. *Journal of Marriage and the Family, 52,* 769-782.

Dwyer, J., & Seccombe, K. (1991). Elder care as family labor: The influence of gender and family position. *Journal of Family Issues, 12*(2), 229-247.

Edelman, P. (1986). The impact of community care to the home-bound elderly on provision of informal care. (Special Issue). *The Gerontologist, 26,* 234A.

Ehrenreich, B. (1983). *The hearts of men: American dreams and the flight from commitment.* Garden City, NY: Doubleday.

Ehrenreich, B., & English, D. (1979). *For her own good: 150 years of the experts' advice to women.* Garden City, NY: Anchor.

Eichler, M. (1987). The relationship between sexist, nonsexist and women: Centered and feminist research in the social services. In G. Nemixoff (Ed.), *Women and men: Interdisciplinary readings on gender* (pp. 21-53). Montreal, Canada: Fetzhenry & Whitside.

Eichler, M. (1988). *Nonsexist research methods: A practical guide.* Boston: Allen & Unwin.

Eisenberger, R., Fasolo, P., & Davis-LaMastro, V. (1990). Perceived organizational support and employee diligence, commitment and innovation. *Journal of Applied Psychology, 75,* 51-59.

Ellison, M. L., Bradley, V. J., Freud, E., Blaney, B., Knoll, J., & Bersani, H. (1991, April). *Testing family support and family empowerment: Key findings across four pilots.* (Available from the Human Services Research Institute, 2336 Massachusetts Avenue, Cambridge, MA 02139)

Emlen, A. C., & Koren, P. E. (1984). *Hard to find and difficult to manage: The effects of child care on the workplace.* Portland, OR: Portland State University, Regional Institute for Human Services.

Englehardt, J. L., Brubaker, T. H., & Lutzer, V. D. (1988). Older caregivers of adults with mental retardation: Service utilization. *Mental Retardation, 26*(4), 191-195.

England, S. E. (1990). Family leave and gender justice. *Affilia: Journal of Women and Social Work, 5,* 8-15.

England, S. E., Keigher, S. M., Miller, B., & Linsk, N. C. (1990). Community care policies & gender justice. In M. Minkler & C. Estes (Eds.), *Critical perspectives on aging: The political and moral economy of growing old* (pp. 227-244). Amityville, NY: Baywood.

England, S. E., Linsk, N. L., Simon-Rusinowitz, L., & Keigher, S. M. (1990). Paying kin for care: Agency barriers to formalizing informal care. *Journal of Aging & Social Policy, 2*(2), 63-86.

Enright, R. B., & Friss, L. (1987). *Employed caregivers of brain-impaired adults: An assessment of the dual role.* (Final Report submitted to the Gerontological Society of America). San Francisco: Family Survival Project.

Estes, C. (1991a). Epilogue. In M. Minkler & C. Estes (Eds.), *Critical perspectives on aging: The political and moral economy of growing old* (pp. 341-345). Amityville, NY: Baywood.

Estes, C. (1991b). The Reagan legacy: Privatization, the welfare state, and aging in the 1990s. In J. Myler & J. Quadagno (Eds.), *States, labor markets, and the future of old-age policy* (pp. 59-83). Philadelphia: Temple University Press.

Estes, C. (1994, May/June). Crisis in health reform and the culture of caring. *Aging Today,* pp. 3, 4.

Estes, C., & Binney, E. (1988). Toward a transformation of health and aging policy. *International Journal of Health Services, 18*(1), 69-82.

Estes, C., & Binney, E. (1989). The biomedicalization of aging: Dangers and dilemmas. *The Gerontologist, 29*(5), 587-596.

Estes, C., Gerard, L. E., Zones, J. S., & Swan, J. H. (1984). *Political economy, health, and aging.* Boston: Little, Brown.

Estes, C., Swan, J., & Associates. (1993). *The long-term care crisis.* Newbury Park, CA: Sage.

Estes, C., & Wood, J. (1990). The non-profit sector & community-based care for the elderly in the U.S.: A disappearing resource. In P. Lee & C. Estes (Eds.), *The nation's health* (3rd ed, pp. 374-381). Boston: Jones & Bartlett.

Estes, C., Wood, J. B., & Lee, P. R. (1988). *Organizational and community responses to Medicare policy.* San Francisco: Institute for Health and Aging.

European Center for Social Welfare Training & Research. (1987). *Report on the conference of European ministers for social welfare, Warsaw, Poland, April 6-10.* Vienna, Austria: Author.

Evans, P. (1991). The sexual division of poverty: The consequences of gendered caring. In C. Baines, P. Evans, & S. Neysmith (Eds.), *Women's caring* (pp. 169-204). Toronto, Canada: McClelland & Stewart.

Eyman, R. K., Grossman, H. J., Tarjan, G., & Miller, C. R. (1987). *Life expectancy and mental retardation.* Washington, DC: American Association on Mental Retardation.

Families USA Foundation. (1993). *Private insurance protection unaffordable report on long term care insurance concludes.* Press Release. (Available from Families USA Foundation, 1334 G Street, Washington, DC 2005)

Featherstone, H. (1980). *A difference in the family: Living with a disabled child.* New York: Penguin.

Feldman, P., Sapienza, A., & Kane, N. (1990). *Who cares for them? Workers, work life problems, and reforms in the home care industry.* Westport, CT: Greenwood.

Fengler, A. P., & Goodrich, N. (1979). Wives of elderly disabled men: The hidden victims. *The Gerontologist, 19,* 175-183.

Ferber, M. A., O'Farrell, B., & Allen, L. R. (Eds.). (1991). *Work and family: Policies for a changing work force.* Washington, DC: National Academy.

Ferree, M. (1990). Beyond separate spheres: Feminism and family research. *Journal of Marriage and the Family, 52,* 866-884.

Ferree, M., & Hess, B. (1987). Introduction. In B. Hess & M. Ferree (Eds.), *Analyzing gender: A handbook of social science research* (pp. 9-30). Newbury Park, CA: Sage.

Finch, J., & Groves, D. (Eds.). (1983). *A labour of love: Women, work and caring* (pp. 53-71). London: Routledge & Kegan Paul.

Finch, J., & Groves, D. (1980, October). Community care and the family: A case for equal opportunities? *Journal of Social Policy 9*(4), 487-511.

Finley, N. J. (1989, February). Theories of family labor as applied to gender differences in caregiving for elderly parents. *Journal of Marriage and the Family, 51,* 79-86.

Finley, N. J., Roberts, M. D., & Banahan, B. F. (1988). Motivators and inhibitors of attitudes of filial obligation toward aging parents. *The Gerontologist, 28,* 73-78.

Fischer, L., & Eustis, N. (1994). Care at home: Family caregivers and home care workers. In E. Kahana, D. Biegel, & M. Wykle (Eds.), *Family caregiving across the lifespan* (pp. 287-311). Thousand Oaks, CA: Sage.

Fisher, B., & Tronto, J. (1990). Toward a feminist theory of caring. In E. K. Abel & M. K. Nelson (Eds.), *Circles of care: Work and identity in women's lives* (pp. 35-62). Albany: State University of New York Press.

Fisher, G. A., Beason, P. R., & Tessler, R. C. (1990). Family response to mental illness: Developments since deinstitutionalization. In J. R. Greenley (Ed.), *Mental disorder in social context* (pp. 155-176). Greenwich, CT: JAI.

Ford, D. E. D. (1991). Translating the problems of the elderly into effective policies. In E. A. Anderson & R. C. Hula (Eds.), *The reconstruction of family policy* (pp. 91-109). Westport, CT: Greenwood.

Foster, S. E., & Brizius, J. A. (1993). Caring too much? American women and the nation's caregiving crisis. In J. Allen & A. Pifer (Eds.), *Women on the front lines: Meeting the challenge of an aging America* (pp. 47-73). Washington, DC: The Urban Institute.

Francell, C., Conn, V., & Gray, D. (1988). Families' perceptions of burden of care for chronic mentally ill relatives. *Hospital and Community Psychiatry, 39*(12), 1296-1300.

Frank, R. G., & McGuire, T. G. (1986). A review of studies of the impact of insurance on the demand and utilization of specialty mental health services. *Health Services Research, 21*(2, P. II), 241-265.

Franklin, S. (1993, February 21). Laboring to lead: Few women climb to top union posts. *Chicago Tribune,* p. C1.

Franks, D. (1978). *Report on economic expenses of families of the chronically mentally ill.* (Submitted to the National Institute on Mental Health [NIMH], Division of Biometry and Applied Science). Rockville, MD: NIMH.

Franks, D. D. (1987). *The high cost of caring: Economic contribution of families to the care of the mentally ill.* Unpublished doctoral dissertation, Brandeis University, Waltham, MA.

Fraser, N., & Nicholson, L. (1988). Social criticism without philosophy: An encounter between feminism and post modernism. *Theory, Culture and Society, 5,* 378-394.

Freedman, R., Litchfield, L., & Warfield, M. E. (1994, May). *Balancing work and family responsibilities: Perspectives of parents of children with developmental disabilities.* Paper presented at the Annual Meeting of the American Association of Mental Retardation, Boston, MA.

Freeman, M. (1990). Beyond women's issues: Feminism and social work. *Affilia: Journal of Women and Social Work, 5*(2), 72-89.

Freiman, M. P., Arons, B. S., Goldman, H. H., & Burns, B. J. (1990). Nursing home reform and the mentally ill. *Health Affairs, 9*(4), 47-60.

Friedan, B. (1963). *The feminine mystique.* New York: Penguin.

Fuchs, V. R. (1989). Women's quest for economic equality. *Journal of Economic Perspectives, 3,* 25-41.

Fuller, M. (1971). *Women in the nineteenth century.* New York: Norton.

Furstenberg, F. F., Jr. (1990). Divorce and the American family. *American Review of Sociology, 16,* 379-403.

Gailey, C. W. (1987). Evolutionary perspectives on gender hierarchy. In B. B. Hess & M. M. Ferree (Eds.), *Analyzing gender: A handbook of social science research* (pp. 32-67). Newbury Park, CA: Sage.

Galinsky, E., Friedman, D., & Hernandez, C. (1991). *The families and work institute family-friendly index.* New York: The Families and Work Institute.

Gallagher, D., Lovett, S., & Zeiss, A. (1988). Interventions with caregivers of frail older persons. In M. Ory & K. Bond (Eds.), *Aging and health care: Social science and policy perspectives* (pp. 167-189). New York: Tavistock.

Gallagher, D., & Thompson, L. (1994). Direct services and interventions for caregivers: A review of extant programs and a look to the future. In M. H. Cantor (Ed.), *Family caregiving: An agenda for the future* (pp. 102-122). San Francisco, CA: American Society on Aging.

Geiser, R., Hoche, L., & King, J. (1988). Respite care and mentally ill patients and their families. *Hospital and Community Psychiatry, 39,*(3), 291-295.

George, L. K., & Gwyther, L. P. (1986). Caregiver well-being: A multidimensional examination of family caregivers of demented adults. *The Gerontologist, 26,* 253-259.

George, L. K., & Gold, D. T. (1991). Life course perspectives on intergenerational and generational connections. *Marriage and Family Review, 17,* 67-88.

Gerson, J. M., & Peiss, K. (1985). Boundaries, negotiation, consciousness: Reconceptualizing gender relations. *Social Problems, 32*(4), 317-331.

Gerson, K. (1985). *Hard choices: How women decide about work, career, and motherhood.* Berkeley: University of California Press.

Gerstel, N., & Gross, H. E. (Eds.). (1987). *Families and work.* Philadelphia: Temple University Press.

Giele, J. Z., Mutschler, P. H., & Orodenker, S. Z. (1987). *Stress and burden of caregiving for the frail elderly.* (Working Paper No. 36). Waltham, MA: Brandeis University.

Gilder, G. (1981). *Wealth and poverty.* New York: Basic Books.

Gilkes, C. T. (1988). Building in many places: Multiple commitments and ideologies in Black women's community work. In A. Bookman & S. Morgen (Eds.), *Women and the politics of empowerment* (pp. 53-77). Philadelphia: Temple University Press.

Gill, D., & Ingman, S. (Eds.). (1994). *Eldercare, distributive justice, and the welfare state: Retrenchment or expansion.* Albany: State University of New York.

Gilligan, C. (1982). *In a different voice: Psychological theory and women's development.* Cambridge, MA: Harvard University Press.

Gilliland, N. (1986). Mandating family responsibility for elderly members, costs and benefits. *Journal of Applied Gerontology, 5,* 26-36.

Gimpel, J. (1991). *Family caregiving: A preliminary report based on the national survey of families and households.* (Working paper prepared for the division of Family, Community, and Long-term Care Policy), Washington, DC: Department of Health & Human Services.

Gittins, D. (1986). *The family in question: Changing households and family ideologies.* Atlantic Highlands, NJ: Humanities Press.

Glazer, N. (1990). The home as workshop: Women as amateur nurses and medical providers. *Gender & Society, 4,* 479-499.

Glenn, E. (1987). Gender and the family. In B. B. Hess & M. M. Ferree (Eds.), *Analyzing gender: A handbook of social science research* (pp. 348-380). Newbury Park, CA: Sage.

Goldberg, A. (1994). Home care for the chronically ill in the U.S. In J. C. Hollingsworth & E. J. Hollingsworth (Eds.), *Care of the chronically and severely ill* (pp. 75-106). New York: Aldine de Gruyter.

Goldberg-Wood, G., & Middleman, R. (1989). *The structural approach to direct practice in social work.* New York: Columbia University Press.

Goldman, H. H. (1982). Mental illness and family burden: A public health perspective. *Hospital and Community Psychiatry, 33,* 557-560.

Goldman, H. H., & Manderscheid, R. W. (1987). Chronic mental disorder in the United States. In R. W. Manderscheid & S. A. Barrett (Eds.), *Mental health, United States,*

1987 (DHHS Publication No. ADM 87-1518, 1-13). National Institute of Mental Health. Washington, DC: Government Printing Office.

Goldstein, J. R. (1982). Adult day care: Expanding options for service. *Journal of Gerontological Social Work, 5*(1/2), 157-168.

Goldstein, J. R. (1994, October 2). Health Reform: Now for Round 2. *NASW News.*

Gonyea, J. G. (1989). Alzheimer's disease support groups: An analysis of their structure format and perceived benefits. *Social Work in Health Care, 14*(1), 61-72.

Gonyea, J. G. (1991, March). *Advancing the elder care agenda: A conceptual model for assessing corporate receptiveness.* Paper presented at the Annual Meeting of the American Society on Aging, San Diego, CA.

Gonyea, J. G. (1993). Family responsibilities and family-oriented policies: Assessing their impacts on the workplace. *Employee Assistance Quarterly, 9,* 1-29.

Gonyea, J. G. (1994a). Making gender visible in public policy. In E. Thompson Jr. (Ed.), *Older men's lives* (pp. 237-255). Thousand Oaks, CA: Sage.

Gonyea, J. G. (1994b). Introduction to special issue on work and eldercare. *Research on Aging, 16,* 3-6.

Gonyea, J. G. (1995). Middle age. In D. Levinson (Ed.), *Encyclopedia of marriage and the family.* New York: MacMillan.

Gonyea, J. G., & Googins, B. K. (1992). Linking the worlds of work and family: Beyond the productivity trap. *Human Resource Management, 31,* 209-226.

Goodstein, J. D. (1994). Institutional pressures and strategic responsiveness: Employer involvement in work-family issues. *Academy of Management Journal, 37,* 350-382.

Googins, B. K., Gonyea, J. G., & Pitt-Catsouphes, M. (1990). *Linking the worlds of family and work: Family dependent care and workers' performance.* Boston: Boston University, Center on Work and Family.

Googins, B. K., & Litchfield, L. (1992). *BULL study: Integrating work and personal life survey.* Boston: Boston University, Center on Work and Family.

Gordon, D., & Donald, J. (1993). *Community social work, older people and informal care.* Aldershot, England: Avebury.

Gordon, S. (1992). *Prisoner of man's dreams: Striking out for a new feminist future.* Boston: Little, Brown.

Gottlieb, N., Burden, D., McCormack, R., & Nicarthy, G. (1983). Distinctive attributes of feminist groups. *Social Work with Groups, 6*(3), 80-85.

Gould, M., & Kern-Daniels, R. (1977). Toward a sociological theory of gender and sex. *American Sociologist, 12,* 182-189.

Grad, J. P. D., & Sainsbury, P. (1968). The effect that patients have on their families in a community care and a control psychiatric service: A two year follow-up. *British Journal of Psychiatry, 114,* 265-278.

Grad, J. P. D., & Sainsbury, P. M. D. (1963). Mental illness and the family. *Lancet, 1,* 544-547.

Graham, H. (1983). Caring: A labour of love. In J. Finch & D. Groves (Eds.), *A labour of love: Women, work and caring* (pp. 13-25). London: Routledge & Kegan Paul.

Grambs, J. D. (1989). *Women over forty: Visions and reality.* New York: Springer.

Granger, J. M. (1990). African American family policy or national family policy: Are they different? *Urban League Review, 13,* 43-51.

Grant, G. (1986). Older carers, interdependence and the care of mentally handicapped adults. *Ageing and Society, 6,* 333-351.

Grant, G. (1990). Elderly parents with handicapped children: Anticipating the future. *Journal of Aging Studies, 4,* 359-374.

Grassi, L. (1988). The frail elderly and long-term care administration. *Caring, 7*(3), 24-30.

Greenberg, J. S., Greenley, J. R., McKee, D., Brown, R., & Griffin-Francell, C. (1993). Mothers caring for an adult child with schizophrenia: The effects of subjective burden on maternal health. *Family Relations, 42,* 205-211.

Greene, V. L. (1983). Substitution between formally and informally provided care for the impaired elderly in the community. *Medical Care, 21,* 609-619.

Greene, V. L., & Monahan, D. J. (1984). Comparative utilization of community based long term care services by Hispanic and Anglo elderly in a case management system. *Journal of Gerontology, 39,* 730-735.

Greene, V. L., & Monahan, D. J. (1989). The effect of a support and education program on stress and burden among family caregivers to frail elderly persons. *The Gerontologist, 29*(4), 472-477.

Grella, C. E., & Grusky, O. (1989). Families of the seriously mentally ill and their satisfaction with services. *Hospital and Community Psychiatry, 40*(8), 832-835.

Grunebaum, H., & Friedman, H. (1988). Building collaborative relationships with families of the mentally ill. *Hospital and Community Psychiatry, 39*(11), 1183-1187.

Grusky, O., Tierney, K., Manderscheid, R., & Grusky, D. B. (1985). Social bonding and community adjustment of chronically mentally ill adults. *Journal of Health and Social Behavior, 26,* 49-63.

Guberman, N., Maheu, P., & Maille, C. (1992). Women as family caregivers: Why do they care? *The Gerontologist, 32,* 607-617.

Gutierrez, L. (1990). Working with women of color: An empowerment perspective. *Social Work, 35*(2), 97-192.

Gutierrez, L. (1991). Empowering women of color: A feminist model. In M. Bricker-Jenkins, N. Hooyman, & N. Gottlieb (Eds.), *Feminist social work practice in clinical settings* (pp. 199-215). Newbury Park, CA: Sage.

Gwyther, L. P. (1989). Overcoming Barriers: Home care for dementia patients. *Caring, 8,* 12-16.

Hagestad, G. O. (1987). Family. In G. L. Maddox (Ed.), *The encyclopedia of aging* (pp. 247-249). New York: Springer.

Hagestad, G. O. (1988). Demographic change and the life course: Some emerging trends in the family realm. *Family Relations, 37,* 405-410.

Hahn, A. (1994). *The politics of caring: Human services at the local level.* Boulder, CO: Westview.

Halamandaris, V. (1991). The power of caring: Management by values. *Caring, 19*(19), 4-6, 8, 10.

Haley, W. E. (1989). Group intervention for dementia family givers: A longitudinal perspective. *The Gerontologist, 29*(4), 478-480.

Haley, W. E. (1991). Caregiver intervention programs: The moral equivalent of free haircuts? *The Gerontologist, 31*(1), 7-8.

Haley, W. E., Levine, E. G., Brown, S. L., Berry, J. W., & Hughes, G. H. (1987). Psychological, social, and health consequences of caring for a relative with senile dementia. *Journal of the American Geriatric Society, 35,* 405-411.

Half of US children in traditional families. (1994, August 30). *Boston Globe,* p. 3.

Hall, D. T. (1990). Promoting work/family balance: An organizational-change approach. *Organizational Dynamics, 18,* 5-18.

Hallfors, D. (1992). *State policy issues in long-term care for frail elders.* Waltham, MA: Brandeis University, Heller School, Center for Vulnerable Populations, Health Policy Institute.

Haracznak, S. (1991). Home medical equipment: Playing a growing role in the nation's health care system. *Caring, 19*(11), 10-12.

Haraway, D. (1988). Situated knowledges: The science question in feminism and the privilege of partial perspective. *Feminist Studies, 14*(3), 578-597.

Hardesty, C., & Bokemeier, J. (1989). Finding time and making do: Distribution of household labor in non-metropolitan marriages. *Journal of Marriage and the Family, 51*(1), 253-267.

Harrington, C., Estes, C., Lee, P., & Newcomer, R. (1986). Effects of state Medicare policies on the aged. *The Gerontologist, 26,* 626-663.

Hartmann, H. I. (1981). The family as the locus of gender, class and political struggle: The example of housework. *Journal of Women in Culture and Society, 6*(3), 366-394.

Hartsock, N. (1979). Feminist theory and the development of revolutionary strategy. In Z. Eisenstein (Ed.), *Capitalist patriarchy and the case for socialist feminism* (pp. 56-77). New York: Monthly Review Press.

Hartsock, N. (1990). Foucault on power: A theory for women? In L. Nicholson (Ed.), *Feminism/post modernism* (pp. 157-175). New York: Routledge, Chapman & Hall.

Hatfield, A. B. (1978). Psychological costs of schizophrenia to the family. *Social Work, 23,* 355-359.

Hatfield, A. B. (1987a). Families as caregivers: A historical perspective. In A. B. Hatfield & H. P. Lefley (Eds.), *Families of the mentally ill: Coping and adaptation* (pp. 3-29). New York: Guilford.

Hatfield, A. B. (1987b). The National Alliance for the Mentally Ill: The meaning of a movement. *International Journal of Mental Health, 15*(4), 79-93.

Hatfield, A. B., & Lefley, H. P. (1987). *Families of the mentally ill: Coping and adaptation.* New York: Guilford.

Hawkesworth, M. (1989). Knowers, knowing, known: Feminist theory and claims of truth. *Signs: Journal of Women in Culture and Society, 14,* 533-557.

Hayden, D. (1981). *The grand domestic revolution: A history of feminist design for American homes, neighborhoods and cities.* Cambridge: MIT Press.

Hayghe, H. V. (1988). Employers and child care: What role do they play? *Monthly Labor Review, 111,* 38-44.

Heagerty, B., & Eskenazi, L. (1994). A practice and program perspective on family caregiving: A focus on solutions. In M. H. Cantor (Ed.), *Family caregiving: An agenda for the future* (pp. 35-48). San Francisco, CA: American Society on Aging.

Health Care Reform Week. (1993, June 14). *Relatives, friends, neighbors may be key to long-term care savings, survey suggests.*

Heller, T. (1993). Aging caregivers of persons with developmental disabilities: Changes in burden and placement desire. In K. A. Roberto (Ed.), *The elderly caregiver: Caring for the adults with developmental disabilities* (pp. 21-38). Newbury Park, CA: Sage.

Heller, T., & Factor, A. (1988). *Development of a transition plan for older adults with developmental disabilities residing in the natural home.* (Public Policy Monograph Series No. 37). Chicago: University of Illinois at Chicago, University Affiliated Program in Developmental Disabilities.

Heller, T., & Factor, A. (1991). Permanency planning for adults with mental retardation living with family caregivers. *American Journal of Mental Retardation, 96,* 163-176.

Hendricks, J. (1990). Gender and aging: Making something of our chromosomes. *Generations, 14*(3), 5-6.

Hendricks, J. (1994). Governmental responsibility: Adequacy or dependency for the USA aged. In D. Gill & S. Ingman (Eds.), *Eldercare, distributive justice: The welfare state* (pp. 255-286). Albany: State University of New York Press.

Hendricks, J., & Hatch, L. R. (1993). Federal policy and family life of older Americans. In J. Hendricks & C. Rosenthal (Eds.), *The remainder of these days: Domestic policy and older families in the United States and Canada* (pp. 49-74). New York: Garland.

Hendricks, J., & Leedham, C. A. (1992). Toward a political and moral economy of aging: An alternative perspective. *International Journal of Health Services, 22*(1), 125-137.

Hendricks, J., & Rosenthal, C. J. (1993a). Introduction: Family life and the public sphere. In J. Hendricks & C. J. Rosenthal (Eds.), *The remainder of their days: Domestic policy and older families in the United States and Canada* (pp. 1-10). New York: Garland.

Hendricks, J., & Rosenthal, C. J. (Eds.). (1993b). *The remainder of their days: Domestic policy and older families in the United States and Canada.* New York: Garland.

Hernes, H. (1984). Women and the welfare state. In H. Holter (Ed.), *Patriarchy in a welfare society* (pp. 26-46). New York: Columbia University Press.

Hernes, H. (1987). *Welfare state and women power.* Oslo: Norwegian University Press.

Herr, S. (1983). *Rights and advocacy for retarded people.* Toronto, Canada: Lexington.

Hess, B. (1990). Gender and aging: The demographic parameters. *Generations, 14*(3), 12-15.

Hess, B., & Ferree, M. (Eds.). (1987). *Analyzing gender: A handbook of social science research.* Newbury Park, CA: Sage.

Hewitt Associates. (1993). *Flexible compensation programs and practices, 1993.* (1992 Data). Lincolnshire, IL: Author.

Hirst, M. (1985). Young adults with disabilities: Health, employment and financial costs for family carers. *Child Care, Health and Development, 11,* 291-307.

Hochschild, A. (1975). The sociology of feeling and emotion: Selected possibilities. In M. Millman & R. M. Kanter (Eds.), *Another voice: Feminist perspectives on social life and social science* (pp. 280-307). New York: Anchor Press/Doubleday.

Hochschild, A. (1979). Emotion work, feeling rules and social structure. *American Journal of Sociology, 85*(3), 551-575.

Hochschild, A. (1989). *The second shift: Working parents and the revolution at home.* New York: Viking.

Hoeffer, B. (1979). Children's acquisition of sex-role behavior in lesbian mother's families. *American Journal of Orthopsychiatry, 51,* 545-551.

Hoenig, J., & Hamilton, M. W. (1966). The schizophrenic patient in the community and his effect on the household. *International Journal of Social Psychiatry, 12,* 165-176.

Hokenstad, M., & Johansson, L. (1990). Caregiving for the elderly in Sweden: Program challenges and policy initiative. In D. Biegel & A. Blum (Eds.), *Aging and caregiving: Theory, research, and practice* (pp. 254-268). Newbury Park, CA: Sage.

Holden, D. F., & Lewine, R. R. J. (1982). How families evaluate mental health professionals, resources and the effects of illness. *Schizophrenia Bulletin, 8,* 626-633.

Hollingsworth, E. (1994). Falling through the cracks: Care of the chronically mentally ill in the United States. In J. Hollingsworth & E. Hollingsworth (Eds.), *Care of the chronically and severely ill* (pp. 145-172). New York: Aldine de Gruyter.

Hollingsworth, J., & Hollingsworth, E. (1994). Comprehensiveness and coordination of care for the disabled. In J. Hollingsworth & E. Hollingsworth (Eds.), *Care of the chronically and severely ill* (pp. 173-230). New York: Aldine de Gruyter.

Holt, S. W. (1986-87). The role of home care in long term care. *Generations, XI*(2), 9-12.

Holter, H. (Ed.). (1984). *Patriarchy and the welfare state.* Oslo, Norway: Universitetsforlaget.

Hooyman, N. (1990). Women as caregivers of the elderly: Implications for social welfare policy and practice. In D. Biegel & A. Blum (Eds.), *Aging and caregiving* (pp. 221-242). Newbury Park, CA: Sage.

Hooyman, N. (1992). Social policy and gender inequities in caregiving. In J. W. Dwyer & R. T. Coward (Eds.), *Gender, families, and elder care* (pp. 181-210). Newbury Park, CA: Sage.

Hooyman, N. (1994). Diversity and populations at risk: Women. In F. Reamer (Ed.), *The foundations of social work knowledge* (pp. 309-345). New York: Columbia University Press.

Hooyman, N., & Ryan, R. (1987). Women as caregivers of the elderly: Catch-22 dilemmas. In J. Figueira-McDonough & R. Sarri (Eds.), *The trapped woman: Catch-22 in deviance and control* (pp. 143-171). Newbury Park, CA: Sage

Horowitz, A. (1985). Family caregiving to the frail elderly. *Annual Review of Gerontology & Geriatrics, 5,* 194-246.

Horwitz, A. V. (1993). Adult siblings as sources of social support for the seriously mentally ill: A test of the serial model. *Journal of Marriage and the Family, 55,* 623-632.

Horowitz, A., & Schindelman, L. W. (1983a). Reciprocity and affection: Past influences on current caregiving. *Journal of Gerontological Social Work, 5,* 5-20.

Horowitz, A., & Shindelman, L. W. (1983b). Social and economic incentives for family caregivers. *Health Care Financing Review, 5,* 25-33.

Howe, C., & Howe, J. (1987). The National Alliance for the Mentally Ill: History and ideology. In A. Hatfield (Ed.), *Families of the mentally ill: Meeting the challenges* (pp. 23-34). San Francisco: Jossey-Bass.

Howe, W. J. (1986). Temporary help workers: Who they are, what jobs they hold. *Monthly Labor Review, 109,* 45-57.

Hu, T., Huang, L., & Cartwright, W. W. (1986). Evaluation of the costs of caring for the senile demented elderly: A pilot study. *The Gerontologist, 26,* 158-163.

Huckle, P. (1991). *Tish Sommers, activist, and the founding of the Older Women's League.* Knoxville: University of Tennessee Press.

Hugen, B. (1993). The effectiveness of a psycho-educational support service to families of persons with a chronic mental illness. *Research on Social Work Practice, 3*(2), 137-154.

Hula, R. C. (1991). Introduction: Thinking about family policy. In E. A. Anderson & R. C. Hula (Eds.), *The reconstruction of family policy* (pp. 1-7). Westport, CT: Greenwood.

Hurtado, A. (1989). Relating to privilege: Seduction and rejection in the subordination of white women and women of color. *Signs: Journal of Women in Culture and Society, 14*(4), 833-855.

Intagliata, J. (1982). Improving the quality of community care for the chronically mentally disabled: The role of case management. *Schizophrenia Bulletin, 8,* 655-674.

Isaacson, W. (1989, November 20). Should gays have marriage rights? *Time,* pp. 101-102.

Jacobs, G. (1990). Aging and politics. In R. H. Binstock & L. George (Eds.), *Handbook of Aging: The Social Sciences* (3rd ed.). (pp. 349-361). San Diego, CA: Academic Press.

Janicki, M. P., & Wisniewski, H. M. (1985). *Aging and developmental disabilities: Issues and approaches.* Baltimore: Brookes.

Jarrett, W. H. (1985). Caregiving within kinship systems: Is affection really necessary? *The Gerontologist, 25*(6), 5-10.

Jennings, J. (1987). Elderly parents as caregivers for their adult dependent children. *Social Work, 5,* 430-433.

Jensen, G. (1994, February 19). *Testimony on health insurance to U.S. Senate's Committee on Finance.* Washington, DC: American Association of Retired Persons.

Jette, A., Tennstedt, S., & Branch, L. (1992). The stability of informal support provided to the frail elderly. *Journal of Aging and Health, 4,* 193-211.

Johnson, A., & Rose, K. (1992). *The emerging role of the work-family manager.* (Report Number 987). New York: The Conference Board.

Johnson, C. (1983). Dyadic family relations and social support. *The Gerontologist, 23,* 377-383.

Johnson, C., & Catalano, D. (1981). Childless elderly and their family supports. *The Gerontologist, 21,* 610-618.

Johnson, C., & Catalano, D. (1983). A longitudinal study of family supports to impaired elderly. *The Gerontologist, 23,* 612-618.

Johnson, C., Klee, L., & Schmidt, C. (1988). Conceptions of parenthood and kinship among children of divorce. *American Anthropologist, 42,* 126-134.

Johnston, W. B., & Packer, A. H. (1987). *Workforce 2000: Work and workers for the twenty-first century.* Indianapolis, IN: Hudson Institute.

Joyner, T. (1994, June 26). Mothers are jilting jobs, opting to stay home with families. *Seattle Times,* p. C4.

Kahana, E., Biegel, D., & Wykle, M. (1994a). Conclusion. In E. Kahana, D. Biegel, & M. Wykle (Eds.), *Family caregiving across the lifespan* (pp. 382-385). Thousand Oaks, CA: Sage

Kahana, E., Biegel, D., & Wykle, M. (Eds.). (1994b). *Family caregiving across the lifespan.* Thousand Oaks, CA: Sage.

Kalleberg, A. L., & Rosenfeld, R. (1990). Work in the family and in the labor market: A cross-national, reciprocal analysis. *Journal of Marriage and the Family, 52,* 331-346.

Kamerman, S. B., & Kahn, A. J. (1978). *Family policy: Government and families in fourteen countries.* New York: Columbia University Press.

Kamerman, S. B., & Kahn A. J. (1987). *The responsive workplace: Employers and a changing labor force.* New York: Columbia University Press.

Kamerman, S. B., & Kahn, A. J. (1989). Family policy: Has the United States learned from Europe? *Policy Studies Review, 8,* 581-598.

Kaminer, W. (1993). Feminism's identity crisis. *Atlantic Monthly, 272,* 51-68.

Kane, C. (1994). Psychoeducational programs: From blaming to caring. In E. Kahana, D. Biegel, & M. Wykle (Eds.), *Family caregiving across the lifespan* (pp. 216-239). Thousand Oaks, CA: Sage.

Kane, R. (1989a). The home care crisis of the nineties. *The Gerontologist, 29,* 24-31.

Kane, R. (1989b). Toward competent, caring paid caregivers. *The Gerontologist, 29*(3), 292.

Kane, R. (1990). *What is case management anyway?* Minneapolis: University of Minnesota, Long-Term Care Decisions Resource Center.

Kane, R., & Kane, R. (1985). *A will and a way: What the United States can learn from Canada about caring for the elderly.* New York: Columbia University Press.

Kane, R., & Kane, R. (1990). Health care for older people: Organizational and policy issues. In R. Binstock & L. George (Eds.), *Aging and the social sciences* (3d ed., pp. 415-437). New York: Academic Press.

Kane, R., & Kane, R. (1994). Financing long-term care: Lessons from Canada. In T. R. Marmor, T. M. Smeading, & V. L. Greene (Eds.), *Economic security and intergenerational justice: A look at North America* (pp. 303-323). Washington, DC: Urban Institute Press.

Kanter, R. M. (1977). *Work and family in the United States: A critical review and agenda for research and policy.* New York: Russell Sage.

Kanter, R. M. (1983). *Changemasters: Innovation for productivity in the American corporation.* New York: Simon & Schuster.

Kaplan, J. (1982, Spring). Female Consciousness & Collective Action: The case of Barcelona, 1910- 1918. *Signs: Journal of Women in Culture and Society, 7,* 545-566.

Karon, S. L. (1991). *The difference it makes: Caregiver's gender and access to community-based LTC services in the Social HMO.* Unpublished doctoral dissertation, Brandeis University, Waltham, MA.

Kaufman, A., Adams, J., & Campbell, V. (1991). Permanency planning by older parents who care for adult children with mental retardation. *Mental Retardation, 29,* 293-300.

Kaye, L. W., & Applegate, J. S. (1990). *Men as caregivers to the elderly: Understanding and aiding unrecognized family support.* Lexington, MA: Lexington Books.

Kaye, L. W., & Kirwin, P. M. (1990). Adult day care services for the elderly and their families: Lessons from the Pennsylvania experience. *Journal of Gerontological Social Work, 15*(3/4), 167-183.

Keating, N., & Jeffrey, B. (1983). Work careers of ever married and never married retired women. *The Gerontologist, 23,* 416-421.

Keefe, J. M., & Fancey, P. (1992, October 24). *Which is more beneficial to caregivers: Financial compensation or home care service?* Paper presented at the Canadian Association on Gerontology Annual Educational and Scientific Meeting, Edmonton, Alberta.

Keigher, S. (1991). Wages or welfare? Compensating caregiving in two conservative social welfare states. *Journal of Aging & Social Policy, 3*(3), 83-104.

Keigher, S., & Murphy, C. (1992, June). A consumer view of a family care compensation program for the elderly. *Social Service Review, 66,* 256-277.

Keigher, S., Simon-Rusinowitz, L., Linsk, N., & Osterbusch, S. E. (1988). Payments to informal versus formal home care providers: Policy divergence affecting the elderly and their families in Michigan and Illinois. *The Journal of Applied Gerontology, 7*(4), 456-473.

Keigher, S., & Stone R. (1993, July 4-7). *Payment for care: The United States of America: A very mixed policy bag.* Paper presented at the International Meeting: Paying for Care. Vienna, Austria.

Kelly, R. M., & Bayes, J. (1988). *Comparable worth, pay equity, and public policy.* Westport, CT: Greenwood.

Kelly, T. B., & Kropf, N. P. (in press). Stigmatized and perpetual parents: Older parents caring for adult children with lifelong disabilities. *Journal of Gerontological Social Work, 23.*

Kemper, P. (1992). The use of formal and informal home care by the elderly. *Health Services Research, 27*(4), 421-451.

Kemper, P., Applebaum, R., & Harrigan, M. (1987a). Community care demonstrations: What have we learned? *Health Care Financing Review, 8*(4), 87-100.

Kemper, P., Applebaum, R., & Harrigan, M. (1987b). *A systematic comparison of community care demonstrations.* (Special Report No. 45, Reprint OM No. 88-0014). Madison: University of Wisconsin, Institute for Research on Poverty.

Kessler, R. C., & McLeod, J. D. (1984). Sex differences in vulnerability to undesirable life events. *American Sociological Review, 49,* 620-631.

Kessler-Harris, A. (1987). The debate over equality for women in the workplace: Recognizing differences. In N. Gerstel & H. E. Gross (Eds.), *Families and work* (pp. 520-539). Philadelphia: Temple University Press.

Kiecolt-Glaser, J. K., Glaser, R., Shuttleworth, E. E., Dyer, C. S., Ogrocki, P., & Speicher, C. E. (1987). Chronic stress and immunity in family caregivers of Alzheimer's disease patients. *Psychosomatic Medicine, 49,* 523-535.

Kingson, E. (1988). Generational equity: An unexpected opportunity to broaden the politics of aging. *The Gerontologist, 28*(6), 768-772.

Kingson, E., Hirshorn, B., & Cornman, J. (1986). *Ties that bind: The interdependence of generations.* Cabin John, MD: Seven Locks.

Kingson, E., & O'Grady-LeShane, R. (1993). The effects of caregiving on women's social security benefits. *The Gerontologist, 33*(2), 230-239.

Kingston, P. W. (1990). Illusions and ignorance about the family-responsive workplace. *Journal of Family Issues, 11,* 438-454.

Kinsey, A. C., Pomeroy, W. B., & Martin, C. E. (1948). *Sexual behavior in the human male.* Philadelphia: W. B. Saunders.

Kirkpatrick, M. (1987). Clinical implications of lesbian mother studies. *Journal of Homosexuality, 14,* 201-211.

Kirp, D., Yudof, M., & Franks, M. (1986). *Gender justice.* Chicago: University of Chicago Press.

Knoll, J., Covert, S., O'Connor, S., Agosta, J., & Blaney, B. (1990). *Family support services in the United States: An end of decade status report.* Cambridge, MA: Human Services Research Institute.

Korczyk, S. M. (1993). Gender issues in employer pension plans. In R. V. Burkhauser & D. L. Salisbury (Eds.), *Pensions in a changing economy* (pp. 59-66). Washington, DC: Employee Benefit Research Institute.

Krane, J. (1991). Feminist thinking as an aid to teaching social work research. *Affilia: Journal of Women and Social Work, 6*(4), 53-70.

Krause, H. (1990). *Family law: Cases, comments, and questions.* Minneapolis, MN: West.

Krauss, M. (1986). Patterns and trends in public services to families with a mentally retarded member. In J. Gallagher & P. Vietze (Eds.), *Families of handicapped persons* (pp. 237-250). Baltimore: Brookes.

Kropf, N. P. (1994a, May). *Family support services: Issues facing older parents.* Paper presented at the meeting of the Young Adult Institute, 15th Annual International Conference, New York City.

Kropf, N. P. (1994b, May). *Older parents of adults with developmental disabilities: Issues for practice and service delivery.* Paper presented at the Meeting of the Young Adult Institute Conference on Social Work and Disabilities, New York City.

Kuhn, M. (with Long, C., & Guinn, L.). (1991). *No stone unturned: The life and times of Maggie Kuhn.* New York: Ballantine Books.

Lakin, K. C., Hayden, M. F., & Abery, B. H. (1994). An overview of the community living concept. In M. F. Hayden & B. H. Abery (Eds.), *Challenges in a service system in transition* (pp. 3-22). Baltimore: Brookes.

Lambert, S. J. (1993). Workplace policies as social policy. *Social Service Review, 67,* 237-260.

Langley, P. A. (1991). The coming of age of family policy. *Families in Society: The Journal of Contemporary Human Services, 72,* 116-120.

LaRossa, R. (1988). Fatherhood and social change. *Family Relations, 37,* 451-457.

Lawton, M. P., Brody, E. M., & Saperstein, A. R. (1989). A controlled study of respite service for caregivers of Alzheimer's patients. *The Gerontologist, 29*(1), 8-16.

Lee, G. (1992). Gender differences in family caregiving: A fact in search of a theory. In J. Dwyer & R. Coward (Eds.), *Gender, families, and elder care* (pp. 120-131). Newbury Park, CA: Sage.

Lefley, H. (1986). Culture and mental illness: The family's role. In H. Lefley & P. Pedersen (Eds.), *Cross cultural training for mental health professionals* (pp. 30-59). Springfield, IL: Charles C Thomas.

Lefley, H. P. (1987). Aging parents as caregivers of mentally ill adult children: An emerging social problem. *Hospital & Community Psychiatry, 38*(10), 1063-1069.

Lefley, H. P. (1989). Family burden and family stigma in major mental illness. *American Psychologist, 44*(3), 556-560.

Leutz, W. N., Capitman, J. A., MacAdam, M., & Abrahams, R. (1992). *Care for frail elders: Developing community solutions.* Westport, CT: Auburn House.

Levine, B. (1990, September 23). They face burgeoning demands at work and at home, they don't feel that men will either help or care. That's why many women say they harbor heavy-duty anger. *Los Angeles Times,* p. E1.

Levitan, S. A., & Gallo, F. (1990). Work and family: The impact of legislation. *Monthly Labor Review, 113,* 34-40.

Levy, J. A. (1988). Intersections of gender and aging. *Sociological Quarterly, 29*(4), 459-486.

Lewis, D. (1994, October 28). Working women's lot found to be not happy one. *Boston Globe,* pp. 69-70.

Lewis, D., Shadish, W., & Lurigio, A. (1989). Policies of inclusion and the mentally ill: Long-term care in a new environment. *Journal of Social Issues, 45*(3), 173-186.

Lewis, J. (1986). Feminism and welfare. In J. Mitchell & A. Oakley (Eds.), *What is feminism? A reexamination* (pp. 85-100). New York: Pantheon.

Lewis, J., & Meredith, B. (1988). *Daughters who care: Daughters caring for mothers at home.* London: Routledge & Kegan Paul.

Link, B. G., & Cullen, F. T. (1990). The labelling theory of mental disorder: A review of the evidence. In J. R. Greenley (Ed.), *Research in community and mental health: Mental disorder in social context.* Greenwich, CT: JAI.

Linsk, N. L., Keigher, S. M., & Osterbusch, S. E. (1988). States' policies regarding paid family caregiving. *The Gerontologist, 28*(2), 204-212.

Linsk, N. L., Keigher, S., Simon-Rusinowitz, L., & England, S. (1992). *Wages for caring: Compensating family care of the elderly.* New York: Praeger.

Lipson L., & Laudicina, S. (1991). *State home and community-based services for the aged under Medicaid: Waiver programs, optional services under the Medicaid state plan, and OBRA 1990 provisions for a new optional benefit.* Washington, DC: American Association of Retired Persons, Public Policy Institute.

Litwak, E. (1985). *Helping the elderly. The complementary roles of informal networks and formal systems.* New York: Guilford.

Litwak, E., Jessop, D., & Moulton, H. (1994). Optimal use of formal and informal systems over the life course. In E. Kahana, D. Biegel, & M. Wykle (Eds.), *Family caregiving across the lifespan* (pp. 96-130). Thousand Oaks, CA: Sage.

Lloyd, M. (1992). Does she boil eggs? Toward a feminist model of disability. *Disability, Handicap and Society, 7*(3) 207-221.

Lobel, S. A. (1992). Editor's note: Introduction to special issue on work and family. *Human Resource Management, 31,* 153-155.

Lobel, S. A., & Googins, B. K. (1994, July). *The future of family and family: Critical trends for practice, policy and research.* Paper presented at the International Congress on Applied Psychology, Madrid, Spain.

Lockery, S. A. (1991). Family and social supports: Caregiving among racial & ethnic minority elders. *Generations, 15,* 58-62.

Longino, Jr., C. F. (1988). Who are the oldest Americans? *The Gerontologist, 28,* 515-528.

Loring, B., & Porter, T. (1994). California advocates coordinate long-term care reform efforts for all ages. *Aging Today, 15,* 1, 6.

Lumsdon, K. (1993). Bridging the Gap. *Hospitals and Health Networks, 67,* 44, 48, 50.

Lurie, E. (Ed.). (1987). *Serving the mentally ill elderly: Problems and perspectives.* Lexington, MA: Lexington Books.

Lurie, E., Robinson, B., & Barbaccia, J. (1984). Helping hospitalized elderly: Discharge planning and informal support. *Home Health Care Services, 5*(2), 25-43.

Luthans, F., & Waldersee, R. (1989). What do we really know about EAPs? *Human Resource Management, 28,* 385-401.

Luttrell, W. (1988). The Edison school struggle: The reshaping of working class education and women's consciousness. In A. Bookman & S. Morgen (Eds.), *Women and the politics of empowerment* (pp. 136-158). Philadelphia: Temple University Press.

Lyons, N. (1983). Two perspectives on self, relationships and morality. *Harvard Educational Review, 53,* 125-145.

MacAdam, M. (1993). Home care reimbursement and the effects on personnel. *The Gerontologist, 33*(1), 55-63.

MacDonald, B. (1988, June). *Caregiving.* Paper presented at working conference on older women, University of Utah School of Social Work, Salt Lake City, UT.

Magnet, M. (1993, March 8). Why job growth is stalled. *Fortune*, pp. 54-47.

Mahoney, T. A. (1988). Productivity defined: The relativity of efficiency, effectiveness and change. In J. P. Campbell & R. J. Campbell (Eds.), *Productivity in organizations: New perspectives from industrial organizational psychology* (pp. 13-39). San Francisco: Jossey-Bass.

Manton, K. G., & Stallard, E. (1992). *The projected demand for cancer care, the supply of facilities and the personnel needed to meet it.* Paper presented at the workshop sponsored by the National Cancer Institute on the burden of formal and informal cost of cancer to American families, Rockville, MD.

Manton, K. G., Vertress, J., & Wrigley, J. (1990). Changes in health service use and mortality among U.S. elderly in 1980-86. *Journal of Aging and Health, 2,* 131-156.

Marcenko, M. O., & Meyers, J. C. (1991). Mothers of children with developmental disabilities: Who shares the burden? *Family Relations, 40,* 186-190.

Mardiros, M. (1985). Role alterations of female parents having children with disabilities. *Canada's Mental Health, 33,* 24-26.

Marmor, T., & Gill, L. (1989). The political and economic context of mental health care in the United States. *Journal of Health, Politics, Policy and Law, 14,* 459-475.

Marsh, P. (1992a). *Families and mental illness: New directions in professional practice.* New York: Praeger.

Marsh, P. (1992b). *Families and mental retardation: New directions in professional practice.* New York: Praeger.

Marshall, N., Barnett, R. C., Baruch, G. K., & Pleck, J. H. (1990). Double jeopardy: The costs of caring at work and at home. In E. Abel & M. Nelson (Eds.), *Circles of care: Work and identity in women's lives* (pp. 266-278). Albany: State University of New York Press.

Martin, D., & Lyon, P. (1972). *Lesbian women.* New York: Bantam Books.

Martinson, M., & Stone, J. (1993). Small-scale community living options serving three or fewer older adults with developmental disabilities. In E. Sutton, A. Factor, B. Hawkins, T. Heller, & G. Seltzer (Eds.), *Older adults with developmental disabilities* (pp. 223-235). Baltimore: Brookes.

Mascia-Lee, F., Sharpe, P., & Cohen-Ballerino, C. (1989). The postmodern turn in anthropology: Cautions from a feminist perspective. *Signs: Journal of Women in Culture and Society, 15*(1), 7-31.

Massachusetts Women's Health Care Coalition. (November 1993). *Statement on Health Care.* Boston: Author.

Matson, J. L., & Frame, C. L. (1986). *Psychopathology among mentally retarded children and adolescents.* Beverly Hills, CA: Sage.

Matthaei, J. A. (1982). *An economic history of women in America: Women's work, the sexual division of labor and the development of capitalism.* New York: Schocken.

Matthews, S. H. (1987). Provision of care to old parents: Division of responsibility among adult children. *Research on Aging, 9,* 45-60.

Matthews, S. H., Wekner, J. E., & Delaney, P. J. (1989). Relative contributions of help by employed and nonemployed sisters to their elderly parents. *Journal of Gerontology, 44,* S36-S44.

McBride, T. D. (1989). *Measuring the disability of the elderly: Empirical analysis and projections into the 21st century.* Paper presented at the Population Association of America meetings, Baltimore, MD.

McConnell, S., & Riggs, J. (1994). A public policy agenda: Supporting family caregiving. In M. Cantor (Ed.), *Family caregiving: An agenda for the future* (pp. 25-34). San Francisco: American Society on Aging.

McDaniel, S. (1993). Caring and sharing: Demographic aging, family and the state. In J. Hendricks & C. Rosenthal (Eds.), *The remainder of their days: Domestic policy and older families in the United States and Canada* (pp. 121-144). New York: Garland.

McElroy, E. (1987). The beat of a different drummer. In A. Hatfield & H. Lefley (Eds.), *Families of the mentally ill: Coping and adaptation.* New York: Guilford.

McFall, S., & Miller, B. H. (1992). Caregiver burden and nursing home admission of frail elderly persons. *Journal of Gerontology: Social Sciences, 47,* S73-S79.

McLaren, J., & Bryson, S. E. (1987). Review of recent epidemiological studies of mental retardation: Prevalence, associated disorders, and etiology. *American Journal on Mental Retardation, 92,* 243-254.

McLean, C. S., Greer, K., Scott, J., & Beck, J. C. (1982). Group treatment for parents of the adult mentally ill. *Hospital and Community Psychiatry, 33*(7), 564-568.

Mead, L. (1986). *Beyond entitlement: The social obligations of citizenship.* New York: Free Press.

Mechanic, D. (1987). Challenges in long-term care policy. *Health Affairs, 6*(2), 22-34.

Mechanic, D., & Rochefort, D. (1990). Deinstitutionalization: An appraisal of reform. In W. R. Scott & J. Blake (Eds.), *Annual Review of Sociology* (pp. 301-327). Palo Alto, CA: Annual Reviews.

Medical center adds domestic partner benefits. (1993, October 13). *National Report on Work & Family* (p. 8). Washington, DC: Business Publishers.

Meisenheimer II, J. R., & Wiatrowski, W. J. (1989). Flexible benefits plans: Employees who have a choice. *Monthly Labor Review, 112,* 17-23.

Menolasciro, F., & Potter, J. (1989). Mental illness in the elderly mentally retarded. *Journal of Applied Gerontology, 8,* 192-202.

Meyers, J. W, Ramirez, F. O., Walker, H. A., Langton, N., & O'Connor, S. M. (1988). The state and the institutionalization of the relations between women and children. In S. M. Dornbusch & M. H. Strober (Eds), *Feminism, children and the new families* (pp. 137-158). New York: Guilford.

Miller, B. (1979). Gay fathers and their children. *The Family Coordinator, 28,* 544-552.

Miller, B. (1992). *The distribution of family-oriented benefits.* (Number 130). Washington, DC: Employee Benefits Research Institute.

Miller, B., & Cafasso, L. (1992). Gender differences in caregiving: Fact or artifact? *The Gerontologist, 32,* 498-507.

Miller, B., McFall, S., & Montgomery A. (1991). The impact of elder health, caregiver involvement, and global stress on two dimensions of caregiver burden. *Journal of Gerontology, 46,* S9-S19.

Miller, B., & Montgomery, A. (1990). Family caregivers and limitations in social activities. *Research on Aging, 12,* 72-93.

Miller, D. (1990). *Women and social welfare: A feminist analysis.* New York: Praeger.

Miller, D. (1994). What is needed for true equality: An overview of policy issues for women. In L. Davis (Ed.), *Building on women's strengths* (pp. 27-56). New York: Haworth.

Mills, C. W. (1959). *The sociological imagination.* New York: Oxford University Press.

Mindel, C. H. (1980). Extended familism among urban Mexican Americans, Anglos and Blacks. *Hispanic Journal of Behavioral Sciences, 2,* 21-34.

Minkler, M. (1991). "Generational equity" and the new victim blaming. In M. Minkler & C. Estes (Eds.), *Critical perspectives on aging: The political and moral economy of growing old* (pp. 67-80). Newbury Park, CA: Sage.

Minkler, M., & Estes, C. (Eds.). (1991). *Critical perspectives on aging: The political and moral economy of growing old.* Amityville, NY: Baywood.

Minkler, M., & Roe, K. (1993). *Grandmothers as caregivers: Raising children of the crack cocaine epidemic.* Newbury Park, CA: Sage.

Minnick, E. K. (1990). *Transforming knowledge.* Philadelphia: Temple University Press.

Mollica, R. L., Riley, T., & Rydell, C. (1994). *The impact of health reform on vulnerable adults: Volume I.* Waltham, MA: Brandeis University, Center for Vulnerable Populations.

Mollison, A. (1993, June 6). Large gap still lingers in equity of earnings: Thirty years later, women still don't get equal pay. *The Orlando Sentinel,* p. F1.

Montgomery, R. (1989, October 31). As AARP grows, so does criticism of its priorities. *Seattle Times,* p. 12.

Montgomery, R., & Borgatta, E. (1989). The effects of alternative support strategies on family caregiving. *The Gerontologist, 29*(4), 457-464.

Montgomery, R., & Datwyler, M. (1990). Women and men in the caregiving role. *Generations, 14,* S 34-38.

Montgomery, R., Gonyea, J. G., & Hooyman, N. R. (1985). Caregiving and the experience of subjective and objective burden. *Family Relations, 34,* 19-26.

Montgomery, R., & Hatch, L. R. (1986). *Caregiving career lines.* Paper presented at the 30th Annual Scientific Meeting of the Gerontological Society of America, Chicago, IL.

Montgomery, R., & Kosloski, K. (1994a). A longitudinal analysis of nursing home placement for dependent elders cared for by spouses vs. adult children. *Journal of Gerontology: Social Sciences, 49,* S62-74.

Montgomery, R., & Kosloski, K. (1994b). Outcomes of family caregiving: Lessons from the past and challenges for the future. In M. Cantor (Ed.), *Family caregiving: An agenda for the future* (pp. 123-136). San Francisco: American Society on Aging.

Montgomery, R., & Prothero, J. (Eds.). (1986). *Developing respite services for the elderly.* Seattle: University of Washington Press.

Moon, M. (1990, Summer). Public policies: Are they gender neutral? *Generations, 14,* 59-63.

Moore, L. (1971). Social policy and the politics of social development. In *International Social Development Review. Volume 3: Unified Socio-Economic Development and Planning—Some New Horizons* (pp. 41-46). New York: United Nations Publications.

Morell, C. (1987, March). Cause is function: Toward a feminist model of integration for social work. *Social Service Review,* pp. 144-155.

Morgen, S. (1988). Its the whole power of the city against us! The development of political consciousness in a women's health care coalition. In A. Bookman & S. Morgen (Eds.), *Women and the politics of empowerment* (pp. 97-115). Philadelphia: Temple University Press.

Morgen, S., & Bookman, A. (1988). Rethinking women and politics: An introductory essay. In A. Bookman & S. Morgen (Eds.), *Women and the politics of empowerment* (pp. 3-32). Philadelphia: Temple University Press.

Moroney, R. (1980). *Families, social services and social policy.* Washington, DC: Department of Health and Human Services.

Morrissey, J., & Goldman, H. (1984). Cycles of reform in the care of the chronically mentally ill. *Hospital and Community Psychiatry, 35*(8), 785-793.

Morton, D. (1988). *Analysis of the fiscal impact of S. 1673 on Illinois* (Draft No. 2). Unpublished manuscript.

Moscovice, I., Davidson, G., & McCaffrey, D. (1988). Substitution of formal and informal care for the community-based elderly. *Medical Care, 26*(10), 971-981.

Motenko, A. K. (1989). The frustrations, gratifications, and well-being of dementia caregivers. *The Gerontologist, 29,* 166-172.

Mott, F. L., & Shaw, L. B. (1986). The employment consequences of different fertility behaviors. In L. B. Shaw (Ed.), *Midlife women at work: A fifteen year perspective* (pp. 23-36). Lexington, MA: Heath.

Murray, C. (1984). *Losing ground, American social policy 1950-1980*. New York: Basic Books.

Murray, C. (1988). *In pursuit of happiness and good government*. New York: Simon & Schuster.

Mutschler, P. H. (1994). From executive suite to production line: How employees in different occupations manage elder care responsibilities. *Research on Aging, 16,* 7-26.

National Academy for State Health Policy. (1992). *The status of America's vulnerable populations: A chartbook*. Portland, ME: Center for Vulnerable Populations.

National Association of Social Workers. (1994, April 15). *Mental Health Care Transition Statement* (pp. 1-5). Washington, DC: NASW Government Relations.

National Center for Health Statistics. (1989). *Health, United States, 1988*. (DHHS Publication No. PHS 89-1232). Washington, DC: Government Printing Office.

National Committee to Preserve Social Security and Medicare. (1993). *View point: Long-term care*. Washington, DC: Author.

Naylor, R., Jr. (1994, October 15). U.S. working women cite anger, unfairness in poll. *The Boston Globe,* p. 4.

Neal, M., Chapman, N., Ingersoll-Dayton, B., & Emlen, A. (1993). *Balancing work and caregiving for children, adults, and elders*. Newbury Park, CA. Sage.

Nelson, G. (1982). Social class and public policy for the elderly. In B. Neugarten (Ed.), *Age or need? Public policies for older people* (pp. 101-129). Beverly Hills, CA: Sage.

Newman, S. J., & Stuyk, R. (with Wright, P., & Rice, M.). (1990). Overwhelming odds: Caregiving and the risk of institutionalization. *Journal of Gerontology, 45*(5), S173-S183.

"News analysis." (1994, February 17). *Report on disability programs* (p. 25). Silver Spring, MD: Business Publishers.

Neysmith, S. (1991). From community care to a social model of care. In C. Barnes, P. Evans, & S. Neysmith (Eds.), *Women's caring: Feminist perspectives on social welfare* (pp. 272-299). Toronto, Canada: McClelland & Stewart.

Neysmith, S. (1993). Developing a home care system to meet the needs of aging Canadians and their families. In J. Hendricks & C. Rosenthal (Eds.), *The remainder of their days: Domestic policy and older families in the United States and Canada* (pp. 145-168). New York: Garland.

Nicola-McLaughlin, A., & Chandler, Z. (1988). Urban politics in the higher education of Black women: A case study. In A. Bookman & S. Morgen (Eds.), *Women and the politics of empowerment* (pp. 180-201). Philadelphia: Temple University Press.

NIMH Steering Committee on Chronically Mentally Ill. (1980). *Toward a national plan for the chronically mentally ill*. Rockville, MD: National Institute of Mental Health.

Noddings, N. (1984). *Caring: A feminine approach to ethics and moral education*. Berkeley: University of California Press.

Noelker, L. (1994). The interface between health and social services and family caregivers. In M. H. Cantor (Ed.) *Family caregivers: An agenda for the future* (pp. 77-88). San Francisco: American Society on Aging.

Noelker, L., & Bass, D. (1989). Home care for elderly persons: Linkages between formal and informal caregivers. *Journal of Gerontology, 44,* 563-570.

Noelker, L., & Bass, D. (1994). Relationships between the frail elderly's informal and formal helpers. In E. Kahana, D. Biegel, & M. Wykle (Eds.), *Family caregiving across the lifespan* (pp. 356-385). Thousand Oaks, CA: Sage.

Number of telecommuters pegged at 4.5 million. (1993, October 13). *National Report on Work and Family*. Washington, DC: Business Publishing.

Older Women's League & American Federation of State, County & Municipal Employees. (1988). *Chronic Care Workers: Crisis among paid caregivers of the elderly*. Washington, DC: Author.

Older Women's League. (1989). *Failing America's caregivers: A status report on women who care*. Washington, DC: Author.

Older Women's League. (1990). *Heading for hardship: Retirement income for American women in the next century*. Washington, DC: Author.

Olson, M. H. (1983). Remote office work: Changing work patterns in space and time. *Communications of the Association of Computing Machinery, 26*, 182-187.

Omnibus Budget Reconciliation Act of 1980, Pub. L. No. 100-203 (1981).

O'Reilly, B. (1992, August 24). The job drought: Why the shortage of high-wage jobs threatens the U.S. economy. *Fortune, 126*, 62-74.

Orodenker, S. Z. (1990). Family caregiving in a changing society: The effects of employment on caregiving stress. *Family and Community Health, 12*, 58-70.

Osterbusch, S., Keigher, S., Miller, B., & Linsk, N. (1987). Community care policies and gender justice. *International Journal of Health Services, 17*, 217-232.

O'Toole, J. (1985). *Vanguard management: Redesigning the corporate future*. New York: Doubleday.

Painton, P. (1993, April 26). The shrinking ten %. *Newsweek*, pp. 26-29.

Parker, G. (1993). *With this body: Caring and disability in marriage*. Buckingham, UK: Open University Press.

Parker, V., & Hall, D. (1993). Workplace flexibility: Faddish or fundamental? In P. H. Mirvis (Ed.), *Building the competitive workforce: Investing in human capital for corporate success* (pp. 122-155). New York: John Wiley.

Parks, H., & Pilisuk, M. (1991). Caregiver burden: Gender and the psychological costs of caregiving. *American Journal of Orthopsychiatry, 6*, 501-509.

Pascall, G. (1986). *Social policy: A feminist analysis*. London: Tavistock.

Pearlin, L., Lieberman, M., Menaghan, E., & Mullan, J. (1981). The stress process. *Journal of Health and Social Behavior, 22*, 337-356.

Pearlin, L., Mullan, J., Semple, J., & Skaff, M. (1990). Caregiving and the stress process: An overview of concepts and their measures. *The Gerontologist, 30*, 583-594.

Pearlin, L., & Schooler, C. (1979). The structure of coping. *Journal of Health and Social Behavior, 19*, 2-21.

Pendleton, S., Capitman, J., Leutz, W., & Omata, R. (1990). *State infrastructure for long term care: A national study of state systems*. Waltham, MA: Brandeis University, Institute for Health Policy.

Pepper Commission (U.S. Bipartisan Commission on Comprehensive Health Care). (1990). *A call for action*. Washington, DC: Government Printing Office.

Perkins, K. (1993). Recycling poverty: From the workplace to retirement. *Journal of Women & Aging, 5*, 5-23.

Petch, A. (1994). The best move I've made: The role of housing for those with mental health problems. In M. Titterton (Ed.), *Caring for people in the community: The new welfare* (pp. 76-90). London: Jessica Kingsley Publisher.

Petty, D., & Friss, L. (1987). A balancing act of working and caregiving. *Business and Health, 15*, 22-26.

Pfeiffer, E., & Mostek, M. (1991). Services for families of people with mental illness. *Hospital and Community Psychiatry, 42*(3), 262-264.

Pharr, S. (1988, December). Column. *Transformation, 3*, 1.

Pifer, A. (1993). Implications for policy and practice. In J. Allen & A. Pifer (Eds.), *Women on the front line: Meeting the challenge of an aging America* (pp. 241-252). Washington, DC: The Urban Institute Press.

Platt, S. (1985). Measuring the burden of psychiatric illness on the family: An evaluation of some rating scales. *Psychological Medicine, 15*, 383-393.

Pleck, J. H. (1985). *Working wives/working husbands.* Beverly Hills, CA: Sage.

Polansky, E. (1985). *A feminist analysis of hospital discharge planning: Women as caregivers of disabled family members.* Paper presented at the Women's Symposium, the Annual Program Meeting of the Council on Social Work Education, Washington, DC.

Posner, C. M., Wilson, K. G., Kral, M. J., Lander, S., & McIlwraith, E. D. (1992). Family psychoeducational support groups in schizophrenia. *American Journal of Orthopsychiatry, 62*(2), 206-218.

Potasznik, H., & Nelson, G. (1984). Stress and social support: The burden experienced by the family of a mentally ill person. *American Journal of Community Psychology, 12*(5), 589-607.

Poulshock, S. W., & Deimling, G. T. (1984). Families caring for elders in residence: Issues in the measurement of burden. *Journal of Gerontology, 39,* 230-239.

Poulshock, S. W., & Noelker, N. (1982). *The effects of families caring for impaired elderly in residence.* Cleveland, OH: Benjamin Rose Institute.

PR Newswire. (1991, December 10). *Reports of men taking on increased responsibilities largely a myth* [On-line]. Available: NEXIS Library: NEWS File: PRNews

President's Commission on the Status of Women. (1963). *Report of the Committee on Home and Community.* Washington, DC: Government Printing Office.

Pruchno, R., & Resch, N. (1989). Husbands and wives as caregivers: Antecedents of depression and burden. *The Gerontologist, 29,* 159-165.

Purdy, J. K., & Arguello, D. (1992). Hispanic familism in caretaking of older adults: Is it functional? *Journal of Gerontological Social Work, 19,* 29-43.

Quadagno, J. (1989). Generational equity and the politics of the welfare state. *Politics and Society, 17*(3), 353-376.

Quadagno, J. (1990). Race, class and gender in the U.S. welfare state. *American Sociological Review, 55,* 11-28.

Quadagno, J., & Meyer, M. H. (1990). Gender and public policy. *Generations, 14,* 64-66.

Quadagno, J., Meyer, M., & Turner, J. (1991). Falling into the Medicaid gaps: The hidden long-term care dilemma. *The Gerontologist, 31,* 521-526.

Qureshi, H., & Walker, A. (1989). *The caring relationship: Elderly people and their families.* Philadelphia, PA: Temple University Press.

Raabe, P. H. (1990). The organizational effects of workplace family policies: Past weaknesses and recent progress to improved research. *Journal of Family Issues, 11,* 477-491.

Raffel, N., & Raffel, N. (1987). Elderly care: Similarities and solutions in Denmark and the United States. *Public Health Reports, 102*(5), 494-500.

Rapp, R. (1978). Family and class in contemporary America: Notes toward an understanding of ideology. *Science and Society, 42,* 278-300.

Reeser, L. (1988). Women and social work activism in the 1980s. *Affilia: Journal of Women and Social Work, 3*(3) 51-63.

Rein, M., & Rainwater, L. (1986). *Public/private interplay in social protection: A comparative study.* New York: M. E. Sharpe.

Rexroat, C., & Shehan, C. (1987). The family life cycle and spouses' time in housework. *Journal of Marriage and the Family, 49,* 737-750.

Rice, T. (1989). The use, cost, and economic burden of nursing-home care in 1985. *Medical Care, 27,* 1133-1147.

Ries, P., & Stone, A. J. (Eds.). (1992). *The American woman 1992-1993: A status report.* New York: Norton.

Riessman, C. K. (1989). From victim to survivor: A woman's narrative reconstruction of marital sexual abuse. [Special Issue] *Women & Clinical Practice, 59*(3), 232-251.

Riley, T., & Mollica, R. L. (1994). *The impact of health reform on vulnerable adults: Volume II. An analysis of national health reform proposals.* Waltham, MA: Brandeis University, Center for Vulnerable Populations.

Rinck, C., & Calkins, C. (1993). Family satisfaction with case management and service provision. In K. Roberto (Ed.), *The elderly caregiver: Caring for adults with developmental disabilities* (pp. 125-145). Newbury Park, CA: Sage.

Rivlin, A., & Wiener, J. (1988). *Caring for the disabled elderly: Who will pay?* Washington, DC: Brookings Institute.

Roberto, K. A. (1993a). Family caregivers of aging adults with disabilities: A review of the caregiving literature. In K. A. Roberto (Ed.), *The elderly caregiver: Caring for adults with developmental disabilities* (pp. 3-18). Newbury Park, CA: Sage.

Roberto, K. A. (1993b). Older caregivers of family members with developmental disabilities: Changes in roles and perceptions. In K. A. Roberto (Ed.), *The elderly caregiver: Caring for adults with developmental disabilities* (pp. 39-50). Newbury Park, CA: Sage.

Rodeheaver, D. (1987). When old age became a social problem, women were left behind. *The Gerontologist, 27*(6), 741-746.

Rodgers, C. S. (1992). The flexible workplace: What have we learned? *Human Resource Management, 31,* 183-199.

Rosenblatt, R. A. (1993, June 16). Benefits studied for part-time workers. *Los Angeles Times,* p. D1.

Rosenson, M. K., Kasten, A. M., & Kennedy, M. E. (1988). Expanding the role of families of the mentally ill. In J. S. McNeil & S. E. Weinstein (Eds.), *Innovations in health care practice* (pp. 116-133). Silver Spring, MD: National Association of Social Workers.

Rosenthal, C. J., & Hendricks, J. (1993). Conclusion. In J. Hendricks & C. J. Rosenthal (Eds.), *The remainder of their days: Domestic policy and older families in the United States and Canada* (pp. 223-227). New York: Garland.

Rosenthal, M. G. (1994). Single mothers in Sweden: Work and welfare in the welfare state. *Social Work, 39,* 270-278.

Rossi, A. (1980). Life span theories and women's lives. *Signs: Journal of Women in Culture and Society, 6*(1), 4-32.

Rossi, A. (1985). Gender and parenthood. In A. Rossi (Ed.), *Gender and the life course* (pp. 161-192). New York: Aldine.

Rothman, S. M. (1978). *Women's proper place: A history of changing ideals and practices.* New York: Basic Books.

Rothman, S. M., & Marks, E. M. (1987). Adjusting work and family life: Flexible work schedules and family policy. In N. Gerstel & H. E. Gross (Eds.), *Families and work* (pp. 469-477). Philadelphia: Temple University Press.

Rowitz, L. (1987). The American mental retardation service system. *Journal of Mental Deficiency, 31,* 337-347.

Ryan, R. (1987). *Clients or service providers: How case managers view the relatives of frail elders.* Unpublished doctoral dissertation, University of Washington, Seattle.

Sacks, K. (1988). Gender and grassroots leadership. In A. Bookman & S. Morgen (Eds.), *Women and the politics of empowerment* (pp. 77-97). Philadelphia: Temple University Press.

Salisbury, C., & Intagliata, J. (1986). *Respite care: Support for persons with developmental disabilities and their families.* Baltimore: Brookes.

Saltzman, A. (1991, June 17). Trouble at the top. *U.S. News & World Report,* pp. 40-48.

Salvo, J. J., & McNeil, J. M. (1984). Lifetime work experience and its effect on earnings. U.S. Bureau of the Census, *Current Publications Reports* (Special Studies, Series P-23, No. 136). Washington, DC: Government Printing Office.

Samuelson, R. J. (1993, July 5). R. I. P. : The Good Corporation. *Newsweek,* p. 41.

Sands, R., & Nuciro, K. (1992). Postmodern feminist theory and social work. *Social Work, 37*(6), 489-494.

Scanzoni, J. (1982). Reconsidering family policy: Status quo or force for change? *Journal of Family Issues, 3,* 277-300.

Scanzoni, J. (1991). Balancing the policy interests of children and adults. In E. A. Anderson & R. C. Hula (Eds.), *The reconstruction of family policy* (pp. 11-22). Westport, CT: Greenwood.

Scanzoni, J., & Marsiglio, W. (1991). Wider families as primary relationships. *Marriage and Family Review, 17,* 117-133.

Scharlach, A. E., & Boyd, S. L. (1989). Caregiving and employment: Results of an employee survey. *The Gerontologist, 29,* 382-387.

Scharlach, A. E., & Fredriksen, K. I. (1994). Elder care versus adult care: Does care recipient age make a difference? *Research on Aging, 16,* 43-68.

Scharlach, A. E., Lowe, B. F., & Schneider, E. L. (1991). *Elder care and the work force: Blueprint for action.* Lexington, MA: Lexington Books.

Scheyett, A. (1990). The oppression of caring: Women caregivers of relatives with mental illness. *Affilia: Journal of Women and Social Work, 5(1),* 32-48.

Schmidt, W. (1990, December 25). Hard work can't stop hard times. *New York Times,* p. A1.

Schneider, R. (1993, May 2). Statistics that hid the 'hidden' minority. *Boston Globe,* p. 75.

Schor, J. B. (1991). *The overworked American: The unexpected decline of leisure.* New York: Basic Books.

Schorr, A. L. (1980). *Thy father and thy mother: A second look at filial responsibility and family policy.* Washington, DC: Department of Health and Human Services.

Schulz, R. (1990). Theoretical perspectives on caregiving: Concepts, variables, and methods. In D. E. Biegel & A. Blum (Eds.), *Aging and caregiving: Theory, research and policy* (pp. 27-52). Newbury Park, CA: Sage.

Schulz, R., Tompkins, C. A., & Rau, M. T. (1988). A longitudinal study of the psychosocial impact of stroke on primary support persons. *Psychology and Aging, 3,* 131-141.

Schulz, R., Williamson, G. M., Morycz, R., & Biegel, D. E. (1993). Changes in depression among men and women caring for an Alzheimer's patient. In S. H. Zarit, L. I. Pearlin, & K. Warner Schaie (Eds.), *Caregiving systems: Informal and formal helpers* (pp. 119-140). Hillsdale, NJ: Lawrence Erlbaum.

Schuping, J. A. (1992, June 8). Industry-at-large: Information integration: Key to business success. *Electronic News, 38,* (1915) 11-12.

Schwartz, F. (1989, January-February). Management women and the new facts of life. *Harvard Business Review,* 65-76.

Seaberg, J. R. (1990). Family policy revisted: Are we there yet? *Social Work, 35,* 548-554.

Seccombe, K. (1992). Employment, the family and employer-based policies. In J. Dwyer & R. Coward (Eds.), *Gender, families, and elder care* (pp. 165-180). Newbury Park, CA: Sage.

Segal, E. A. (1989). Welfare reform: Help for poor women and children? *Affilia: Journal of Women and Social Work, 4,* 42-50.

Seltzer, G. B., Begun, A., Seltzer, M. M., & Krauss, M. W. (1991). Adults with mental retardation and their aging parents: Impacts of siblings. *Family Relations, 40,* 310-317.

Seltzer, M. M., & Krauss, M. W. (1987). *Aging and mental retardation: Extending the continuum.* Washington, DC: American Association on Mental Retardation.

Seltzer, M. M., & Krauss, M. W. (1989). Aging parents with mentally retarded children: Family risk factors and sources of support. *American Journal on Mental Retardation, 94,* 303-312.

Shaddish, W., Lurigio, A., & Lewis, D. (1989). After deinstitutionalization: The present and future of mental health long-term care policy. *Journal of Social Issues, 45,* 1-15.

Shalala, D. (1994, October 12). Top 10 reasons to keep health care reform alive. *Seattle Times,* p. 4B.

Shao, M. (1994a, April 3). New US workers: Flexible, disposable—Temping of America rolls on. *Boston Globe,* pp. 1, 18.

Shao, M. (1994b, April 3). In Cambridge, new take on temps. *Boston Globe,* p. 18.

Shapiro, I., & Greenstein, R. (1991). *A painless recession: The economic downturn and policy responses.* Washington, DC: Center on Budget and Policy Priorities.

Shapiro, J. (1993). *No pity: People with disabilities forging a new civil rights movement.* New York: Random House.

Shellenbarger, S. (1992). Lessons from the workplace: How corporate policies and attitudes lag behind workers' changing needs. *Human Resource Management, 31,* 157-170.

Shellenbarger, S. (1994, February 16). The aging of America is making elder care a big workplace issue. *Wall Street Journal,* pp. A4-5.

Shelton, B. A. (1990). The distribution of household tasks: Does wife's employment status make a difference? *Journal of Family Issues, 11*(2), 115-135.

Shelton, B. A., & Firestone, J. (1989). Household labor time and the gender gap in earnings. *Gender & Society, 3,* 105-112.

Sherman, J. (1992). *Medicare's mental health benefits: Coverage, utilization and expenditures.* Washington, DC: American Association of Retired Persons, Public Policy Institute.

Short, P., & Leon, J. (1990, September). Use of home and community services by persons age 65 and older with functional disabilities. *National Medical Expenditures Survey.* Rockville, MD: U.S. Department of Health and Human Services.

Short, P., Monheit, A., & Beauregard, K. (1989). A profile of uninsured Americans. *National Medical Expenditures Survey* (Research Findings I). Rockville, MD: U.S. Department of Health and Human Services.

Silicon electronics firms develop two near-site child care centers. (1993, October 13). *National Report on Work & Family* (pp. 3-4). Washington, DC: Business Publishers.

Silliman, R. A. (1984, March). *Family caregivers and their frail elderly.* Paper presented at the Annual Meeting of the American Geriatrics Society, Denver, CO.

Simon, R., & Danziger, G. (1991). *Women's movements in America.* New York: Praeger.

Singer, G. H., & Irvin, L. K. (1989). Family caregiving stress and support. In G. H. Singer & L. K. Irvin (Eds.), *Support for caregiving families* (pp. 3-25). Baltimore: Brookes.

Sipila, J., & Simon, B. (1993). Home care allowances for the frail elderly: For and against. *Journal of Sociology and Social Welfare, 20,* 119-134.

Skaff, M. M., & Pearlin, L. I. (1992). Caregiving: Role engulfment and the loss of self. *The Gerontologist, 32,* 656-664.

Smeeding, T. (1983). The size distribution of wage and nonwage compensation: Employer cost versus employee value. In J. E. Triplett (Ed.), *The measurement of labor cost* (pp. 237-285). Chicago: University of Chicago Press.

Smeeding, T., Torrey, B., & Rein, M. (1988). Patterns of income and poverty: The economic status of children and the elderly in eight countries. In J. L. Palmer, T. Smeeding, & B. B. Torrey (Eds.), *The vulnerable* (pp. 89-119). Washington, DC: Urban Institute.

Smith, D. (1987). Women's inequality and the family. In N. Gerstel & H. E. Gross (Eds.), *Families and work* (pp. 23-55). Philadelphia: Temple University Press.

Smith, G., Smith, M., & Toseland, R. (1991). Problems identified by family caregivers in counseling. *The Gerontologist, 31*(1), 15-22.

Smith, G., & Tobin, S. (1989). Permanency planning among older parents of adults with lifelong disabilities. *Journal of Gerontological Social Work, 14*(3/4), 35-59.

Smith, J. P. (1989). Women, mothers, and work. In M. N. Ozawa (Ed.), *Women's life cycle and economic insecurity* (pp. 42-70). New York: Praeger.

Snyder, B., & Keefe, K. (1985). The unmet needs of family caregivers for frail and disabled elders. *Social Work in Health Care, 10,* 1-14.

Soldo, B., & Myllyluoma, J. (1983). Caregivers who live with dependent elderly. *The Gerontologist, 23,* 607-611.

Sommers, T., & Shields, L. (1987). *Women take care: The consequences of caregiving in today's society.* Gainsville, FL: Triad.

Spain, D. (1988, December). *Women's demographic past, present and future.* Paper presented at the Radcliffe Conferences on Women in the 21st Century Defining the Challenge: Emerging Needs and Constraints, Cambridge, MA.

Spakes, P. (1989a). A feminist case against national family policy: A view to the future. *Policy Studies Review, 8,* 610-621.

Spakes, P. (1989b). Reshaping the goals of family policy: Sexual equality, not protection. *Affilia: Journal of Women and Social Work, 4,* 7-24.

Spakes, P. (1991). A feminist approach to national family policy. In E. A. Anderson & R. C. Hula (Eds.), *The reconstruction of family policy* (pp. 23-42). Westport, CT: Greenwood.

Spakes, P. (1992). National family policy: Sweden versus the United States. *Affilia: Journal of Women and Social Work, 7,* 44-60.

Spanier, G., & Furstenberg, F. F., Jr. (1987). Remarriage and reconstituted families. In M. B. Sussman & S. K. Steinmetz (Eds.), *Handbook of marriage and the family* (pp. 419-434). New York: Plenum.

Spencer, G. (1989). Projections of the population of the United States by age, sex, and race, 1988 to 2080. U.S. Bureau of the Census, *Current Population Reports* (Series P-25, No. 1018). Washington, DC: Government Printing Office.

Spender, D. (1985). *For the record: The making and meaning of feminist knowledge.* London: Women's Press.

Spitze, G. (1986). The division of task responsibility in U.S. households: Longitudinal adjustments to change. *Social Forces, 64*(3), 689-701.

Stacey, J. (1993). Good riddance to "The Family": A response to David Popenoe. *Journal of Marriage and the Family, 55,* 545-547.

Stacey, J., & Thorne, B. (1985). The missing feminist revolution in sociology. *Social Problems, 32*(4), 301-316.

Starr, P. (1989). The meaning of privatization. In S. Kamerman & A. Kahn (Eds.), *Privatization and the welfare state* (pp. 15-48). Princeton, NJ: Princeton University Press.

Starrels, M. E. (1992). The evolution of workplace family policy research. *Journal of Family Issues, 13,* 259-278.

Steiner, G. (1981). *The futility of family policy.* Washington, DC: Brookings Institute.

Stewart, D. L., & Burge, P. L. (1989). *Assessment of employee satisfaction, stress, and child care at Dominion Bankshares Corporation.* Blacksburg, VA: Virginia Polytechnic Institute & State University.

Stober, M. H. (1982). Market work, housework and child care: Burying archaic tenets, building new arrangements. In P. W. Berman & E. R. Ramey (Eds.), *Women: A developmental perspective* (pp. 207-219). Bethesda, MD: National Institute of Health.

Stoller, E. P. (1983). Parent caregiving by adult children. *Journal of Marriage and the Family, 45,* 851-858.

Stoller, E. P., & Gibson, R. (1994). *Worlds of difference: Inequality in the aging experience.* Thousand Oaks, CA: Pine Forge Press.

Stoller, E. P., & Pugliesi, K. (1991). Size and effectiveness of informal helping networks: A panel study of older people in the community. *Journal of Health and Social Behavior, 32,* 180-191.

Stone, R. (1989). The feminization of poverty among the elderly. *Women's Studies Quarterly, 17*(1,2), 20-34.

Stone, R., Cafferata, G., & Sangl, J. (1987). Caregivers of the frail elderly: A national profile. *The Gerontologist, 27,* 616-626.

Stone, R., & Keigher, S. (1994). Toward an equitable, universal caregiver policy: The potential of financial supports for family caregivers. *Aging and Social Policy, 6*(1/2), 57-76.

Stone, R., & Kemper, P. (1989). Spouses and children of disabled elders: How large a constituency for long-term care reform. *Milbank Memorial Quarterly, 67*(3-4), 485-506.

Stone, R., & Short, P. (1990). The competing demands of employment and informal caregiving to disabled elders. *Medical Care, 28*(6), 513-526.

Strasser, S. (1982). *Never done: A history of American housework.* New York: Pantheon.

Strawbridge, W. J., & Wallhagen, M. I. (1991). Impact of family conflict on adult child caregivers. *The Gerontologist, 31,* 770-777.

Susser, I. (1988). Working class women, social protest and changing ideologies. In A. Bookman & S. Morgen (Eds.), *Women and the politics of empowerment* (pp. 257-271). Philadelphia: Temple University Press.

Sweet, J. A., & Bumpass, L. L. (1987). *American families and households.* New York: Russell Sage.

Swoboda, F. (1993a, July 11). U.S., others struggle with choice of creating more jobs or good jobs. *Washington Post,* p. H2.

Swoboda, F. (1993b, September 5). For growing ranks of part-time workers, more burdens and fewer benefits. *Washington Post,* p. H2.

Taeuber, C. M., & Allen, J. (1993). Women in our aging society: The demographic outlook. In J. Allen & A. Pifer (Eds.), *Women on the front lines: Meeting the challenge of an aging America* (pp. 11-45). Washington, DC: Urban Institute.

Taube, C. A. (1990). Funding expenditures for mental illness. In R. W. Manderscheid & M. A. Sonnenschein (Eds.), *Mental Health, United States, 1990* (DHHS Publication No. ADM 90-1708, pp. 216-226). National Institute of Mental Health. Washington, DC: Government Printing Office.

Tellis-Nayak, V., & Tellis-Nayak, M. (1989). Quality of care and the burden of two cultures: When the world of the nurse's aid enters the world of the nursing home. *The Gerontologist, 29*(3), 307-313.

Tennstedt, S. L., Crawford, S. L., & McKinlay, J. B. (1993a). Determining the pattern of care: Is coresidence more important than caregiver relationship? *Journal of Gerontology, 48,* S74-S83.

Tennstedt, S. L., Crawford, S. L., & McKinlay, J. B. (1993b). Is family care on the decline? A longitudinal investigation of the substitution of formal long-term care services for informal care. *Milbank Quarterly, 71,* 601-624.

Tennstedt, S. L., & Gonyea, J. G. (1994). An agenda for work and eldercare research: Methodological challenges and future directions. *Research on Aging, 16*(1), 85-108.

Tessler, R. C., Gamache, G., & Fisher, G. (1991). Patterns of contact of patients' families with mental health professionals and attitudes toward professionals. *Hospital and Community Psychiatry, 42*(9), 929-935.

Thompson, E. H., & Doll, W. (1982). The burden of families coping with the mentally ill: An invisible crisis. *Family Relations, 31,* 379-388.

Thompson, L. (1993). Conceptualizing gender in marriage: The case of marital care. *Journal of Marriage and the Family, 55,* 557-569.

Thorncroft, G., Ward, P., & James, S. (1993). Care management and mental health. In T. Groves & R. Griffiths (Eds.), *Countdown to community care* (pp. 76-87). London: BMJ.

Thorne, B. (1982). Feminist rethinking of the family: An overview. In B. Thorne & M. Yalom (Eds.), *Rethinking the family: Some feminist questions* (pp. 1-24). New York: Longman.

Thornton, C., Dunstan, S. M., & Kemper, P. (1988). The evaluation of the national long-term care demonstration: The effect of channeling on health and long-term care costs. *Health Services Research, 23*(1), 129-142.

Thurer, S. L. (1983). Deinstitutionalization and women: Where the buck stops. *Hospital and Community Psychiatry, 34,* 1162-1163.

Tice, K. (1990, Spring/Summer). Gender and social work education: Directions for the 1990s. *Journal of Social Work Education,* (2), 134-144.

Titmuss, R. M. (1968). *Commitment to welfare.* London: Allen & Unwin.

Torres-Gil, F., & Pynoos, J. (1986). Long-term care policy and interest group struggles. *The Gerontologist, 26*(5), 488-495.

Torrey, E. (1988). *Nowhere to go: The tragic odyssey of the homeless mentally ill.* New York: Harper & Row.

Torrey, E., Wolfe, S., & Flynn, L. (1988). *Care of the seriously mentally ill* (2nd ed.). Arlington, VA: National Alliance for the Mentally Ill and Public Citizens Health Research Group.

Toseland, R., & Rossiter, C. (1989). Group interventions to support family caregivers: A review and analysis. *The Gerontologist, 29*(4), 438-448.

Toseland, R., Rossiter, C., & Labrecque, M. (1989a). The effectiveness of peer-led and professionally-led groups to support caregivers. *The Gerontologist, 29,* 457-464.

Toseland, R., Rossiter, C., & Labrecque, M. (1989b). The effectiveness of two kinds of support groups for caregivers. *Social Service Review,* 415-432.

Townsend, A., Noelker, L., Deimling, G., & Bass, D. (1989). Longitudinal impact of interhousehold caregiving on adult children's mental health. *Psychology and Aging, 4,* 393-401.

Traustadottir, R. (1988, August). *Women and family care: On the gendered nature of caring.* Paper presented at the First International Conference on Family Support Related to Disability, Stockholm, Sweden.

Traustadottir, R. (1991). Mothers who care: Gender, disability, and family life. *Journal of Family Issues, 12,* 211-218.

Travail, familles, patries. (1994, May). *Le Monde de l'education, 215,* 41-44.

Travelers Insurance Companies. (1985). *The Travelers employee caregiver survey: A survey on caregiving responsibilities of Travelers employees for elder Americans.* Hartford, CT: Author.

Treas, J. (1975). Aging and the family. In D. S. Woodruff & J. E. Birren (Eds.), *Aging, scientific perspectives, and social issues* (pp. 92-108). New York: Van Nostrand.

Troll, L. E. (1987). Mother-daughter relationships through the life span. In S. Oskamp (Ed.), *Applied social psychology annual: Vol. 7. Family processes and problems: Social psychological aspects* (pp. 284-305). Newbury Park, CA: Sage.

Troll, L. E., Miller, S., & Atchley, R. (1979). *Families in later life.* Belmont, CA: Wadsworth.

True, J. M., III (1993, December 13). Contingency workers' frayed safety net. *Legal Times,* pp. 7-8.

Turner, B. F. (1994). Introduction. In B. F. Turner & L. E. Troll (Eds.), *Women growing older: Psychological perspectives* (pp. 1-34). Thousand Oaks, CA: Sage.

Twigg, J., & Atkin, K. (1994). *Carers perceived: Policy and practice in informal care.* Buckingham, UK: Open University Press.

U.S. Bureau of the Census. (1988). Money income and poverty status in the U.S.: 1988. *Current Population Reports* (Series P-60, No. 166, p. 88). Washington, DC: Government Printing Office.

U.S. Bureau of the Census. (1989). Changes in American family life. *Current Population Reports* (Special Studies, P-23, No. 163). Washington, DC: Government Printing Office.

U.S. Bureau of the Census. (1990). Money income and poverty status in the U.S.: 1989 (pp. 49-59). *Current Population Reports* (P-60, No. 168). Washington, DC: Government Printing Office.

U.S. Bureau of the Census. (1991a). 1980 and 1990 censuses of the population. *General Population Characteristics.* (PC80-1-B1, Table 45). Washington, DC: Government Printing Office.

U.S. Bureau of the Census. (1991b). *Statistical abstracts of the United States: I* (111th ed.) Washington, DC: Government Printing Office.

U.S. Bureau of the Census. (1991c). Studies in American fertility. *Current Population Reports* (P-23, No. 176). Washington, DC: Government Printing Office.

U.S. Bureau of the Census. (1992a). *Households, families, and children: A 30-year perspective.* (P. 23, No. 181.) Washington, DC: Government Printing Office.

U.S. Bureau of the Census. (1992b). How we're changing—demographic state of the nation: 1992. *Current Population Reports* (Special Studies, Series P-23, No. 177). Washington, DC: Government Printing Office.

U.S. Bureau of the Census. (1992c). Marital status and living arrangements: March 1992. *Current Population Reports* (Series P-20, No. 468). Washington, DC: Government Printing Office.

U.S. Bureau of the Census. (1992d). Marriage, divorce and remarriage in the 1990s. *Current Population Reports* (Series P-23, No. 180). Washington, DC: Government Printing Office.

U.S. Bureau of the Census. (1992e). Population projections of the United States, by age, sex, race and Hispanic origin: 1992 to 2050. *Current Population Reports* (Series P-25, No. 1092). Washington, DC: Government Printing Office.

U.S. Bureau of the Census. (1992f). Sixty-five plus in America. *Current Population Reports* (Series P-23, No. 178). Washington, DC: Government Printing Office.

U.S. Bureau of the Census. (1992g). *Statistical abstract of the United States: 1992* (112 Ed.) Washington, DC: Government Printing Office.

U.S. Bureau of the Census. (1993a). How we're changing: Demographic state of the nation: 1993. *Current Population Reports* (Series P-23, No. 184). Washington, DC: Government Printing Office.

U.S. Bureau of the Census. (1993b). U.S. population estimates by age, sex, race and Hispanic origin: 1980 to 1991. *Current Population Reports* (Series P-23, No. 1095). Washington, DC: Government Printing Office.

U.S. Bureau of Labor Statistics. (1988). *Employment and Earnings, January 1988.* Washington, DC: Government Printing Office.

U.S. Bureau of Labor Statistics. (1991). *Employment and earnings, January 1991, 38*(1). Washington, DC: Government Printing Office.

U. S. Bureau of National Affairs, Inc. (1990, February 7). Experts say labor-management relations must undergo fundamental change in 1990s. *Daily Labor Report,* 26, p. C-1.

U.S. Department of Labor. (1993). *Employee benefits in medium and large private establishments, 1991.* Washington, DC: Government Printing Office.

U.S. General Accounting Office. (1991). *Long-term care insurance: Risks to consumers should be reduced* (GAO/HRD-92-14). Washington, DC: Government Printing Office.

U.S. General Accounting Office. (1992a). *Elderly Americans: Health, housing and nutrition gaps between the poor and nonpoor.* Washington, DC: Government Printing Office.

U.S. General Accounting Office. (1992b). *The changing workforce: Comparison of federal and nonfederal work/family programs and approaches* (GAO/GDD-92-84). Washington, DC: Government Printing Office.

U.S. House of Representatives, Select Committee on Aging, Subcommittee on Health and Long-Term Care. (1988). *Exploding the myths: Caregiving in America: A study* (100th

Congress, 1st session., Comm. Pub. No. 99-611). Washington DC: Government Printing Office.

U.S. Senate Special Committee on Aging. (1990). *Developments in Aging: 1989* (Vol 1). Washington, DC: Government Printing Office.

U.S. Senate Special Committee on Aging. (1992). *Aging America: Trends and projections, 1990-1991.* Washington, DC: U.S. Department of Health & Human Services.

Ungerson, C. (1987). *Policy is personal: Sex, gender, and informal care.* New York: Tavistock.

Urquhart, M. (1984). *The employment shift to services: Where did it come from?* (Bureau of Labor Statistics). Washington, DC: Government Printing Office.

Van Den Bergh, N., & Cooper, L. B. (1986). Introduction. In N. Van Den Bergh & L. B. Cooper (Eds.), *Feminist visions for social work* (pp. 1-28). Silver Spring, MD: National Association of Social Workers.

Verbrugge, L. (1989). Recent, present and future health of American adults. *Annual Review of Public Health, 10,* 333-361.

Voydanoff, P. (1988). Women, work, and family: Bernard's perspective on the past, present, and future. *Psychology of Women Quarterly, 12,* 269-280.

Waerness, K. (1984). Caring as women's work in the welfare state. In H. Holter (Ed.), *Patriarchy in a welfare society* (pp. 67-87). Oslo, Norway: Universitetsforlaget.

Waerness, K. (1985). *Informal and formal care in old age: What is wrong with the new ideology of community care in the Scandinavian welfare state today.* Paper presented at the Conference on Gender Division and Policies for Community Care, University of Kent, Canterbury, UK.

Walby, S. (1989). Theorizing patriarchy. *Sociology, 23*(2), 213-234.

Waldo, D., Sonnefeld, S., McKusick, D., & Arnett, R. (1989). Health expenditures by age group, 1977 and 1987. *Health Care Financing Review, 10*(4), 111-120.

Walker, A. (1982). *Community care: The family, the state and social policy.* Oxford, UK: Blackwell/Martin Robertson.

Walker, A. (1985). From welfare state to caring society? The promise of informal support networks. In J. Jonker, R. Leaper, & J. Yoder (Eds.), *Support networks in a caring community* (pp. 41-49). Lancaster, UK: Martins Nijhoff.

Walker, A. (1990). The economic "burden" of aging and the prospect of intergenerational conflict. *Aging and Society, 10,* 377-396.

Walker, A. (1991). The relationship between the family and the state in the care of older people. *Canadian Journal on Aging, 10,* 94-113.

Walker, A. (1992). Conceptual perspectives on gender and family caregiving. In J. Dwyer & R. Coward (Eds.), *Gender, families, and elder care* (pp. 34-49). Newbury Park, CA: Sage.

Wallace, S. (1990). The no care zone: Availability, accessibility and acceptability in community-based long-term care. *The Gerontologist, 30*(2), 254-261.

Watkins, S. C., Menken, J. A., & Bongaarts, J. (1987). Demographic foundations of family change. *American Sociological Review, 52,* 346-358.

Wedenoja, M. (1991). Mothers are not to blame: Confronting cultural bias in the area of serious mental illness. In M. Bricker-Jenkins, N. R. Hooyman, & N. Gottlieb (Eds.), *Feminist social work practice in clinical settings* (pp. 179-186). Newbury Park, CA: Sage.

Weeks, W. (1994). *Women working together.* Mellowing, Australia: Longman Cheshire.

Weick, A. (1987). Reconceptualizing the philosophical perspective of social work. *Social Service Review, 61,* 218-230.

Weissert, W. G., Elston, J. M., Bolda, E. J., Cready, C M., Zelman, W. N., Sloan, P. D., Kalsbeck, W. D., Mutran, E., Rice, T. H., & Koch, G. G. (1989). Models of adult day care: Findings from a national survey. *The Gerontologist, 29*(5), 640-649.

Wethington, E., McLeod, I., & Kessler, R. (1987). The importance of life events for explaining differences in psychological distress. In R. Barnett, L. Biener, & G. Baruch (Eds.), *Gender and stress* (pp. 144-159). New York: Free Press.

Whitehead, B. D. (1993). Dan Quayle was right. *Atlantic Monthly, 271,* 47-84.

Whitlach, C. J., Zarit, S. H., & von Eye, A. (1991). Efficacy of interventions with caregivers: A reanalysis. *The Gerontologist, 31*(1), 9-14.

Wiatrowski, W. J. (1990, March). Family-related benefits in the workplace. *Monthly Labor Review, 113,* 28-33.

Wiener, J. M., & Illston, L. H. (1994a). Health care reform in the 1990s: Where does long-term care fit in? *The Gerontologist, 34*(3), 402-408.

Wiener, J. M., & Illston, L. H. (1994b). How to share the burden: Long-term reform in the 1990's. *The Brookings Review, 12*(2), 17-21.

Wiener, J. M., Illston, L., & Hanley, R. (1994). *Sharing the burdens: Strategies for public and private long-term care insurance.* Washington, DC: Brookings Institution.

Wilensky, H. L. (1985). *Comparative social policy: Theories, methods, and findings.* Berkeley, CA: University of California, Berkeley, Institute of International Studies.

Winston, K., & Bane, M. J. (1993). *Gender and public policy.* Boulder, CO: Westview.

Wisensale, S. K. (1988). Generational equity and intergenerational policies. *The Gerontologist, 28,* 773-778.

Wisensale, S. K., & Heckart, K. E. (1993). Domestic partnerships: A concept paper and policy discussion. *Family Relations, 42,* 199-204.

Wittig, M. A., & Lowe, R. H. (1989). Comparable worth, theory, and policy. *Journal of Social Issues, 45,* 1-21.

Wolfe, J. (1993). *The coming health crisis: Who will pay for care for the aged in the 21st century.* Chicago: University of Chicago.

Women Employed Institute. (1988). *Occupational segregation.* Chicago: Author.

Wood, J. B. (1993). Planning for the transfer of care: Social and psychological issues. In K. A. Roberto (Ed.), *The elderly caregiver: Caring for adults with developmental disabilities* (pp. 95-107). Newbury Park, CA: Sage.

Wood, J. B., & Estes, C. L. (1983). The private non-profit sector and aging services. In C. L. Estes, R. J. Newcomer, & Associates (Eds.), *Fiscal austerity and aging: Shifting government responsibility for the elderly* (pp. 227-249). Beverly Hills, CA: Sage.

Wood, J. B., & Skiles, L. L. (1992). Planning for the transfer of care. *Generations, 16*(1), 61-62.

Wright, B., & King, M. (1991, February). *Americans with developmental disabilities: Policy directions for the States.* Denver, CO: National Conference of State Legislatures.

Zarestsky, E. (1982). The place of the family in the origins of the welfare state. In B. Thorne & M. Yalom (Eds.), *Rethinking the family: Some feminist questions* (pp. 188-224). New York: Longman.

Zarit, S. H. (1994). Research perspectives on family caregiving. In M. H. Cantor (Ed.), *Family caregiving: Agenda for the future* (pp. 9-24). American Society on Aging.

Zarit, S. H., Pearlin, L. I., & Schaie, K. W. (Eds.). (1993). *Caregiving systems: Informal and formal helpers.* Hillsdale, NJ: Lawrence Erlbaum.

Zarit, S. H., Todd, P. A., & Zarit, J. M. (1986). Subjective burden of husbands and wives as caregivers: A longitudinal study. *The Gerontologist, 26,* 260-266.

Zarit, S. H., & Toseland, R. W. (1989). Current and future direction in family caregiving research. *The Gerontologist, 29*(4), 481-483.

Zavella, P. (1988). The politics of race and gender: Organizing Chicana cannery workers in Northern California. In A. Bookman & S. Morgen (Eds.), *Women and the politics of empowerment* (pp. 202-226). Philadelphia: Temple University Press.

Ziral, D. Lieberman, A. & Rapp, C. (1989). Respite care for the chronically mentally ill: Focus for the 1990s. *Community Mental Health Journal, 25*(3), 171-184.

Name Index

Subject Index

405

About the Authors

Nancy R. Hooyman is Professor and Dean at the University of Washington School of Social Work in Seattle. She holds a BA from Denison University in Ohio, an MA in Sociology from the University of Pennsylvania, and an MSW and PhD in Sociology and Social Work from the University of Michigan. Nationally recognized for her scholarship related to aging, family caregiving of dependents, feminist social work practice and administration, and community organization, she has coauthored or edited seven books, one of which is the text for the first national telecourse on aging. Her book *Taking Care of Aging Family Members* (coauthored with Wendy Lustbader) is widely used by both professionals and families. She is a Fellow of the Gerontological Society of America. Highly regarded for her national leadership regarding social work education, she was selected by the Washington State Chapter of the National Association of Social Workers as Social Work Educator of the Year in 1992, was a board member of the Council on Social Work Education, and chaired that council's national Commission on Women. She serves on numerous local and national boards related to social work education, gerontology, and women's interests, and is a frequently requested speaker in these areas, nationally and internationally.

Judith G. Gonyea is Associate Professor and Chair of the Social Research Department at the Boston University School of Social Work. She is also a Fellow at the Boston University Center on Work and Family. She received her MSW and PhD in Social Welfare from the University of Washington in Seattle. Her research interests are in aging, family, and gender studies. She is especially interested in the phenomena of family care, the intersection of family and work roles, and the effect of social policies on women's lives. Her recent publications include: "Linking the Worlds of Work and Family: Beyond the Productivity Trap," *Human Resource Management Journal*; "An Agenda for Work and Elder Care

Research: Methodological Challenges and Future Directions," *Research on Aging*; "The Paradox of the Advantaged Elder and Feminization of Poverty," *Social Work*; and "Making Gender Visible in Public Policy," *Older Men's Lives*. She was the guest editor for a special issue of *Research on Aging* (March 1994) devoted to the topic of work and elder care. She is a Fellow of the Gerontological Society of America and currently serves on the editorial boards of *Research on Aging, Journal of Gerontological Social Work, Health Care in Later Life,* and the National Academy on Aging's *Public Policy and Aging Report.*